manuel puig and the spider woman

manuel puig and the spider woman

his life and fictions

suzanne jill levine

farrar • straus • giroux   new york

Farrar, Straus and Giroux
19 Union Square West, New York 10003

Library of Congress Cataloging-in-Publication Data
Levine, Suzanne Jill.
    Manuel Puig and the spider woman: his life and fictions / Suzanne
Jill Levine.
        p.   cm.
    Includes bibliographical references and index.
    ISBN 0-374-28190-4   (alk. paper)
    1. Puig, Manuel.   2. Authors, Argentine—20th century Biography.
I. Title.
PQ7798.26.U4Z772   2000
863—dc21
[B]   99-39130

Excerpts from Pauline Kael's review of the movie *Kiss of the Spider Woman* are reprinted
by permission: copyright © Pauline Kael. Originally published in *The New Yorker*.

contents

introduction

Mothers of America. Let your kids go to the movies . . .
it's true that fresh air is good for the body
but what about the soul
that grows in darkness, embossed by silvery images
—Frank O'Hara, "Ave Maria"

"This dream is short but this dream is happy" are the last, redemptive words uttered in *Kiss of the Spider Woman*, Manuel Puig's most famous novel. This dream reached a vast audience as an Oscar-winning film and then as a Broadway musical hit, but its dreamer never saw the musical that opened in 1992 and won seven Tony Awards—he died July 22, 1990, at the age of fifty-seven, in Cuernavaca, Mexico. The film was his "entrance into immortality."[1] Whether or not his name is remembered by the public, his prison romance under the stars of Hollywood nostalgia—in which William Hurt as a gay window dresser falls in love with Raul Julia, a Marxist journalist who looks like Che Guevara—still remains. The novel was Manuel Puig's most affirmative, most daring, and the only one with heroes: the Marxist, prejudiced by his politics or blind to their contradictions, learns that tolerance for the Other is essential for true political action, while his gay cell mate is liberated by a selfless act.

Movies made from novels prolong their sources' literary lives even as they reduce them to marketable images; to the surprise of both the author and the makers of the film, when it opened in September 1985 at the height of the Reagan era, it captivated not only gay but mainstream audiences. The conservative First Lady's rueful reaction after viewing it upon the passionate recommendation of White House aide Mike Deaver was perhaps the film's highest praise. Deaver recalled that he

> did not attempt to describe the plot, knowing how distasteful
> it might sound . . . The homosexual has nothing in life he de-

sires except to give and receive love with another human being. The radical couldn't care less for that kind of love; for
him life is a cause . . . In the end, the radical discovers there is
grace in giving of yourself—not necessarily in a physical way.
And the homosexual finds that he is willing to take a risk for
a cause . . . In the end, both die, the homosexual while trying
to deliver a message for the radical . . . They had a print delivered to Camp David and watched it one weekend. Nancy
could not wait to see me that Monday morning. "Mike," she
almost gasped, "how could you recommend that film? It was
dreadful. We turned it off halfway through the reel." "Once
you get past the subject," I said, "it was an incredible picture."
She shuddered slightly. "How can you get past that?" she
asked.[2]

Manuel's childhood, he always said, was rescued by his discovery of the
movies. "I grew up on the pampa in a bad dream, or rather a bad western"
was the fable he invented, hoping to wake up to find that real life was
the daily matinee imported from Hollywood. On the flat silver screen the
world became three-dimensional, peopled with glamorous men and
women. Like many children, he was able to construct a safe and imaginary
paradise, an idyll to which he would always return. More than simply loving
the movies, he wanted to live in them; he would have liked to be a diva like
Norma Shearer, but more than that, he wanted to be the character she
played.

He would immerse himself in movie magazines,

anticipating the great moment of the next show. I even went
so far as to cut out ads for the coming attractions in Buenos
Aires. Since we lived 12 hours by train from Buenos Aires we
always received the newspaper a day late. I would organize
them in piles and one day somebody who was mad at me
messed them up! But at age 6 or 7 I would remember the order of the openings in Buenos Aires—what a futile use of
memory, but it just shows what an outsider I felt.[3]

This apparently useless exercise of memory would serve the future novelist well; from life's harsh contrast with these engrossing fantasies, his first novel, *Betrayed by Rita Hayworth* (1968), would emerge. Manuel's childhood friends took for granted that he would have a career in music or movies: "I didn't choose literature . . . Literature chose me. I never fantasized about writing fiction. My only fantasy about writing was that in my old age, after directing many masterpieces, I would write my memoirs."[4]

He would not reach old age, but his first novel remains as a fictional chronicle of his childhood. More than a memory machine, writing turned out to be a way of life in which he was continually creating himself—in visions that would vanish like the image of Rita or Greta after the lights went on—as if he were one of his own fictions.

It was a hot summer day in November 1995 when I visited Manuel's hometown in the pampa, General Villegas, seeking glimmers of him. My guide was a former schoolmate of Manuel's, a short, energetic gray-haired woman named Hebe "Chiquita" Uriarte, a schoolteacher. Chiquita informed me, in a brisk, proud manner, that in 1925 the Prince of Wales made a special visit to the region's most impressive *estancia*, the Drabble ranch, in recognition of its contribution to the Empire. Before lunch, we strolled along dusty streets in the glaring midday sun, revisiting the three-block radius along which home, movie house, and school stood, consecrated sites that native Villegans easily recognize from Manuel's descriptions in *Betrayed by Rita Hayworth* (whose name they pronounce, lovingly, as "Highword"). Lecturing me on local history, Chiquita explained that language, as well as cultural differences, kept the English isolated from town life on their rambling estates. Never integrating, by the time of the drought of 1927 most of their heirs had sold the ranches and left General Villegas for town houses in Buenos Aires or had migrated back to the old country.

To reach Villegas (there is no airport, and the trains are still slow and infrequent), I took an overnight split-level bus whose reclining cloth seats were surprisingly comfortable, if well-worn. For six hours the lumbering vehicle sped across infinite plains, and from my window all I could see in the moonlight was a landscape speckled with low shrubs, sparse hamlets, and sporadic telephone poles. As the moon peeked in and out of the clouds, I nodded off, but an occasional jolt awakened me; groggily I glimpsed what beyond the fogged dusty window could be either land or sea—or was I dreaming a Dalí-scape? I had a sense of Manuel's claustrophobia—and that of those British ranchers who fled to bustling Buenos Aires or lush English countrysides.

The task of the biographer is tricky, to say the least. The danger is to testify only "to the long worldly corruption of a life, as documented deeds and days and disappointments pile up," John Updike recently observed: the ideal, to "convey the unearthly lunar innocence that attends, in the perpetual present of living, the self that seems the real one." Biography then must be fiction as well as fact—for how can the intensity, the passion, the "self that seems the real one" be resurrected without conjecture? Like a translation, a literary biography can be measured against (to paraphrase Borges) a visible original, can be measured with a cold eye against not one but at least two "visibles": the life itself (the reader wants facts) and the corpus. No biography, for example, can resurrect more vividly the world of Manuel Puig's childhood than *Betrayed by Rita Hayworth*, his own fictional autobiography. But by retracing his life, we may gain further insights into the person behind the mask of literature.

In the fall of 1968, a budding enthusiast of Latin American literature in graduate school at Columbia University, I had the good fortune to be assigned to a bibliographical project directed by Professor Gregory Rabassa, John Alexander Coleman, and the Uruguayan literary critic Emir Rodríguez Monegal, who had recently accepted a chair at Yale University. The bibliography was never finished, but Emir and I became romantically involved and remained intimate friends until his death in 1985. The author of many scholarly and critical books on Latin American writers and culture, Emir had recently written an insightful review of Manuel Puig's first novel, which, as Manuel wrote to Emir, made the new novelist feel that "for the first time, my intuitions and my conscious life seem perfectly integrated."

Emir first introduced me to Manuel on a wintry night one year later, in December 1969, at a Chinese restaurant on University Place in Greenwich Village, near the office of our friend John Coleman at New York University. Many years later, researching this biography, I learned that in the spring of 1963 Manuel had lived on upper Riverside Drive in Washington Heights, not far from the neighborhood where I grew up; our paths might even have crossed then. During that year he often saw movies at the RKO on 181st Street or Loew's on 175th, the same theaters where I too escaped temporarily into glamour, from everyday routine in a lower-middle-class neighborhood and from my loneliness as the youngest in a family of adult siblings who had all moved out and on to their life adventures.

Manuel was in New York in December 1969 for a ten-day visit, on his way from Buenos Aires to Europe. Emir had told me that the Argentine writer was handsome, and so I recognized him when a Latin-looking Tyrone Power type with thinning hair, a slight fellow in a leather jacket and a scarf up to his nose, swept into the restaurant and approached our booth with a sprightly step. Manuel said "Hola" shyly and I was immediately captivated by his beautiful, expressive, flirtatious eyes. I could tell he was surprised by the dramatic age gap between his older friend, who looked his age—forty-eight—and this American girl, who looked very young, so different from Emir's former wife, a sophisticated Uruguayan society lady. Manuel took it all in in a split second, of course, as the two chatted and laughed; I chimed in occasionally, usually with a nervous giggle, both thrilled and overwhelmed. Emir later heard from a mutual friend that Manuel's first impression was that we were "una pareja llamativa," a striking (odd) couple. "Llamativa" was an old-fashioned euphemism, typical of the speech of his mother's generation. Upon meeting the exuberant Mrs. Puig in Buenos Aires two years later, I realized she was the source of the language Manuel mimicked so perfectly in his writing, those spoken words I had, by then, recently translated. Manuel explained my delight to her: "You sound like my novel!"

In the following years restaurant dates with Manuel were rare occasions, not because we didn't see each other frequently in the seventies, before he moved to Brazil, but because for Manuel restaurants were an unnecessary expense—and unhygienic, a fact he had learned working in commercial kitchens as a dishwasher in London and Stockholm. After our Chinese dinner Emir, Manuel, and I next met, the following afternoon, to see a movie at the Film and Cultural Center on Columbus Circle, a special showing of Ben Hecht's screwball satire *Nothing Sacred* (1937), with Carole Lombard and Fredric March, two of Manuel's favorites. He sat silently, staring with those big eyes as the audience laughed continuously at the rapid-fire dialogue and shenanigans. Suddenly—during a nightclub scene in which the svelte, in-

ebriated Lombard stands up, daintily tottering, and the audience quietly
await the next wisecrack—Emir and I heard an exclamation pitched beside
us in the dark vast hall: "¡Ay, qué traje divino!" (What a divine dress!). We
looked, startled, at Manuel, his eyes lit by his own enthusiasm even more
than by the luminous screen. "Divino"—another of those over-the-top Argentine utterances—meant that, as far as he was concerned, the satin gown
clinging to immortal Carole's sleek curves was the only note worth taking
on this occasion.

During the early seventies I translated his first three novels: *Betrayed by
Rita Hayworth*, or "Cansino"—Miss Hayworth's real, Hispanic surname—
as he would call it; *Heartbreak Tango*; and *The Buenos Aires Affair*. My first
attempt to read *Betrayed by Rita Hayworth* was halting, however, and I was
nearly defeated by one-sided dialogues and slangy Faulknerian run-on Argentine monologues in the early chapters. In those dialogues, the speakers
were not identified, hence I had to grope along, gradually figuring out who
was who from hints dropped by the characters speaking from within their
world and not to an author or reader who, like a little child hiding behind
the sofa, is obliged to play the role of eavesdropper.[5] Manuel's capacity to
mime speech in his writing was almost hyperreal, but only a fellow Argentine could understand every word on the page. I despaired at first, even with
Emir there to guide me, and not until reading Manuel's seductive second
novel, *Heartbreak Tango* (1969), did I truly gain entrance, on my own, to the
fictive town of Colonel Vallejos.

I got to know Manuel (often in the company of his mother or friends)
quite well, especially when he moved back to New York in the mid-
seventies; my close association with him has given me an advantage as a
chronicler of his days and nights, and has opened doors to correspondence
and interlocutors, sources which might otherwise remain unknown. This
intimacy, as translator and friend, is also an added responsibility. I am only
too aware of the closeted nature of his private life and of that of many of his
friends, whether in Argentina, Italy, or even New York. Indeed, some
names have been changed to protect the privacy of certain individuals. Today, survivors of Manuel's generation, particularly fellow Argentines, still
fear exposure, and his family continues to maintain a veil of discretion over
his personal life.[6]

The photo of Manuel that ran in early publications of the Spanish and

English editions of his novels is Manuel in his prime: he is in his mid-thirties, still very handsome, with a full head of hair. The picture was taken outdoors at his friend Pepe Lamarca's estate by the sea—the background could be either the foam of the sea or waving pampa grass. Manuel is smiling widely—a smile that is more like a laugh—and is showing shining white teeth and a slight five o'clock shadow (he had spent the night in the rustic overseer's hut with Pepe, hence no shave); he is joyous, full of life. The image was to be replaced with updated photos as he gained fame and confidence enough not to conceal his age. The last photo on book jackets featured a gentle middle-aged intellectual—a squinty smile, the vertical line on his brow ever deeper.

Are we fascinated with the lives of writers because we want to be writers? The writer's life seems ideal, free; he or she seems to have minimal material needs—and can travel, live anywhere—in order to work.

Manuel wanted to make music, then movies; then, as a failed screenwriter, he became a novelist. Like his own characters, he embraced a model idealized in Western culture, shaping his life around the myth of the Writer. The reader's biographical curiosity, then, is probably to find out the "truth" behind the fictions, compare the life lived and the life written, understand why the writer feels compelled to make life over in fiction, to "add another room to the house of life," as another Argentine storyteller, Adolfo Bioy Casares, once explained his writerly urge. Dylan Thomas was struck cold when a friend said to him: "If you didn't write those poems, nobody would know you." As Manuel wrote in his penultimate novel, *Blood of Requited Love*, "Death is the worst thing because people forget you."

What made Manuel Puig a disarming figure in modern Latin American literature was that he was the continent's first literary pop novelist. The distinction is no longer salient as we enter the millennium in a cultural environment that has obliterated the classical, but in the sixties he dared, almost out of innocence, to defy the innate elitism of the Argentine and Hispanic intelligentsia—both the left and right political wings. He reinvented literature out of the nonliterary, living culture of his times. He understood how movies, soap operas, and popular songs seductively manipulate our hearts and minds, how the language of the melodramas on radio and in films programmed intellectuals and housemaids alike. Hence he would always combat stereotypes of how a writer, particularly a Latin American writer, should present himself on the world stage. But he would also complain of being misunderstood, of being pegged as nonliterary. His narrative tricks were mostly inspired by popular genres, the movies, and a strong desire to make films, but in his youth he had read extensively and was drawn to a wide variety of styles, from the economy of Gide to the labyrinthine prose of Faulkner. He stopped reading (he explained only half in jest) because writing ruined it for him; he would read any written page—even by Proust!—always with pencil in hand. Old movies, on the other hand, were often perfectly constructed inventions—without need of revision—and he could simply sit back and enjoy. He began writing as a way of understanding how, in so many ways, we have been molded by the persuasive images on screen, and, in the process, his love for those glamorous old stars has perhaps deepened for his readers the pleasure of seeing movies.

He molded his fiction out of the makeshift, the devalued, and though, like many writers, he was always creating himself, that self was more a child of celluloid than a man of letters. He was the writer as playful mime. Whether channeling, in his novels, the voices of shopgirls or, in private display for his friends, the hip-thrusting of redheaded Rita Hayworth when the lights came up on *Gilda* or the mesmerizing facial expressions of Greta Garbo, the "Divine Woman," Manuel was a performer, a magician who could resurrect the ephemeral.

the pampa . . . promises: 1932–49

The Argentine way of life is what I would call the concrete futurism of each individual. It is not the generic futurism of a common ideal, a collective utopia, but rather, each person exists within his illusions as if they were already reality. —José Ortega y Gasset

green pampas, arid pampas

Juan Manuel Puig, named after his paternal grandfather, was born on the pampa at 2:00 a.m. on a hot summer night, December 28, 1932, the Feast of the Holy Innocents. The family's one-story house stood on the corner of Moreno and Arenales in a flat dusty town of around 15,000 inhabitants called General Villegas, about halfway between the Andes mountains and the Atlantic Ocean, in the vast province of Buenos Aires. To appear slightly younger in the public eye, Manuel would later claim his year of birth as 1933. He was *almost* born in 1933, and the birth certificate was signed three days later, on the eve of the new year. Juan Manuel was a healthy round-faced infant with big brown eyes "like grapes," his father's thick black curls, and his mother's fair complexion. Her side of the family was proud of that complexion, the coloring of their northern Italian ancestors, and considered it a mark of class distinction, so valued in Argentine society. In the bureaucratic rhetoric Manuel would someday subvert as a writer, the first declaration of his existence imprinted his gender: "child of the male sex."

María Elena Delledonne and Baldomero Puig, his parents, were proud and relieved. It had been a long and difficult birth; Juan Manuel was their first child. That night, so as not to disturb his exhausted wife and newborn infant, Baldomero slept in the next room with his six-year-old nephew Jorge. When Baldomero saw the dark curly hair of the cherub in his beaming wife's arms, he gave him the nickname normally assigned to Jorges—Coco—as part of his patriarchal heritage. María Elena, or Malena as she was known in General Villegas, was called Malé. The nickname was a common abbreviation, but, considering the bond that would form between mother and son, its suggestion of androgyny (in English) is uncanny. From La Plata, Malé's mother, Annunziata, her sister María Carmen, and María Carmen's son Ernesto had all embarked on the twelve-hour train ride to General Villegas, almost 600 kilometers due west, across endless plains that at night looked like the sea.

In his first and most directly autobiographical novel, *Betrayed by Rita Hayworth*, Manuel would attempt to recapture his aunt's impression when she first got off the train at Colonel Vallejos, his fictional mask for General Villegas, in that summer of 1932:

> My first impression was awful, there's not a single tall building. They're always having droughts there, so you don't see many trees either. In the station there are no taxis, they still use the horse and buggy, and the center of town is just two and a half blocks away. You can find a few trees that are hardly growing, but what you don't see at all, anywhere, is real grass.[1]

Longing for the fragrance of the linden trees in La Plata, the provincial city where she grew up, his mother would try futilely to make grass and plants grow in the patio where Manuel played "by watering the pots practically twenty times a day."

After life on the plains, Manuel, like Malé, would make it a point to live surrounded by flora; at first this meant plant-filled apartments in big cities; later, in Rio de Janeiro, they found the perfect antidote to the bleak contours of General Villegas, a place

> very far away from the sea and the mountains and from Buenos Aires. There was no landscape there, everything was flat. Only the sky was very bright and the air very dry. The town was ugly too . . . It was like living in exile. Anyone born there who never goes away has no idea what life is or of what there is in the world. That's why, when my mother took me to the cinema for the first time—I was four—I thought that was where life was, it all seemed so real to me.[2]

In this absence of landscape, referents like *lake* or *hill* were poetry, not real; the term *city* implied a forbidden faraway place filled with dangers, almost a word one couldn't utter. If you died without ever leaving the town, you would barely know what water was. There was the relentless midday sun, the stars at night, and "wind and dirt blowing all day long." The arid landscape was reality but also a metaphor, the harsh void of the human horizon; there was grass for the cattle, "but for people there is nothing."

Several frontier towns in the region were named after colonels and generals who had been awarded land grants for their campaigns during the nineteenth-century Indian Wars. General Villegas was named after a zealous colonel who had been born in neighboring Uruguay of Canarian origins. A dashing Custer of sorts with a handlebar mustache, he was known as both the Titan and the Bull of the Pampa, and received the rank of general in the 1880s after twenty years of service. He founded Trenque Lauquen as well as Villegas, after leading his gaucho troops to decimate large numbers of Ranquel and Araucana Indians on the plains near the town that honors his name. The Indians of this region had migrated from Chile (according to Caucasian landowners, they invaded the "pampa verde," or fertile green plains); these indigenous peoples fiercely defended what they considered their *pampa*—a Quechuan word meaning "flatland" or "space." They attacked and ravaged scores of new settlers whose reprisals were no less rabid. The Indians' disastrous history has much in common with the legacy of North America's devastated nomadic tribes, though Caucasian immigrants in South America coupled more readily with indigenous peoples than in the northern hemisphere. The Spaniards had fewer compunctions than the British about miscegenation, and their faith, Catholicism, was always avid for converts. The mestizo offspring of such unions in Argentina, labeled *negros*, joined the ranks of the country's servant and worker class; they were the *cabecitas negras* for whom Juan and Evita Perón would symbolize salvation.

In Argentina the upper-class *estancieros*, or landowners—some British but mostly criollos, descendants of Spaniards who had come to Argentina several generations before—virtually ruled until 1945. While the principal European immigrants were Spanish and Italian, the English had brought the technology that would modernize Argentina and make possible the exportation of its riches. These British expatriates, as well as the Argentine criollos of Spanish ancestry, constituted the highest economic rank in a country where class was determined by the amount of land you owned and how much income you produced. Around 1886, when General Villegas was officially founded, the English began buying up ranches, or *estancias*—vast parcels of 10,000 to 30,000 acres—which became grazing land for Aberdeen and Shorthorn cattle. Like other frontier towns it provided a support system for the surrounding region's grain, dairy, and livestock industries. By 1895, farmers, merchants, and professionals from Spain and Italy had begun to migrate to towns in the pampa, like General Villegas, to usher in a network of services and small businesses.

A veiled chronicle of General Villegas in soap opera format, Manuel's second novel, *Heartbreak Tango*, records the declining British presence in the story of solidly middle-class Mabel, who almost marries an English ranch owner. The Englishman is forced by circumstances to file a suit against her father, an auctioneer, for the sale of diseased cattle, thus thwarting her social ascension. Mabel's father's fall from grace reflects what happened to many middlemen during the droughts of the twenties and thirties, which had a direct impact on Manuel's early years: his father, Baldomero, failed at first to rise above his humble station when his youthful attempts in the livestock and dairy business were thwarted by the harsh pampa as well as his older brother's mismanagement.

The landowners remained a unified class through marriage—hence marriages out of their class were frowned upon. The middle and lower-middle class supplied the storekeepers, merchants, tailors, and grocers who ran small businesses and serviced the principal industries: cattle ranching and agriculture. Their ties were looser, and while they formed ethnic social centers such as the Italian Society, the Basque Society, and the Syrian-Lebanese Society, these associations tended to foster formal gatherings rather than a genuine sense of belonging. In the microcosm of Villegas, the landowners were typically in control of the government and the Church, as well as the legal system, medicine, and commerce, professions to which middle- or, more likely, upper-middle-class people could aspire. *Aspire* is the operative word: just as there was no landscape in the pampa, there was also no past, and no present; in this artificial landfill of immigrants—a mere handful on the endless plain—reality was the future; since there was nothing to see, the perceiver projected a mirage.

The state was also a mirage, an abstraction which Argentines, more individuals than citizens, tended to distrust. Manuel's childhood, in the thirties and forties, was spent in a middle-class ambience caught in the fierce struggle between conservative landowners and populist movements. The years 1945, when General Perón and Evita rose to eminence, and 1946, when the general took over the presidency, marked the beginnings of the *proceso*, a crisis-ridden process of economic and political democratization. The Peróns presided over what would be the last prosperous years in Argentina: in the thirties Argentina had been the fifth-richest country in the world, with a per capita income equal to that of France.[3] From the nineteenth through the mid-twentieth century Argentine aristocrats, as citizens of a polyglot and wealthy nation, were frequent travelers to Europe. The Argentine ranch owners who brought their own milk cows to their hotel in Paris were almost a cliché, like the figure of the rich Brazilian in the musical *French Cancan* (1955).

"We were middle-class," Manuel's childhood friend Elena Piña, or Elenita, told me with a warm, crinkly smile, and explained, "I was Alicita in the novel," referring to *Betrayed by Rita Hayworth*. This novel, centered around a little boy in love with the movies, follows Manuel's childhood up until age fifteen and is, for those friends and family members who figured in his early life, a clearly identifiable roman à clef: Juan Manuel Puig, or Coco, becomes the principal character, José Casals, or Toto; his father, Baldo, is Berto; Malé is Mita; cousin Jorge is Hector; Aunt Carmen is Clara; Quica, the maid, is Felisa; and cousin Bebé is Teté. Still vivacious and slanty-eyed in middle age as she was in Manuel's portrait of her as Alicita in *Rita Hayworth*, Elenita is proud to have been Manuel's friend:

> Manuel was from an even better class than my family because
> his mother was a professional and mine was only a housewife,
> and his father owned a business while mine worked in the
> bank as a clerk. But, despite our more conservative parents,
> we shared the same liberal values, in part because we went to
> Public School No. 1 with poor children who lived in huts on
> dirt roads, and we felt sorry for them.

The girls from these poor families—called "negras" or "criollas"—immediately went to work as maidservants and were as young as Bebé. Bebé, Manuel's pretty half-cousin from his father's side of the family, still an attractive blonde in her mid-sixties, remembers that, at age eleven when she spent a couple of months in Villegas, she and nine-year-old Coco talked constantly about how badly some of these girls were treated by their employers.

Bebé's maternal grandparents were "upper-upper-class," particularly her grandmother, whose family owned two vineyards in Mendoza, and her grandfather, whose ranch "was larger than the whole town of Villegas, 2,000 acres."[4] On her visits to Villegas, Bebé would go horseback riding with Coco, bareback, out onto the pampa, the wind in her hair as the horse broke into a gallop: "I was really rich . . . but when Grandfather died, my parents went bankrupt and I got to be very poor. A horrible matter for me; for me money is tied up with emotions, feelings, impotence, a sense of power."[5] Bebé's reversal of fortune provided Coco, keenly aware of his parents' uphill battle for class status, with yet another early realization about the power of money. Associated with class and money worries, Bebé would also be an unconscious rival for Coco in his struggles for sexual identity. Parrying with Teté (Bebé) for making him feel ashamed about being a sissy, Toto tauntingly repeats to her what he had heard among the grown-ups: "Your grandfather didn't want your mom to marry your dad, because he was poor."[6]

Prior to Bebé's family crisis, however, Manuel dated the awakening of his class consciousness to when he realized the maid couldn't go with him and his mother to the movies. The movies were the only escape from that dusty, dreary place, and Quica couldn't share this escape. Simple, earthy Quica was four-year-old Coco's sole companion when his mother went off to work in the morning, the only person at home whom he could talk to during those long hours, or at siesta time when mother and father were in bed. Quica listened to Coco's movie chatter but could not contribute much more than "How nice," and, besides, she had to do her housework. The good-natured young servant was treated as an equal, everybody in the house ate together, and there was no distance. But, Manuel recalled,

> I always thought it was unfair that she couldn't go with us to
> the movies in the afternoon; Quica had to work in the
> kitchen. Everybody had to work. Also Dad and his workers.
> That marginalization [of the worker] didn't hurt until I was
> old enough to transform it into guilt . . . I'm persecuted by the
> idea of privilege or escapism, the feeling that I'm taking time
> away from reality.[7]

Compared with Quica and his father's employees, Coco knew he was a relatively privileged member of local society, but at the same time he felt like an outsider, estranged from the workaday existence of "normal" boys and men. This sense of culpability or difference may have led him, in part, to redeem his escape into the movies by turning this dalliance into his life's work.

If Baldo's principal struggle during Coco's childhood was to achieve solid middle-class status, one could see why Coco might be made to feel guilty about frivolous moviegoing. In contrast to his father's austerity and the stinginess of other characters populating the small town of his memory, Manuel portrays Mita (Malé) in an early draft of *Betrayed by Rita Hayworth* as an indulgent, generous spender: "Mita's the one who spends on what she shouldn't, particularly the daily meals, which were lavish, since they were eaten up, and nothing was left to show for it!"[8] Malé was also a teller of elaborate tales. Her expansive, chatty nature played a crucial role in the transformation of Coco, dreamer and movie lover, into Manuel Puig, novelist. By age twenty Manuel, like most homosexuals of his culture and generation, was living a double life to maintain his social and family relations. The way he handled this was to "embroider," to disguise and transform facts into fiction.

Manuel's material life as an adult would oscillate between the yin and yang of parental economy acquired early on: a penny-pincher in everyday life, he indulged in the luxuries of travel, entertainment, cultural life, and, last but not least, making art.

malé and the delledonnes

In that town what alternatives did I have? It was really a harsh place, like the Far West, on the dry pampa, where it never rains. An almost desert-like plain where the only thing that grows is grass—and it's not even green—that's good only for the cattle, which is why the region survives and is inhabited.

Movie images and the words in books had to compensate for all that was missing in Villegas: whose message was this? It was Malé who took Coco every evening to the movies even before he began going to school, so that she could escape for a few moments from a town where she couldn't smell the orange blossoms and linden flowers of La Plata. Villegas was so dull that the local newspaper published a column called Travelers, announcing the travel plans of its inhabitants, even if this meant only a day trip to the next town! For both mother and son, General Villegas was a bad B movie that had to end.

The movies were where they felt most at home; where, indeed, Manuel wanted to live. The notion of his place of origin as a place of exile might seem surprising, but it is native to Argentina. Like many Argentines confronted by their geographic isolation, Manuel became a relentless traveler as an adult, though he would never be able to shed completely the condition of exile. For a while the new home would be paradise, but sooner or later, paradise would crumble. "He suffered the cities he settled in as one who suffers the setbacks of a house, on a private scale, the same way a sick person reduces the horrors of the world to the portable, idiosyncratic format that the symptoms of his own illness take on."[9] Exile and home would always be two sides of the same coin for him.

The saying goes: The Mexicans descended from the Aztecs, the Peruvians from the Incas, and the Argentines from the boat. At the turn of the last century, over 70 percent of Argentina's population was composed of first-generation immigrants, including "Russians" and "Turks" but mostly Spaniards and Italians.[10] Doña Malé Delledonne's family came from the fertile Po valley in northern Italy. Her father, Ernesto Delledonne—the surname means "of women"—was a country boy from a farm near Busseto, Verdi's birthplace. Don Ernesto and his fiancée, Annunziata Marenghi, had married in her hometown, Piacenza, near Cremona, the city famous for its Stradivarius violins. They remained childless for several years, which had everyone concerned. But, as soon as they disembarked in Buenos Aires in the late 1890s and (with the help of cousin Giorgio who had preceded them) settled in La Plata, thirty miles south of Buenos Aires, the Delledonne couple lived up to the family name. Annunziata gave birth, in quick succession, to five daughters. A patriotic deed, because emigrants were encouraged to populate sparse La Plata, the new capital of the province of Buenos Aires.

A big city in comparison to Villegas, though only a suburban town compared to Buenos Aires, La Plata was the only planned urban center in the country. Manuel and Malé loved visiting La Plata: for both it was an oasis. Symmetrical streets crisscrossed *diagonales*—broad angling avenues—punctuated deliberately with squares, parks, and stately monuments. There were theaters, several movie houses, and an "acclimatized" pool in the neighborhood gymnasium where Malé did her daily laps while Coco took swimming lessons. Like his mother, his Delledonne aunts and cousins were more genteel than the Puigs, more modern and less *machista*. Manuel would always feel more affection for his mother's family than for his father's.

The sheltering bosom of the Delledonne home in La Plata would be the setting for the opening scene of *Betrayed by Rita Hayworth*. Manuel, in the first draft of his novel, let Aunt Clara (Carmen) tell the family history, from the point of view of the Italian side and its critique of the Spanish Puigs; she explains Toto's "strangeness" as coming from the difficult Casals family (the Catalan name he substitutes for Puig). While his father saves every penny, struggling to build up capital, his mother, serving steaks and whiskey, appears more generous. The *gallegos* (Spaniards) are more brutish, rowdier, unpredictable; the Italians more easygoing and trustworthy.

In an early draft Manuel sketched typical Argentine prejudices among different national minority groups, but in the final version he toned down the overt rivalry between Spaniards and Italians, turning petty ethnic frictions into a more personal opposition between mother and father. Life's experiences might modulate his feelings about Spaniards and Italians, but he would remain more allied to his maternal origins. He makes this preference clear in the first draft of *Betrayed by Rita Hayworth*, in which Aunt Clara tells a kind of fragmented family history; but discretion as well as economy shaped the novel's final version, in which most of his family history was excised, and only the essential—such as Toto's "movie-crazy" passion and devotion to the arts under the influence of the Italian matriarchs—was left intact.

Grandpa Ernesto, an illiterate greengrocer, was a humble, simple man. Ernesto's grocery adjoined the house, and chickens in the patio provided eggs for the family as well as for customers. Young Ernesto, his grandson, watched them grow up from little chicks popping out of their shells; they would become his friends and eventually, to his horror, Sunday stew.[11] That is how simple people lived then, cousin Ernesto said to me when we met in November 1995; Grandpa Ernesto's goal was to provide for his family. But he was more gregarious than industrious, and spent hours in the café chatting with friends, which exasperated Annunziata.

While they were "more like Papa's family, from Busseto," Aunt Clara's monologue revealed that "Mama" (Manuel's grandmother, Annunziata), who was from a more cosmopolitan background, was the preferred parent, the one Mita (Malé) felt closest to. "Mita knew how to give herself time for everything, like Mama. Because Mama always has her clothes ready to go out . . . mostly to the movies."[12] Malé had Annunziata's drive and intelligence, and shared her passion for theater and her daydreams about movie actors: "Who knows who [Annunziata] would have liked as a husband. She never said anything . . . but she was crazy about [the actor] López Lagar." A dark virile gallego whose heavy-lidded, almond-shaped eyes made hearts throb in the thirties, Lagar had fled Franco's Spain with Margarita Xirgu, remaining in Argentina to become a matinee idol.[13]

Annunziata missed her family but, like most Italian immigrants, was not sentimental about returning to the old country: having to make your own bread every day was not romantic. Sentimentality had no place in the harsh origins of these immigrants, but deep down everyone believed in the redeeming value of sentiment. In the first draft of *Betrayed by Rita Hayworth*, Aunt Clara responds defensively to her sister Mita's friend Sophia, who criticizes Victor Hugo for being too sappy: "I think a romantic person, who has feelings, can't be bad, because he knows what it means to suffer and will try not to make others suffer." Clara reminisces about how she met her husband but then contrasts these feelings with her immigrant mother's experience:

> A woman like Mama had no time to be romantic. The work
> in Italy was hard, everything they had in the house they had
> to make, you couldn't just buy bread, you had to make it . . .
> I'd like to know how that was, but now we're not educated to
> live that way, though I do my sewing very well: what a pity
> there's no time to make a pretty tablecloth.[14]

This mention of embroidery, a daily chore that had some aesthetic function in the limited lives of these homebound women, would give Manuel *Betrayed by Rita Hayworth*'s deliberately plain first sentence: "A brown crossstitch over beige linen . . ." The first dialogue, a conversation among practical-minded family members who have no choice but to be down-to-earth, establishes the book's antiromantic yet nostalgic feel—nostalgia for the old country, Mita's nostalgia for the family home in La Plata, and the family's nostalgia for Mita far away in Villegas.

The strong-willed Annunziata Marenghi Delledonne, uneducated like her husband, pushed him to work so hard in this fresh city of opportunity that Grandpa Ernesto was considered a saint—a euphemism for henpecked husband. He was to outlive Annunziata, but not before she embarked her girls on their respective life voyages. To ascend socially, to compete successfully with Spaniards, Eastern Europeans, and native Argentinians, the descendants of these Italian immigrants needed to leave behind the past. For her children to leave behind peasant origins and enter the middle class, education was essential. Public education in Argentina, as in the United States during the same period, promoted assimilation: immigrants had to adapt to their new country, which, after all, had adopted them.

Aida was the eldest daughter, called Pety, short for Petisa (Shorty), and known for being a "bit absent-minded." Next came Emma: she and middle daughter Malé were tall and blond, the ones who inherited Annunziata's ambitious nature, shrewd intelligence, enthusiasm for the arts. Emma, sketchily represented by Adela in chapter 1 of *Betrayed by Rita Hayworth*, which takes place in the family home in La Plata, used her eyes too much, according to Grandmother. This was a typical complaint mothers made about studious daughters who ruin their looks with too much reading in bad light. If on the one hand daughters had to be educated, they also had to become desirable wives.

After Malé came María Carmen, nicknamed Chiquita—or Little One, a common diminutive for girls in patriarchal Argentina—followed by Annunziata's youngest daughter Regina (Reya). Aside from Manuel, Malé's constant companion on many trips would be María Carmen, the mother of Manuel's cousin Ernesto, with whom he played as a small child. The last of Malé's sisters to die, she was the aunt whose voice initiated Manuel Puig's first novel and whose death inspired his last, *Tropical Night Falling*.

Malé was born on September 8, 1907, astrologically a Virgo, destined to be both creative and fussy, as she summed it up. Malé with the laughing light eyes, the only daughter to attend the university and the one who most took after Annunziata—intelligent, hard-nosed, and "movie crazy." With a flair for drama that Manuel would inherit, Malé wanted to be an actress. Cut in the final version of *Betrayed by Rita Hayworth*, this revelation appears in Aunt Clara's monologue in the first draft of the novel: "[It was] a good thing Mita didn't decide to get involved with the theater as she was determined to at one point, before becoming friends with Sophia and going crazy over novels, because if Mita had gone into the theater where they're all hyenas, as in all job markets, if you really look at it, they would have eaten her alive."[15] Because Malé loved to draw and paint too, her best friend in La Plata encouraged her to study literature and the arts at the university. Her lifelong interest and enthusiasm would inspire not only Manuel but her nephew Ernesto, who, though he studied to be an engineer, was also an amateur painter. In his third novel, *The Buenos Aires Affair*, Manuel not only caricatures himself as Gladys Hebe D'Onofrio, a collage artist of Italian descent, but perhaps also Malé, as Gladys's mother, Clara Evelia, a bombastic poetry reciter.

Despite her artistic aspirations, Malé had to be pragmatic, to help support the family that had sacrificed so much for her education. So instead of devoting herself to her true vocation, Malé majored in biochemistry at the University of La Plata, one of the largest universities in Argentina, and received a degree in pharmacology. But every spare moment or peso she would spend, like her mother, on the theater, which at that time meant not only the movies but also popular zarzuelas, or music hall operettas.

"Mama wasn't from town," as Manuel described her, casting her in a cosmopolitan light. "She was from the capital of the province, La Plata." Even though it was a quiet, provincial city, La Plata was Paris compared to General Villegas, where a pharmacist like Malé was a novelty. Service industries were becoming more professionalized throughout the nation; up until the twenties, the local pharmacist could get away with some pharmaceutical knowledge, but now such persons had to be legally certified. Argentine universities were churning out qualified professionals at a faster rate than they could be absorbed by an infrastructure that afforded relatively few positions. Malé had to accept an opening 600 kilometers away, at the other end of the province of Buenos Aires, at Farmacia Moderna, the town drugstore in General Villegas, on Rivadavia Street, the same street where Malé and Baldo would eventually buy a house. It was a big leap for Malé, attached as she was to her family, particularly her mother, and she wrote home every three or four days. Years later, when he was living far away from home, Manuel would adopt his mother's practice of letter writing. His copious correspondence with friends and family is an illuminating (though still unpublished) part of his written legacy.

With Coco, Malé would repeat the intense connection that Annunziata, cut off from her family in Italy, had with her daughters. By the late thirties, contact with Europe was even more difficult; "Poor Mama," Aunt Clara says,

> to think that she didn't see her family again and who knows if she will. And now with the war . . . the poor things must be suffering terrible hunger . . . Each one has her cross to bear, and poor Mita has to live faraway from us, and [I] especially feel bad for Mother because Mita was very attached to her.[16]

Initially Malé decided to go to General Villegas for one year, in 1929, "to earn a little money . . . and return to La Plata and live the life she wanted, going to lectures and working at some lab or continuing her studies."[17] While continuing to work at the drugstore Malé accepted another position, as head chemist at the town's hospital pharmacy on the morning shift; though determined to escape from General Villegas, she was generous and even philanthropic in the workplace, often giving medicines to poor people in the hospital who could not afford to buy them. When Annunziata and María Carmen came three years later, to witness Coco's birth, they supported Malé's desire to make the best of her situation. Even though they didn't like the place, they recognized that life there was "easy," a viewpoint Manuel evokes in his novel: "Mita has a maid who cooks and cleans while she works in the hospital. All the poor people in Vallejos love Mita since she isn't stingy with the cotton and antiseptics and bandages."[18]

The Spanish owner of the pharmacy was a heavy drinker with an invalid wife. When Malé's sisters heard about him—she sent letters home every two or three days—they feared for their sister's fate. Her reports of his bad breath and a group photograph revealing a short fat fellow in a beret reassured them, however. Idolizing silent films stars such as Ramon Novarro and Antonio Moreno, Malé was particular about looks, and had criticized her sister Carmen for marrying a mousy-looking fellow, even if he was nice. But this faint rumor about his mother and the pharmacist, which little Manuel would later overhear, would become raw material for *Heartbreak Tango*.

A year before she had left for Villegas, young Malé flirted in La Plata with a young actor, who followed her on the street, named José Gola. Called Carlos Palau in *Betrayed by Rita Hayworth*, with the looks of Tyrone Power and the "tough but tender" touch of John Garfield, "Gola began to work in the Argentine movies, and since he was so handsome he was very successful."[19] The young man soon became a national film star, but his career was cut short: he died on tour in northern Argentina of some mysterious tropical disease. When Malé sent a photo of her new boyfriend in Villegas, her sisters smiled because he was the spitting image of her adored José Gola.

When she first arrived in Villegas, Malé lived at the Hotel Estrella, which belonged to the six Iriarte sisters. These girls shared Malé's theatrical bent and she joined their amateur theater group. In an early draft of *Rita Hayworth* Manuel related the story of the Iriartes, supposedly "loose" girls known for throwing wild parties, and insinuated that the hotel was considered, for all practical purposes, a brothel. In the final version Manuel eliminated the Iriartes, just as he toned down Malé's flirtation with Gola, to avoid associating his mother with shady behavior. He condensed this aspect of Malé's life to a phone conversation between Mita and her best friend Choli, the cosmetics saleswoman. The pharmacy where Malé worked, today still standing on Rivadavia Street, was next door to the perfume shop where she made friends with the "interesting" (that is, sexy) cosmetics saleswoman who, in the novel, had affairs with traveling salesmen. Like the Iriartes, this woman left town, leaving Malé without a local confidant—though she did have little Coco.

Malé's association with the Iriartes would lead some Villegans to brand this outsider as promiscuous, particularly since Malé joined in their parties and unwittingly, according to Clara's monologue, went on at least one outing in a car with traveling salesmen:

> Ay, the things that happened to Mita, the fright . . . Because
> who would have thought it, three of the Iriartes (who knows
> what the others were doing) go off with Mita to take a ride

with a salesman and Mita totally trusting, but afterwards they
stopped at a pastry shop [café] at the end of the paved road,
and there were other salesmen there and they all went . . . in
four cars to race. But what racing, on those dirt roads . . . The
thing is they went far out of town.[20]

In her family's eyes Malé was a decent girl: at least, as Clara clarifies, Mita
refused to go on further excursions like this one, and the Iriartes were good
sports about it, even letting Malé play a starring role in one of their musical
comedies. While the Iriartes were erased from the novel, the traveling salesmen incident reappeared in a more disguised and—one could say—more
vengeful form in *Heartbreak Tango*, the novel whose "indiscretions" most
scandalized the inhabitants of General Villegas.

Here the story of a local Don Juan, Juan Carlos Etchepare, and his
erring sister Celina, who gets into cars with traveling salesmen, is closely
based on gossip Coco would overhear (usually at home, from a hiding place)
about the well-respected, upper-crust Caraveras. They were nice people and
nice-looking, beloved and admired in town; one daughter, Marina Caravera, a pretty coquette, was the most popular girl, hence set up by other un-
married girls as newcomer Malé's rival for male attentions. The rivalries in
Heartbreak Tango between lower-middle-class Nené and upper-middle-class
Mabel, as well as the clashes between Nené and Celina, dramatize Marina's
supposed competition with Malé. Indeed Ma(bel) and (Ce)lina conjoined
phonetically suggest both Marina and Malena. Marina's sister married and
moved to Buenos Aires, as does Nené in the novel, while Marina, the party
girl, stayed behind in Villegas, though she too eventually married. The vivid
rivalries between the girls were heightened by Coco's sense of Malé's discomfort.

It was in a play put on by the Iriartes that Baldo first saw Malé, the new
girl in town. She apparently stole the show by playing the role of *catalana*, a
woman from his father's native Catalonia, and she, in turn, saw his handsome face as the only beacon among "all those faces that looked alike when
one is missing people . . . [faces] that looked at you in an unfriendly way."[21]
A few days later, leaving the post office where she went regularly to send off
her homesick letters to La Plata, she ran into him again—and sparks flew.
She accepted a date to play tennis with him in the Plaza de la Cruz (today

Plaza San Martín), and at the social gatherings organized by the Iriarte sisters, he always showed up. Malé seemed not to mind that he was the darling of all the girls in town, with the reputation of being a Don Juan. Charming and dynamic, with movie-star looks, Baldomero Puig was the event that changed Malé's plans forever.

Malé and Baldo, born respectively under the signs of Virgo and Aries, were opposites drawn by mutual attraction: she, fair, feminine, elegant with a romantic air, but earthy and practical; he, strong and dark with intense eyes, described by some as fiery and tenacious. They were the archetypal couple of the afternoon radio soap opera. They fell in love, and when Malé went home after a little over one year in Villegas in early 1931, four days later Baldo showed up on the Delledonne doorstep in La Plata, unable to be apart from her. He had come to ask for her hand in marriage. Even though he had only a modest job selling livestock and dairy produce, he managed to convince Annunziata that he had business smarts. They married right then and there at the San Ponciano church in La Plata—though Malé resented the fact that the priest married them in the small chapel simply because they couldn't afford the high altar.

The newlyweds reappear in *Heartbreak Tango* in the figures of Nené and Massa, who, like Malé and Baldo, went to Buenos Aires for their honeymoon. Nené and Massa are a less romantic match than Malé and Baldo were at first, however, as if Manuel were shedding a harsh light, condensing early and later stages of their relationship. Nené marries for convenience and doesn't like marital sex since her true beloved was Juan Carlos; at the beginning of her own romance, Malé was smitten with handsome Baldo, who was equally smitten with the pretty girl he had first seen dressed as a peasant lass from his father's homeland. But would this flame smolder into true love? Even if it could have, Malé quickly became embittered with life in Villegas, but, like Manuel's fictional Nené, she had to be practical. The fire that first fused his young parents would lead to heated discord and, in their mature years, to separation.

How newcomer Malé was seen in General Villegas had as much impact on her firstborn—and the books he would someday write—as did her response to those desolate circumstances. Like voluptuous Gradisca in Fellini's *Amarcord*, Malé in her house on Rivadavia Street now filters through memory's veil as a creature of glamour for several elder Villegans. Among them,

Manuel's schoolmate Hebe "Chiquita" Uriarte remembers one cold day coming in the front door and then turning into the room on the right with the balcony overlooking Rivadavia, where "his mother was sitting by a gold-arabesqued heater; she always wore a white blouse, and her blond hair was combed back. Always impeccable. Sometimes she wore white clogs." Quica Brown, grateful to have worked for the liberal Puigs, recalls a lovely Malé who was, nonetheless, a rigorous employer: "Malé was a model housewife. She liked the house to be orderly, she liked to cook, clean, decorate. She starched all the clothes. She was pretty, good, gentle." Manuel's playmate, Elena, admired Malé's education and culture, and how they always listened to music on the Victrola at Coco's house. Sprightly Nelly Ortea, wife of Jorge López, the swimming instructor, remembers how friendly Malé was to her mother, always generously lending her women's magazines like *El Hogar* (Home)—which young Coco would also read cover to cover.[22]

Malé was outgoing and intelligent, a graceful dancer and an excellent tennis player; she was warm, generous, accomplished; she recited poetry and acted in plays. She was a dynamo in that small town, bound to provoke admiration but also the flipside, envy. Villegas was like a family, and some members, mostly women, resented that she had married the best-looking bachelor. Such an independent professional woman, so attuned to culture, was too different. Nelly, an in-law whose sister married Manuel's cousin Antonio "El Gordo" Grippo, noticed that Malé changed drastically after her marriage, became more withdrawn, less of a social butterfly: "Why, she stopped playing tennis and didn't take it up again until 1952!" Malé was devoted to supporting her family and to educating Coco, arranging for music and English lessons as well as sending him every morning to school. Like most housewives, she prepared elaborate midday meals (luscious homemade ravioli filled with calves' brains and spinach, followed by breaded veal cutlets, or rich homemade canelloni followed by beef stew, and for dessert, dulce de leche), listened to soap operas on the radio, and went to the movies. The excursion to the movie house, three blocks away, was her excuse to put on a nice dress. What was viewed as somewhat unusual, however, was that she would take her little boy with her every evening, five days a week, even after Coco was old enough to go with friends. The son was proud and enamored of his elegant mother, but also implicitly sensed that they stood out like sore thumbs in the small town.

Malé was considered "too progressive." Her secularism, shared with her liberal-minded sisters and nourished by the university, where religion was not discussed, went against the grain of a largely Catholic population. More than an atheist, Malé, like many immigrants reacting against their Catholic backgrounds, was anticlerical. But her sons were baptized, and she made all of them, including nephew Jorge, take Communion; because he was already "different," she was particularly eager for Coco to go to catechism school. And though she disapproved, she later respected her youngest son Carlos's post-hippie religious phase.

In oppressive Villegas, however, Malé couldn't stand Catholic fanaticism and the hypocrisy of the supposedly religious society around her, especially its lack of charity and tolerance. Despite her neighbors' indignation she never went to church on Sunday, and on days when the town turned out to celebrate a saint's day with processions, carrying the effigy of the saint from house to house, Malé would close her window and hide. At Jorge's Communion, which preceded Coco's by six years, it was Malé's turn to be indignant when "one of those old bags" who spent the whole day in church, organizing and arranging everything, separated the boys who were all spruced up from those who were more simply attired, pushing the better-dressed ones into the first row. Malé was furious at such discrimination and wanted to drag Jorge from the church. Baldo and the other family members present had to stop her before a scandal ensued.

Her atheist tendencies created a confusing situation for Coco at the Nuns' School. He won a prize for being the "most religious boy" when he took Communion on December 8, 1942, and yet his family was not religious and his mother made fun of the nuns. Her resistance to this Catholic environment permeates Manuel's early novels: in *Betrayed by Rita Hayworth* Toto jokes about the nuns but is terrorized by their fire-and-brimstone sermons; in *Heartbreak Tango* hypocritical Mabel tells lies even in the confessional, and Nené daydreams, with blasphemous naïveté, of meeting Juan Carlos in heaven, where the two lovers are finally united in the flesh. Like Malé, Manuel was a skeptic who wished he had the consolation of religion, as he confided later in life to his devout cousin Bebé. His childhood fear of death would come up in *Betrayed by Rita Hayworth*, where Toto tries to ignore the nuns' stories but "the only thing that bothers Toto is the end of the world."[23]

If Malé was coquettish, Baldo was actually unfaithful. He was a big flirt, said Quica, and the occasional affair on his business trips did not count against him, whereas in that conservative society a liberated woman was a loose woman. From an oligarchic Spanish or British colonial perspective, Malé was considered déclassé on other grounds. A former resident of General Villegas named Luisa, from a Spanish Catholic family, still speaks disparagingly of Malena, who worked at the hospital instead of owning her own pharmacy.

Those ill-disposed toward Malé saw her as a bossy outsider who had married a simple local boy, who looked small next to overbearing Malena; Manuel would appear in retrospect as another weak male, just like his father. This opinion seems to jibe with Malé's supposed similarity to her mother as a strong woman frustrated by a wishy-washy husband, and, though an unsympathetic view (almost diametrically opposed to Quica's fond memory of gentle Malé and virile Baldo), it corresponds in part with Coco's early sense that Malé was the tough mate and Baldo had to struggle to overcome his vulnerabilities.

baldo and the puigs

Baldo's favorite tango, "El Aguacero" (The Rainstorm), written by two brothers, José González and Cátulo Castillo, in the twenties, told a sad, stoic tale about spartan life on the pampa: "La pampa is a green handkerchief / hanging from the sky / out in the sun . . . How life sometimes is / without shade or wounds, / without suffering or love! . . . And the pampa is a green handkerchief / hanging from the sky / that wants to cry." There may well have been times when Baldo wanted to cry but couldn't, because he was a man.

His father, Jorge Juan Manuel Puig, of Catalan origin, was known in his time as the most handsome man in Villegas. As a recent immigrant in the 1880s, Grandfather Puig married Eulogia Cortés in the city of Córdoba in the mountains of northern Argentina. Fresh off the boat from Galicia, in northwestern Spain, young Eulogia had left her family behind in the Orense town of Carballino, where her mother, Rosa, had been the town beauty. These Catalan and Galician peasants settled in colonial Córdoba instead of the port town of Buenos Aires (founded in the sixteenth century on the Plata River delta as the Puerto de Nuestra Santa María de los Buenos Aires, or Port of Our Lady Saint Mary of the Good Airs). Córdoba, like Mendoza, was also founded by the Spanish in the sixteenth century, as a strategic link to the precious metal mines in Peru and Bolivia; both Córdoba and Mendoza were as vital as Buenos Aires before it became the country's megalopolis in the late nineteenth century.

Eulogia had arrived with her nephew, Camilo Cortés, a merry boy with a beautiful singing voice, and his friend Fernandez Blanco, who would one day compose the tango "Marinero, Adiós," or "Goodbye, Sailor." Homesick sailors would sing this tango in a thirties Mexican film that Manuel loved, *Woman of the Port*, a truculent melodrama ending in incest and suicide. For Camilo, born out of wedlock, the new world meant a fresh start, far from dubious origins. Here Camilo could start a family: he would also be more of a brother to his cousin Baldomero than Baldo's own siblings.

High up in Córdoba, Jorge Juan Manuel and Eulogia gave birth to their first son, Juan, in 1889. A few years later they moved south to the flat pampa to resettle with a colony of Catalans in the frontier boomtown of General Villegas, and lived in a rambling one-story farmhouse, its typical long wooden gallery lined with bedrooms and its large inner courtyard populated by cackling hens and chickens.

Jorge Juan Manuel worked as the town postman, which in those days meant taking the mail off the train and distributing it on horseback. He rode tall in his saddle from the station to the town; his son Andrés and his grandson Carlos, Manuel's younger brother, would inherit the proud patriarch's height, and his youngest son, Baldo, his stalwart, austere air. The formidable postman eventually saved up to buy a hotel in a nearby town, Fortín, between Villegas and Trenque Lauquen. Old-timers also remember that Don Jorge Juan Manuel had bought a wagon to travel back and forth from Villegas to Fortín; he'd often take along his sons Juan and Andrés. They were an imposing trio commanding the respect of the men and the admiration of the ladies as the wagon raised dust along the streets of Villegas. Among their ardent admirers was Carmen Grippo, a plump young woman from a prosperous Italian family in Villegas, who would soon become Juan's wife.

Baldomero, the youngest of seven children, was born in Villegas on April 6, 1906. Three years later his father died, and after Eulogia's death in 1922, Baldomero was left in the care of his oldest brother Juan, who became a kind of stepfather to Baldo. Later, Baldo would take care of Juan's son Jorge, and during the years when Coco was growing up, Jorge was more like a brother than a cousin to him.

Men wore guns in those days; living in Buenos Aires in the forties, Juan still carried a gun. Stories about the "macho" Puig men are remembered in the family, as when Juan, who worked in his boyhood in Villegas as a postman, told his brothers about some hooligans who were throwing stones at him as he went about his job. "Tell me who they are," said Andrés, the tallest and most macho of all; needless to say, he "took care of them" and the hooligans never bothered Juan again.

Juan had married well; his in-laws, the Grippos, supported and housed an early business venture in the twenties, *El Comentario*, the "radical" town newspaper, in opposition to the conservative *La Idea*. Juan, Andrés, and Baldomero, as well as their four sisters, Anselma, Ramona, María, and Mercedes, worked on the paper for several years. From northern Spain, the Galicians had the reputation for being hardy and brutish, and the family elders remember Mercedes in particular because she was considered slightly masculine, or a *gallega hombruna*: while her sisters handled clerical duties, Mercedes ran the manual printing press and had no qualms about doing a man's job.

Camilo Cortés, the musical gallego who had journeyed to the New World with his aunt Eulogia, was the editor in chief and also wrote poems, or rather verses, like "Churri, You're My Queen" ("Always singing, always sprightly, all day long, adorable Churri"). In 1929 lyrical Camilo would marry Dora Lariguet, a member of an affluent landowning family in the town of Colonel Granada, and in 1930 Dora would give birth to cousin Bebé: Teté in *Betrayed by Rita Hayworth* mentions, "Daddy worked in a printing press in this town and published a newspaper and wrote long articles and sometimes poems under another name."[24] Camilo was more a dreamer than a businessman, however, and after Dora's rich parents died, he and Dora eventually went bankrupt.

But the ineffectual Camilo was at least a decent person; shady Juan would cause young Baldo much anxiety and insecurity. The final chapter of *Betrayed by Rita Hayworth*—"an adornment" Manuel modestly called it (in a letter to Malé in 1964) in the heat of finishing the novel—is an unsent letter that Berto (Baldo) supposedly writes to Jaime (Juan). This adornment would be an essential key to the novel—the theme of a father's betrayal of his son. As Marlon Brando reproaches Rod Steiger with his climactic lament "I could've been a contender" in *On the Waterfront*, so Berto complains bitterly to his older brother Jaime, who failed him by not providing for his education, obliging him to work as a ranch hand in his adolescence, and then proceeding to mishandle business and neglect their economic welfare: because of Jaime's mismanagement they lose their livestock in the droughts of 1927 and 1933.

According to Berto, Jaime was also an irresponsible womanizer: "I imagine there won't be a sacred corner in Madrid when you're through with it, you must have corrupted half the women there . . . How different we are in that respect, Jaime. Since I met Mita I've forgotten that other women exist."[25] But the factual betrayal behind the fiction was even more onerous. While Juan did make a trip to Spain in 1929, "womanizing" stands in for a more sordid truth: Juan left his invalid wife and his son with Baldo and Malé to manage a business which cast great shame upon the family—"the white slave trade," as it was called, or prostitution.[26] One of the last film projects Manuel conceived—*Naked Tango* (1989)—would portray a fatal filial rivalry between the patriarchal boss and a young pimp in a Buenos Aires brothel in the twenties and thirties, the period of his father's youth. *Betrayed by Rita Hayworth* would be hailed and censored for its frankness, but this family skeleton was even more scandalous, too shocking to reveal explicitly. Shame no doubt fanned Baldo's sense of betrayal (or abandonment), heightened further by town gossip; one can see how such wounds might open again when Malé and Baldo's first son would show early signs of sexual ambiguity in the small world of this remote town. Intentionally or not, Manuel was to avenge this atmosphere of petty humiliations in his first two novels about the fictional town of Colonel Vallejos.

By the forties, Juan had established his "trade" in Buenos Aires, wearing the obligatory pistol, and brought his adolescent son Jorge to live with him in a succession of cheap hotels or boardinghouses. For Jorge, it meant the end of the idyllic period of his life, his safe childhood in Villegas. Jorge's story not only provided a starting point for *Betrayed by Rita Hayworth* but would spark the second novel, *Heartbreak Tango*, which Manuel began upon returning to Argentina after his years in Europe. Though desirous of adventures abroad, Manuel had also felt he had no choice but to leave home. Seeing the winners of the past end in bitter defeat in the present provided a new perspective and perhaps a certain guilty satisfaction. Jorge, the athlete and the ladykiller, had Manuel's handsome looks, but was a huskier, more masculine version of his cousin. Never successful at any career, he would always depend on the charity of his family; his fate dramatized the ordinary lives of those Manuel left behind in Argentina.

The child of immigrants, Baldo dreamed of having a roof over his head, a house of his own. To save on rent so as to be able eventually to buy a house, hardworking newlyweds Baldo and Malé were first obliged to live in a large old house on Arenales Street with Baldo's family: sister Anselma, or Selma, brother Juan, Juan's now invalid wife, Doña Carmen de Grippo, and small son, Juan Jorge. Baldo was understandably preoccupied with raising enough cash to move out; shortly after Juan Manuel was born, they were able to rent a house on their own, down the block on San Martín Street. Doña Carmen, bedridden with a "circulatory disease" that manifested itself as mental illness, passed away, and the money she left for her son, Jorge, was "borrowed" by Baldo, caretaker of his brother's family, to boost his new business—Vinos Viñaflor—as a wine distributor.

Feeling unworthy of his educated wife, Baldo was determined to make a comfortable life for his family, to live up to his wife's expectations, and to her family's, as Berto expresses in a letter in the first draft of *Betrayed by Rita Hayworth*: "Mita's mother wrote her from La Plata saying they were so happy they trusted me when I went to ask for Mita's hand. You know they wanted the best for Mita and they sacrificed a lot so that she could study; after that it's not so easy to give her away to the first bum that comes along." And further: "Mita keeps harping on going to La Plata so I can get any old job while I finish college at night and then go to law school, which I always wanted; but I can't stick her in her parents' house, living off charity, in a home that's not our own, living from hand to mouth, until I graduate almost seven years later."[27]

On the one hand, the real Baldo had little to offer this dynamic young woman, and on the other, it was his manly duty to support her. Berto writes in his unsent letter: "Do you know that before things got bad I had Mita send all she wanted to her mother every month, but it's not my fault if the tide's against me and lately she's been giving me her whole salary."[28] Malé was head pharmacist at the hospital for almost ten years, until March 1939, when she was officially dismissed because of her frequent trips home to Annunziata in La Plata. By this time Baldo's business was successful enough to support the family anyway: distributing wines in bulk from Mendoza, Baldo first sold the wine in barrels in the surrounding towns; then he bottled it by hand; and finally he was able to finance the machinery to automate the bottling process. Now Malé could spend more time at home, attending to six-year-old Coco.

By the time Coco was three, his parents had bought the Grippo family house, next door to the Italian Society on Rivadavia Street. In this house, where they lived until they moved to Buenos Aires in 1949, Baldo set up his wine factory. Today a high school has replaced the Italian Society, and all that's left of the Puig house, in which much of *Betrayed by Rita Hayworth* transpires, is a staircase and a well. The cellar staircase, once part of the winery, leads nowhere; in the patio where Malé had her garden stands the original well that supplied the house with the "sparkling" water Toto compares with the lights in his friend Alicita's hair.

Handsome and athletic, Baldomero was a ladies' man but also a man's man who spent his spare time with his employees or with buddies at the Rotary Club. He was a good swimmer and a regular on the tennis courts; in the eyes of his Villegan men friends, Baldo was outgoing, worldly, enterprising; in 1946, when the first (non-British) cars with left-sided steering wheels arrived, Baldomero was the first in town to buy a Dodge. Unlike his unreliable older brother Juan, Baldo was a responsible husband and father, and, unlike progressive Malé, he was a good Catholic in public, if not at home. But while the fictional Berto claims fidelity to his wife, Mita, in his letter to his disloyal brother, Baldo, a skirtchaser, resented his brother in part for leaving him saddled with responsibilities. Baldo's philandering is played down in the final draft of the novel, perhaps because what made a greater impact on Coco was not Baldo's infidelities but his anger at home and, implicitly, his sense of inadequacy.

If something went wrong at work, Baldo vented his frustration at home.

After all, weren't women supposed to serve their husbands' every need, as well as nurture children? In the old country the womenfolk didn't even sit down to have dinner with the men, but ate before or afterward, sitting by the hearth. Years later Manuel remembered the Delledonne aunts' stories about northern Italy, about women who were conditioned to believe in their husbands' authority. The worst irony of his parents' relationship, Manuel always felt, was that they shared more than their society allowed them to recognize. His father was a daydreamer, his mother a pragmatist, but they were each forced to play the opposite role, which confused everything. Particularly confusing were the "strange authority games" his father played, barking orders. For Coco his father seemed to be acting, at work as well as at home, and also his workers, all men, imitated this act in their homes. As Manuel joked, "at least the movies were more straightforward," and one knew that everybody in the movie was supposed to be acting.

Baldo the dreamer had no choice but to harness his dreams for practical use. After the winery was under way, he began experimenting with metals and found an efficient way to anodize aluminum for more durable and attractive pressure cookers; this discovery, preceding the arrival of foreign patents, spelled prosperity. Trained as a mechanical engineer, Manuel's cousin Ernesto speaks admiringly of Baldo's tenacious ability to get ahead: "He had no education but he had a scientific imagination; he was inventive in business, which meant success and money." Eager to move his family to Buenos Aires, Baldo set up a factory on the outskirts of the big city called Olla Puig (Puig Pressure Cooker), where eventually he employed over fifty workers. After years of effort Baldo was able to secure a solid financial standing for his family and provide for his sons' education. The family had a comfortable apartment in Buenos Aires and eventually owned a modest country house forty kilometers outside the city. Determined to forget his small-town hardships, Baldo never returned to Villegas, nor did he even visit nearby La Plata: he wanted complete independence from Malé's family, and he wanted her to depend completely on him.

Manuel's drive, cousin Ernesto said, came from his father, and it was "peasant" tenacity, reinforced by an apprehension about any aspect of his affairs over which he did not have direct control. Horacio Contratti, a schoolmate of Coco's whose father bought Vinos Viñaflor from Baldo, said: "When they left Villegas, Baldo didn't want the money in the form of a bank check but rather took the cash with him on the train." Years later in Brazil, Manuel, with similar distrust, would carry cash in suitcases, buying real estate with "ready money." This same psychology—or "sweet craziness," as one literary agent would later put it—made him reluctant to hire an agent; particularly in the early stages of his career he insisted, often to his detriment, on handling his own book deals. A work addict, he would follow a rigid schedule no matter where he made his home. In a way, this created order was home, a space where he wrote books and watched movies with the same discipline, often late at night and even into the morning.

If his inventive drive came from his father, Coco's pragmatism and devotion to music and movies (amalgam of all that was good) came from Malé. He had no interest in science and technology, and would not listen when Baldo tried to explain his aluminum experiments. In 1946 when his father's Dodge arrived by train, everybody except Coco went to the station to see it. In *Betrayed by Rita Hayworth*, Toto speaks disparagingly of the people of Villegas who are only interested in "eating, sleeping, and cars." By the time Baldo realized the gap between himself and his son, it was too late to bridge it.

made at the movies

There is much to be said for the suggestion that the true oedipal situation is not the primal scene but parents talking to each other in words the child does not understand.   —Margaret Mead

Even before starting school at age four, in 1936, Coco was a regular movie-goer who saw everything there was to see at the "one movie house in town, with a different show every day: mostly American stuff."[29] Malé and Coco were not alone: almost every weekday evening at 6:00 p.m. they would walk three blocks to the Teatro Español and always sit in the same seats—row 15, in the middle—where they were surrounded by friends and neighbors like Elena and Raquel Piña and Nelly Ortea. Today the Teatro is a community center—there were actually two movie theaters during Manuel's childhood, but now there are only video rental clubs in Villegas. While on the outside it is one of the few elegant buildings in Villegas, inside, the simple hall looks like a school auditorium with banks of hard wooden seats, the stage veiled by a frayed red curtain with gold fringe. Yet for Malé and Manuel this was the only place during the day where they felt at one with the town.

"Every day we went and we all sat close together," Nelly Ortea reminisced. With his girlfriends Coco would exchange pictures of stars, and cut and paste them in albums. Elena Piña added, "When we used up all the notebooks we'd paste them in magazines." Coco loved the same golden-age actresses and actors that his mother and friends loved: Vivien Leigh, Laurence Olivier, Clark Gable, Olivia de Havilland, Carole Lombard, Robert Taylor, Tyrone Power, Rita Hayworth. From the movies Coco and his friends learned that women could be irreverent as well as glamorous, that little guys could challenge men in power. These dreams were in many cases the inventions of Eastern European immigrants and their sons: Hollywood moguls such as Samuel Goldwyn, Louis B. Mayer, David O. Selznick, and Irving Thalberg helped create an image of America as the land of justice and opportunity. In the eyes of Coco Puig, who also wanted to flee his roots, these movies were not commodities or products of alienation but rather visions of salvation, a cheap ticket to paradise. Europe, on the threshold of war, was closing down, and Latin America constituted a large percentage of Hollywood's foreign audience.[30] Hollywood had, in some ways, more impact in Latin America than at home because it presented both "the real world" (New York, Chicago, London, Paris) and a romanticized paradise, a comforting universe of familiar faces.

There was another connection: Hollywood had adopted Mexico, the Caribbean, and South America as an exotic other world, a place of tropical exuberance, romance, sin, and decadence. Fred Astaire loved the Latin beat and introduced South American rhythms into American popular music in movies like *Flying Down to Rio* and *You Were Never Lovelier*. Both romantic and comic characters, played by stars like Cesar Romero and Carmen Miranda, came from south of the border; Latin American actresses like Dolores Del Rio were among the highest paid in the Hollywood of the thirties and forties; the Brooklyn-born daughter of a Spanish dancer, Margarita Cansino, became Rita Hayworth. Latin audiences enjoyed movies like Hayworth's *Blood and Sand* (1941), which represented Spanish culture in glamorous if fantastic terms.

The film industry in Argentina, more developed than in other Latin American countries except for Mexico, made every effort not only to market these Hollywood melodramas but to reproduce them. *Canto del Cisne* (Swan Song, 1950), with Argentine star Mecha Ortiz, for instance, was a variation on Joan Crawford's *Humoresque* (1946). Before she became Evita Perón, Eva Duarte was a second-rate actress who attempted to imitate, first for radio soap operas, heroic roles immortalized by the likes of Norma Shearer (*Marie Antoinette*) or Vivien Leigh (*That Hamilton Woman*).[31]

Evita, an illegitimate child from a lower-middle-class family, grew up in Los Toldos, not far from General Villegas, and regarded the big city as a marvelous paradise where lower-middle-class people had perfect lives. She too went to the movies to dream of a world where women were beautiful as long as they had jewelry and fur coats; Evita and her sisters also collected and exchanged photographs of actresses. The movies, national as well as foreign, were a place where love existed, where social barriers crumbled. Charisma was the ultimate star quality; the actress was the role she played, or rather it was her personality that made the role. People went to the movies to lose themselves in enchanting fairy tales and, even more, to lose themselves in the enchanting persona of the star.

The movie screen was young Coco's window, both to the world and to pleasure, inspiring his earliest ambition: to make music or movies. As a child playacting with his chums, he had already adopted the role of director. Coco loved playacting, piano playing, and performing, and "had a great need to express himself," Raquel Piña said. "We used to play a game called 'el pueblito' [the little town], a game where we had little houses, a castle, paths, a river. Coco would make up the scripts; since I was skinny and blond he always made me play Cinderella." Yet another way to transform the dreary town, these games foreshadowed the grown-up game Manuel would play, writing his first two novels about the "little town," using real-life actors, replaying episodes from the movies, transforming them to represent what he perceived. Manuel stayed in touch with the Piña sisters until he left the country permanently in the early seventies, and Raquel reminded

Manuel years later of the line that he would direct her, as Cinderella, to re-cite: "My sisters are off to the ball, the great King's Ball." The Cinderella fa-ble struck home for these children of the pampa, desiring a meaningful place in the world and finding their models in the Hollywood fairy tales that danced before their eyes at the Teatro Español at six o'clock every evening.

At age four, though, Coco was just learning to read, and these movies were usually subtitled. The process was cheaper than dubbing and most South American audiences did not like dubbed films; Borges once joked that he hated seeing Queen Cristina played by Greta Garbo played by Al-donza Lorenzo (alluding to the real name of Don Quixote's Dulcinea).[32] In order to enjoy the movies, Coco was doubly motivated to learn to read and to study English. In addition to his classes at public school, in 1942 he began private English lessons (with Elsa Corradi, a Villegan whom Coco and Malé called Fat Face) "because it was the language of films," and though he was still twelve hours away from Buenos Aires by train, it made him feel as if "he had one foot in Hollywood."

Malé's voice explained whatever he did not comprehend, so that one could say he saw these movies through his mother's eyes. As a spectator he absorbed, at first, more than he could understand. Manuel recaptures these experiences in *Betrayed by Rita Hayworth* where Toto repeats the plots of movies, changing them to interpolate his version—something Malé in-evitably must have done when she explained the movies' plots to her little son. The voice of Toto explaining movies is also his mother's voice, a device which becomes central to *Kiss of the Spider Woman*, where Toto grows up to be Molina, in a sense, but is also still Mother. When Malé raved about a movie, so did little Coco; when she praised a female star, so did he. The male actors he preferred were "the strong, gentle types" like Tyrone Power and Robert Taylor, and here again, Coco's taste followed his mother's: he couldn't stand violent movies, only the romantic ones and the musicals.

High on Coco's list of favorites "were [Ginger] Rogers musicals (I never noticed Astaire)": while he of course admired the agile genius of Fred Astaire, Coco, sitting beside Malé in the dark theater, watched these movies, destined largely for a female audience, with a female gaze, his eyes on Gin-ger—her gowns, facial gestures, movements, her natural charm. The musi-cals (Eleanor Powell was another fave) were the ultimate escape; *The Great Ziegfeld*, a biographical melodrama about flamboyant showman Florenz

Ziegfeld, with its fabulous Busby Berkeley numbers studded with beautiful girls, was, for Coco, the greatest show of 1936.[33]

The women characters they saw in these movies were not only beautiful but spirited, much more diverse and empowered than they would be in the postwar forties and fifties. In classic screwball comedies like *The Awful Truth* (1937; Irene Dunne), *Midnight* (1939; Claudette Colbert), *Ninotchka* (1939; Greta Garbo), *The Lady Eve* (1941; Barbara Stanwyck), women could desire to be something, could leave restrictions behind.[34] The premise of these films, however, was the innate inequality of the sexes. Coco's and Malé's favorite melodramas—for example *Rebecca* (1940), *Gone With the Wind* (1939), and Greer Garson's *Blossoms in the Dust* (1941)—all imparted manifold messages about men, women, love, and marriage. Men had greater power and freedom, while women were emotionally superior precisely because they were willing to be the weaker sex. Women could easily dupe men, but if they fell in love, they got trapped. The dream makers conned their audiences, at once endorsing the female viewer's strengths and yet driving home the message that their ultimate fulfillment lay in submission to men.

Luise Rainer, who won an Oscar opposite William Powell as Flo Ziegfeld's faithful, jilted wife and went on to be loyal spouse to Fernand Gravet's Johann Strauss in *The Great Waltz* (1938), would play an important role in Manuel's first novel. Sweet and sensitive, she was the perfect victim with whom Malé—hence Coco—could identify: he "adored the subdued yet heroic woman, who in the thirties was Norma Shearer and in the forties became Greer Garson. I protected the waif Luise Rainer." In *Betrayed by Rita Hayworth* Toto imagines a happy ending in which Rainer is rescued from her cruel fate. As part of his spontaneous repertory of impersonations, Manuel could later meticulously mimic her Austrian accent and melancholy demeanor when, hurt but brave, she phones her urbane ex to congratulate him on his new wife, and tries to greet him with a casual "Hello, Flo."

Coco's (and Malé's) favorite dramatic stars in the thirties were the glamorous European imports like Rainer, Marlene Dietrich, Greta Garbo—"the unearthly ones." Garbo—like Hedy Lamarr, Rita Hayworth, and, much later, Marilyn Monroe—was unreal, a dream image, a supreme object of desire, appealing to men but also an ideal to which women aspired. As an adult, Manuel would articulate the nuances of their allure:

> For me it is the fantasy that stars embody. The constellation of vices and virtues . . . As for Garbo and Lamarr, they were too strong and too beautiful; they didn't need me. Unless they died in the end, like Garbo in *Camille* or Lamarr in *Lady of the Tropics*. Then they suffered glamorously. They died, and I died with them, only to go to heaven along with them. Very, very dangerous clichés. Because the enjoyment of suffering was there; there was a streak of masochism.[35]

With Garbo, Manuel said, "it was different: I didn't admire her; it was more like being in the presence of a god." At the same time, the enigmatic diva was just a simple Swedish peasant girl (a point Marlene harped on) who had made good. She was a free spirit, an eccentric, a camp hero; following the Garbo formula, Dietrich was also an androgynous rebel.[36] In movies like *Morocco* (1930), where she cross-dresses in a cabaret performance to titillate Gary Cooper, Dietrich insinuated, unrestrained by gender, that "male" and "female" were largely a matter of costuming. Coco was vividly impressed by such exquisite images—Josef von Sternberg's direction and photography were largely responsible for Dietrich's glow—but also by their not so subliminally subversive gender signals.[37] Coco was a sensitive if naive receptor to the film world's underlying bisexuality, the ambiguous personae behind the masks of heterosexual glamour. Many golden-age films of the thirties, relatively free of censorship before the Hays Code, featured scandalous ménages à trois and oddball dandies or sissies played by quaint stock actors. Edward Everett Horton—the name already a lavender banner—played fey Astaire's fussy sidekick, serving alternatively as impediment or go-between to the budding romance between Ginger and Fred in Mark Sandrich's musical gems *Top Hat* (1935) and *The Gay Divorcee* (1934). Eric Blore consistently played a fawning butler who was perhaps too attached to his master. These clowns in frock coats were delightfully zany, and Coco felt an irresistible bond with them.

The glamour girls of the thirties were succeeded by the drama queens of the forties, like Joan Crawford in *Mildred Pierce* (1945), anger and self-sacrifice radiating from her mask-like face and severe angular attire, often designed by Adrian of *Grand Hotel* fame (whose name in scrolling film credits invariably caused Malé to squeeze Coco's hand). Greer Garson was exaggerated too, in her noble, warm, maternal, yet sexy guise; she was, in her own words, "Metro's Glorious Mrs." Garson was the virtuous spirit of wartime Britain, or, in Vincent Canby's words, "invariably serene, polite, elegant in a slightly unreal way, too good to be true, always prepared to meet any emergency and staunchly middle-class."[38] Coco's favorite actresses of the forties were, again, Malé-identified. Garson was ladylike on the surface and something else (perhaps a bit whorish) underneath, just as Malé could be feminine and frivolous on the surface, but tough and calculating to the core. To succeed, "a woman," as Manuel would often refer to himself, had no choice but to be duplicitous.

Former sirens played spinster or career-woman parts in the forties and fifties and appealed, particularly as they aged, to older women audiences. They acted out the spectators' rage and rebellion for them, suffered the consequences for them too, and allowed them to go home when "The End" came on the screen, so that they could continue to make dinner and do the household chores. While Katharine Hepburn attracted both men and women as the upper-class feisty American woman, Ginger Rogers was the middle-class version of everywoman. In the forties she pioneered the image of the natural working-girl heroine, a refreshing change from the cult of larger-than-life personalities like Joan Crawford and Bette Davis. Rogers embodied for a wartime audience the down-to-earth young woman who had to make an honest living (as Anna Magnani did for postwar Italy). Manuel admired her dramatic work, especially her close-ups, and praised the naturalness with which she embodied the suffering of the average woman in *Kitty Foyle* (1940) and *Tender Comrade* (1944). In *Kitty Foyle*, he picked out the melodrama's underlying social critique: Rogers, a secretary, enters a doomed marriage with an aristocrat who can't adapt to their class difference. She's going to have his baby, but the baby dies in childbirth, and the culminating moment is a close-up of Rogers's face when she receives the tragic news. Manuel added a naughty aside—"Evil tongues say that Astaire wanted to steal the scene by playing the nurse!"[39] He would quote in *The Buenos Aires Affair* the climactic monologue from *Tender Comrade* in which brave Rogers tells her baby boy about the absent father he'll never know. Rogers, brilliant at playing characters unable to express their true feelings, had the ability to articulate her audience's unhappiness and to teach them how to live with it; likewise, Malé was able to put on a brave face in a hostile town.[40]

Rita Hayworth, on the other hand, was not, at first, one of Coco's favorites: she was beautiful, but not trustworthy. After he saw her in *Gilda*, in 1946, he would realize there was more to her; her beauty and personality were as classy as they were sexy. Both a musical star and a femme fatale, she had Rogers's versatility, but, more important, she was the sexy *mala mujer*—of exotic Latin origins—who proved to be good-hearted and whose fate was tragic. She would epitomize the mysterious woman, the broken doll who had wasted her youth, beauty, life by marrying the wrong men and being abused by Hollywood moguls. Caught between Hollywood and her Hispanic roots, she was a relevant alter ego for Manuel, who, some of his friends claim, *was* Rita Hayworth.[41]

"Coco would leave the theater happy," Elena Píña remembers. "It had taken us out of our reality and we were happy; we wanted to dance." In order to screen out the "awful truth" of dreary Villegas, Coco molded life into a continuation of the movie he had just seen: he would re-create his child's capacity for a happy, imaginary world in *Betrayed by Rita Hayworth*, as when Mita throws a paper streamer and Toto sees Ginger Rogers twirling around in a musical, or when the picture of a saint on a printed card at Hector's First Communion reminds him of his beloved Norma Shearer. In the dreamworld of the cinema, Toto becomes someone else, and so does everyone around him, even the fish in an underwater documentary: "How badly that little fishie behaves, he doesn't love anybody, his uncle died and the fishie didn't even cry and just went on playing."[42] Elena recalled in particular the night they all went to see *The Great Waltz* (1938). After the movie they went to pick up Baldo at the local club. Coco left the theater dancing a waltz, the "Emperor" or "Tales from the Vienna Woods," dancing along the sidewalk all the way to the club, until he suddenly encountered Baldo. "It was a brutal awakening," Elena said. The abrupt contrast between men in top hats in gay Vienna and his censuring father on the dusty, deserted Villegan street was a harsh one.[43]

blood and sand

I understood . . . the moral world of movies where goodness, patience, and sacrifice were rewarded. In real life nothing like that happened. Mama would take me to the movies in the afternoons to entertain me, and herself, and I, at a certain moment, decided that reality was what was on the screen and that my fate—to live in that town—was a bad impromptu movie that was about to end. What was real was what happened for an hour and a half every day at the movies.

Baldo did sometimes go with Malé and Coco to the movies. In chapter 5 of *Betrayed by Rita Hayworth*, Manuel resurrected the memory of an occasion when the six o'clock show was *Blood and Sand*, which was based on the Spanish novel by Vicente Blasco Ibáñez and starred, at the height of their popularity, Tyrone Power as Juan Gallardo and Rita Hayworth as Doña Sol. Manuel chose this event—significant in that his Hollywood stars were playing roles close to home, as it were, Spanish hero and heroine—as a fictional turning point in the tense relationship between father and son: the boy was anxious for his father to like the movie, so that he would go with them again, essentially so that he would approve of the movies—and of his son. Baldo liked the movie, but what he enjoyed most (according to Manuel's fictional version) was the gorgeous, "wicked" seductress Rita Hayworth.

Until Hayworth, the good were always beautiful, the bad ugly. Toto agrees that she is pretty, but he is disturbed by her betrayal of the good and good-looking Tyrone Power; what is not said in the novel is that the real Coco was excited, sexually, by her seduction of Tyrone Power. In her sensual flamenco dance he discovered the "joy of having a body," and his memory of the movie is associated with his first masturbation, at age nine:

I felt this sweet sensation as I rubbed against the sheet in bed, reconstructing and improving scenes from *Blood and Sand*. Thinking of Rita Hayworth strumming her guitar and

singing "Verde Luna" in her Andalusian residence; thinking
also of Linda Darnell, praying on her knees for the bull not to
wound Tyrone Power . . . I conserve the stimulating sensation
of her fabulous body; Rita, the supreme enchantress, the goddess of love . . . but as much as I admired her, what stimulated
me more was Tyrone Power.[44]

The fantasy was tinged with masochism; the sexy, manipulative woman's seduction of the handsome male to whom he was attracted (and who slightly
resembled his father) excited him: the bad bullfighter (a young Anthony
Quinn), who steals Doña Sol from Juan Gallardo, resembled Baldo even
more.

In the movies, bad guys usually looked like bad guys and usually got
punished; on the real-life stage of General Villegas, sometimes a good person had a bad guy's face and was good or, as in his father's case, was handsome but often angry. In real life, people like his parents seemed
uncomfortable with their roles, unlike the actors in movies. Of course, while
imparting straightforward messages—love conquers all, women need men,
men protect women—the movies also flashed subliminal messages: women
should have their economic freedom, and men could be "weak" or sensitive
and yet be men. After this movie outing, Berto "betrays" Toto in the novel
by not sharing the experience of the movies; though, from Baldo's adult
point of view, the main reason he often didn't attend the evening show in
real life was practical—he needed to work and to save money.[45]

Camilo, Bebé's father, and Baldo were very close, and it was Camilo, the
least macho man in the family, who first made Baldo aware of Coco's "tendencies." He warned Baldo that it was wrong to leave his son's upbringing
in the hands of Malé or, as Teté reports in Manuel's fictional version: "Papa
told Mita that Toto was too attached to her."[46] Baldo tried, probably in a
brusque way, to correct this situation by challenging Coco to behave in
manly ways. "He was different: he didn't participate in our games," a fellow
Villegan, José Luis Chavarri, recalls, "As kids we'd spend the whole day
biking, we'd go to the park. Coco had a shiny green new chrome bicycle that
he never used." Manuel re-creates these moments in Toto's words—"The
bicycle I like is the smallest one, with little wheels on the side so I won't fall.
Papa doesn't like it, but I do"—and the boy's sarcastic defense: his father

wants to buy him the big bike "that I am sure to fall off."[47] "It takes hard work to make a man," Berto chides Toto in the novel, but the battle is also with his wife, of whom he is simultaneously proud and resentful: "Toto needs to be far away from your skirts." Mita's most telling words in the novel are then uttered: "Boys become men when they go to schools away from home, they say, so wouldn't I lose my boy? At the end of classes would he come back to me a man?"[48]

Malé would be caught in the middle, betraying Coco by transmitting Baldo's wishes, and betraying Baldo by transmitting her grievances to Coco. *Betrayed by Rita Hayworth* is filled with betrayals, even Mita's betrayal of Toto, in the sense that in some way he wanted to possess her but could not. By age six he came to this realization (he later told a psychiatrist friend) when he interrupted her conversation with a neighbor to make a joke, and she inadvertently humiliated him: "Your joke does not amuse me."[49] Bebé relates another incident: During her visit to Villegas in the winter of 1942, her mother, Dora, had given Malé a gift, a biography of Napoleon. Malé, always more ebullient when old friends and family visited, was also thirsty for culture and normally too busy to read; she waxed with enthusiasm over the biography and Napoleon as they were all taking a walk together, Malé, Dora, the two children. At one point, in inspired poetic mode, Malé looked up at the wide pampa sky and commented on the shape of a cloud, how it looked like a horse. Nine-year-old Coco, by this time boiling with possessive jealousy, wielded his already-evolved sense of irony: "How strange that you haven't seen Napoleon riding the horse too!"

The Puigs grew irreversibly polarized—and cousin Jorge played no small part. Jorge hated his own father, Juan, because of the disorderly life he forced him to share, particularly when they moved to Buenos Aires, but he remembers with nostalgia Coco's father and his idyllic childhood in Villegas. Even before Coco's birth, Baldo, to compensate for his brother Juan's negligence, treated his nephew as his own child. Jorge was an athlete and popular with the girls. He was also lazy, always playing when he should have been working; Baldo tried in vain to guide the young "good-for-nothing" and employed him after school at the winery. As Quica tells it, her husband would drive the truck, distributing wine in the nearby towns, accompanied by Jorge, who inevitably fell asleep in the passenger seat after the revels of the night before; eventually he would wake up, singing tangos.

Jorge says Manuel aggrandized him as the virile Hector in the novel, but that is how Coco saw Jorge as a child: the quintessential male, a perfect Puig.

Jorge remembers the same demanding Baldo in another light: "Baldo protected his boys like a lion"; he was overbearing for their sake, to make them men for the tough world out there. In the summertime, except for trips to La Plata and the coast, life revolved around the pool at the Club Atlético. When Jorge was eight, Baldo would not let him continue to jump into the pool but forced him to dive in; they would not go home for lunch until he had dived. Years later, Coco, ever observant, saw Baldo repeat the same scene with his baby brother, Carlos. Sitting at the pool's edge, feet dangling in the water, he watched Baldo dive in with Carlos on his shoulders, to teach Carlos to be a man, he said, but Coco sensed it was to confront him. Not to make "the same mistake twice," Baldo would develop a close bond with his younger son, which caused Coco to feel even more excluded.

Malé too treated Jorge as a son. He went to the same primary school as Coco and was king of the swimming pool, and as he grew into a big, strong adolescent with hairy arms and legs, there may have been an attraction, certainly an affection. Malé's admiration for Jorge produced a painfully rivalrous situation for "el Coco"; their heterosexuality underscored his own sense of inadequacy. Jealous, he felt betrayed by both cousin and mother. The two cousins were a version of Cain and Abel: Jorge was protective and impatient, while Coco both admired and envied the bigger boy: "I watched my cousin Jorge climb up trees and hang like a monkey, play ball and always win, run faster, understand things quicker." Jorge and cousin Antonio "El Gordo" Grippo cavorted at the pool and pursued girls while little Coco sat at the pool's edge, watching. In the years when Malé was working, Chuchiña (a former neighbor) claims that Jorge and Coco seemed like abandoned urchins on the street together. "She'd give them money to go to the movies," Chuchiña said, adding sarcastically, "That's where he acquired his 'cinematic vision.'" Malé placed Coco in Jorge's care, half hoping that Jorge's masculinity would somehow rub off; but at the movies each boy nourished different fantasies: Jorge lusted after Ann Sheridan and Coco wanted to *be* Ann Sheridan.

He saw himself, perhaps, as more of a sissy than he really was, but in any case created such an image in fiction, accentuating it in his autobiographical novel by Toto's fear of diving. Jorge López, Manuel's swimming instructor, recalls, on the contrary, that all the kids were afraid when they began learning to dive, and that although Coco wasn't interested in most sports, he was a very good swimmer and even took risks. But Coco seemed to feel that he was being compared with the bigger, more athletic boys, especially with cousin Jorge. The Club Atlético was where "real" men showed off their prowess and made sexual conquests.

Coco admired his father's entrepreneurial tenacity and egalitarian sentiments toward maidservants and his men at work, but after spending hours on the street, charming his friends, Baldo often brought his ill humor home. Baldo kept Coco at a distance, though in Baldo's view he was busy providing for his wife and child and trying not to spoil the boy. In *Betrayed by Rita Hayworth* Berto comes off as someone ill-equipped emotionally to take on the burden of fatherhood, and this was the Baldo Coco knew as a child, the tantrum-throwing man struggling to succeed in business, a "father-child" whose insecurity was not only professional but personal. Baldo would be proud in later years of the son who became the famous author, but at some point in Manuel's late teens, when Don Baldomero blurted "Better to have a dead son than a gay son," Manuel felt this pronouncement expressed his father's true feeling.

Malé and Baldo were separated by the time Baldo died in 1990. As a well-known writer, Manuel had long since left Baldo's accomplishments in the dust, but would he ever be resigned to their antagonism, or was it a stress he could never quite relieve, a war within? The key to *Betrayed by Rita Hayworth* (as Manuel asserted) was the father as absence, or silence: while Mita has little direct speech, Berto has even less. Manuel wrote *Betrayed by Rita Hayworth* while struggling to prove himself, to transcend the ever-present "critical eye." He would strive, in successive novels, to legitimate his work, and to work through his gnawing sense of vulnerability or alienation from his father. This meant betraying the betrayer; as when he omitted from the final version of the novel the fact that the very first time he went to the movies was not with his mother but rather with Baldo.

In his enthusiasm for technology, Baldo had taken three-year-old Coco with him to visit the recently installed projection room of the Teatro Español. They watched *The Bride of Frankenstein*, and it frightened the hell out of Coco. (For the rest of his childhood Coco avoided horror movies; as an adult, of course, Manuel enjoyed their campy excess.) Years later, writing Toto's monologue about scary movies, Manuel first thought of associating the father figure with Dracula in order to present him clearly as a bad guy.[50] To introduce the theme of sexual repression in *Kiss of the Spider Woman*, Manuel thought *Dracula* should be the first movie gay Molina recounts to the Marxist prisoner, before he decided to use *The Cat People*. *Dracula*, the famous horror tale about the undead, brought together the idea of unfinished mourning—the inability to lay the dead to rest—and Victorian sexual prohibition, and served Manuel initially as a dramatic emblem of unfinished business with one's parental figures, and its possible consequences.

Coco must have sensed very early on that, like the little fishie in Toto's monologue who didn't love anybody and went on playing when his uncle died, he could never hope to love or be loved by his father. In Manuel's penultimate novel, *Blood of Requited Love*, written in Brazil when he had finally "rescued" his mother from an unsound Baldo (then hospitalized with Parkinsonian dementia), the principal character, Josemar, is summed up in these words: "He who is incapable of loving his father is incapable of loving anyone, right?"[51]

siesta time

When the mother's relationship with the boy is too close and too blissful for too long, a disorder may develop in the boy out of rage at having to give up the relationship, out of panic that he will not be able to escape his mother's influence and out of a desire for revenge at her having put him in this predicament.
　　　　　　　　　　　　　　　　　　　　　　　　　　　　　—Mark Booth

Cousin Ernesto's first memory of Coco—Ernesto was three years older—remains a vivid one:

> We would visit my aunt in Villegas at least once a year; I must
> have been around five or six because Coco was two or three
> years old and his thick curls had not yet been cut. We were
> playing upstairs in the bedroom, and at some point I remem-
> ber him wearing his mother's nightgown, much too long for
> him, and a pair of her high-heeled shoes, and he was walking
> and dancing on top of the bed.[52]

Ernesto, now a white-haired gentleman with kindly blue eyes behind thick
glasses, remarked softly, "I guess the umbilical cord was never cut."

Manuel's earliest memories of "dressing up" were always accompanied
by memories of punishment. As an adult he realized, through hypnotherapy
he underwent in the sixties, that he remembered certain musicals as violent
because, after seeing an elegant Fred Astaire–Ginger Rogers movie, he
would attempt to dress up and dance like Ginger with disastrous consequences: an enraged Baldomero would either slap him or, worse, threaten to
beat him to a pulp: "I don't hit, but if I ever have to, I'll kill you." Coco associated not only his beloved musicals with his father's menace of violence,
but also siesta, a quiet time in traditional Hispanic households. "I woke
Mama up during siesta because I was bored," says six-year-old Toto in *Betrayed by Rita Hayworth*, "and Papa shouted, 'I never hit you but the day I
put my hands on you I'll break you in two.' " On another occasion, "Papa's
shouting scared my friend and he doesn't want to come and play in the en-
tranceway; he rang the bell at naptime because I forgot to disconnect it, and
Papa bellowed from the bedroom."[53] Nelly Ortea remembers siesta at the
Puig household:

> At siesta time, which was sacred, we were in the corridor or in
> the patio so as not to make noise, the nanny, Coco, and his
> friends. The word was "Silence." There was a shed and a
> large pear tree. If we were too noisy we went there and gath-
> ered delicious pears.

At siesta time it was most evident that not only did Coco not possess his
mother, but his father did.

When he was very little, Malé would tell him to think of a movie he
liked and to draw pictures, so that he wouldn't get bored, so that he

wouldn't feel lonely. Quica followed Malé's example and, when he was alone with her, would sit the child at the kitchen table with his note-books, into which he would paste, draw, and color his cutouts of actresses from newspapers and magazines. High-strung and short-tempered, Baldo needed to assert himself at home in the years of Coco's early childhood, years of economic insecurity when his wife's professional stance was a source of pride but also further cause for his urgency to prove himself. The death of their second-born would reinforce feelings of insufficiency: if they hadn't been living in the sticks, it would not have happened. So sensitive was Baldo that Malé could barely cry over the death of this child. And if Coco cried or was noisy at siesta time, the one moment of the day he could rest from his worries, Baldo's anger could be unleashed.

Malé would emerge with a pale face from the siesta—she hadn't yet put on her makeup—which led young Coco to surmise something unpleasant and to avoid at all cost crossing the threshold of his parents' bedroom. What should have been a nest of love and safety seemed like a dangerous place. Sex became associated with anticipated harm or terror, and Coco identified even more with the submissive female whose desire, in those movie melo-dramas, seemed to require that she feel "a little afraid" of the male.

Siesta was the time for forbidden games involving dressing up, and also sexual discovery. Around age eight, playacting, or showing off with his girl-friends, was part of an erotic dance that continued in dreams and in movie-sparked daydreams. Coco went through an intense onanistic stage for several months, masturbating to the image of Rita Hayworth's seduction of Tyrone Power.[54] Meanwhile, eroticized games with his pals grew more and more sexual. In *Betrayed by Rita Hayworth*, Manuel would recall the movies, games, and fantasies of his childhood, the seeds of his sexuality: the autobio-graphical sketch that emerged would stress certain fears, rage, or sublima-tion, and perhaps underplay the pleasure he experienced.

His earliest memory of a sexual experience was at age seven, when he was alone (at home or at a friend's house) with a little girl. "We played doc-tor; I was the doctor, she the patient. I examined her tummy, she took down her panties and then I checked the rest."[55] But while girls like Elenita Piña were his best friends, his first sensual feelings were directed toward young women—and even more intensely toward men who, unlike the little girls, had "forms."

He had more vivid memories of his first homosexual experiences. While it was common for schoolboys to masturbate together, Manuel was cast in the "passive" role early on:

> A group of friends would play "making love." It was "first you, then me," in which I was always the first to lower my pants, and then, when it was my turn, the others didn't keep their word. I also remember that sometimes twelve- or thirteen-year-old kids would come, and ask us to let them touch us. The one who always obeyed was me; and when it was my turn they didn't keep their promise. Thus the "round" was always incomplete. But I didn't get angry; on the contrary, I was happy. I remember, with pleasure, when a friend my age—eight or nine—fell in love with me and, for the first time, he gave me his body and I gave him mine. It was a kind of "platonic" love, of course, because physically we couldn't do anything "strong" . . . but we had a good time.[56]

If Coco played a subordinate role in sexual initiations, he played the dominant role, or tried to, when he and his playmates replayed or invented movies. This playacting developed alongside his love for dressing up:

> I didn't want so much to own personal toys, clothing, disguises . . . and even treasures for keeps like medallions or rings, as to use them for playacting, in that constant exercise of imitating grown-up models or connecting with them somehow . . . I really valued those things that belonged both to me and the grown-ups, temporary gifts that sooner or later would return to them.

For his imaginary world of movies and plays he wrote the script, directed, played the male lead. Bebé remembers playing the female lead in a jungle movie in which the good guys had to save the girl from being swallowed by a menacing crocodile. When there was no one else to play the role, Coco had to play the crocodile, which swallowed the female lead with ferocity, but he didn't like to take a secondary role. In *Betrayed by Rita Hayworth* Manuel elaborated this game, making it clear that Toto manipulated others because he couldn't manage his sexual fears. He had been excited by the sight of an older girl's developed body and vulva; the crocodile's gaping jaws in this scene in the novel almost suggest a *vagina dentata*:

> "Let's change places so the girl's the crocodile" and she became a crocodile. They have those mouths that swallow a man in one piece and are scarier than lions, but even scarier are the carnivorous plants at the bottom of the sea.[57]

In little Toto's imagination, the crocodile game becomes associated with an underwater documentary he had seen as the trailer of a scary murder movie:

> Mama, don't look, the murder movie is scary and somebody comes into a dark room and the murderer's behind the door and Mama and me we don't look because it's a scary movie and before the long movie once they showed a short movie about the bottom of the sea and Mama lowered her eyes because there was a plant that moved in the nice clear water at the bottom of the sea and it had hairs . . . and the fishies . . . get caught . . . don't look . . . What does "fucks" mean . . . naughty Pocha doesn't want to tell me what the boy with the hairs did.[58]

How did young Coco feel about the mother who adored and protected him and yet had expectations he could not fulfill? Cousin Bebé insists that she remembers clearly an incident recorded almost verbatim in *Betrayed by Rita Hayworth*, when Malé passes Baldo's message on to nine-year-old Coco: Malé and Coco are in the bathroom, she is shaking and scolding him, telling him that he can't play with girls and dolls anymore, that he has to play with boys. Bebé remembers not hearing a sound out of Coco, and thinking that he had drowned in the bathtub. She remembers that he ran out very pale—with fear? with rage? with shame?—and that he got sick.[59]

Emotional upsets tended to make Coco nauseous, as if he literally couldn't stomach the stress. Whether genetic or dietary, a sensitive digestion would always plague him. In hindsight, the banal mention of family digestive ailments in the first chapter of his first novel no longer seems trivial, particularly in the more detailed first draft. Annunziata Delledonne, in real life, died of a liver ailment: "Poor maids," Aunt Clara rambles, "when they get a little money, they all fill their stomachs on anything and get sick in the liver like Mama."[60] In the same breath she says that her husband's "stomach is a mess . . . it runs in the family." In the final version the ailment is transferred to Toto's father, who "has a very weak stomach too."[61] Toto speaks of liking sweets (in his monologue), but Papa doesn't because they make him sick, and Toto eats Mama's cake—rich food that sometimes makes the real Coco sick. Baldo had ulcers later in life, and Malé was operated on for gallstones—the same routine operation that would prove fatal for her son.

Like most children, Coco cherished the regularity of rituals and, according to Quica, was very particular, even rigid about his food, always requesting "mashed potatoes with breaded veal cutlet. If he had peas, they had to be prepared with hard-boiled eggs." The constant playmate of his early years, Elenita, remembered how important food was for them, and when she first read in *Kiss of the Spider Woman* the scene where Molina tries to gain Valentín's love by feeding him canned peaches, she laughed because this was one of Coco's favorite desserts:

> We were neighbors on Rivadavia Street and became friends at
> age five. Coco would come running, take me by the hand, and
> we'd cross the square. We'd sit on benches there with roofs
> over them or on the steps of the bank. We'd have long conver-
> sations in the square, about food, especially about what we ate
> at home that day and about movies.

Coco was very observant, "much more than me," said Elena, and she liked being with him because he was smart and she could learn from him. They were kindred spirits, although Elena felt slightly inferior because Coco's mother was a professional and Coco would get annoyed at her "vulgar way of saying things." But if Coco was better at reading and writing, his friend was better at math, which Coco would ask her to help him with, she claims, even on his vacations home after he went off to boarding school in Buenos Aires.

Coco initiated their rivalry, said Elena. They both teased each other, but she felt that if anything, "Coco was the bully," relying on intellect, not force, while—she added—"I won out in the romance department." Once when they were listening to one of his favorite musical pieces, Mussorgsky's *Pictures at an Exhibition*, Coco tried to frighten her by acting out the sinister moment when the "gnomus," or dwarf, enters. He was always trying to pull her leg, she said, and he could be spiteful. Particularly upsetting was the fib he invented about her father:

> One day he showed up with a map of Argentina and Brazil and a Brazilian flag. Brazil had entered the war [World War II] and he said to me: "Look how close Brazil is to Argentina. Now they're going to send your papa to war." When he wanted to lie, he was a big liar and I was an easy target.

Betrayed by Rita Hayworth presents another point of view, however. Toto "wants to be Alicita's boyfriend" but he doesn't quite trust her. He thinks she's laughing at him behind his back. She has pretty teeth but they are sharp like a dog's, and the climax of his disappointment is when she hides in the bathroom to play with another, bigger boy, who bullies him, and he runs off, retreating into his daydreams about *The Great Ziegfeld*. In Toto's complicated fantasies, the suffering Luise Rainer, abandoned by her beloved Flo Ziegfeld, is rescued by Alicita's handsome uncle, and Toto, identifying with delicate Rainer, who dies in the movie, becomes the bellhop at the hotel who helps the handsome rescuer by feeding the lady Toto's favorite foods. The bellhop has a "nervous stepfather"—Berto is disguised and demoted to stepfather—unlike the handsome guy who takes a protective liking to the bellhop and who, in the end, holds the bellhop in his arms. As if by magic the bellhop becomes one with him, and then Toto fantasizes that Alicita comes in to kiss her uncle but doesn't realize that she's kissing Toto (the bellhop). This kiss opens a Pandora's box of gender confusion: was Toto a boy in love with a man, or a man being kissed by a girl, or . . . ?

Who is this handsome uncle who supplants the "nervous stepfather"? "At least 15 percent of invention" went into the re-creation of his childhood in this novel, according to Manuel, and perhaps a good deal more, considering subjectivity and the sieve of memory. But what Manuel didn't invent was the feeling behind his rivalry with Elenita and her sister Raquel. Toto's principal monologue, chapter 5, begins: "Alicita's father is a father of girls."[62] "Father of girls" was a way of saying a father capable of love and understanding, a harmony lacking in Manuel's upbringing.

Toto's fictional rivalry with a bigger boy for Alicita perhaps displaces what was Coco's real longing for a father who caressed and touched. According to Elena and Raquel, Coco envied the warmth and lack of tension in the Piña household, the way the girls' father played piggyback with them when he came home from work. Their mother was home all day, and both parents appeared to share nurturance and discipline; there was a balance between her character and his gentleness. At Coco's house, his working mother was not home during the day; more than nurturer, Malé was an educator, introducing her son to music, movies, and the arts; his father was too busy and too harried to spend time with the boy.

When Elena visited Manuel in Buenos Aires in 1969, he explained to her that he had exaggerated her "lively" qualities to create drama. While an older boy would sometimes come to Elenita's house (with his mother, who would visit Elena's mother), she didn't get along with him. She had chosen Coco as her playmate, just as he had chosen her, but in the novel he invents a combative relationship, makes her into a flirt who spurns him, conflating his envy of the parental love his friend received and his discomfort as an outsider among the boys.

Coco developed a sharp sense of irony early on as a defense against boisterous schoolmates, but he turned it on those he loved too, as when he poked fun at his mother's poetic waxings about clouds in the Napoleon incident. This mockery would resurface mischievously in the portrayal of the poetry-reciting mother of artist Gladys in *The Buenos Aires Affair*. Gladys outdoes her mother, just as Manuel would go beyond both his parents, being a greater artist than his mother and a more successful man than his father.

Beneath his sarcasm one glimpsed a lonely child, Elena said. "He was always lively and laughing, but had a sadness in his eyes." Manuel became famous and saw the world, while Elena stayed in Villegas, married young, and never even had children. When she heard about his death she was shocked, and she thought: "You should have stayed in Villegas, like me, then you'd still be alive, less famous, but with a life." Raquel recalled a strikingly unsympathetic letter Manuel wrote from Brazil in the eighties, upon hearing of the death of one of her sons: "I'm sorry to hear about Robertito, but you will get over this, Raquel, because you had a *luxurious childhood*." In the eyes of his childhood friends, Manuel achieved fame and even fortune, like Citizen Kane, but Raquel and Elena had constant love; Charles Foster Kane would forever long for his sled Rosebud, or lack mother's love, and Coco Puig had only the cut-out images of actresses.

i was number one at school

"School was a block away from home and I'd go and come alone. I was always the best student. I was always afraid of no longer being so." The poet in Coco made an early debut at age five, at the Mother's Day celebration in school. On such occasions in Argentine schools the children dressed formally, which, for the boys, meant starched military uniforms. All the pupils stood in a line as Coco stepped up to the podium, dressed and groomed impeccably, and proceeded to read clearly, with a slight tremor in his voice, a poem his teacher had given him, in praise of Mother. "He put so much emotion into his reading, he recited with such feeling, he was all sensitivity, and when he finished, the audience, filled with parents, many of them practically in tears, exploded in applause," remembers Ana María Ladaga, Manuel's third-grade teacher, now in her eighties, with benevolent tears in her bespectacled eyes. "Such a sensitive little boy, so sweet and handsome. So devoted to his mother."

Manuel's grammar school years began in 1939 at School No. 1, which he attended until fifth grade and where "after the second week in class I proved to be the best student." He was driven to be the best student, as if he needed to comply with some outside measure of success, to create an ideal self, or, at the very least, to escape the cul-de-sac he found himself in, where he felt he did not belong, where he was alienated, alone.

Coco's most vocal fan at school was the kindly, soft-voiced Ladaga, whom Elenita and Coco first laughed at for being a goody-goody but whom they soon adored. In *Betrayed by Rita Hayworth* Manuel humorously jumbled Toto's misunderstandings of anatomy lessons with his sexual doubts: mild-mannered Ana María claims that it was a fabrication—that "he had a lot of imagination"—because she never taught anything having to do with animals' reproductive organs. He was her most attentive student, the kind who always came up after class to ask questions, and his appreciation for music and poetry was exceptional. Ana María was among the Villegans Manuel stayed in touch with as an adult, appreciative of her devotion. With her he was teacher's pet—raising resentments, apparently, among the rougher boys.

Aware of his poetic and theatrical gifts, Ana María Ladaga encouraged him to act in school plays, but when he was nine years old, Malé put an end to this: Jorge told her that he had seen Coco making "a fool of himself" (read: gesturing effeminately) in some rehearsal. Malé went to school, and, even though the schoolteacher complained to her that Jorge was to blame, Malé insisted that, if she permitted this behavior, it could be potentially harmful for Coco—a "harm" (she did not realize or could not admit) which was already irreversible.

Jorge chaperoned Coco even more when he was sent to high school in Buenos Aires: overprotective Malé felt that twelve-year-old Coco was too young to go to movies and theaters alone in the big city. Jorge, now a white-haired man in his seventies, still blushes remembering his embarrassment when they attended live musicals, and Coco would resolutely walk up to the stage, as he did after the show *Dos Corazones* (Two Hearts), to congratulate the actors and musicians. Chatting with the director and even more enthusiastically with Argentine actress and tango singer Tita Merello, Coco stood looking intensely up at the actress, praising the play, the music, her performance, as his eighteen-year-old cousin hung back sheepishly like an awkward rube, waiting on the side, in the dark, hat in hand.

At grammar school, Manuel received excellent grades in reading, writing, drawing, singing and music, language, history, and mathematics, but only passing grades in everything else, notably the sciences and physical education. Nelly López, Manuel's sixth-grade teacher in 1945, agreed with Ana María that Manuel was an "excellent student, very serious and responsible . . . outstanding in writing," but stressed that "he needed to be the best." If he wasn't the best in some subject, he accepted it gracefully, as if aware of his strengths and weaknesses: what was most memorable was the intensity with which he worked and "fought to stand out."

Headstrong, opinionated, insatiably curious, as Quica remembers Coco, "he would throw a tantrum if he couldn't understand or do something, and would ask questions endlessly until he understood, try until he succeeded." This perfectionism spelled enterprising determination to her, but it also meant that he was a pest—or, as good-natured Quica put it tactfully, "He always had his personality." Nelly López insinuated, winking, that his attention to detail was effeminate: he had "very nice handwriting," he was "very serious, and always came to class with a scarf and gloves, impeccable." Quica would follow Malé's strict orders, preparing his clothes and buffing his shoes for school in the morning, or for the afternoon outing to the movies. She remembers him always "well dressed, in his black velvet pants with suspenders and white shirts, hair always combed back in the style that was fashionable then."

Manuel was seen as a lonely little boy by many, a boy whose mother was away for much of the day, and who entertained himself by talking to older girls. "Coco did not have a childhood," declared Luisa Strubolini. The Strubolinis lived next door to the Puigs, in the building belonging to the Italian Society, of which Luisa's father was the director. He played the violin, an instrument that fascinated Coco. Then a woman in her early twenties, Luisa noticed that the little neighbor boy was often alone or trying vainly to persuade older girls like Chiquita Méndez to play with him, never playing with the boys. Luisa "took pity" on him and arranged with Malé to give the eight-year-old boy piano lessons. She was one of the few in Villegas with whom Coco could connect, the only person other than his mother who had interests besides "eating, sleeping, and cars." She was another "betrayed" one too: in her adolescence she had an American suitor of whom her religious Catholic Italian father did not approve; she was sent away to Catholic school in the town of Lincoln, and when she returned, the boyfriend had a new girlfriend.

Now an elderly recluse, Luisa remembers that Coco was lively like his mother, adding, not without some malice, that Malé molded him as if he were a daughter. By organizing a full schedule of lessons for him after school, Malé felt she was ensuring her son's prospects and helping him to rise above the stultifying level of the town. But most of the locals saw that, as his mother's secret sharer in a town where she was an outsider, he was too limited to adult, and female, company.

While he liked to visit the Italian Society, to see the violin, and to take lessons, he learned to be good "technically," Luisa said, but performing music wasn't his passion. He studied piano out of curiosity but also, as Raquel said, because he liked to perform, to be theatrical. More than anything he talked about movies, read a lot, and listened to records, "like his mother." When Baldo came back from business trips to Buenos Aires, he often brought new books and records which Coco and Malé had requested. Coco would invariably invite Luisa over to listen to the new music. She had similar tastes but also was a sounding board, an intellectual equal against whom he could sharpen his wits. He was always trying to outsmart her: he was "a know-it-all . . . We frequently argued about music." Luisa's father would side with Coco on questions of musical taste, a "manly" conspiracy, quips the elderly Luisa, still conserving her irony. While she preferred Chopin and the Romantics, Manuel preferred Mussorgsky's *Pictures at an Exhibition*, or moody, impressionist pieces like Debussy's *Submerged Cathedral* and *Claire de Lune*. Coco was very sure of himself in these arguments; Luisa would say, "You're just a kid, what do you know," but he'd spout his opinions and reasons, apparently unflappable.

At school Manuel soon hated his nickname because the bigger boys taunted him with the alliteration Culito de Coco (Coco, the Little Ass).

> In grammar school I encountered a violence I never ceased to hate. The systematic humiliation of anyone who was sensitive or weak, uniting groups, whole grades or schools into a single horde against the fat kids or the sickly, the little or delicate kids, always terrified me. I identified that horde with a whole generation and have never been able to forgive their incapacity to understand what is not like them.[63]

Manuel would later depict in fiction something that might have happened, when he was around ten, which coincided with a period when he barely grew for three years and was one of the smallest boys in his class: "The first time he saw fucking, he said he saw the Mansilla kid standing against the wall looking like he had an upset stomach and dripping tears, Noziglia grabbing him from behind and pumping him."[64]

According to his own statements, and the rumors that went about town, a fifteen-year-old boy had almost succeeded in raping him in the school bathroom. It had gotten around, apparently, that Coco liked to masturbate bigger boys. But anal sex with inexperienced boys who could hurt him was, at first, too frightening: "I refused to do it out of fear; he had little experience and didn't take his time."

Excitement and fear seemed inseparable—not an unusual combination—even regarding his fantasies about girls: he felt stimulated by a woman's body when he caught an illicit glance after sneaking into a twenty-year-old neighbor's house (this could have been Luisa's). But most thrilling were games with male schoolmates; one version of his "first time," at age eight or nine, was an incident with a seventeen-year-old boy (which he recalled through the enhancing sieve of memory):

> . . . too old for my little husband and wife games. And yet there was a special relationship between us . . . he was very handsome and I was very much in love . . . he was the brother of a little friend of mine. One day he took me into a park and at one moment he made me touch him. From there on I began to seek his company more and more, or that of boys his age, and move away from the "childish" games with my other friends . . . I had never experienced before such a bewitching, magical sensation.[65]

The school bathroom scandal occurred around the same year Coco's baby brother died. It was the winter of 1943, marked by a military coup in Argentina that would pave the way for the Peronist regime. Manuel would use this temporal setting for the chapter in *Betrayed by Rita Hayworth* that presents Mita's point of view, a monologue following the death of her second son.

In the novel, the mother's sorrow over her lost baby intensifies her disappointment with her darling Toto. Mita, in her monologue, intertwines the loss of her "little man" and the fear that her beloved Toto's "angel face" is a "woman's face." The effects of the school incident, the loss of his little brother, the fact that he stopped growing, and his mother's grief all feed Toto's sense of guilt. In the margin of the first draft of the Mita chapter,

Manuel jotted down a neologism "machification," shorthand for the fact that Mita seemed to favor macho cousin Hector from then on.

For Malé and Baldo as a couple, however, the emotional impact of this mischance, and their growing fears about Coco, would alienate them even more from Villegas, and from each other. The resentments between them as well as Baldo's feelings of guilt and resentment toward the Delledonnes, who blamed him for the misfortune, were the breeding ground for Coco's own feelings. Baldo and Malé arranged, well in advance, to have their next child delivered in a private hospital in Berisso, an upper-middle-class suburb of La Plata. In January 1945, Malé gave birth to their son Carlos, surrounded by loving parents and sisters, with whom she and Coco had spent the Christmas holidays, celebrating Coco's birthday and awaiting the happy event. Baldo could never wholeheartedly enjoy a trip to La Plata, however, because of his discomfort with his in-laws.

Manuel also speaks of this period as the end of "blissful" childhood because he was taken out of School No. 1, leaving his favorite teacher, and placed in the only other school in town, No. 17, on the outskirts of Villegas. Today Ana María Ladaga still tries to protect Manuel from scandal by explaining that after fifth grade they separated the sexes, so he had to move. But Julia B. de Méndez Boffi, the director of School No. 17, insists upon town lore: because of "a problem in the bathrooms," Coco's mother said to her, "Lula, I'm sending him to your school." Méndez Boffi's typically long Italo-Hispanic name was the kind Manuel would later satirize with playful revenge in *Heartbreak Tango*, as Laura P. de Baños, the name he gives a school administrator. Baños, the surname of another Villegan family, also means "baths."

The end of blissful childhood meant, ultimately, assuming a sexual identity.

the valley of decision

Fiction is an art of emphases and omissions: while Manuel played up Jorge's masculine attributes in *Betrayed by Rita Hayworth*, he underplayed Coco's— or rather, he suspended the narrative at the point when Coco, at age fifteen, was becoming aware of the inner "truth" while developing on the outside into a "handsome boy with broad shoulders," as one of his former girl-friends commented in Villegas. His shoulders were broad but there was al-ready a soft roundness about them which his stoop-shoulder posture would accentuate as he got older. Germán Puig, not a relative but a Cuban friend and a photographer Manuel met in Paris, described Manuel in his mid-twenties as having a "handsome masculine Roman head and large eyes" while his body gave a "flimsy, soft impression."

As his sexual desires grew more apparent, Coco could no longer confide in his mother. Years later, in the process of turning Johann Strauss's love tri-angle into Toto's Oedipal affair in chapter 13 of *Betrayed by Rita Hayworth*, Manuel jotted down the following: "The Great Sadness: 1947–8 Casals: he realizes he cannot tell his mother everything. HE'S ALONE. Because it would hurt her, he prefers not to communicate more to avoid communicat-ing PAIN."[66] The only family member he could confide in was pretty Bebé. After he had his first love affair—somewhere between the ages of eighteen and twenty—he told Bebé that on the one hand he felt good, relieved, and on the other, horrible. A devout Catholic, Bebé felt anguish not only for him but because she had to keep this guilty secret from the rest of the family.

Bebé (her Christian name is Alda) to this day still speaks with the psy-chosomatic breathlessness that developed early in her life. In *Betrayed by Rita Hayworth* Teté's mother has tuberculosis and Teté, imagining that she's suffocating like her mother, claims that she can't breathe. Teté hears from her grandmother that her mother got ill when she was born; Manuel leads his reader, through Teté's free-associating monologue, to understand that she connects her mother's illness not only with her existence but with her "sinful" thoughts about sex as well. In the same monologue she fantasizes that Toto is choking to death when Mita gives him his bath, shaking him and ordering him not to play with girls and dolls anymore; ultimately he's choking because he is somehow sinful too: like his mother, he doesn't be-lieve in God. Bebé claims she became a psychologist to work through the neuroses of a guilt-ridden Catholic childhood, in which her cousin's strug-gles with his sexuality played a major role: her first research paper discussed whether homosexuality should be classified as disorder or illness. Coco's conversations with Bebé were to provide him with psychological back-ground for his writing, most evident in the technical detail of the footnotes in *Kiss of the Spider Woman*.

In 1946, thirteen-year-old Coco was sent away to one of the best private secondary boarding schools in the country, Colegio Ward (called George Washington in the novel), located in Ramón Mejía, a western suburb of Buenos Aires. There was nothing beyond grammar school in Villegas, and Malé and Baldo wanted Coco to have the best education possible, which they could now afford. Ward was notorious for its upper-class snobbery, and Coco felt alone there. The children were cruel, he missed his mother, and the movies, where he'd go with a cousin or friend on Saturdays, were his only consolation and "escape from an impossible system of machismo, aggression, and dominance."

His favorite stars in the mid to late forties included Joan Crawford, Ingrid Bergman, and "forever Hayworth"; the films he preferred were women's melodramas and romantic adventures. Though Manuel would caricature Crawford's cardboard impenetrability, in his early adolescence her conflictual role as mother and career woman in *Mildred Pierce* and her obsessive, almost incestuous feelings for her ungrateful daughter Veda struck home. Another favorite, the adventure *Frenchman's Creek* (1944), starring Joan Fontaine and Latin leading man Arturo de Córdova and directed by Mitchell Leisen, also explored a woman's dilemma, but in a lighter vein. While contrasting male and female worlds in typical Hollywood fashion, this "feminized" pirate movie, based on a best-seller by Daphne Du Maurier (*Rebecca*), romanticizes a woman's temporary escape from her motherly-wifely role. The normally demure Joan Fontaine wears men's clothing and goes off with a pirate lover, but her motherly instinct draws her back: "Women may play and wander for a time," warns her pirate, "but in the end instinct is too strong for them. They must make their nest."[67]

These dramas about mothers and children, about home versus the dangerous world, were, for Coco, a refuge. Homesickness at Ward prompted, in *Betrayed by Rita Hayworth*, his fusion of Johann Strauss's story with Toto's retelling of the movie *The Great Waltz*. To seek consolation after his disappointment in love, Johann (German for "Juan") returns from Vienna to the house in the country where he was born, but when he enters his room, the despotic duke who stole his beloved away begins to haunt him, as does his mother, a disheveled ghost in an apron. In the more explicit first draft Toto says: "My room: How pretty the room in 'Vallejos' is; remembering it from Ward, of course it's so beautiful with everything in matching tones, but when I enter, all my phantoms enter with me." These become Johann's thoughts in the novel.

Coco was at Ward for his own good, but he felt vulnerable and abandoned: in a letter from New York almost twenty years later, these feelings remained vivid, as he reminds his "Dear Family" (which is how he often addressed letters home, even though his main correspondent was Malé):

> Yesterday and today I received letters, how nice; every day, like when I was at Ward. If it hadn't been for those letters I would have died in that boarding school, beautiful as it was; the teachers and wardens were all insane. When I remember how they'd make us take off our undershirts to sleep and put on our freezing pajamas "for hygiene," I die laughing; not only was one sneezing all the time but the colds and viruses never let up.[68]

No longer teacher's pet, Coco found it daunting to keep up and to fit in at Ward, infused as it was with the fascist atmosphere that overshadowed the country. Perón had assumed the presidency on June 4, 1946, ushering in a climate of intensified nationalism (sanctioning embargoes against foreign economic intervention, notably the United States' Standard Oil), along with xenophobia and anti-Semitism—already strong in Argentina, which, as a neutral country in World War II under Perón's predecessor, Edelmiro J. Farrell, had sympathized with the Axis powers. In *Betrayed by Rita Hayworth* a poor, tough Jewish boy named Cobito (nickname for Jacobo), who hates the Catholic gallegos, and Esther, a worker's daughter and a Peronist, represent the underdog at exclusive, anti-Semitic Ward. From their point of view Toto is a middle-class twit and social climber. Cobito is also sexually violent and tries to rape Toto. Manuel joked while we were working on the translation of this difficult chapter: "I thought my Jewish friends would appreciate being represented by a macho type!" Manuel presents class and racial prejudice as it is experienced by Jewish Cobito and Peronist Esther— and exposes, by extension, the tension between Argentine *criollo* natives and first- or second-generation immigrants, between a Catholic majority and a Jewish minority, between the working classes and the privileged.

His run-in with snobbery in those formative adolescent years (1946–50) at Ward would reverberate in his sensitivity about class throughout his life and work. Ana, the protagonist of his fifth novel, *Pubis Angelical* (1979), is an exiled Argentine woman in Mexico, hospitalized with cancer. Her best friend, Beatriz, is modeled after Manuel's friend the Mexican socialite Elena Urrutia. Class envy as well as annoyance at Beatriz's "superior" maternal attitude attenuate Ana's feelings for her friend, with whom she competes by putting Beatriz down for speaking a *cursi* (corny, or kitsch) upper-class lexicon. Ana's thoughts echo Manuel's reaction to Ward:

> My home was just like all the other middle-class homes, however comfortably middle-class it was. It was when I switched to that private secondary school that I found out I wasn't as privileged as I'd thought. It was there that I learned those distinctions. An expensive school where there were girls from the upper class. It was their scorn that taught me the difference.[69]

Coco was not devoid of anti-Semitic sentiments, endemic to his cultural background, nor did he avoid clichés about Jewish looks and character; the flipside was his admiration for his Jewish schoolmates at Ward, and the affinity he felt with some of them as outsiders—sensitive, marginalized, intellectual—among them his bench mate Raquel Hodari, who, years later, remarked that she and Manuel had "liked the same boys."[70]

One of the last girls he ever fell in love with, at age fourteen, was a Jewish girl named Laura Kacs—in Esther's diary, or chapter 13, she's called Laurita and is also identified as a white Russian, whom tough Cobito thinks is really Jewish but trying to pass. Coco seemed to be seeking rejection. Laura was older and taller, or, as he confided to Luisa Strubolini, "elegant like Mama," and, unlike the girls his age, she was his intellectual equal.[71] Bebé, who lived in Buenos Aires at the time, tried to introduce Coco to girls during those secondary school years. Once, when she took him to a dance, he stood on the side like a wallflower. After an hour or so, when Bebé asked him if there was any girl he liked, he replied sarcastically. "There's one who's divine!" and pointed to the seven-layer chocolate cake on the table.

A chubby schoolmate named Hernán convinced him to go to a prostitute; it was a traumatic experience, which later resurfaced as an incident in *The Buenos Aires Affair*, part of a case history Manuel constructs for the sexually dysfunctional male protagonist, Leo:

> At age sixteen [Leo] went with some classmates to a construction site where a prostitute and her manager were waiting for them. It was Leo's first time and he became inhibited when he got near the woman; he came out of the room and asked the manager to return his money, which the man refused to do, giving Leo a tongue-lashing . . . the boy . . . walked away crestfallen.[72]

There would be brief romances with girls in Manuel's late teens and early twenties, but Laura's rejection was a turning point: Coco tried to prove he could fall in love with a girl, and the one he chose was unavailable. Bebé remembers that the day Laura turned him down he was sick to his stomach and lay in bed for days. After this episode, according to Bebé, he began to question himself with increasing panic, and joked compulsively about homosexuals.

A few years after leaving Villegas, in 1951, he sent Luisa Strubolini a copy of *Moira*, the latest novel by Julien Green. *Moira* (Greek for "Grace") begins with a student's attraction to an older woman who also repulses him: filled with self-loathing and religious guilt over sex, the student turns out to be a repressed homosexual, and violently misogynist. Speaking to both Luisa's repressive faith and Manuel's sexual angst, Green's novel depicted a crisis of faith, the forced choice between (homo)sexuality and religion, a choice which led to madness as the only liberation. Adolescent antihero Joseph loses control and unintentionally kills the "temptress" Moira after raping her, a brutal scene that perhaps reflected Manuel's anxiety and anticipated his own depiction of sexual violence in *The Buenos Aires Affair*, where Leo loses control and kills a homosexual, and later attempts the same against a woman lover. Such a gift to Luisa carried a loaded message, to say the least. While it was a recognition of their bond and shared marginality, it seems mischievous if not spiteful: in part because of the caricatured older woman in the novel, in part because Coco was showing off his knowledge of the latest hot writer.

The Ward years were difficult, but they had expanded Coco's horizons. "By then the fashionable authors in Buenos Aires were Hesse, Huxley, Sartre. I read them all, and essays in psychology as well." Particularly significant was his discovery, in 1947, of Freud—in Hitchcock's *Spellbound*. "Discussing this film with a Jewish schoolmate, I found out that my friend knew everything about Freud." This was a turning point: he realized being the best pupil didn't mean he knew everything, and he started to read voraciously. In *Betrayed by Rita Hayworth* he would associate Toto's discovery of Freud with Herminia's (Luisa's) repression of sexual self-knowledge. *Spellbound* was his introduction to the "talking cure" and led him to read Freud's *The Interpretation of Dreams* and *Introductory Lectures on Psychoanalysis*. In the cherished medium of the movies he encountered a director—Hitchcock—who introduced psychological trauma and cure as raw material for entertainment (*Spellbound* was the first of his "pop Freud" thrillers, followed by *Vertigo*, *Psycho*, and *Marnie*). In the same vein, Manuel was captivated by Ginger Rogers in the musical *Lady in the Dark*—"dollar-book Freud" in a phrase coined by Orson Welles—and an over-the-top Olivia de Havilland in *The Snake Pit*.

Despite Manuel's later claims that literature had no influence on him, he read widely in his adolescence and twenties. This anti-literary image was partly a defense, once he became a public figure, against academic inquisitors and the judgments of the Argentine literati. Manuel didn't read Argentine writers, nor did he read much in Spanish. The point was to learn "the languages of the cinema" as he had already begun to do—English as a child and, from 1946 on, "Italian and French, because post-war European films began to arrive in Argentina."[73]

Manuel's facility and determination to learn languages was not only a gateway to the movies but a way out of Argentina. As a homosexual, an outsider, he was drawn to foreign languages, to otherness, and to other places where he could be himself, where he wouldn't hear unbearable words like *puto*, or where its connotations were more bearable—*fag* in English or *folle* in French—set at a linguistic distance, mediated by camp humor.

In order to learn these languages he read the literatures, and it wasn't till he was in the full fever of becoming a writer (during the Boom of the early sixties) that he began to read contemporary Latin American writers. Paradoxically there seemed to be more of a dialogue "in underdevelopment," he quipped, that is, among Latin American writers on neutral soil, and, also, he needed to be au courant. By the time Manuel was writing his second novel, however, he says he developed "professional deformation of reading everything with a pencil in his hand."[74] He was also beginning to be sure of his own enterprise and increasingly jealous of time not spent on his own projects.

Film versions of literary works did lead the adolescent Manuel to read the books they were based on; in Villegas he read mainly novels that had been adapted for children—the international classics from Cervantes to Dostoevsky—and thought of the marvelous films they could become, developing intuitively his early interest in plot and narrative. The first unabridged novel he read was *The Pastoral Symphony* by the famous homosexual writer André Gide; here was a role model. He discovered literature could be enjoyed for itself and not only as raw material for a film:

> I read literature seeking something that would awaken my intelligence. The movies were where one yielded to a sensual abandon, not for thinking, but to feel . . . I read *The Pastoral Symphony* because the film had just earned first prize in Cannes for Michèle Morgan's performance. Gide had won the Nobel Prize that same year.[75]

Gide showed him how effective spare writing could be, while, when a few weeks later he read *The Sound and the Fury*, Faulkner was "equally marvelous" for his baroque extravagance. "But I never thought of writing. I read as a common reader, and watched movies wanting to learn how to make them." Manuel's heart still belonged to the movies, but his concept of the movies was also expanding:

> My friend also pointed out that film didn't only mean Hollywood. I was reluctant to see a film featuring no stars, but *Quai des Orfèvres* (*Jenny Lamour* in the United States), a French thriller by Clouzot, dazzled me. In that film the star was the director, and at least I knew what I wanted to become: a film director. I couldn't be Tyrone Power or Ginger Rogers or Robert Taylor or Eleanor Powell, but I could be Clouzot.

> First step: study French, English and Italian—the languages
> of the cinema.[76]

After Ward, he would take full advantage of resources in cosmopolitan
Buenos Aires, studying at the Alliance Française, the British Institute, and
the Dante Society—and the latter would provide him with his first real
crack at glory.

a writer is born: 1950–61

Passion is better in the movies than in life; you only suffer for 90 minutes.

buenos aires: an affair to remember

By 1949 the Puigs had moved to Buenos Aires, settling in a small two-bedroom apartment on Bulnes, a quiet tree-lined street in the Barrio Norte. Now seventeen, Manuel shared a room with his five-year-old brother, Carlitos—nicknamed "el chino" for his almond-shaped eyes and olive complexion—as he finished his last year at Ward. Cousin Jorge lived with his father at a boardinghouse downtown; there were frequent visits to the Delledonnes in La Plata on weekends, and on many afternoons Coco went to the movies on Corrientes with his friends and cousins as well as Malé. There were concerts too, operas at the majestic Teatro Colón, shopping on bustling Santa Fe or downtown on Florida, and movies at the fabulous Versailles, the only theater that showed foreign films during the Peronist years.

Coco spent a lot of time with his cousin Bebé, who had blossomed into a beautiful young woman; the cousins shared romantic secrets and career aspirations: "Coco wanted to be a director in those days." He practiced directing with Bebé as his lead actress, and the plays they rehearsed were no longer "el pueblito" but serious contemporary theater. Tennessee Williams was his favorite, in particular, Bebé recalls, *The Glass Menagerie*, "the great homosexual playwright's family psychodrama about a repressed daughter."

In late adolescence Manuel liked to "dress up and act like a grown-up" with Bebé. He would cast himself as dapper man-about-town, but he also took charge—in the same way he had bossed his girlfriends in Villegas when they played "el pueblito"—of his female companion's wardrobe. He advised Bebé on her hairstyle and makeup: "I was one of Coco's first real-life dolls." One evening he rented a tuxedo, and the two youngsters—he was eighteen, she twenty—sneaked into a nightclub pretending to be of legal age. They stayed out late drinking cocktails, eating rich foods; both got sick. Bebé, who spent the night vomiting, remembers that her cousin again lay in bed for days; Coco's stress always seemed to take its toll on his digestive system.

Under Coco's influence, before her marriage and her career as a psychologist, Bebé worked as a fashion model and, at the time, cultivated an elegant gamine look à la Audrey Hepburn. At first she wore her hair in Rita Hayworth or Veronica Lake style, long and wavy off the brow; but the trendsetter was the "princess who wanted to live," after Audrey's sparkling debut in the arms of handsome Gregory Peck in *Roman Holiday* (1953).[1] (Years later, after *Funny Face*, Manuel changed his mind about Audrey: how could he have loved this "anemic" waif?) Bebé had to be up on the latest fashion, so now she wore irregular bangs and a beret in French existential mode. Manuel wanted to be her, envied her, she sensed, or, as he said one day, staring at her, watching her put on her makeup: "You're beautiful, very desirable. But I don't desire you; I want to be you." Perhaps Manuel gave Bebé the name Teté in *Betrayed by Rita Hayworth* because she was almost his twin; not only his secret sharer, but the one he wanted to be.

Bebé was dating a military officer who was friends with Juan Duarte, Evita's brother. Through this connection Bebé obtained a pass for Coco to see a film in the making, starring Duarte's mistress at the time, a leading Argentine actress, Fanny Navarro. Manuel and Navarro would become good friends—and years later, though he did not share her devotion to Peronism, he was the only friend from former days who came to visit her when she was ill and dying. But this first venture onto a movie set was uncomfortable; apparently someone uttered a sarcastic remark about there being too many people on the set, and he was an outsider.[2] He was embarrassed: whenever he felt insecure, as on this occasion, he could hear himself speaking in a *marica*, or faggy, way and he hated his own voice. He sensed that his manner had provoked the sarcasm.

In 1950, when Juan and Evita Perón were at the height of their power, Manuel entered the School of Architecture at the University of Buenos Aires. Baldo would have preferred that he study engineering, the career cousin Ernesto pursued, but Manuel was dead set against the sciences. Architecture, a fashionable middle-class profession, seemed a fair compromise between art and pragmatism, and he tried it out, partly to make his parents happy. By this point, the comfort of home and Malé's cooking were increasingly offset by his father's disapproving glances and the small room he had to share with his little brother.

He dropped out of Architecture before the end of the academic year, relieved, though remorseful about disappointing his parents.[3] Only foreign languages could motivate him to study, hence he transferred in 1951 to the School of Philosophy and Letters, convinced that by mastering English, French, and Italian, the "languages of cinema," he would eventually gain a foot in the door. At school, he struck up what would be a lifelong friendship with Alfredo Gialdini, a sensitive classmate and dilettante of the arts who, after interrupting his studies to do military service, went on to become an insurance salesman. Manuel dropped out of the university definitively in 1952, and studied language and literature at private institutes—the Alliance Française, the Dante Alighieri Society, and the British Institute.

"On the sly" he bought *Photoplay*, seduced by the latest fashions and gossip about his glamorous movie stars. But even this arena was overcast with shadows. Most Hollywood movies were embargoed in Argentina under Perón's policy to promote national industries, and, moreover, the fifties were the "dark ages" because Manuel's stars were "growing old with no replacements—except for Monroe."[4] Only Marilyn Monroe radiated an authentic charisma, risqué yet innocent, sexy yet poignantly vulnerable. But the material prosperity of the postwar era in the United States, epitomized by Hollywood's new busty blondes, was brash and abrasive.

With the advent of television in the fifties, nostalgia for the glamorous thirties and early forties began to spread. Television producers in the United States had discovered that a cheap way to fill airtime was to run old movies, which had an emotional appeal for millions of viewers. *Million Dollar Movie* was perhaps the first series of this kind, with its musical theme from *Gone With the Wind*, the biggest blockbuster in motion picture history. At the university Manuel found kindred spirits like Alfredo, young men who shared his secret life and the ecstasy of the silver screen, fellow fans equally attentive to the pulse of the distant Western world, and even more nostalgic for the prewar European and American cinema than for the Parisians or New Yorkers they longed to be.

With his new city friends Manuel rushed to see not only the few Hollywood movies shown in those years in Buenos Aires but everything from European imports to Mexican and Argentine kitsch. Wednesdays were almost always reserved for Malé and the special double bill at the Lorraine. An energetic culture-vulture, Malé adopted and was adopted by Manuel's university comrades like Alfredo and, later, Alfredo's dapper friend, Hugo Sottotetti, a bank teller, but she never openly acknowledged her son's orientation. Even recently, commenting on a gay character in a film, she mentioned to a visitor, "Coco understood those people so well." Alfredo recalls that he and Manuel discovered Ingmar Bergman together, when they attended the opening of the sex farce *Smiles of a Summer Night*, the Swedish director's first international success, in August 1955. They left the theater in a lyrical daze. The film had won first prize at the international Punta del Este Film Festival, at the elegant Uruguayan seaside resort, and inspired two young Uruguayan journalists, Emir Rodríguez Monegal and Homero Alsina Thevenet, to write the first book in Spanish on Bergman.

With equal enthusiasm Alfredo and Manuel relished the trite Argentine soft-porn flicks of the well-endowed Isabel Sarli—notably *Mujer* and *¡Fuego!* The more statuesque or exaggerated an actress was, like the divine Garbo, the more worthy of adoration. Any kitschy attribute or contradiction made the divas all the more enthralling or amusing. The voluptuous Sarli, for example, was more enamored of her gaggle of poodles than of any *hombre*. After drama diva Mecha Ortiz—Argentina's Joan Crawford—Alfredo and Manuel's most idolized native *artista* was Niní Marshall, a gifted radio comedienne during the late thirties and forties. Marshall mimicked to perfection the foibles and, especially, the inflections of Argentine women, inventing a pantheon of characters ranging across the social strata. Most famous for her strident lower-middle-class Catita, Marshall was possibly the first popular media artist to make the Argentines laugh at themselves. Manuel would often imitate her imitations for his friends, and she inspired, however indirectly, his first novels, particularly his "soap opera," *Heartbreak Tango*.

As democratically attentive to obscure actresses like Ann Harding as he was to Crawford or Ortiz, Manuel talked about these ladies as if they were next-door neighbors. For Malé and Manuel it was a personal affront as well as a Peronist injustice that the films of sentimental chanteuse Libertad Lamarque were banned in Argentina after Lamarque criticized Eva Duarte on the movie set of *Circus Cavalcade* for her third-rate acting. When Duarte became Evita Perón, Lamarque fled to Mexico, where she continued to be a star, playing the role of the mother in soap operas until she was very old. Libertad would gain the title (the ninety-year-old Malé recalls with proud erudition) Mexico's Mother. Like other faithful Argentine fans of Libertad, Coco discovered Mexico's musical melodramas thanks to Evita's banishing act.

While Perón was ruling Argentina from 1946 to 1955, Western Europe was rising out of its ashes under the Marshall Plan. Uncle Sam used tax benefits to encourage American entrepreneurs to invest in Europe and to make use of its cheap labor. Astute American producers, eluding the McCarthy trials, set up shop in Rome to produce schlock epics with low-cost extras, sets, and locations. Competing, in color, for its position in a marketplace threatened by black-and-white television, the Hollywood that stayed home degenerated over the next several years into sugary musicals, stilted comedies, and bland melodramas. While some older names like Ginger Rogers and Fred Astaire braved color technology with their fading charms, new cardboard stars like Rock Hudson and Doris Day, or Doris Día (as Manuel and his friends called her), took center stage.

In Europe commercial movies could be made cheaply, especially in Italy and Spain, but art films also flourished. Postwar Italian neorealism critiqued Hollywood's "frivolous escapism"; a decade later François Truffaut and the French New Wave paved another artistic way, parodying but also paying homage to Hollywood's bygone glories with fond nostalgia. By the early sixties, perceptive critics were recognizing directors like Federico Fellini, Michelangelo Antonioni, Jean-Luc Godard, Truffaut, Robert Bresson, Eric Rohmer, Bergman, and Luis Buñuel as "auteurs"—authors, each with a distinctive style—and certain movies were becoming, more respectably, classic "films." Big studio directors like Ernst Lubitsch, Howard Hawks, William Wyler, George Cukor, Fritz Lang, Billy Wilder, and Alfred Hitchcock, once just talented craftsmen on a payroll, were now revered virtuosi. A new public venue, the art theater or film society, cropped up in cosmopolitan cities and college towns to accommodate the expanding educated audience for the new films—such as Truffaut's *400 Blows* and Godard's *Breathless*—and Hollywood classics like *Casablanca* were resurrected as art by the critical sensibility of film buffs.

By the late fifties the notion of classic Hollywood—the Hollywood of the thirties and forties—arose simultaneously with an appraisal of the thriller as high art, as a proper genre called film noir. Such box office hits as *The Maltese Falcon* (1941), *Laura* and *Double Indemnity* (both 1944), *The Big Sleep*, *The Blue Dahlia*, and *Gilda* (all 1946), seething with violence, veiled perversion, and social corruption, fiercely reacted to an earlier, more innocent age. Though made in Hollywood, these thrillers struck a relevant chord not only in France but in Latin America: gangsters and crooked capitalists were close cousins to *caudillos* like Perón and Batista, who ruled by mob or military coercion. These film adaptations of the *roman noir*, or the hard-boiled detective fiction of the Depression era, written by high stylists like Raymond Chandler and Dashiell Hammett, were superbly crafted. In an era when color was still a more costly process, these films were shot inexpensively in ordinary, yet exquisite, black and white. The use of light and shadow summoned a dark, cynical, pessimistic mood, hence André Bazin and postwar French intellectuals coined the apt term *film noir* in 1946. An invention of misogynistic or masochistic masculinity, film noir women were featured as predatory yet self-destructive femmes fatales, played by glamour queens Rita Hayworth, Barbara Stanwyck, Ava Gardner, and Veronica Lake. The male characters were tough yet vulnerable antiheroes portrayed by *beaux ténébreux* like Robert Mitchum, Alan Ladd, and Humphrey Bogart. In *Breathless*, Godard's homage to Paris as well as to film noir antiheroes, Bogie inspired Jean-Paul Belmondo's narcissistic soliloquy—delivered as he looks at himself in the mirror, but also at a picture of Bogart.

Europe and America played a shifting game of nostalgic mirrors; if, before, European figures like Dietrich had brought charm to Hollywood, now American figures like Bogart took on a new poignancy in jaded Europe. Culture capital of the fin de siècle, haven of the American "lost generation" of the twenties, Paris continued to be La Ville Lumière to young Argentines with artistic aspirations. Among them, a new writer named Julio Cortázar, born in Belgium, where his father held a diplomatic post, had fled Perón's regime in 1951 to seek out *la vie de boheme* in "gay Paree"—he would immortalize the angst of expatriate Argentine artists and intellectuals on the Left Bank in his 1963 *roman comique, Hopscotch*.

In the meantime, Perón capitalized on xenophobic, particularly anti-Yankee sentiments in Argentina to maintain the support of the military and the adulation of the working classes. Films from Hollywood were embargoed and, because of the Peronist affiliation with the nationalist models of Nazism and Italian fascism, most of the foreign films Coco got to see in those years were from Germany, Italy, and Vichy France. His adolescent romance with cinema was contaminated by the "fascinating fascism"[5] of Germany's star Zarah Leander and France's Arletty.

At the end of World War II, Argentina infamously offered refuge to Nazis; what is less well known is that the Argentine military imitated the German police state's strategies of torture and mass control:

> Among the elements of European regimes imported into Argentina [during the Perón years] were concentration camps (for a short period), anti-Semitism (which Perón unconvincingly repudiated), a Gestapo-style secret force called the Control (del Estado), torture, and the suppression of civil liberties. Behind all these was the Argentine version of the nationalistic attitude of German national socialism. Clearly, this was very likely to appeal to a population conscious of its lack of roots; indeed, in 1946, when the United States published the famous *Blue Book*, reporting on Argentina's pro-Nazi activities, this increased Perón's popularity among his followers, for their natural resistance to foreign intervention was by this time turning into rampant xenophobia. Perón actually designated his new policies "the nationalist revolution."[6]

In a footnote to *Kiss of the Spider Woman*, Manuel would ironically dub Hitler the Conductor, after Perón. The Conductor's xenophobia followed the criteria characteristic of his German and Italian models: intolerance of foreignness, hostility to otherness—including those who were "different," like Jews and homosexuals. Authoritarian systems require conformity, as Alberto Moravia, the Italian novelist, reminded readers in *The Conformist*, and machismo has remained a perennial value in the Catholic cultures of the Latin world, to which all men must conform.

Machismo's flipside is homophobia, not only because homosexuals are offensively effeminate, or considered so, but because, uncomfortably, homosexual practices are not incompatible with machismo, as long as the macho is an "active" sodomist. Homophobia, in this context, guided Perón's anti-clerical policies: determined to resolve the problem of sexually transmitted diseases and, in passing, to provide an alternative to the spread of homosexuality, Perón legalized brothels.[7] This measure was aimed particularly at working-class men who indulged in indiscriminate sex with either street-walkers or homosexuals, but it also undermined the Church, which, Perón claimed, was "benevolently tolerant" of homosexuality among the priesthood. Perón was selective when it came to perversions: not averse to corrupting schoolgirls before, during, and after his marriage to Evita, he was notorious for picking up young girls as he roamed the city on his motorcycle.

Perón's personal behavior provoked moral indignation, and ultimately his fatal error in Argentina was his anticlerical attitude. Both he and Evita had suffered the humiliation of illegitimate births. Perón took his revenge by instituting reforms in the legal organization of the family so as not to favor legitimate over extramarital offspring, but his ultimate slap in the face to the Church was to authorize remarriage by divorcées. Peronist measures seemed marked by drastic contradiction: liberalize certain mores but foment intolerance; sustain the workers' unions but guarantee total power for Perón; promote social reform but control it under the dictatorial aegis of nationalist fascism, which appealed to compatriots both on the extreme right and on the extreme left. Evita was an essential ingredient in this recipe: she elicited admiration as a woman of the people who rose out of illegitimate obscurity from a small town in the pampa; she secured suffrage for Argentine women, but mainly to guarantee more votes for Perón; she won the love of the workers, whom she called her *descamisados*, or shirtless ones. She stole from the rich to give (some) to the poor or underprivileged *cabecitas negras*, or "Greaseheads," from the interior, the Rabas and Panchos (characters in *Heartbreak Tango*) whom Coco and Bebé had felt sorry for as children.

Middle-class Argentines, critical of Perón's authoritarianism, were caught between the urgency for social and political reforms, to which Perón paid lip service, and the fascist corruption that continued to undermine the country's stability. By 1953 inflation had intensified and the middle class, disillusioned by diminishing economic leverage, became increasingly reactive, siding with the old oligarchy and the Church against Perón to remove him from office in 1955. Peronism was (and still remains) a knotty paradox for Argentines; in the early seventies Perón would return briefly to power, backed by an uneasy coalition of the right-wing military and Marxist intellectuals.

One victim of Perón's "nationalist revolution" was Argentina's greatest writer, Jorge Luis Borges. Dismissed from his municipal job as librarian, he had been appointed poultry inspector—intentionally degrading, of course, for an upper-middle-class intellectual. Refusing to accept such humiliation, he was forced to teach for a living, a terrifying prospect for this timid man with a stutter. In 1952 Manuel met Borges, not realizing till years later the significance of their chance encounter.

Many avid readers and intellectuals in Buenos Aires attended Borges's lectures in the fifties, before he became a world-famous figure; most of them were friends associated with *Sur* magazine, such as Adolfo Bioy Casares, Silvina Ocampo, and José Bianco. Among Manuel's current and future friends at these lectures at the Colegio Libre de Estudios Superiores (Free School of Advanced Studies), on elegant Santa Fe Avenue, were his university buddies Alfredo and Hugo, as well as film critic Alberto Tabbia and writer/filmmaker Edgardo Cozarinsky, who later compiled Borges's articles on film in a volume called *Borges in/and/on Film*.[8]

To keep up his studies of English at the Argentine Association for English Culture, also on Santa Fe, Manuel, not yet twenty, took a course from Borges on the detective novel. Here he encountered the works of Wilkie Collins.[9] Manuel's future novels, *Heartbreak Tango*, subtitled "A Serial Romance," and *The Buenos Aires Affair*, subtitled "A Detective Novel," would be compared to Collins's work. Borges's readerly enthusiasm for detective stories was infectious and stimulated Manuel's own budding fascination with well-wrought plots and seductive suspense. Many years later, asked to contribute an homage on the occasion of Borges's death in 1986, Manuel wrote this tribute:

> I met Borges in 1952 . . . He was around fifty-three, I figure, but at times he seemed much younger (when he read) or much older (when he walked with a stoop, dragging his feet). The only Argentine lecturer in the institute, he gave the talks in English. At that time only a few initiates knew him as a writer; for the young people in class he was just another pro-

fessor. What first drew my attention was how shy he was: we were merely a few attentive, depersonalized, silent adolescents, but we managed to make him tremble. Next I noticed the threadbare sleeves of his jacket, the shoes that threatened to lose their soles in the middle of the class. His eyes were different then; he saw, but he didn't look at anybody until he felt completely ensconced in his lecture of the day. Then his eyes would roam the class until they rested upon some girl in the group, where they remained for the duration of the class. At that point a transformation would occur: little by little his apprehension disappeared and with simple, dispassionate words, always avoiding hyperbole, he communicated gradually his hyperbolic joy as a reader of those authors. He lingered with special delight upon Wilkie Collins. He would narrate the plots of his novels, analyzing them in such pleasurable terms for his listeners that one avoided the original text for fear of disappointment (or so I reacted, at least). That man in a few minutes would change, become one more adolescent in the room, discovering those passionate stories and vibrating with surprise like the rest of us. But he always curbed emphasis, communicating emotion through some secret, subterranean quality that permeated his words. Perhaps that quality was simply the modest expressivity of a person who was very passionate and very shy at the same time. It never failed that when he referred to some heroine's physical attributes, he'd blush. The girls in the class always made comments about this, and we waited for such moments as the climax of the spectacle.

Around then I had older friends who knew something about the literary world and I asked them about this strange and endearing character. They told me he was someone who lived to read, that because of this he was going blind, and to beware of approaching him because he was very sarcastic. The course ended and I didn't see him again.[10]

Whether or not Manuel bothered to read *The Moonstone* and *The Woman in White*, he absorbed from the older man's fervor a valuable lesson about the weaving of plots, odd characters, engaging suspense, and the passionate threads of gothic romance. Trickling down through his own delight in movies and radio soap operas, these narrative arts would shape the architecture of Manuel's future novels.

In 1953, while continuing his language studies, Manuel began, at the same time as his friend Alfredo, his compulsory term of military service. Thanks to the influence exerted by cousin Bebé's military fiancé and to Manuel's knowledge of languages, he was assigned a clerical position in the offices of the Air Force, where he translated documents and evaded the potential hazards, as an effeminate youth, of the barracks. Bebé claims her marriage ("at the late age of thirty") to a *militar*, a naval officer, saved her life after the military coup in the seventies. In those precarious years, her friendships with left-wing intellectuals could have easily endangered the whole family. In *The Buenos Aires Affair* Manuel alludes to Bebé (or Alda) in the figure of Leo's sister Olga, who "intervened with her influential friends."[11]

Bebé's penchant for men in uniform disturbed the family (Manuel included), though not as acutely as Manuel's sexuality. The cousins continued to feel bonded by their respective conflicts with the family. Unable to speak about the unspeakable, Manuel had to lead a double life, and Argentina, a country with a split personality, was to blame.

Early in the nineteenth century this new nation, the first in the New World to overthrow the hegemony of a Spain depleted by the Napoleonic wars, willed itself to emulate the libertarian models of France, England, and the United States. By the end of the nineteenth century, waves of immigrants had helped shape Buenos Aires into a clone of Paris, Rome, and London grafted with New York or Chicago, and make it the refuge of polyglots who spoke several European languages as well as Spanish with an Italian accent.

But Argentina, in hard economic times, would always fall back on its feudal Spanish past: The *cursi* pretensions of an insecure, never-quite-Europeanized middle class, the machismo inherited from Mediterranean grandfathers and fostered by the harsh life of the pampas, and the colonial overlay of British decorum produced a stifling society, one that valued elegant facades and proper appearances more than civil liberties. Up until the late forties and even fifties, when Perón's shirtless workers movement marked a new populist era, men were obliged by law to wear jackets in public places, and could be fined if they appeared in their shirtsleeves.

In this constraining atmosphere, Manuel learned early on the protective uses of irony—in particular, camp. At its best, camp delicately balances frivolity and discernment, recognizes the value of discards, whether songs or wanton women. Camp sensibility empathizes with the foibles of humanity, relishing rather than judging "the little triumphs and awkward intensities" of character.[12] Like Ernst Lubitsch, a favorite comedic director and consummate campster, Manuel had tender feelings toward his objects of mimicry.[13] The other face of love is often hate, though, and Manuel's camp wit had its lethal side, just as his loving, devoted bond with Malé served as defense against women and shrouded his rivalry with her and all women for "real" men. Placing Joan Crawford or opera diva Maria Callas on a pedestal empowered or "augmented" woman as a means to empowering the campster capable of appreciating such "degraded artifacts."[14]

When Evita became first lady of Argentina and then saint, camp became particularly subversive in a country obsessed with propriety and blind (like most nations) to its own kitsch, its own *cursilería*. Simply mentioning Perón's police state in a novel that also portrayed sexual perversity was justification enough for censorship in Argentina.

The homophobia that Coco weathered as a youth in Buenos Aires would figure most prominently in his third novel, *The Buenos Aires Affair*. The plot bridged the fifties—corresponding to Manuel's early career and sexual history—and moved on through the political upheaval of the late sixties and early seventies, when, after a brief democratic hiatus, authoritarian military rule returned in full force. Leo Druscovich, a Freudian cliché of neuroses, is born at the expense of his mother's life, and he never resolves his burning guilt, fanned by an absent father who speaks to his son only to chastise him explicitly for his sexual precocity, and implicitly because his beloved wife died in childbirth. Leo attempts to elude the turmoil of his emotions through his vocation; he becomes a stern, highly respected art critic who first exalts and then censors Gladys Hebe D'Onofrio, an artist. Manuel depicts her as the daughter of a narcissistic mother and judgmental father, whose emotional fragility provides sadistic Leo with his masochistic complement.

Leo's "case history"—including his initiation with a prostitute—seems an exaggerated distortion of Manuel's adolescence. Soon after Leo suffers humiliating failure with a hooker, he attends a political meeting, "in the home of an ex-professor dismissed from the university for his socialist leanings, during which General Perón's recent elected government was passionately accused of Nazism. Leo found that these accusations had a firm basis."[15] Later, after Leo rapes and unintentionally kills a homosexual in a vacant lot one night, he joins the Communist Party with friends at the university who are opposed "to the President, General Perón."[16] Feeling guilt for his unpunished crime, he attains temporary relief when he is caught distributing clandestine political pamphlets. When Perón's secret police brutally apply the infamous electric prod to his genitals, he fears (and hopes) he may become impotent and, unbeknownst to his torturers, pay for his crime.[17] The personal motivates political action once more when, a year later, in order to obtain work as "layout designer for an official evening newspaper," Leo takes up "compulsory membership in the Peronist party." Soon after, however, he befriends a draftsman who introduces him "to an artistic circle, clearly anti-Peronist, since the general conviction was that 'Perón uses the ignorant masses to attain power for himself.' "[18] Through the sadomasochistic affair of his characters Leo and Gladys, male and female alter egos (a handsome, sexually conflicted male; a depressed, strange-looking female), Manuel would psychoanalyze the inextricable knot of Argentine fascism and sexual repression.[19]

Leo's encounter with the nameless homosexual was not only the fodder of crime pages: it was the ultimate fantasy that both terrorized and fascinated Manuel, drawn, by age twenty, to risky assignations on the buses and policed streets of Buenos Aires. He was a "size queen" drawn to anal sex and rugged men with large penises—an obsession depicted in graphic detail in *The Buenos Aires Affair*. In Argentina this could lead to arrest or assault, or, at the very least, the humiliation of being labeled a *puto*, a word that would always make him cringe. One youthful experience Manuel remembered—or perhaps invented—was when he was followed down a dark street in La Boca by a beautiful woman who turned out to be a transvestite. On this nocturnal adventure he barely escaped being cornered by a gang, he claimed; he threw a brick at someone's chest and ran like lightning: "I lived in fear, for me it was a kind of sport then, though now I feel faint when I think of it. I was trying to provoke a final vertigo which maybe had something to do with my traumas."[20] It's hard to know whether such a thing happened, but such a brick did show up in the novel as Leo's fatal weapon. Fear and desire were always connected in Manuel's jokes and intimate conversations about the well-endowed men he either had encounters with or heard rumors about.[21]

Out walking one night (in chapter 6), the well-endowed Leo notices "a slight blond person of the masculine gender" who looks repeatedly at Leo's fly. He gets an erection and, to escape the situation, gets on a bus, but the person follows:

> The bus was full, the person pressed against Leo's body. Leo got off and the other did the same. Leo suddenly turned around and in a gruff tone asked him what he wanted. The other said to Leo that if it didn't offend him he could suck his member: Leo could not restrain a smile of relief, faced with the proximity of a sexual discharge. The person took courage and said that he would also let himself be penetrated, if that gave him more enjoyment. They walked in silence for several minutes; a dark lot appeared, near Leo's house. At a moment when nobody was passing by, they entered, and Leo opened his fly and took out his erect member. The person began to suck.[22]

When the other man sees the considerable size of Leo's member he refuses to be penetrated but Leo insists, takes him by force, and, as he is brutally sodomizing his victim, to keep him from biting his hand, he smashes the weaker man's head with a brick.

The "case histories" of Leo and Gladys together can be understood as a disguised sexual autobiography of Manuel. Guilt and sex seem inseparable for Leo, who cannot ejaculate with any woman who wants to have a relationship with him, and who can't even visit a prostitute a second time: "He preferred the distrust they showed on a first date while the lascivious eagerness they expressed in any subsequent encounter repulsed him." Leo also postponed ejaculations when masturbating "because two times produced decidely unbearable migraine headaches."[23]

As a child Manuel dreamed of sex with girls too, and as a youth, he dated them, but after his twenties these encounters grew rare, as he told a friend who asked if he ever slept with women: "Now I think that if I did it,

I would only do it once, out of curiosity, to know what it's like. Twice would seem a perversion to me."[24] His sexual humor was an expanding repertory of obscene euphemisms (for the amusement of sexual playmates of both sexes) such as calling the penis, when thick like his own, an eggplant, or the distended vagina, after a lengthy coitus, a juicy tomato. Speculating about the petite wife of a Chilean art critic, he confided to a friend his "theory" about vagina size: short women were spacious, tall women, narrow because "in the beginning" God had made all women walk over a sword. An Argentine academic in Brazil remembers a joke Manuel made upon being introduced to a student named Rosa, "Ah the rose, so narrow!" The shy student blushed with embarrassment.

He explained his infrequent "digressions" with young women to a New York gay friend, saying: "For every thrust I give, the Holy Mother rewards me with two in return!" Witty and good-looking, Manuel was irresistible to women, who liked to think they could convert him. His "conquests" as a newly famous author in Argentina in the late sixties included Marcela López Rey and Libertad LeBlanc, *cursi* B-movie actresses. Foxy, neurotic Marcela would emigrate in the seventies, to Mexico, where she and Manuel renewed their friendship. LeBlanc, an Argentine Zsa Zsa Gabor, or a buxom bleached-blond version of Isabel Sarli, once claimed with narcissistic bravado that Manuel had told her, "You're the only woman who has awakened my libido," though apparently they had only flirted and "kissed." Manuel may have said the same things to other women, since he had a few casual "lesbian" affairs. But even if girlfriends stimulated him sexually, his imagination translated that excitement into the pursuit of "real men." A pastime Manuel indulged in with female companions—as did effete Sebastian in Tennessee Williams's *Suddenly, Last Summer*—was to use them as "bait," though mostly for make-believe cruising, a pursuit begun with his older childhood chums and his pretty cousin, Bebé.

He was a *flâneur*, a city lover who enjoyed wandering the streets of Buenos Aires alone or with friends, day or night, particularly La Boca, the traditional southside barrio on the western bank of the mouth of the river, where he could hear the strains of the tango as he passed a tavern or dance hall. La Boca was the barrio of sin, where the tango had originated as an obscene sexual rite which only *guapos*, tough guys, could dance in public; a barrio of *compadres*, or gangsters, Italian pederasts and prostitutes, *putos* and *putas* from all over Europe, often Polish or Jewish, but also always associated with Italian gangsters: "La Boca meant lust, especially when we went into some brothel, always run by Italians and women of the Italianate underworld."[25] He loved the ships entering and leaving port, the bustle of people, the colorful tenements with clothes hanging out windows, the gulls screaming, the flea market in San Telmo, vendors hawking their wares, the old cobblestoned streets and dark winding staircases, the noises of ship horns and buses, the foul smells of the big muddy river. On these walks he collected images but also characters, like Quinquela Martín, a folksy neighborhood artist who painted dock scenes with muscular sailors and stevedores and who told stories about the immigrants coming off the boats in the nineteen-twenties. Years later Manuel still remembered a sad anecdote about a little orphan boy who had come alone, from far away.

In the summer the Puigs would often vacation a few hours away from Buenos Aires in Mar del Plata, a populous beach resort. It was here, according to cousin Bebé, that Manuel had his first real love affair. He told her it was wonderful, but also horrible, for he realized that this was what he wanted. Elsewhere Manuel stated that his first affair began in Buenos Aires one Sunday afternoon on fashionable Florida Street. He had stopped to look at the window of a fine men's clothing shop when another man appeared next to him reflected in the window, looking at the display:

> He was elegant, upper-class, robust, around thirty-five, neither short nor tall, medium height. He looked at me and said, "Do you like . . . ? Pick what you want, I'll buy it for you," and he smiled, showing off a perfect set of teeth. Shocked and trying to look poised, I answered, "Yes, I like it," and smiled back. He added in an almost vulgar way: "Looking for chicks? . . . Come with me, you'll have a better time than with a woman." His direct manner put me off at first but then when I saw him smile and the way he looked at me, which enticed me, I followed him. "I live right around the corner from here," he said, and we walked toward San Martín Street. Meanwhile we didn't say a word. At the door of the hotel—not the room-by-the-month kind—he said, "Don't be afraid. Everything's fine. I'm a man of quality." He had a permanent

suite. Later I found out he was from one of those aristocratic families with three last names, that he liked music and was known in the jet set by the name—shall we say—White Keys. He played piano like a god . . . He was a total gentleman: sweet, delicate, and strong at the same time, both gentle and wildly temperamental. Not only an excellent pianist but a true artist in the delicate art of lovemaking. He taught me the "anatomy lesson" like no one else; he initiated me in the most luminous and darkest of pleasures. He was a kind of god for me. He healed my wounds and erased bad memories . . . I think it was then I discovered my true sexuality; after him I no longer had doubts; he helped me to define and assume my identity.[26]

In this (perhaps apocryphal) admission Manuel speaks in the idealizing, kitschy tones he would lend to Molina in *Kiss of the Spider Women*: "A playboy with both men and women, he never hurt me deliberately; he treated me with respect . . . I discovered with him pleasure, music, and 'naughty' night life."

He always remembered his first romance with a certain nostalgia for youth, more idyllic in memory of course, and something he felt he could never recapture. Manuel would remark in later years: "In life you must have been well fucked at least once; if it doesn't happen again, it doesn't matter: you live by that memory"—wonderful, but (as he told Bebé) also a horrible realization.[27]

escape to cinecittà, or hollywood, italian style

In 1955, the year of Perón's fall, Manuel finished his Italian language and literature courses at the private Dante Alighieri Society, and won a scholarship to study for a year in Italy. This was the chance he had been waiting for, the chance to flee his father's "paralyzing stare" across the dining room table,

which might have been bearable if the Buenos Aires of his Villegan daydreams had not turned out to be so limited, so constraining. Mecca, or something like it, had to be somewhere else. Skeptical Baldo was unwilling to
finance his son's daydreams—and Manuel was too proud to accept money
from his father—but Baldo also favored his son's plan to expand his horizons beyond the borders of Argentina. All roads seemed to lead to Rome, to
the sensual land of his ancestors and the capital of the film world. The first
Italian neorealist movies had come to Argentina in 1948. If Paris was still
the capital of literary culture, Rome in the fifties was "Hollywood on the
Tiber" and Europe's most important film school—the Centro Sperimentale
di Cinematografia—was next door to Cinecittà, the most celebrated producer of neorealist films. The Centro's prestigious instructors included the
great talents of the day such as Vittorio De Sica, Roberto Rossellini, Ingrid
Bergman, and Jean Renoir. Manuel's Dante Society scholarship covered his
tuition fees at the Centro and a minimum of travel and living expenses.
With his knowledge of French, English, and Italian, the eager twenty-
three-year-old was confident that he would become a film director in the
more ample European arena.

In August 1956 he boarded the *Federico C*, an Italian ship, and disembarked almost three weeks later in Genoa. Up until the sixties, air travel was
for the rich and famous, and most Latin Americans traveled to Europe by
boat: it was a grand occasion, and the family went to see him off. For
mother and son the parting was difficult, but they comforted themselves by
planning, as soon as he was settled, for Malé to visit. Manuel would make a
career for himself and have an exciting adventure in Europe, and the family
would be able to join him and visit the Delledonnes who had remained in
Busseto and Cremona. Europe meant culture and romance, and Busseto was
also the birthplace of Verdi, composer of the fabulous operas Malé and Coco
had attended at the Teatro Colón in Buenos Aires and would soon get to see
at La Scala.

From the tourist-class deck, Manuel watched the Queen of the Plata disappear on the horizon. He would make the crossing a few more times over
the following years until airplane travel became more accessible, particularly
when he became an employee of Air France. Seasickness was the downside
of these long maritime voyages, with stops in several ports on both sides of
the Atlantic. But they were also floating parties, and often the perfect setting

for shipboard romance—a staple of those sophisticated romantic comedies of the thirties and forties which had fed Coco's dreamlife. The Delledonnes and Luisa Strubolini sent gifts with Manuel to relatives in Italy, and references from the Dante Society would open the doors of the Argentine embassy in Rome.

In Genoa he stayed at a student hostel for four days and then took a train to Rome, arriving early in the morning of August 23. The run-down outskirts were "horrible," as was the squalor on the tram route from the center of Rome to Cinecittà, where he went immediately upon arrival because the hostel he had been referred to had no vacancy. But Rome itself was marvelous, and before the first day was over he had spent several hours wandering narrow winding streets that emptied into magnificent piazzas.

He was impressed too by the size of the Centro, "a big building that covers a whole city block," and once there an employee offered him lodging in her parents' apartment downtown at Piazza Regina Margherita, where they often rented a room to students. He was in luck because it was still summer and they hadn't rented it out yet. That afternoon he went to see the apartment and moved in instantly. His room faced a typically lively, noisy courtyard. In his first letter home, written the next morning, Friday, August 24, he described the place:

> A poor, humble family, but very clean, good people: two old ladies, the old husband of one of them, the daughter, around 30, and a little girl. It's one of those old, spacious apartments, and I'm in a very nice, private room, with a little nighttable and lamp, a big wardrobe, a table, a vanity with _3_ mirrors and a small bookshelf—super-comfortable. The apartment building is right on the Piazza Regina Margherita, in the heart of Rome; it also has a telephone. I have a window with five lovely plants where the beautiful sun comes in early until midday.

From his apartment he could walk to the stunning Piazza Navona, to the famous Spanish Steps at the Piazza di Spagna, and to the glamorous Via Veneto, where he could mingle with the gods:

Rome was seething with moviemakers from all over the
world. It was like Hollywood, New York and Cannes all
rolled into one. Most deals were made on Via Veneto, over
Campari or espresso. Every player had to make an appearance. On Sunday mornings, sidewalk cafes on both sides of
the street were filled to overflowing . . . In Hollywood, the
stars would only assemble at premieres or awards ceremonies,
but along the Via Veneto it was common to see Greg Peck, Ingrid Bergman, Bill Holden, Anna Magnani, Gene Kelly, Silvana Mangano, Clark Gable, Audrey Hepburn, Gary Cooper,
Jennifer Jones, or Errol Flynn turn out for the sidewalk show,
often on the same afternoon. The six blocks between the Ex-
celsior and the Porta Pinciana were the center of the motion
picture industry.[28]

On the Via Veneto it was just as important to be seen as to see, and even
more important to be photographed by the paparazzi, those intrusive
voyeurs depicted so justly by Fellini in *La Dolce Vita* (1960). In those first
sultry days Manuel felt enveloped by a double aura: ancient Rome and modern movie mecca.

Rome was a nocturnal city and, for young Manuel, the luminous
Fontana di Trevi was as romantic in real life as in the movies, as decadent
and glamorous as luscious Anita Ekberg emerging like Venus into the arms
of a nearly swooning, equally stunning Marcello Mastroianni. Manuel was
in love with the Romans, and they reciprocated, but after the first thrilling
weeks, peppered with flirtations and spontaneous assignations, he started
to feel homesick. In the bourgeois neighborhood where he lived, people
seemed huffy or reserved, so unlike the Barrio Norte back home, where
everybody chatted with everybody. He missed Malé, Bebé, and intimate
friends like Alfredo, and wrote frequent, almost daily letters, staying in
touch with those who loved him and expressing himself in his own language. These letters became a lifeline, and not only for Manuel: it was his
way of taking care of Malé when he was far away from her, keeping her entertained, providing the kind of gossip and stimulation she so enjoyed. The
Argentine embassy on Piazza Inquilino was a provisional home base during
those first months, where he could receive his overseas mail and speak his
native tongue with other Argentines at embassy cocktail parties.

In late September, classes at the Centro began, where he was thrilled to encounter famous directors like Roberto Rossellini and Vittorio De Sica. He also met Pasolini (whom Manuel soon concluded was a "false poet" and a "terrible" filmmaker) and the admirable screenwriter/novelist Alberto Moravia, with whose second wife, Dacia Mairani, Manuel established a warm friendship; forty years younger than the consecrated Moravia and a budding writer, she was, in Manuel's words, "a great lady."[29] Unlike most of these celebs, De Sica showed him how "an enormous talent" could be a simple person, kind to those around him: "He was making sexy little comedies without putting his name on them. He only signed the big neo-realist films. I liked *Anna of Brooklyn*, with Gina Lollobrigida, which was called *Fast and Sexy* in the U.S."[30] Manuel would remember De Sica with fondness, especially after he saw him sit with Gina for almost an hour at a table on a set— "Lollo" was dumb (a *burra*, Manuel informed Malé)—and patiently explain a scene to her over and over again until she understood. Another episode associated with De Sica, this time as actor, involved none other than Marlene Dietrich, dubbing scenes with De Sica in a projection room for a B movie, *The Monte Carlo Story*. Seeing Shanghai Lil in the flesh was disenchanting:

> She was very dissatisfied [with the film]. As a person she's a monster, very skinny, and her face is deathly yellow and she had no makeup on, but she dubbed several scenes with such precision that it leaves one speechless; she was very nervous but she focused in a way I've never seen in anyone; she's a hard worker and repeated things as many times as she needed to get them precisely right.[31]

Marlene had grown old and could be nasty but behind the frayed glamour she was a professional. There would be many such stellar glimpses, but the Roman honeymoon soon turned bittersweet.

The Centro had been founded by Mussolini's son, and emerged out of Italy's *prise de conscience* over the recently fallen Fascist regime. As Manuel put it: "Nothing was legal outside of neorealism." The social realism taught as gospel at the Centro was much too leaden and dogmatic for his taste— and didn't even have much to do with the exciting new directors of the late fifties like Fellini and Antonioni. While Manuel disdained most of the films

coming out of postwar Hollywood, even those by directors he formerly worshiped, he idolized, even before the term "auteur cinema" had been coined,
"the great figures like Lubitsch, Hitchcock, and Fritz Lang."[32] Among his
favorites was Lubitsch's disciple Billy Wilder, whose *Sunset Boulevard* (1950)
could be considered the last great Hollywood classic. A tragic satire of Hollywood, written by Wilder with Charles Hecht, its martyrs are an aging
silent-screen diva, Gloria Swanson, for whom this film was a swan song,
and a washed-up young screenwriter, played brilliantly, and against character, by handsome young William Holden.

A shining exception in Hollywood's fifties was the work of European
émigré Douglas Sirk. His German films of the early forties, starring kitschy
Swedish-born chanteuse Zarah Leander, who had an unusually deep, androgynous voice, had already captivated Manuel.[33] Back in the late thirties,
opposed to fascism, Sirk feared the worst if he remained in his homeland,
and so he headed west to join the expatriate community of Eastern Europeans in Hollywood. He would enrich the Hollywood melodrama with his
exposés of race prejudice and class injustices, and his satirical representa-
tions of gender inequity and sexual repression. In *Magnificent Obsession*, for
instance, the archetypal virility of Rock Hudson, a closeted gay postwar
matinee idol, becomes ambiguous to the observant eye, not least of all because his leading lady, Jane Wyman, though considered pretty in the steril-
ized aesthetic of the fifties, was bland, if not plainly asexual. Sirk penetrated
the glossy surface of the American way of life. His fifties films are "still the
best of Hollywood," Malé asserted in 1995, because they entertain and also
enlighten: *All That Heaven Allows* (1955), a heavy drama (about a widow—
Wyman—and her younger lover—Hudson) with a positive ending, helped
her through her mourning for Manuel. Manuel's favorite was one of Sirk's
last, *Imitation of Life* (1959)—starring the beautiful and bad actress Lana
Turner—which juggled the taboo subject of racial prejudice and the story of
a woman caught between career and "real" fulfillment.

Glamour and ecstasy, however, had been supplanted in the fifties by a
kitschy mélange of stilted realism, garish extravaganza, and sensationalist
melodrama, all tempered by a predictable puritanism. And while the brutal
lyricism of Cinecittà's *Rocco and His Brothers*, or the raw poignancy of the
early Fellini, as in *Nights of Cabiria*, were a refreshing alternative, Manuel
found himself caught between a rock and a hard place at the Centro:

From the first films by De Sica and Rossellini, which had been totally personal, the Italians had formed a theory . . . My teachers were mainly Camerini and Blasetti . . . teaching us Zavattini's neorealism as if it were dogma. While initially it fulfilled an important function, to portray social and political unrest in works like *The Bicycle Thief*, *Bitter Rice*, and *Paisà*, by this time it had become petrified into strict norms that had ceased to work . . . Cinema had to be a means of exposing reality and denouncing what society did to individuals. The author had to disappear behind the camera. Hollywood was condemned for being escapist, and French cinema was condemned for being too personalized. The author's presence was an obstacle, too self-complacent . . . The art of narrative, with Hitchcock as the supreme example, was synonymous with reactionary cinema, without any political or social content. A total misunderstanding on the part of Zavattini, the theoretician.[34]

"Everybody blindly accepted Zavattini," Manuel said in an early interview, "and didn't even pay any attention to Fellini and Antonioni."[35] Against the grain, Manuel rejected Zavattini, and would ultimately reject Fellini and Antonioni. The early Fellini had humor, lyricism, and grace, as in *The White Sheik*, or Ekberg and Mastroianni's famous fountain scene in *La Dolce Vita*. But Manuel felt that from *8½* on, Fellini's films were, like Antonioni's, pretentious.[36]

Manuel soon clashed publicly with his professors' dogmatic rejection of Hollywood's studio system, standing out among his classmates as a frivolous nonconformist. When the students were asked to do a monograph on some prestigious film by a European master like Eisenstein, Dreyer, or Renoir, Manuel chose Charles Vidor's *The Swan*, just released that year by MGM. He liked this mild remake of Ferenc Molnár's minor play because it was also Grace Kelly's last role. But his choice shocked fellow students as well as the professor: in the midst of discussions about serious European cinema here was this foreign boy, practically a savage from the pampa, who insisted, "But what about Grace Kelly in *The Swan*!?"

Caught between the crass commercialism of sanitized Hollywood and the Centro's "theoretical terrorism," Manuel became disenchanted. But years later, as an established author, he said, "My stay in Italy served me in that I found my own position, between Zavattini's rigors and the newer avant-garde tendencies in film, when I began writing my novels."[37]

> In some way that ideological purity, that absence of a personal point of view, that lack of narrative devices made the focus real, but purely photographic. That photographic reality was not dramatic. One remained on the surface of the problems and without drama the audience lost interest. This social message, directed to a wide audience, wanted to awaken consciences, but that audience withdrew and no longer went to see neorealist films . . . They were boring and programmatic . . . For me, narrating, telling a story, is a way of knowing.[38]

Movies weren't movies if they didn't invite you to dream. The irony is that the social realists with "such clear ideas and such pretensions" and filmmakers like Carlo Lizzani or Pietro Germi have been forgotten.[39] The neorealists' failure provided Manuel with a clue to success, perhaps, and the desire to produce art that, without ceasing to be engagé, was also entertaining.

Manuel had an ally in his low opinion of the highly respected Cesare Zavattini: a tall, earnest classmate and fellow Latin American named Nestor Almendros. With intense myopic eyes and an aquiline profile, Nestor Almendros would one day win an Oscar for his cinematography. A Cuban born in Catalonia, Spain—his family had fled Franco after the Civil War—Nestor became not only one of Manuel's closest friends, but the one who had the biggest role in launching his literary career. In the early sixties Nestor's first major break was the film *More*, directed by young French New Wave auteur Barbet Schroeder; from there he went on to work with Rohmer and Truffaut. Years later Nestor wrote in his memoir, *A Man with a Camera*, that the Centro had taught him "technical clichés":

> In these circumstances Luciano Tovoli—my best friend among the Italians—the Colombian Guillermo Angulo, the Argentine Manuel Puig and I rebelled. In this contrary frame of mind we decided that we were learning only ossified techniques.[40]

The Cuban and the Argentine bonded in solidarity against an intellectual climate that was polarized between right-wing papal Christian Democrats and dogmatic Italian Stalinists. Because of their indifference to politics— "Manuel was even more indifferent than me," Nestor clarified—and their enthusiasm for escapist Hollywood movies (though Nestor liked adventure flicks as much as women's pictures), both were scorned by most of their colleagues at the Centro. But, as was the case for Manuel, Nestor's rebellion helped him develop his own ideas:

> Eric Rohmer has the odd idea that bad schools can have a positive effect, because a bad school—unjust, intolerant, and old-fashioned—provokes reactions and makes students rebel, so that in the long run bad teaching can produce good results.[41]

Another aspiring Argentine writer, working as a reporter in Rome, was Ernesto Schoo—whose family name derives from the Irish Shaw. Schoo recalls how Manuel felt alienated by his bourgeois Italian classmates, who tagged him "Cinderella" because at lunchtime, instead of sitting down decorously at the table with the others to have a proper midday three-course *pranzo*,[42] Manuel would go off by himself and usually sit on the sidelines of some set where he could watch the moviemaking as he ate his sandwich.

Neorealist fanaticism and bourgeois conformism aside, Manuel dropped out during his first year at film school because of the scarcity of work at Cinecittà for non-Italians. He even won a prize for the best script in his class but, because of chauvinism and limited postwar resources, preference was given to Italian students, and he never got to practice making a film. He scrambled for a few odd jobs over the next years as assistant director, or, as he joked, "assistant to the assistant," but mainly, like Nestor and the other foreign students, he was allowed only to watch the important directors' shoots.

If he had expected magic behind the scenes, what he experienced was a loss of innocence. In the artists he worshiped he reencountered, in a way, the hated specter of authority, which (incarnated first in his father, then in Perón) he thought he had escaped. Directors and producers, it seemed, needed to be dictators. Initially enthusiastic when assigned to the special effects unit for *A Farewell to Arms*, produced by the mythic David O. Selznick, Manuel soon had regrets:

I was on the set of *A Farewell to Arms*, with Jennifer Jones and
Rock Hudson. It was a stormy set. Selznick disagreed with
the director, Charles Vidor, after he had already replaced John
Huston. Jennifer Jones didn't agree with Vidor's concept of
her role and they fought constantly. For me, Selznick was
Gone With the Wind and *Rebecca*, and I was disappointed. I
didn't like all the strife . . . What's more, I hate authority. I
like to deal with people on an equal basis. I can't tell people
what to do.[43]

Manuel's relationship with authority would always be complex. He couldn't
deal with others' authority because, in part, he wanted it and yet hated the
inequity it perpetrated. He retreated from being an authority himself, he
claimed, because he felt too embarrassed to shout orders at large groups of
people; since adolescence, he still smarted from shame about sounding effeminate. In any case, he made a big discovery at Cinecittà: he related to the
movies as a spectator, not as a filmmaker.

When Jean-Luc Godard's *Mépris* (*Contempt*) came out in New York, in
1965, Manuel as spectator found reasons to rave, not the least being the camera's love affair with Brigitte Bardot's beautiful bronzed buttocks, which began in Roger Vadim's titillating . . . *And God Created Woman* (1956).[44] (On
the latter, he and Malé—for whom the nudity was a bit much—had parted
ways.) Based closely on Alberto Moravia's autobiographical novel *Il Dis-
prezzo* (1954), which had already been made into a play, *Contempt* portrays a
screenwriter's struggles at Cinecittà, where he is commissioned to write a
modern interpretation of *Ulysses*. Godard alludes satirically to *Ulysses*, Dino
De Laurentiis's 1954 schlock epic directed by Mario Camerini, in which producer Dino exploited talented writers Ben Hecht and Irwin Shaw for this
spectacle, whose most striking feature was a monstrous Cyclops. Starring
Kirk Douglas, acting in English to guarantee the film's "international success," and dubbed in Italian, *Ulysses* was, as Moravia quipped, "a technical
circus replete with naked women, King Kong, and belly dancers."

Like Moravia, Godard criticized the making of *Ulysses* by focusing on a
pompous American producer named Prokosh, played by the snarling Jack
Palance. The writer (Riccardo Molteni in Moravia's novel), nostalgic for the
golden age of filmmaking and played by the suavely intense French actor

Michel Piccoli, fights over aesthetic principles with Prokosh (Battista in the novel) and a German expatriate director (Rheingold), played in the film by Fritz Lang himself. The producer, "dictator, not friend," crassly manipulates the writer to accept his (re)interpretation of the *Odyssey*; Piccoli capitulates and even passively stands by as Prokosh seduces his wife, Bardot. In Prokosh's "modern" version—the film within the film—Penelope does not remain faithful, because Ulysses loses his way and never returns.

Like *Sunset Boulevard*, *Contempt* was a film about the film world, in this case a satire of Cinecittà as well as of Hollywood, in which a crass entrepreneur corrupts artistic innocence, or purity, just as he degrades Homer's ancient hero; Michel Piccoli's character personifies alienated modern man, diminished by his environment. *One-Dimensional Man*, Herbert Marcuse's groundbreaking study, had enormous impact in the post-existential sixties and strongly impressed Manuel, who read it shortly after moving to New York in 1963, anguished about what seemed to be his failed career. "In today's world," Piccoli's character laments, "we are forced to do what other people want us to do; why does money decide everything we do?" In this poetic film, Godard spoke to Manuel's own frustrations about the movie business, run by money and abusive authorities who compromise art. But while Manuel was disillusioned with the men behind the camera whom he had once idolized, he disdained the political reductionism of left-wing European intellectuals like Godard.

Toward the end of his life, Manuel would return to his dispute with neorealist dogma. In 1990, the Italian novelist and journalist Alberto Arbasino asked him to write about the history of pre–World War II Italian cinema for *Chorus*, a fashion magazine, and what resulted was a series of short fictionalized dialogues. They were collected in a posthumous little volume called *The Eyes of Greta Garbo*, published first in Italy, then translated after his death into Spanish.[45] In one dialogue, a long-distance telephone conversation between Anna, an Italian professor in Colorado, and Carlo, her former boyfriend in Rome, Manuel reevaluates the "unknown," or suppressed, cinema of the fascist thirties, in this case Italian salon comedies.[46] Anna mouths the opinions of Manuel, who, in the seventies, also taught at American universities: discussing the merits of the forgotten director Mario Camerini, Anna defends that period of so-called decadent cinema against the neorealists' judgment. Because the "French were better at advertising themselves than the Italians," they received much more recognition, and yet Camerini's *Men: What Scoundrels* and *Mister Max*, starring the charming De Sica and made in the early thirties, were just as sophisticated as Jean Renoir's classic 1939 satire *Rules of the Game* or the witty Lubitsch farces in Hollywood. Furthermore, in 1932, in these "artificial" drawing room comedies, Camerini was already shooting real-life scenes in the street, preempting neorealist techniques by more than a decade. Camerini also produced "awful" propaganda in the thirties, such as *The Great Muster*, and his reputation was completely demolished by postwar flops like *Ulysses* or *Il Brigante Musolino*. But then again, the first neorealist film, Anna continues, was Rossellini's pro-Mussolini *The White Ship* (1942), in which Il Duce makes a speech as Nazi soldiers march arm in arm with Italian soldiers. Anna (or Manuel) concluded, in brief, that artistic worth does not always accompany correct politics—and that the politically self-righteous are often hypocrites.

a friendship is born

Orlando Berlingieri, an acquaintance of Manuel's at the embassy, had told him about another Argentine in Rome whom he was sure Manuel would enjoy meeting; in October 1956, Manuel telephoned Berlingieri's friend, Mario Fenelli. They made a date to meet a few days later, in front of the Central Post Office in Piazza San Silvestro. To recognize each other they agreed that Manuel would carry the latest issue of *Cinema Nuovo* under his arm. It was a cold, drizzly afternoon and the two young men immediately ran for shelter in the nearest bar, chattering nonstop under Mario's umbrella, Manuel joking that he first thought (or hoped) Fenelli was Fellini, a relative of the great Federico. Bantering back and forth they realized they had much in common, and, as it continued raining, they went on to another and yet another café until, before they knew it, it was 2 a.m. They finally went home to bed (each to his own, Mario clarifies), but continued where they left off the next day. Aside from finding in Mario a tall, handsome, witty playmate with whom he could joke freely about sexual matters,

Manuel had met someone who could talk about seeing *Dinner at Eight* or *Rain* when they first appeared, who could discuss literature and all the arts that interested Manuel.

Both had been bewitched by Hollywood at age eight. As he was six years older than Manuel, Mario's key year was 1933, and the films were *Grand Hotel*, with Greta Garbo, and Busby Berkeley's musical dream-extravaganza *Gold Diggers of 1933* with Ruby Keeler. For Manuel the definitive year was 1940, and the films were *Two-Faced Woman*, with Garbo, and *Intermezzo*, with Ingrid Bergman, whom he could now see frequently in person, "walking like a Viking" along the Via Veneto. She had become persona non grata in sanitized Hollywood because of her scandalous affair and stormy marriage with Rossellini. Both boys were in love with this Nordic beauty, but Mario proclaims that his favorites were Ginger Rogers and Joan Crawford, while Manuel was stuck on Garbo.

While not a boy from the sticks like Manuel, Mario had been born on the outskirts of Buenos Aires, in La Paternal, a dreary lower-middle-class neighborhood, so that he too felt that the movie house had been a refuge from humdrum reality. They compared and were delighted to discover their similar childhood experiences as well as their shared Parmesan origins—Mario's on his father's side, Manuel's on his mother's. Manuel listened with vicarious pleasure as Mario recounted his early adventures as a sailor: through his father, a broker for the Onassis shipping line, Mario shipped as a crew member to Cape Town in 1945, where he arrived the day the atom bomb was dropped on Hiroshima. Here was another errant Argentine, brimming with desire to see the world, a fellow globetrotter. Not all was movie and travel talk, though.

Listening to Mario's history, Manuel realized that his friend's background was perhaps even more difficult than his own. Family tensions and repressive machismo had darkened Mario's adolescent years as well, and after he broke up with a girlfriend at the university, an identity crisis and a suicidal depression led him to Dr. Tagliaferri, one of the pioneers of psychoanalysis in Argentina. In 1950 Mario had arrived in Rome to study at Cinecittà with his friend Fernando Birri, and he shared a flat near glamorous Via Veneto with Cinecittà classmate Luigi Bazzoni.[47] Among his other classmates in 1951 were Domenico Modugno, later famous for composing "Volare," and Sophia Loren—who had failed an entrance exam because they didn't think she was actress material! Mario had taken courses with Rossellini, De Sica, Ingrid Bergman, and Jean Renoir, and got to see the filming of *Quo Vadis?* and *Roman Holiday.*

But his flight from Argentina (five years after his boyhood escapade in South Africa) and his immersion in Roman life had not resolved his emotional problems. In 1955 he spent several months in Zurich undergoing analysis at the Jung Institute, where he also managed to procure two sessions with Professor Bienswanger, Jung's successor as director of the institute. Back in Italy he worked as a translator for the Vatican newspaper to pay the rent, with an extra perk thrown in: the Vatican *cucina*, or cafeteria. For penniless students in postwar Rome, this soup kitchen was a salvation, and Manuel would join Mario regularly there for a hot lunch. Mario occasionally interviewed celebrities for the Vatican paper—among them, Tennessee Williams—and directed documentaries with Bazzoni, some of which received prizes in São Paolo and at the Venice Film Festival. And he wrote stories in his spare time.

In Buenos Aires he had written "The Hole," in which a man observes life through a hole in the wall without participating (he commits suicide, covering with his hands the little hole that links him to the world).[48] In Rome he had begun a story about autograph hunters, expressing the Argentine tendency to fabricate idols at the expense of one's own identity—a theme that would come to fruition in Manuel's novels. Little did Mario know that his literary aspirations would play a decisive role in the birth of a famous writer.

Although Manuel and Mario started flirting the minute they met— Manuel was apparently more infatuated than Mario—they became not lovers but, as Manuel put it, "sisters" who shared romantic woes, laughed at the world together, deeply respected each other's intelligence, and utterly delighted in each other's company. Most important, they invented a language all their own—a mixture of several languages and some imaginary ones. After Manuel left Rome, they corresponded passionately, especially throughout the early sixties—until Manuel blossomed into a successful and very busy writer. Upon receiving a letter from Mario, in 1960, assuring Manuel of the depth of their friendship, Manuel's response reveals how much Mario meant to him: "Your letter is a monument which I shall conserve always: it contains all that is fundamental in our relationship. I feel as if I had been given a chain-watch or a ring, something that will accompany me my whole life."[49]

Nestor Almendros was Manuel's other lifetime friend made in Rome, though their friendship was less intimate than Manuel's with Mario. The three cineastes were almost inseparable for the next two years, meeting daily at cafés and film events; in the summer they spent almost every Sunday at the crowded beach in Ostia, "where the boys were." Nestor's nickname was Cubchapi (or Kubchapi), which, in a mixture of Catalan, Parmesan, and Argentine pig latin, meant "Cuban butt."[50]

Manuel usually had more than one nickname for friends he spent a lot of time with: one of Mario's many tags was Chela, after a gossip columnist who had a radio show in Argentina, a kind of Louella Parsons of the pampa. Mario, like Nestor, Alfredo Gialdini, and Manuel's more closeted friends in those days, did not like to be feminized—"Most of us," Mario claims, were irritated or embarrassed by this mania. But they "put it into perspective," since Manuel feminized famous men as well: la Moravia, la Fellini, la Borges, la Neruda. Mario was also Eve or Hebe, a *cursi* name Manuel later used for Gladys Hebe D'Onofrio in *The Buenos Aires Affair*.[51] Nestor and Mario in turn called Manuel "Sally"—connoting frivolous flapper Sally Bowles or saucy strawberry blonde Rita Hayworth in *My Gal Sal*.

Mario and Manuel's secret language became even more ornate in their letters—Argentine Spanish and Italian mixed with English, Italian dialects, French, German, even Turkish words, as well as obscure cinema references. After Mario got to know Malé, the boys turned Malé into Mele (apples in Italian), then Apples, or Apfel, and finally Tif (apples in Arabic). *K*, the hard Anglo-Germanic consonant, substituted for *c* in their letters, to make words look more "komic"; and the past participle "ida" became "lupino"—a play on the name of actress Ida Lupino, noted for her glazed intensity—hence *perdida* (lost) became *perdlupino* in this elaborate, clandestine code.

Humor was all-important to spiritual survival, and in Europe Manuel now realized how Argentine his was, as he wrote home:

> I'm going out this evening with some Argentine boys. I never thought that I would have anything to do with Argentines, and now all I want is to see "compatriots." With Italian people I can't fool around, I don't have a good time. That happens with all foreigners, because each country has its own sense of humor.[52]

With his fellow Argentines, he shared a language and a sensibility. Mario's group of friends, who immediately adopted Manuel, included Mario's French girlfriend Olga and also his best friend from grade school in Buenos Aires, Jorge "Coco" Krimer, an aspiring playwright, whose witty camaraderie had helped Mario survive his difficult boyhood years in Argentina. They were all young and poor, many of them gay or bisexual, and when Manuel first arrived in Rome with his pockets full he gave his money away, without a thought, to his newfound friends in need. Soon he too needed to earn lire, if he was to remain in Rome.

His first job, tutoring Spanish, came to him by way of Luisa Strubolini; his first student was Margherita Muzi, whom he met through Chuchi, Luisa Strubolini's sister in Rome. Miss Muzi worked for an electrical company and wanted to learn Spanish so that she could someday visit friends and relatives in Argentina. Manuel tutored her twice a week at teatime, at the modest but cheery little apartment on Via Commercio in the Testaccio quarter, which Margherita shared with her two sisters, Elena and Adela. The Muzis, in their fifties and sixties but single, or "spinsters" (except for Adela, who was a widow), nurtured the enchanting young man on these occasions with comforting tea and delicious homemade pastries. Mario remembers fondly that he first met the Muzis when Manuel invited him to join them for Easter dinner, and the little party went on for hours, everyone painting Easter eggs. Sunday lunch at the Muzi sisters' apartment became a custom for both Mario and Manuel, who mischievously called them the "Tecoñacs" because, along with heaping portions of pastries, they would serve the tea with a shot of cognac. (Mario confesses that he participated in this adopted family life mostly for the free meal—Manuel was the true Muzi fan.)

One chilly day Mario and Manuel came by to take the Tecoñacs out to the movies, and Margherita, to practice her Spanish, said she had to put on her *bombacha*—bloomers—instead of *bufanda*—scarf; this became the standard Muzi joke, still remembered by cousin Ernesto and his wife, Nelva, in La Plata. For Manuel "las Margas"—because Margherita was the real friend in the trio, or the "superstar"—were "aunties," a warm refuge from the cold Roman bourgeoisie, a home away from home, comforting replicas of his mother and aunts. For years Margherita would send Manuel care packages at Christmas, as when he spent his first Christmas in London in 1958: "a fine wool scarf, a statuette of the Virgin Mary (!), and a box of typical Roman

Christmas candies, those Muzi are too much!" Later, when Malé began traveling to Rome, in September 1964, the Muzis adopted her too, and subsequently she'd always visit them on her trips to Italy. Even when Manuel was living in New York, in November 1965, Margherita and her sister Elena visited Argentina and stayed with the Puigs.

As fond as she was of the Muzis, however, coquettish Malé adored even more the gallant attentions of Manuel's handsome new friend, Mario, whose latest nickname was Daniel Denis—an invented glamorous actor's name—or D.D. for short. When she came with Aunt Carmen to Italy in 1964, D.D. met them at the airport and took them everywhere. Carmen in particular, who was very petite, appreciated leaning on his strong arm as they toured the marvels of Rome, Florence, Venice, Padua, and Vicenza. When Mario finally returned to the Buenos Aires he sorely missed, to visit his mother after a fifteen-year absence, he also visited Carmen in La Plata. Manuel told him that she considered him the ideal son she never had, that she had always envied Malé for having Coco. Mario was family; before moving to New York Manuel regularly visited Mario's parents, who lived on the same street as the Puigs, and, from New York, Manuel kept urging his homesick friend to visit his family while he still had them, repeating the words of Mario's father: "Before, I was opposed to Mario's path in life, but now MY GREATEST WISH is for him to be happy and HONEST." To which Mario's mother added: "We want so much to have him here, we want to enjoy him, to enjoy his presence in our remaining years." "Don't be silly," Manuel wrote to Mario. "Come see them, they're angels."[53]

In the summer of 1956, Mario rented a minuscule attic apartment in elegant Aventino, on one of Rome's seven hills, overlooking the Testaccio, the picturesque working-class neighborhood where Manuel lived. Mario's pied-a-terre, on Piazza Sant'Anselmo down the street from Vittorio Gassman's palatial villa, would later become a ritzy hotel. The attic study was so tiny that it could only accommodate a bed, a table, a little wardrobe, and a microscopic bathroom. Here the two friends would cook their daily pasta and, for lack of chairs, eat on the little side table, sitting on the edge of the bed. Manuel would walk up the hill with a bag of groceries from the Testaccio, and they would dine together, talking endlessly. Mario talked most; Manuel asked questions, and remembered everything about Mario's life. In retrospect Mario recognizes the budding novelist in his observant listener: "He recorded in his memory the episodes of my life which I recounted, with such precision it was as if he himself had lived them. His identification was so strong that he remembered the names of my relatives and friends (even the maids) as if he himself had known them."[54]

first screenplay

During those first months at film school, Manuel had written a draft of his first script, "Ball Cancelled," a sort of *Wuthering Heights* set in an English country manor, with a modern twist. He wrote it in English, "for Vivien Leigh." "I didn't know it then, but what excited me in film was to copy, not to create." Copying Hollywood models turned out not to be so easy, however: he could not avoid using broken English or revealing his personal mark—not yet a style, but even so—as a Spanish American imitating in 1956 the Hollywood writers of the thirties. In "Ball Cancelled" Manuel transported his mother-son baggage into British gothic romance. The Hollywood country-manor setting of the story, Manuel's naive idea of what he called the glamour touch, was also a typically Argentine fantasy. In *Heartbreak Tango*, middle-class vamp Mabel would aspire to live in such a manor, transplanted to a vast *estancia*, by marrying the veddy British Cecil. *Wuthering Heights*, a childhood favorite of Coco's, was the ultimate romantic melodrama, about love made impossible by social repression and class differences, yet invincible by death.[55] He borrowed in his first script from *Tea and Sympathy* the modern touch of a sensitive adolescent's difficult rite of passage to adult sexuality.

Tea and Sympathy, audacious in the prudish fifties, was ultimately about prejudice against those who are different. A play by Robert Anderson, it portrays a shy adolescent's sentimental education at boarding school in the hands of a compassionate faculty wife who sacrifices her unsatisfying but stable marriage to rescue the boy from suicide. In the 1956 film, co-starring Deborah Kerr in her luminous prime and newcomer John Kerr (no relation)—both of whom had been in the original Broadway cast—John Kerr plays the role of Tom Lee, who has been singled out by his rough-and-tumble classmates at an exclusive all-boy's academy as "sister boy." Manuel was so taken when he saw the movie that first year in Rome that he later attended two versions of the play, one performed by Ingrid Bergman in Paris in 1957, where he sat in the third row.[56]

The faculty wife's happiness has been marred by the early loss of her first husband, a sensitive young man who died in war "trying to prove his manlihood." Her second husband, a sports coach, is closed off emotionally. These story elements stayed with Manuel; in *Betrayed by Rita Hayworth* he would exaggerate his own mother's early regrets about matinee idol José Gola to dramatize her disappointment with his father. What was particularly compelling for Manuel in *Tea and Sympathy* was the quasi-incestuous relationship which helped the boy to pass successfully into adulthood. Petrified notions about manliness in a fifties private boys school in New England replayed for Manuel the oppressive sex roles in Villegas in the thirties. The boy's suicidal crisis is set off by his father's humiliating disapproval when Tom wants to play a female role in the school production of a Restoration farce. If Cousin Jorge's vigilance cost Coco a part in a school play, Tom's father's refusal to let his son perform not only reduces the boy to passive obedience but also to a suicide attempt.

For the pre-feminist fifties, this movie had a subversive message, uttered by Deborah Kerr at a climactic moment to her husband: "If [Tom] were manly, then you would have to question your own kind of manliness." The film ends with her unsent letter to Tom as a man, years later, a device of romantic literature Manuel would use in the last chapter of *Betrayed by Rita Hayworth*. The woman explains her "sacrifice" to Tom, now a successful novelist who has written a book about his boyhood, clarifying that she wasn't a saint, that she chose the boy over her husband for her own reasons. Like Malé, she received from a boy the affection and understanding her husband could not give her.   •

Manuel's first two scripts, "Ball Cancelled" and "Withered Roses for Apollo," the latter co-written with Mario, who had his own Oedipal issues, both revolved around mother-son incest. Hoping to break into the Italian film industry, and because Mario wrote better in Italian than in English, the inseparable duo collaborated in Italian over the next few years under the pseudonyms Stuart and Rafferty on a "deliberately commercial" but, as

Mario jested, "not deliberately terrible" play. An illicit affair between an older woman and a young man in "Ball Cancelled" ("Balls Cancelled" should have been the title, Mario jokes) reappeared in their kitschy Italian script ("Rose Appassite per Apollo") for which they wanted Rita Hayworth to play Sheila, the mother. The rest of the pipe-dream cast of "Roses" included Hedy Lamarr and Joan Fontaine, as well as the then-popular, handsome Italian actor Giuliano Gemma. Ironically, Gemma would consider the role of Valentín twenty years later in a never-realized Italian film version of *Kiss of the Spider Woman*.[57]

Incest showed up in several projects over the years, and was finally given fuller treatment when a father supposedly rapes his daughter in Manuel's sex farce "Under a Mantle of Stars," written in the eighties. Whether used as a stand-in for other perversions or as a metaphor for filial obsession, incest was a visceral subject ripe for melodrama, as it had been for Greek tragedy. Instead of gods and nobility, melodrama's sons and lovers are middle-class, ordinary, but driven by the same tensions—between passion and duty, good and bad, love and power—toward fates they cannot control.

Don't keep writing screenplays in a thirties style for the fifties, Mario and Nestor scolded, and Manuel tried to follow his friends' advice in his next script, "Summer Indoors." Written again with "witty" dialogue in broken English, this was (as Manuel later wrote) a "sophisticated (?) comedy" about a ménage à trois. In the summer of 1957 he had seen at the Paris Cinématèque several thirties screwball comedies starring his current favorite, Irene Dunne—"charming, natural, piquant."[58] *The Awful Truth* (1937), a wise screenplay about marriage and divorce by one of Hollywood's many unsung women writers, Viña Delmar, directed by Leo McCarey and enhanced by co-star Cary Grant, was the most screwball of them all. But this time Manuel tried to give his script a fifties feel, to make it like *Pillow Talk*. Having just been in Switzerland—where he hitchhiked for three months, keeping an eye out for Garbo's summer home—Manuel situated this screenplay in yet another unreal, glamorous European locale, beautiful Lucerne, where, thirty years later, in *Tropical Night Falling*, his last heroine (Luci) would die. "Summer Indoors" centered around a woman torn between propriety and her desires—like her creator. The battle between private and public life—the core of melodrama, the core of his own double life—was a theme to which Manuel would return obsessively.

Manuel was only in his mid-twenties, but later he reminisced: "My friends were quite worried about me by then."[59] Mario especially was urging him to write about places and situations he knew, in his own language. "Summer Indoors" featured another motif of his future work: the desperate desire to triumph over obscure provincial origins, which he would express more successfully in *Heartbreak Tango*, set in a world he knew. His letters home referred to these first scripts as *bodrios*, boring trash. He knew they were not works of art; he wanted commercial success.

arrivederci, roma

The Dante Society scholarship was for one year only, but Manuel was determined to stay longer in Italy. He refused to accept money from his family except as a last resort and, through the agency Mario worked with, started translating movie subtitles. He continued tutoring, as the translation work was sporadic, and waiting for paychecks was nerve-racking; by 1957 Manuel was complaining to Malé that the atmosphere in Rome was "suffocating." Having crossed the Atlantic—the *charco* (puddle)—he wasn't going to leave without seeing the rest of Europe, especially France, England, and Spain, where his Catalan and Galician cousins lived.

In the next two years, Manuel moved from France to Spain to England to Sweden. A quintessential Argentine globetrotter, he took any sort of job to make ends meet, from translator and language tutor to restaurant dishwasher. He even washed windows on tall buildings when he lived in London, Alfredo Gialdini recalls, admiring Manuel's courage and persistence in adverse circumstances. After Rome, Paris was his next stop. Mario had film contacts there, where he had watched legends Jean Marais and Michèle Morgan on a set, and Nestor encouraged him to visit fellow Cuban film buff, Germán Puig, now living in the City of Light. Around 1951 Nestor, Germán, Tomás Gutiérrez Alea (who, in the sixties, became Cuba's premier film director), and budding writer Guillermo Cabrera Infante had founded the first film club in Havana. Germán, a photographer, had been the first of these young enthusiasts to go to Paris, to establish relations with the legendary founder of the Cinématèque Française, Henri Langlois.

Manuel left Rome on the morning of June 6, 1957, en route to Paris by train—and later by thumb. His first impressions were typically exuberant: France felt more *moderne*, more like Argentina than Italy, which he now branded soporific, so boringly middle-class. But Cannes, Juan-les-Pins, Antibes, the glamour spots of Picasso and the "lost generation," were disappointing, especially the beaches. At the beach in Cannes, however, he chanced upon a classmate from Cinecittà, and she and her companions offered him a ride to Paris, where he arrived on June 14.

His new friend in Paris, Germán, was studying filmography with Langlois and, as he proudly declared, was "the youngest cinématèque director [of the Cuban cinemateca] in the world." He worked part-time at UNESCO in order to support his statuesque blond wife, Adoración, and their baby son, Adrián, in one cramped room in the Cuban dormitory of the Cité Universitaire. Germán was funny, theatrical, full of vitality, and a fellow devotee of Hollywood's golden-age divas and movies. Of Catalan ancestry like Nestor, he was tall, debonair, exuberantly bisexual; with striking matinee-idol looks à la John Barrymore, he described himself to Manuel as having no face, "just two profiles stuck together." The Cuban photographer was immediately struck by Manuel's "perfect, handsome Roman head and profile." Germán had procured a room for Manuel for a month in the Argentine dormitory. This campus of drab pavilion-like buildings, built between the wars to house Sorbonne students, was in the 14th Arrondissement, only a bus ride or a few Metro stops from the busy Latin Quarter.

Ecstatic about his new quarters, a spartan dorm room with a bunk bed, Manuel wrote home:

> Dear folks: I am wild with joy! Here I am writing to you from my room in *La Cité Universitaire*. I'm like a king, I can't believe I got this. I've been in Paris since Friday night. It's marvelous—I never imagined anything like it. The difference between Rome and Paris is the same as between Villegas and Buenos Aires. I feel totally at home and never want to leave; this is a palace, the Argentine Pavilion, and it's mine; I have a

bedroom as big as the master bedroom on Bulnes Street, with a bathroom and hot water all the time. The showers are a few steps away, down the hallway.[60]

In this "palace" Manuel not only mingled with French and Argentine students but had lots of opportunities to meet young men from every corner of the globe since there was only one dining facility. The beds were narrow, but the rules were lax, and he didn't lack, as he wrote home, for "companionship." At the end of July Manuel had to move out of his Argentine quarters, and roomed temporarily with Germán, while Adoración—called Dora—and Adrián were away visiting relatives in Spain. The Cuban Pavilion, Manuel reported home, was not as clean but more relaxed, and there was less gossip and backbiting than among his fellow Argentines. The two friends were working different shifts, so that when one left the bed, the other got in—though a few times they coincided and, according to Germán, "slept like angels."

Soon after he arrived in Paris, Manuel tried out for a small role "sitting at a table in an airport cafeteria and looking surprised" as an extra in a low-budget film, or a little more than an extra, he explained in a letter home, upon whom the camera actually focused for a few seconds. Starring Pierre Fresnay, *Les Fanatiques* (1957) was a film about a plot to assassinate a Latin American dictator, "vaguely about Perón and Argentina," Manuel wrote to Malé, though the movie could have been inspired by more than one South American dictator. He would make several thousand francs more than as a normal extra, but, in the end, he didn't get the part: "The director didn't find me Argentine enough (!?), and chose instead a Mexican Indian with a mustache, à la Pedro Armendáriz. Hollywood's idea of 'South American.'" As Manuel later reminisced, in mock despair, "I had no connections, knew nobody. The European film industry was rejecting me; American films didn't please me. What was left that was sacred?"[61]

To stay afloat (and to improve his French) Manuel temped for the month of July as a receptionist at a small press that serviced the official magazine of the Comédie Française; in August, while he roomed with Germán, he temped again as a night telephone operator in a hotel, and then as a secretary for a leather goods store, dispatching business correspondence in English, Italian, and Spanish. He was a student without a work visa, an illegal alien, which meant that he could obtain temporary jobs easily because employers "took advantage." The pay was still pretty good, he told Malé: the executive secretary at the store was a gorgeous blonde who, unlike the typical Parisian, was very good-natured and let him work only six hours a day.

Mario's and Nestor's connections and Manuel's credentials as a student from Cinecittà got him onto a movie set in Paris, where he watched René Clément direct, and several months later he watched director Stanley Donen on the set of *Once More, with Feeling* in both London and Paris. As he wrote to Malé in October: "Here in Paris I have violent attacks of wanting to leap over to London. V. Leigh and L. Olivier are currently onstage, but I'll save it for another time." He needed to return to Rome first because De Sica had promised to let him attend the filming of *Anna of Brooklyn*. He also planned to take advantage of autumnal travel bargains to Greece and Turkey. Christmas, over the years, was always his loneliest time when away from home and family, especially because each December 28—"a horrendous day," he often remarked—he was one year older. He wanted very much to spend the holidays with Malé's relatives in Busseto, Italy, as he wrote in the same letter: "I'd like to spend Xmas at Luigi's (I'm bringing a good gift) and afterward put up with the Gallegos"—alluding to the brutish "gallego" side of the family he expected to find in Spain. He planned to go to Spain in winter when "it will be perfect, less cold" than in Italy, he wrote to Malé from Rome, before leaving for Greece:

> I want to know if Grandpa was from Barcelona or some-
> where nearby. I've been finding out prices and it's all very
> cheap. I'm dying to go, and to see where Grandma lived be-
> fore they emigrated [Galicia]. I want the address of that uncle
> Camilo (Camilo Cortés is going to love this). The itinerary
> will be fabulous, I won't even miss Majorca!! Then I want to
> spend quite a while in London.[62]

By October 24, 1957, back in Rome—"the tomb"—he was missing the bohemian ease and *cinématèques* of Paris, on top of which, now that he had given up the trip to London, De Sica's project was postponed once again. Cinecittà was a "desert" where lots of actors were out of work, and they were only making horrendous epics like *Ben-Hur*. He quenched his thirst for entertainment—Rome couldn't hold a candle to Paris—by resorting to literature. Taking up membership at the English Library, he read, and recommended to Malé, Henry James's "The Lesson of the Master" and Stephen Crane's *The Red Badge of Courage*. He also delved into Romantic poetry, an anthology of Byron and Shelley, whose exoticisms heightened the appeal of his upcoming escape to Greece and Turkey. Mario had described his summer travels around southern Italy, Greece, and Turkey, Istanbul, the Bosporus, Smyrna: images of Dionysian *hammami*, or public baths, Byzantine splendors and the film-noir ambience of *The Mask of Dimitrios* (1944) all sparked Manuel's travel fever. He left for a two-week trip early in December.

From Brindisi, "desolate, unlike the rest of Italy," he took the boat to Athens via Corfu, "another world."[63] Even more than the actual experience, the idea of going east was exciting. In Athens, "a dirty city," he met up with friends from the Centro and toured the "magnificent" Parthenon and the museums. The Greek sculptures, those perfect male bodies he would describe so meticulously in a novel one day, impressed him enormously, as did the harmonious blend of architecture and landscape throughout Greece, from Adelphi to Salonika to Corinth, which was basically "a village like Villegas." He was intrigued to travel not only in space but in time, to the places of myth: Argos, Olympia; Mycenae, with the palace of Electra and Clytemnestra, was the "best of all."

But being for the first time in more "primitive" countries, where he did not speak the language, was also formidable. It was nearly impossible to communicate with anyone "in any language, including hand signals," and bus, train, and boat schedules seemed completely unreliable. In Istanbul he loved the minarets of Santa Sophia and the splendid Topkapi Palace, "turned into a museum filled with treasures like Ali Baba's cave." He lunched and dined on "Turkish delights" dispensed by street vendors amid the bustling and elbowing of the teeming populace. And the Turkish baths, particularly the "Cukurcum" (also called the Suck-or-Come), had their charms.[64] But the dirt and poverty, which had already been disturbing in Greece, was even worse in Turkey. Danger lurked everywhere; the city was charged with the "chaotic frenzy of an anthill." "The women all had empty expressions and everybody dressed in rags," he wrote, safely back in Italy at Christmas, from the ancestral home near Busseto.

Besides, when he arrived on a crowded boat in Smyrna, he discovered that his suitcase had been "stolen or grabbed by mistake." He told Malé that the police took him on a Keystone Kops jeep ride around the slums of Smyrna, apparently seeking the suspect, the delinquent stevedore. They finally found the missing item at a depot, ransacked: "Luckily I had my money in my small pants pocket." Another mishap occurred on the return trip from Smyrna to Athens: a new Turkish law forced him to pay in dollars for a special visa to get off the boat at Athens, thus delaying his boat connection to Brindisi, where he missed his train and had to use his last penny to take a costly express back to Rome.

After passing through Rome and staying overnight at Mario's, he reached Zibello by Christmas Eve, as he wrote on December 26: "I arrived at 7 p.m. and luckily Uncle Luigi picked me up at Busseto, having left Rome at 6 a.m.—trains were delayed, as usual. I was so exhausted, I've been sitting ever since I arrived here; fortunately, here I've finally been able to get some rest." The food everywhere was delicious and he worried that the family back home would find him fat: "In Greece and Turkey, where I kept eating at ubiquitous street stands, I gained two kilos from all that grease, and then another two at Luigi's, where Christmas dinner was ferocious; five different dishes including ravioli in broth, veal in an exquisite sauce, stuffed chicken, another roasted chicken with potatoes, salad, three cakes, etc. etc. . . . I left B.A. weighing 64 kilos, and now I weigh 72 kilos."

He delighted Malé with tales of their affectionate, picturesque Italian relatives: "I had a wonderful time: the 28th I spent very peacefully, fortunately; Sunday, the 29th, we went to visit Grandma's brother and Pety's godfather, Pietro, who's very old and can barely talk, but he's sweet, the spitting image of Geppetto in *Pinocchio*. The same eyes as Grandma's. All the children with all their families were there; there were around thirty of us at the table. They asked me millions of questions, told me not to leave you in peace until you came to Italy."[65]

He didn't stop in the Italian village for long; the day after New Year's he took the train to Spain. He reached Barcelona by ten in the morning, "trembling" with excitement not only because of the city's fame but because Catalonia was the land of his forefathers. "It's so modern, with fascinating buildings by that crazy architect Gaudí from 1920," he observed. "But there's not that much to see," he concluded. "It's a big, impersonal city." His biggest disappointment: "The people are ugly, they don't look at all like the Puigs . . . I hope I find the family features in Galicia." On the other hand, "the Spaniards are fun, the salt of the earth . . . After checking out the Costa Brava on the 4th I took a night boat—10 hours!—to Majorca, some beautiful spots, not Palma, ugly, the most beautiful was Valldemosa, where Chopin was with G. Sand."

January 18, around the time of his thirteen-year-old brother's birthday, he was still in Spain, in Málaga, where he wrote a letter to Carlitos about how homesick he felt, and how he had not received a letter from the family since before Christmas, nearly a month earlier. Birthdays and holidays always made him forlorn: "All I can think of is your birthday. Today I was remembering when we celebrated your first birthday in Villegas: we bought a cake with one little candle (puff pastry with *dulce de leche*!), and we ate it in the evening when we got back from the pool. Next year we'll eat one 30 stories high for revenge." Manuel regretted not being in Argentina for his brother's early adolescence; he was curious to know how he was doing at school, and surprised to see how tall Carlitos had grown in his photos, advising his mother not to spare money in dressing him well and insisting that he learn English. He tried to encourage Carlitos's interest in school, particularly since the boy was a wavering student. In his correspondence home, first from Europe, then from New York in the sixties, Manuel would try to bridge the generation gap with his brother, but Carlitos was as ambivalent toward his older sibling as he was toward his own goals. Though Malé was affectionate with both, Carlitos knew Manuel was her favorite, the brilliant son, her soul mate.[66]

He stayed overnight in Madrid, and took a two-day tour of Old Castile: "the most impressive of all. I saw the three main spots: Ávila, El Escorial, and Segovia, three small towns but unique. The best of Europe till now, in terms of castles, monasteries, medieval walls, the landscape. The people are wonderful; there are families who rent rooms and I always try to do that to have a more direct contact and see how they live." While it was obviously more economical to rent rooms at people's houses, curiosity was another motive for the Coco who had listened behind doors, and who continued to be an observer of the everyday details of people's lives. Back in Madrid, he complained that he had received no letters from the family at the consulate, only a card from Mario Fenelli and Margherita Muzi saying a letter had arrived "from you, Mama!! . . . Madrid is not typical, almost all modern, and you can see it all quickly, but it's still charming because it's so lively, especially at night." He was staying in a cheap hotel in the center of town, the Puerta del Sol, an ideal place to cruise, though discreetly, but in his letters home he kept to appropriate topics like family and cultural highlights. True to form, he was drawn more to kitschy Spanish folk culture than to the treasures of the Prado:

> I saw musical revues—with Nati Mistral and an old Argentine dame Celia Gámez; and I'm not going to miss, in Seville, La Piquer![67] What surprises me is that the people all over Spain are quite plain, the women in Madrid are the best but nothing special. I saw Papa's eyes a little in Granada, but not much. Can't wait to get to Galicia.

In Andalusia, he

> liked Granada, though the Moorish stuff doesn't catch my fancy as much, but the dancing Gypsies in Sacromonte were the best. Granada pales next to Seville, where I spent only a day and a half because I was dying to see Lisbon . . . Andalusians are talkative but not as lively as the Madrileños; all they say is "I shit on this, I shit on that"; the poverty is the same as in Italy, worse in the south than in the north. The climate in Andalusia in midwinter is wonderful, warm, flowers everywhere, the fragrance of orange blossoms in Seville. Well, I hope a helicopter passes by and drops me a letter, somewhere along the route from Seville to Portugal, and then to northern Spain (without family addresses!!!).

Because they hadn't sent him the addresses of the Puig/Cortés side of the family, he would have to wait for his 1961 European trip to meet "los gallegos."

Back in Paris for a few days in late January 1958, Manuel shared a room at the Sorbonne, again at the "Maison de Cuba," where a letter from Aventino awaited him, filled with news that made him anxious to get back into career mode: Mario was making documentaries with Bazzoni, had received the OK to be on the set of *Ben-Hur*, and had befriended Stephen Boyd—who (it was later revealed) contrived with the director to make his scenes with Charlton Heston charged with homoeroticism. Paris continued to be lively: thanks in part to cultural divas like Jean Cocteau, Jean-Louis Barrault, and Jean Genet, gay life among artists and intellectuals was hopping on the Left Bank, where the hub was the block from Café Flore to the Deux Magots in St.-Germain-des-Prés, only a few Metro stops from the Cité Universitaire. As it entered the sixties, Paris was a haven for exiles of every nation and persuasion, a refuge where Latin American artists could establish closer ties with each other than in their home countries. A hand-typed underground tabloid for and about gay Latins in France was circulated through the early sixties by Pedro Consuegra, a Cuban maître de ballet in Marseilles. A pal of Germán's, Consuegra cultivated bitchy banter: Nestor, for example, who had a penny-pinching reputation even before Manuel became similarly notorious, was not amused when Consuegra compared him with a concierge and called him that "miserly old French woman." But when it came to speaking in the feminine, Manuel commanded a wittier lexicon: Germán was "Pau," alluding to an exaggerated Italian actress, Germana Paulina. Like Mario, Germán laughed but felt uncomfortable. After he became a famous writer, Manuel would espouse openly, if ironically, the worldview that all people were female, the real ones with vaginas, and the "others" with penises—the only real man was the one who, someday, would love him.

Germán introduced Manuel to another slight, dark-eyed, dark-haired Argentine cinephile he had recently met, Nino Franqui, a short man with large expressive eyes who struck Germán as a less scintillating version of Manuel.[68] Nino crossed the ocean to Europe in circumstances similar to Manuel's, with a scholarship, in this case from the Alliance Française in Buenos Aires, to study at the Sorbonne. He initially intended to become a professor of French literature in Argentina, but through a temporary job at UNESCO in Paris (like Julio Cortázar's), he gained a permanent position as a translator and made Paris his home.

Playing the matchmaker, Germán thought Nino's and Manuel's commonalities might ignite a romance and take the heat (so to speak) off Germán, with whom Nino was smitten. Nino had first approached Germán in

the corridor outside the UNESCO radio station, where the two had temporary jobs as announcers for broadcasts to Latin America. He had already
seen Germán once before, in the Metro, play-boxing with his little boy, and
accompanied by Dora—this vivacious, charming trio had been a warm vision for the young Argentine, newly arrived in Paris and living in a small
room in the Argentine student quarters. Nino wondered who they could be,
so European-looking and yet so spontaneous, not stiff like the French. In
their first conversations, about cinema of course, Nino was especially delighted to learn how much this Cuban knew about Argentine movies of the
late thirties and early forties, and how much impact Argentine women's
magazines like *El Hogar*, *Para Ti*, and *Maribel* had in Cuba.[69]

Manuel would put off his return to Argentina until November 1958,
even though he knew it was disappointing for Malé, as he wrote her "I'm always thinking of the first moment of being with you again, the first days
chatting like crazy, the first meal, but there's so much left to see here . . . I'm
in no rush to return to Buenos Aires . . ."

For now, he was off to England.

london, london

Manuel arrived in London on Sunday, February 2, 1958, in the dead of winter, with a suitcase and the address of the family of a young Englishman he
had met during the filming of *A Farewell to Arms*. This new friend had

> found lodging for me, an old-fashioned two-story flat I'm
> renting with two other students—an English boy, Gil Brad-
> ley, and a Swede—furnished, with a big kitchen with all the
> pots and pans, big bathroom too, a living room and three bed-
> rooms, hot water, and heat *all day long*. A convenient, and ex-
> clusive neighborhood, near Park Lane. Very expensive, but
> worth it. It will be easy to clean, with a wall-to-wall carpet
> and a vacuum cleaner included.[70]

His first impression of the English—"so quaint, so charmingly polite"—on the train from Dover to London was one of utter delight. He was particularly struck by their "warmth and hospitality," for as soon as he set foot in his friend's family home, they insisted he stay with them until he moved into his new place, and welcomed him with a party "to introduce the stranger to all the people who could be helpful to him."

Three days after getting off the train from Dover, he moved into 37 Gloucester Place in an elegant West End neighborhood near Kensington Park (not far from 53 Gloucester Road, where the Cuban Guillermo Cabrera Infante would make his permanent residence in exile several years later). Manuel had already lined up four language students and planned to teach "in the morning, to have the afternoons free for snooping around the sets." As he wrote reassuringly to Malé on the same day he moved:

> Now I have six students, Spanish and Italian, and possibly one more because it's expensive here, but wonderful, because I've fallen in with a theater crowd, and the two students I took on yesterday are screenwriters; I'm hoping to get something [a *tajada*, or "cut"] out of that—oh I hope something comes out of all this! Today it began to get cold, but not too bad yet, and so far no London fog. Yesterday I received a letter, no, Monday, so that Thursday is the best day for you to send letters; [it takes] only 4 days. The house is great, nobody is ever here, but so expensive . . . 3 pounds a week. But here all the rents are like that. But I stay home and cook a lot; I've stocked up on milk, butter, bread, jam, tea, sugar, oil, eggs and salt.

One of Manuel's pupils, Paul Dehn, was a poet and ex-spy who had just written his first screenplay, *Orders to Kill*, directed by Anthony Asquith. This obscure poet turned flamboyant screenwriter became Manuel's first guide to the London film world. For Manuel, Dehn was an inspiring model, whose life (he had learned Norwegian as a boy from his nanny and had served as a British spy in Norway) had motivated his first script; his second script was taking a few years to finish, but it would be a James Bond hit, *Goldfinger* (1964). Dehn's career took off with *The Spy Who Came In from the Cold* (1965) and *The Taming of the Shrew* (1967), and the Taylor-Burton team went so far as to buy him a Bentley and fly him to Acapulco to cajole him into writing *Macbeth*. As Manuel wrote ten years later in his coyly ironic chronicle "London, London," Paul Dehn was a patriot: "He writes two or three screenplays a year and is considered one of the unknown soldiers of the national economy together with Rex Harrison, Carol Reed, and other contributors of Hollywood dollars to the British treasury."[71]

In his first letter home from London, Manuel's exuberance was tempered by his lament over recent deaths in the family which Malé had reported in her last letter; the news was upsetting especially because he had "no close friend nearby to confide in." He sympathized, too, over ne'er-do-well cousin Jorge's latest predicaments with women and money, assuring Malé that he himself was managing on his modest earnings, with a glimmer of his boyhood rivalry with Jorge for parental admiration: "It doesn't surprise me about Jorge, he's always had the devil in him."

> Mama: you ask me about money—I'm still living on what I saved in Paris and from the translations in Rome. I'm invited to the Old Vic by my students and their friends; I still don't understand why the English are so unbearable abroad—here they're generous, simple-hearted. Maybe it's too uncivilized for them when they're abroad—here everybody is respectful; you never have any discord in public, just like Buenos Aires.

London was a little bit of home, reminding him of the Anglo-Argentine civic cordiality of Buenos Aires. Aside from tutoring film and theater people in Spanish and Italian—from unemployed actors to John Gielgud—Manuel worked as a dishwasher four nights a week at a Soho theater restaurant frequented by unemployed actors. Not everybody was respectful: fellow kitchen workers made fun of him because he couldn't understand their cockney banter. Worse than these taunts was the risk he ran of deportation, working any odd job that came along. Manuel had a three-month work visa but stayed for fourteen months, "trembling for fear of immigration officers" until he did obtain an extension.

His language skills were still his "foot in the door," as was the cachet of having been at Cinecittà. With his classic Roman features, big expressive eyes, and winning smile, the twenty-five-year-old Manuel looked like a young Latin movie star, and moved as easily in high society as in thespian circles. Reminiscing years later, he modestly admitted, "I wasn't bad-looking, and on occasion people would even turn around on the street as I passed." His many conquests included a few celebrities, among them actors Stanley Baker and Yul Brynner.[72] Except with close confidants, he was as discreet about names—in a homophobic universe—as he was graphic in describing his trysts. One of his longest London affairs, with a married expatriate Anglo-Argentine doctor, would end in the early seventies, when Manuel was on a brief "businesswoman" trip: in their hotel room the doctor, a burly fellow, "presented" himself to Manuel on all fours for variety's sake; shocked, Manuel—more swisher than switcher—couldn't conceive of changing roles, from passive to active, with such a big man!

In London he was frequently invited to plays and theater parties—he wrote Malé detailed reports—to liven things up among the staid Brits:

> I'm changing students because some wanted only a few lessons before going to Italy on vacation. I have a new one who's a scream, a member of Parliament—Fletcher Cooper. He and his wife have one of those cases of desperate "Englishitis," serious stiffs, but I didn't follow their lead and I joked with them. They reacted incredibly, really livened up: how witty they are and how they like to fool around. But at first they're like death warmed over like most of the English, and if you don't shake them out of it, years could pass without going beyond a formal relationship. This has happened to me with other people here; I've always had to take the initiative to melt the ice, and they like that (and need it) because they're always inviting me to parties and tea, and this couple has extended a permanent invitation to their weekend house in Surrey.[73]

While movies were Manuel's magnificent obsession and the British film industry was flourishing, London was, first and foremost, the capital of theater, not to mention opera and all the performing arts. Manuel watched countless stars in person, registered the gestures of those who fascinated him, and heard every nuance of the most brilliant dialogues in the language he wanted to master for his screenplays. He attended all manner of spectacles, from avant-garde experiments to popular musicals:

Last week I saw *My Fair Lady*: superbly wonderful, the music fabulous, one song better than the next; the same goes for the dances. Her [Eliza Doolittle's] introduction to society had me rolling in the aisle and the song he [Henry Higgins] sings angrily because he misses her (almost at the end) is a jewel . . . A lot of the credit belongs to Rex Harrison, who's very funny and has you laughing every minute. The father (Stanley Holloway) is brilliant, and the girl, though not a wonder, does fine, her voice is very good, her name is Julie Andrews, and it's too bad she's not more alluring. They couldn't give the role to another girl because they needed a good voice. They say Kay Kendall (Mrs. Harrison) is moving heaven and earth to do the movie, dubbed.[74]

George Cukor chose Audrey Hepburn, who would also be dubbed.

Luchino Visconti's Covent Garden production of the opera *Don Carlos* was truly marvelous, but Manuel's opera climax that season was la Callas in *La Traviata*:

[She is] charming, her acting is perfect, like an actress, and she sings with such feeling that she could make stones cry. I thought she would strut like a grand diva, but on the contrary she was simple and *human* . . . ruined a little in contrast with the rest of the cast, who acted in the usual style. I can imagine now what she must be like with Visconti in Italy; they've worked a lot together. She's a vision on the stage and the applause and bravos are something else. What they say about her voice is true, it's not perfect; in the first act (the party) she shrieks big time. Her strong point is pathos, when she plays the tragic moments; there she's different from all the rest— she cries without distorting the voice. The whole last act was incredible.[75]

At the Old Vic or in the West End, Laurence Olivier, Vivien Leigh, John Gielgud, Claire Bloom, and other consecrated or new talents performed the classics as well as the latest engagé productions of the "angry young men" like playwright John Osborne. After seeing, on the same day, a pretentious Hollywood movie, *The Long Hot Summer*, with "dour-faced" Joanne Woodward, and an excellent Russian production of Chekhov's *Uncle Vanya*, he evaluated, with equal sobriety, the virtues of Konstantin Stanislavsky's Moscow Art Theater—"which initiated method acting at the start of the century"—and the defects of this realist approach when applied to trashy American postwar film production.[76]

London was still a decorous city, but on the eve of the pop art and fashion revolution on Carnaby Street and King's Road (the Beatles, Twiggy, and miniskirts), it was fast becoming "swinging London," as depicted in *Darling*, with shining starlet Julie Christie, and *Blowup*, with the "divine" Vanessa Redgrave. The young Argentine would later refer to himself as sexy newcomer Christie: just as seductive Darling rose to great fame, Manuel was determined to charm his way to the top and sell his first script, "Ball Cancelled." He was hoping that one of his students, the distinguished silver-haired producer Anthony Havelock-Allan, would be "the ticket," as he writes home in early June, complaining as usual about the changeable weather, how summer came and then went, "cold and hot, rainy and sunny everyday," almost quoting Garbo in *Camille*: "I'm always nervous or sick, sad or too gay."

> If the visa doesn't arrive I'm going to shoot myself because this week the Italian lessons with *THE PRODUCER* began, Anthony Havelock-Allan, the one who did *Brief Encounter*, *Great Expectations*, and *Orders to Kill*. He's a distinguished old Brit, very important, and seems to be a good person, down to earth. He was Valerie Hobson's first husband and now he has an American wife who's here. Every day from Monday to Friday we have a teatime chat for an hour at 5 (we take tea with these incredible Danish biscuits!). He was the first to give movie roles to V. Leigh, Alec Guinness, and Trevor Howard. Now he's making [*The Journey*] with la Magnani and possibly Yul Brynner. He tells me all the gossip—I tremble and swoon. Yesterday he told me Brynner wants Litvak as director and I campaigned against it; his ear perked up when he saw how I remembered the work: Litvak really has deteriorated—a

world of difference from *Mayerling* to *Anastasia*—he's become totally cold. How great it would be if I could get something out of all this; I have him on a platter but these big fish are tricky.[77]

A month later Manuel felt certain he had Havelock in his net: following Manuel's advice that, contrary to what la Magnani was saying, Robert Mitchum was a better actor than Brynner, Havelock screened Mitchum's films *Not as a Stranger* and *Heaven Knows, Mr. Allison*. Havelock encouraged Manuel to expand the treatment of his script, and was a delightful source of gossip: "Coral Browne came back [from the plastic surgeon] looking twenty years younger."

By June 15 the visa extension came through, which brought relief but also a twinge of homesickness:

> I'm going to postpone my return home a few more months
> . . . I'm *close friends* now with the wonderful old producer. I
> have more and more connections here and I'm having such a
> good time in London. I'm afraid it's been so long that we
> won't recognize each other! But I'm also afraid of what I'll
> find in B.A. . . . I spoke to the producer about one of my
> screenplay ideas. He seemed mystified and suggested that it
> would be up Visconti's alley (which puzzled me).

Diplomatic Havelock evidently both flattered and gently discouraged Manuel by steering him toward Visconti—gay, operatic, Latin. But Manuel persisted: "When he gets back from his trip I'll continue the campaign. His (American) wife seems to have a lot of influence on him and is very nice to me." Manuel often felt more at ease with the wives or girlfriends of the men with whom he had professional dealings.

His workaholic tendency took over in London, with its "disastrous" climate, and where the social life, at first comforting and stimulating, soon became burdensome. With the years and the pressures, Manuel would resolve the tug-of-war between play and work by making his daily schedule rigidly airtight, often to the consternation of friends. On June 25, as vacation season in Europe approached, he wrote: "I'd love to go to Scotland and Ireland, but can't decide yet." It seemed more important to wait for Havelock to come back from Rome and Vienna, where he was signing up Yul Brynner for the film. Manuel distracted himself by revisiting *Irene and Vernon Castle* with Fred Astaire and Ginger Rogers—his favorite flick in 1939. Considering that postwar American "bad taste" was ruining most current film musicals, like *South Pacific*, he had eagerly awaited this jewel, he wrote Malé, especially la Ginger:

> The first part is phenomenal (the comedy part), then it sags a bit, but *she* was something unique, *la simpatía* personified. And just yesterday I ran to see Lubitsch's fabulous *Trouble in Paradise* from 1932 with Kay Francis, H. Marshall and M. Hopkins. It hasn't aged a bit; I don't remember seeing it in Villegas (must have been around '34 or '35). I was very curious to see her [Kay Francis]; beautiful, but dull as a comedian.

Current cinema paled: this time he mentions a "French bore," *The Night Heaven Fell* (1958), the latest Brigitte Bardot–Roger Vadim "recipe," which disappointed him after the erotic, sophisticated . . . *And God Created Woman*.

Another disappointment was an "old and tired" Rita Hayworth in *Pal Joey* (1957), a musical that marked the beginning of the end for the sex queen of his childhood, now approaching forty. Manuel kept the gossip from Malé until after she had seen the movie back home: producer Harry Cohn had humiliated Rita (as revenge after she broke her contract and wreaked financial havoc on Columbia Pictures) by making her play second fiddle to newcomer Kim Novak in the romantic female lead. Adding insult to injury, Joey (Frank Sinatra at the height of his long career) sings to Rita the famous Rodgers and Hart tune "The Lady Is a Tramp." Manuel tried to end the tale on a happier note: "Now Rita seems to be having a comeback, *Separate Tables* . . . a dramatic role."[78]

"Fenelli wants to come to London," Manuel wrote Malé in July. He was eager for the company, and not only so he could talk in his own language with an intimate chum (sometimes Manuel went by the Argentine embassy just to speak in Spanish with compatriots). He was anxious for Mario to read his "boring" "Summer Indoors." While Paul Dehn was helping him with the English dialogue in this new script and in revising "Ball Cancelled," he still needed Mario's "good critical mind" and, even more, his supportive enthusiasm.[79] The downside of a visit was Mario's tendency to dwell on his frustrations, Manuel complained: "He's depressed because his assistant work for *Ben-Hur* fell through, the same story as always, Rome, his depression, the uncertainties of translation work; he's so neurotic but a good person too—he kept Margharita [Muzi] company when she was ill."[80]

London was either too cold or too hot, and by August Manuel was lonely, floundering:

> Last week saw a boring double bill, Diana Dors and one with Bardot–Louis Jourdan; I left the movie house half asleep. La Diana doesn't know what to do anymore to entertain the audience, she's going to the dogs; Brigitte dopey too, no comparison with . . . *And God Created Woman* . . . hate the vacation months (August in Europe is like February in Argentina—many people leave town, the libraries are closed, few shows, what garbage). Also, it's been a while since I've seen anything good and stimulating, which helps me a lot. I don't know if I mentioned I saw *Paths of Glory* two or three months ago. It left me agog, especially the final scene in the bar. How good Kirk Douglas can be when they rein him in . . . I'm not reading anything because my attention lags, and then I can't concentrate on my work. I'm turning into a bundle of nerves, poor me.[81]

Mario arrived in mid-August: "Manuel welcomed me to London with a spectacular candlelight dinner party teeming with theater people. He had told all his acquaintances about me and seemed very proud to introduce me." The next day the two friends attended opening night of *Indiscreet*, a "delightful, sexy" comedy directed by Stanley Donen, with Ingrid Bergman and Cary Grant. With Mario at his side London became again a festive orgy of parties and theater.

Among many star-studded events, they attended a theater party with the real Vivien Leigh, after seeing her act with Claire Bloom in *Duel of Angels*. When Manuel went backstage to pitch Vivien "Ball Cancelled," she wasn't interested in the play but she "made overtures," as she had done indiscriminately with other young men backstage or on movie sets. Suffering from bouts of manic-depressive illness, she *was* Blanche Dubois in *A Streetcar Named Desire* (1951), a brilliant, fatal role for this fading beauty—once so lovely in *Gone With the Wind* (1939) and *Waterloo Bridge* (1940). As Leigh tried to wave him into her dressing room, playing spider woman to the unwary fly, Manuel also saw in her the doomed heroine of Williams's *The Roman Spring of Mrs. Stone* (1961), her penultimate film. Leigh had recently been replaced by Elizabeth Taylor during the filming of *Elephant Walk* (1954) for scandalously pursuing handsome newlywed co-star Peter Finch, causing grief for her husband (Laurence Olivier) and concerned friends. Nymphomania, a term whose misogyny Tennessee Williams exposed in his tragic *Streetcar*, was a misunderstood symptom of her emotional illness—compounded by alcoholism and tuberculosis. More terrified than tempted, he eluded the assignation.[82] Some months later, Manuel reported to Malé what he had heard from a friend who had seen Leigh at a Christmas party: "She's super-nuts; she babbles like an idiot, and they're going to have to put her to sleep for ten days. It's a treatment they do from time to time. When she has those attacks she drinks a lot, gets all puffy, a total wreck."[83] Ravaged, in her early fifties, Vivien Leigh died in 1967.

The actress was the role she played, but she was also a real person: Leigh's emotional ills confirmed Manuel's feeling about actresses he connected with, that the role and the person were one. As he (and his goddesses) grew older, Manuel studied their deterioration on screen and, whenever possible, in person, with almost surgical precision. Hedy Lamarr, for example: it was all over after *Boom Town* (1940), a rousing adventure film with Clark Gable, Spencer Tracy, and Claudette Colbert. Lamarr was never lovelier than in the nightclub scene when she lifts herself, drunk, from a chair and sashays amid the bedazzled men, but it was the beginning of the end, almost as if one became aware of the nature of her beauty at the very moment the flower started to wilt. He spotted Ginger Rogers's first "sign" in 1946, in *Heartbeat* (with Jean-Pierre Aumont): what a shock to see how she had aged. Ginger continued to work for another thirty years but lost her confidence, he felt, and her "enviable" intuition. The spritely, witty Miriam Hopkins was beautiful in 1935, but in 1937 a "hag." The most absorbing decline to watch was Joan Crawford's: on the one hand, la Crawford was one of the most durable and resourceful actresses, a woman who knew how to use sex or her charms in a man's world, but, on the other hand, her mask-like face became more and more wooden, as did her acting, as the years flew by. In contrast, Garbo and Shearer "didn't allow him the satisfaction of seeing them falling apart," retiring discreetly while they were still on top.[84] Manuel would always be shocked by how quickly people aged, disturbed, increasingly, by his own passage through time.

When Mario left for Rome on August 30, Manuel headed north to Scotland, where he visited Edinburgh and Mary Stuart's "bleak" castle. Even more magical, on the way back, was his literary tour of northern England, the Lake District, and, most of all, gloomily romantic Yorkshire: "Haworth, the Brontë house, complete with Emily's French notebook and Charlotte's clothing," he wrote to Malé, with whom he would repeat this pilgrimage almost thirty years later.

> From there walking four kilometers you enter a completely wild region of moors, where they always went, barely a little path; anyone who wants to see it has to walk. Completely desolate and one kilometer farther, you can see the Grange house that inspired *Wuthering Heights*. It leaves you breathless; how could those poor girls not have been dazzled? This marvelous surprise was one of the most beautiful things I've seen in all of Europe.[85]

His enthusiasm for his English gothic "Ball Cancelled" was revived by Mario's action-packed visit but also by this voyage to "Wuthering Heights."

A year among the English had led Manuel to conclude they were "nice but incomprehensible." The Brits suffocated him with their teas and parties, with their attempts to marry him off, and especially with their exaggerated Christmas rituals. His students and friends invited him to countless dinners and parties from the twenty-fifth to the thirty-first—"the biggest of all, half of London is invited." He sounds a bit like Scrooge in this pre-Christmas letter to Malé:

> Here I am in the midst of the fog . . . It's very cold and gets dark at 3 p.m.!!! One of these days will be the shortest of the year and then they'll get longer again. Hateful Christmas approaches. When will it be over! . . . I'm sick of London with

damn Christmas, everybody rushing around buying out the
stores, overdoing it big time, and the high point is sitting
down to dinner where nobody has anything to say.

London's foggy winter and predictable social life again inspired him to immerse himself in writing and reading: motivated by the film of a play he had
seen, starring a young new actress named Julie Harris, he read Carson
McCullers's *A Member of the Wedding*. McCullers's autobiographical treatment of a young girl's coming-of-age in a small Southern town and her
vivid use of regional speech brought to life the story of an eccentric "misfit"
with humor and compassion. The literary American South had produced
this play, Manuel wrote Malé, "about a twelve-year-old girl, but it can be enjoyed just the same by those who are allergic to stories about children." He
would soon begin the "failed" screenplay that became his own autobiography of childhood, *Betrayed by Rita Hayworth*.

Contemplating his eventual return to Argentina, he was glad to hear
that his father's factory was doing well, but worried about the country's new
president, a lawyer named Arturo Frondizi. While Perón's distributionist
policies had had disastrous results, Frondizi's open-door policy to foreign
investment was not reassuring either: "Gialdini wrote me overwhelmed by
the political situation; who could have expected such chaos."[86] He wished
his parents could stop working and take a vacation as the English did, for
the Christmas holidays as well as in the summer, even if only to some scenic
place in northern Argentina, Chile, or Rio de Janeiro.

Early in 1959 he was relieved to return to Paris, to the welcoming arms
of Germán and family, where he felt freer, more relaxed than with the English. Like Mario, Germán also encouraged his writing, a boost after his last
conversation with Havelock before leaving London, when the producer
gently advised him to write about more "modern subjects." It was now
April in Paris, and Manuel was thrilled to attend the filming of *Once More,
with Feeling* (1960):

Suddenly so hot here, the changes of temperature in Paris are
incredible. Some news: the filming of *Once More, with Feeling*
began, a comedy by Stanley Donen (*Indiscreet*), and I couldn't
resist the temptation; I had never seen a sophisticated American comedy being filmed and it's very interesting. The leads

are Y. Brynner and Kay K. I left my job in London but I'm thrilled—I told them 100 lies to get out of it. Here I introduced myself as a graduate of the Centro and they immediately let me on the set. I'm writing from a corner—the set's a luxurious house, how innovative for a comedy!

Manuel had already enjoyed Kendall in Vincente Minnelli's *The Reluctant Debutante* (1958), working with her debonair husband, Rex Harrison. As a lowly assistant on the set of *Once More, with Feeling*, Manuel gladly ran to the deli for hamburgers and sandwiches for la Kay: she was ravenous all the time, a symptom of the leukemia that would kill her, months later, at the age of thirty-two. In the brief time Manuel had gotten to know her, she had been an inspiration: "Seeing Kay Kendall act was definitive for me; she always improvised, but had the virtue of being able to repeat her improvisations over and over again."[87] Watching the filming of *Once More, with Feeling*, he wrote Malé, "has been a goodbye gift from Paris, and has given me more techniques to study. Do you realize I've now seen the best of Italy (De Sica), France (Clément) . . . and 2 American ones: drama in *A Farewell to Arms* (directed more by Selznick than the real director) and now comedy. Donen is so gentle and patient."

Manuel continued to revise "Ball Cancelled," and to connect with American and European filmmakers and actors, from Suzy Parker to Fernando Rey, who became a lifetime friend. Unswerving from his goal to see the rest of Europe before crossing the Atlantic again, he planned an itinerary that included Munich, Vienna, Berlin, Copenhagen, and then Stockholm by the end of May. His vertiginous capacity to weave work with travel left his friends reeling, as he recounts in a letter from Berlin:

> Dear Family: I'm exhausted but I don't want to let another moment go by without at least beginning this letter; I don't know where to. Well, I'm very happy because despite all the complications (borders, money changing, the iron curtain!) everything's going smoothly. The last days in Paris were nuts between the filming, visa, and organizing the coming months with a thousand complications . . . An Egyptian friend from the Centro had proposed a translation of subtitles in Cairo for September (three movies from Arabic to be subtitled to Span-

ish) but I couldn't accept because the C Line wouldn't postpone my return trip any longer. I insisted a thousand times until they gave me a final deadline, the end of October, so in November my dear parents and brother will have to put up with me in Bulnes. I can't believe I'll be celebrating New Year's with my family . . . The passage from Marseilles to Alexandria is quite expensive and they're paying me very little (because half of it goes to a friend who's translating the Arabic to English or Italian for me to translate to Spanish), but I'm thrilled about the trip. I'll be able to see Israel on the way back, etc. This Egyptian thing was bothering me for some time—I didn't want to give it up. My Paris friends were speechless, my London friends even more, and my Rome friends went directly into a coma; I'll be passing through Israel, Lebanon, the Greek isles (Rhodes, Delos, etc.); it'll be the crowning glory of these three years. I'm missing you all a lot but I couldn't pass this up.[88]

He insists on hearing what Malé thinks about his going to New York; he hates to be a foreigner, he says, but he fears work will not go well in Argentina, whose movie industry is "half dead." He again pushes Malé and Carlitos to learn English: hadn't they always wanted to see those sumptuous musicals on Broadway? The next letter, from Hamburg, speaks of his fascination with German cities (particularly Cologne and Nuremberg), the mixture of Gothic architecture and war ruins, the liveliness and energy of the people, the boîtes and the café life. The Rhine was a letdown, and so was Austria, or at least his first impression of Vienna, which was "a big disappointment: except for one beautiful baroque neighborhood, the rest lacked personality."

On the contrary Czechoslovakia the people divine, a village, Tabor, and Prague—six wonderful days, a good impression of Communism. But from there to East Germany, an abyss. East German people sad sad, HELL ON EARTH, it upset me so much I got sick to my stomach. Those Russians are the worst. Communism is an interesting idea but the Russians, no!! The Czechs were more autonomous . . . You know what would be wonderful? For the four of us to spend the holidays in Rio!!!!! Kisses, Coco

assistant to the assistant

Sweden, the birthplace of Greta Garbo and Ingrid Bergman, and the setting of Ingmar Bergman's oneiric, evocative masterpiece, *Wild Strawberries*, was where Manuel spent the summer of 1959. His Swedish roommate in London had given him helpful leads in Stockholm, where, during the tourist season, he had no trouble finding work as a dishwasher. He also taught Spanish and Italian in the university's summer sessions. The majestic beauty of Stockholm and the blond Swedes made a big impression on Manuel, and so did the country's sexual permissiveness. He rented a room in a private home and went everywhere on bicycle. He was amazed, he wrote Malé, when a girl renting another room in the same house spent the night with her boyfriend and in the morning came downstairs for breakfast with him and everyone else as if nothing special had occurred. Nino, fluent in Swedish, visited Manuel in the land of the midnight sun, also to take advantage of the fact that dark-haired Latins like himself were exotic and desirable among those tall blonds. The only drawback was the heavy "basic" food, usually grilled fish with sauces, "worse than England if that's possible!"[89]

Almost every morning Manuel biked to the American library to work on "Summer Indoors." The film collection included the screenplay of *All About Eve* and he carefully studied Joseph Mankiewicz's "three or four tricks for lightening and spicing up dialogue." Manuel felt for the first time since he started writing in 1956, that he was beginning to enjoy it:

> When I sit down to write I do it w. pleasure & the hours fly by.
> Before I was afraid of writing & what I loved was to work
> thru the plot in my mind, continuity, etc. Now, happily, I like
> the second phase too. I feel more & more the need to devote
> time to my own work. The marginal jobs become unbear-
> able—like the one at the Folkes Universitat.[90]

In Stockholm he felt depressed less frequently than in Paris, where he only worked at odd jobs and saw many tempting movies and shows, which led to disillusionment. He was glad to leave the Scandinavian north, though.

In Stockholm he had begun the process of obtaining a visa so that he could go to New York, and pressed Malé for information from Cuquín, a cousin of Baldo's who had business connections in New York. Europe was wonderful to visit, he wrote Malé, but he didn't see how he could make any of the cities home—Rome had been the closest to his temperament, though still suffocating and too full of obstacles.

He had no choice, financially, but to return to Argentina toward the end of the year, and he did so urgently because Malé, diagnosed with a cervical malignancy, was about to have a hysterectomy. When he got home he was relieved to find that the operation had been successful and that the cancer had been completely eradicated. Not all was smooth sailing, however.

On the voyage back, Manuel became entangled with a young woman named Vera. With no privacy in their respective bunk cabins, Manuel told me years later, they met secretly on deck at night to have sex in a lifeboat. Vera, a pleasant but plain young schoolteacher returning from her holidays, lived in a poor suburb of Buenos Aires. She was in love, but Manuel was not. Bebé remembers that after they returned home, Manuel made fun of the way Vera dressed, and he told a friend that he felt embarrassed to be seen with her in public. She discovered, soon after they were back in Buenos Aires, that she was pregnant. Manuel panicked, and offered to help arrange for an abortion, causing a minor scandal at home when he asked Baldo to lend him the money. At the same time, of course, this event raised false hopes that Coco was "normal" and that he simply didn't want to marry a girl who was unworthy of him.

Manuel's shipboard dalliances would resurface in nine-year-old Toto's monologue in *Betrayed by Rita Hayworth* (chapter 5), where he fantasizes during naptime about Raúl García, a young "bum" from the wrong side of the tracks, almost a replica of his virile cousin Jorge. Toto invents a movie in which he identifies with the pretty first-grade teacher—who looks to him like Rita Hayworth—in which she becomes a poor chorus girl, bossed around by some gangster; but then a boy in the gang "falls in love with her, he's Raúl García, they decide to escape together . . . , they stow away in a ship . . . and decide to marry secretly before God in the middle of the sea, and . . . they hide in a lifeboat."[91] The trip is so long that she has a baby on board, but in this case the enamored young couple have prayed for the baby, and—a Moses touch—God has left the baby "cozily hidden inside a coiled rope." The couple eventually escape to a paradise island to live "happily ever after."

On the real ship Manuel and Vera hid inside a coiled rope (uncomfortable in Manuel's recollections), but while he could enjoy sex with and feel attracted to women, they did not inspire lasting passion or romantic love. The "real" couple in the daydream are not Toto and the teacher, nor even Raúl and the teacher, but rather Toto and Raúl García living together blissfully in a lumberjack's cabin, overcoming not only the same-sex taboo but the class barrier. Toto is middle-class and Raúl is so poor he's never even been to Buenos Aires, but Toto entertains Raúl at night by telling him about Buenos Aires: "Every night I'd tell him the plot of a different play and then I'd start telling him the stories in the movies and we'd play the game which movie is the best and we'd make a list, and then we'd play which actress is the most beautiful."[92] In the party scene that follows this daydream, Alicita rejects Toto for a bigger boy, and Toto flees in humiliation. But he doesn't want to go home and have to admit defeat, so he hides in Raúl's backyard, where he spies on the young ruffian's aggressive seduction of one of Toto's older female playmates, Paqui.

"He never looked handsomer," Bebé recalls, than when he returned that year (1960) from Rome. He was twenty-eight years old. At the same time, while the rest of the family still held out hopes, Bebé sensed, not only from what Manuel had told her but from his aura, that he was no longer ambivalent about his sexuality. Manuel would later remark that in London he reached the peak of his popularity, which would gradually decline: like Hedy Lamarr, the moment he reached full bloom was when, like the rose, he began to wilt.

He decided that he would come out to those in the family he felt closest to—Malé, cousin Jorge, and Carlos, his teenage brother—but Bebé warned him that his revelation would fall on deaf, if not unsympathetic, ears. In fact, Jorge and Malé pretended they didn't hear what he was saying, and when he tried to explain it to Carlitos, his brother told him point-blank that he didn't want to know. His family did not want to abandon hope that he might marry, and he felt obliged to sustain that fiction. Five years later, when he was working for Air France, he sent a letter to Aunt

Aida from New York, mentioning a pretty French girlfriend (he had roped into) bringing a fine bottle of whiskey to Papa in Buenos Aires. "Finally Coco has a girlfriend," they all thought, but never heard her mentioned again.

As he had feared, Manuel was soon depressed to be back in Buenos Aires (or "Reina"—Queen—as he wrote in his letterheads). It "now seems to me a totally *insignificant* city," he complained to Mario.[93] How backward life was in Buenos Aires. While he enjoyed seeing his old friends like Alfredo Gialdini, he missed talking to Mario and wanted to be with him in Rome or New York. Fortunately Nino had returned from Paris around the same time, and their friendship developed into an affair. Manuel was living with his parents—which is why, according to Nino, Buenos Aires seemed so repressive to Manuel. The second time Nino showed up at the apartment for a rendezvous, Manuel opened the door dressed in a maid's costume, which for Nino was a bit much, and he asked Manuel to change into normal attire. Their relationship soon drifted into an *amitié amoureuse*. Despite his defense of Buenos Aires as a tolerant city, the more closeted Nino would choose to settle permanently in Paris in 1970 and, like Mario, would remain a dependable lifelong friend.

Manuel and Mario continued to fantasize about sharing a bohemian studio in New York, and, while anxious to see more "wonders" in Europe, Manuel planned to find work in New York in hopes that Mario would join him. In one of his infrequent letters, Mario made the following observation:

> Can I tell you something I never said to you until now? I love the way you write your letters; they are so filled with fantasy, wit, a rich erotic Joycean language, and a bubbly spontaneous energy that must come from your mother. I sincerely believe that you could become a very good writer![94]

The only kind of writer Manuel wanted to be, however, was a successful screenwriter.

Promises of work in the unreliable Argentine movie business never materialized, except for occasional subtitle assignments. Through his contacts in

Europe, he was "assistant to the assistant director" on the set of two awful movies, the first an Italo-Argentine production called *America di notte*, filmed on location in the rugged mountains near Lago Argentino in Tierra del Fuego. In Spanish the film (with Egle Martin and Antonio Cifariello, a friend of Mario's from Rome) bore the descriptive title *Casi al fin del mundo*, "Almost the End of the World," or, as Manuel quipped, about the production as well as the location, "almost the asshole of the world."

The other Euro-Argentine fiasco was *Una americana en Buenos Aires* (A Blonde in Buenos Aires), with French leading man Jean-Pierre Aumont and the Hollywood blonde Mamie Van Doren. The movie was so bad that she never included it in her credits. A dizzy blonde offscreen as well, Mamie Van Doren confused Buenos Aires with Rome and asked Manuel if there was "a train or bus we could take to the Coloseum." Manuel was her sidekick during the production and, fleetingly, Aumont's lover. Smitten with Manuel, the suave actor was more smitten with himself, as Manuel quickly surmised, and the affair faded, to Manuel's relief, since he preferred the company of Aumont's charming second wife, Marisa Pavan (sister of actress Pier Angeli).

"The movie finally ended and the director left, not without first promising me work in his next film in Matto Grosso," Manuel joked to Mario, alluding to another "asshole of the world" deal, Matto Grosso being the heart of the Brazilian jungle. Discouraged by these mediocre experiences, Manuel gave in to the advice of Mario and his cousin Bebé, who was now studying psychology, to see a therapist. Little is known about these sessions, which ended abruptly and were to have no sequel. For six months he underwent hypnotherapy. Going against the intellectual trend in Buenos Aires, Manuel would not take psychoanalysis seriously as a solution to personal malaise, and not only because paying to talk to someone you could seduce seemed a rip-off. He resisted the classic Freudian approach to homosexuality as pathology or arrested sexual development. However (as Manuel later claimed), hypnosis shed light on the child in him and on the "demons" he needed to confront, and thus helped liberate him to explore his problems through writing.

Back home in Spanish-speaking Buenos Aires, minding Mario's sensible advice to stop writing in broken English and Havelock's hint to write about modern subjects, Manuel tried first to write about his brother and the younger generation with which he had lost touch during the years in Europe. The problem was, he had lost touch. The Argentina he knew best was the Argentina of his childhood, the Perón years, and so he began his first script set in Argentina, with lots of dialogue, since he felt most comfortable with spoken Spanish. He called it "La tajada," or "The Cut." A slang term for political graft, the title meant "a piece of the action"—something Manuel desperately wanted in the film world. In Argentine sexual jargon it had another connotation: vagina. Manuel later referred to this script as a "shy attempt at social criticism of the Buenos Aires bourgeoisie during the Perón years." He based "The Cut" on gossip about the life of an Argentine starlet, Delia Garcés, who in the forties had married a wealthy young lawyer.[95] Her meteoric rise was not unlike Evita's Cinderella story, and would be easily recognizable to fellow Argentines: poor girl from the provinces gains glory by landing an influential husband.

"The Cut" was his first attempt to depict his reality as an obscure young Argentine from a remote provincial town. While Manuel was not a reader of the populist existential novelist Roberto Arlt (1900–42), this (unpublished) script is strikingly Arltian in that his principal character speaks from within Peronism, and exposes local intellectuals as unsympathetic snobs.[96] His heroine Nélida proudly defines herself at the climax of a bolero she's singing—defying "good breeding"—with the cry "I am *cursi*." This statement about kitsch seems self-conscious on the author's part, voicing an ironic distance as well as empathy with a *cursi* woman. His two previous "Hollywood" scripts read as if he had checked his irony at the cloakroom and merely tried to reproduce soap opera characters. "The Cut" was his first: both Nélida Bilbao (the character based on Delia Garcés) and the potential spectator are aware that Nélida is borrowing song lyrics to spell out who she is.[97] Manuel would soon find a way to show rather than tell his critique, to let his characters speak in their own voice. In *Betrayed by Rita Hayworth*, Esther's 1947 diary would speak from within the Peronist mentality; the character of Nélida in "The Cut" would be a blueprint for the Nélida (Nené) in *Heartbreak Tango*, whose dreams ended in a stagnant housewife's existence. Manuel would explore the pros and cons of Peronism even more explicitly in *The Buenos Aires Affair*.[98]

For the first time he received at least a little professional encouragement: an Argentine film director praised the authenticity of the dialogue, even though he ultimately rejected the script because Manuel "didn't seem to know the subject well." More to the point, Manuel was not a historian but rather a participating spectator (like the young Evita) of history *personified* by Marlene Dietrich playing Catherine the Great or Norma Shearer playing Marie Antoinette. He sought out the intimate melodramas on the margins of history—an apparent weakness later to be recognized as his strength.

Mario had promised him subtitle work in Rome, so he joined Aumont and Marisa on their return voyage to Europe in February 1961. He stopped first in Spain: to finally satisfy his curiosity about his father's side of the family and to try to get "The Cut" produced in Madrid. The ocean voyage—with a delay in Rio for Carnaval ("Just like *Orfeo negro!*" Manuel wrote home)—was a three-week bacchanalia. Passengers from all the classes mingled, boisterous Spaniards and Brazilians, students, actors, directors, sailors, and samba dancers. In March, Manuel disembarked in Galicia, on the northwest coast of Spain, where he was delighted by the earthy charm of Uncle Camilo's distant relatives in the primitive village of Carballino. Here, in the mountainous Orense province, the Cortés family stuffed him with rich food and told him about the legendary beauty of Baldo's grandmother Rosa. Visiting the largest city of the region, Santander, he recognized the family features on every street. But his favorite Spanish city remained Seville, in Andalusia, more exuberant than anything in Italy, with its folklore, churches, orange blossoms, and music: "From the houses they sing *saetas*—flamenco prayers to Christ," he wrote home in April. He urged the family to come visit the lively gallegos in Carballino, especially Bebé, who, recently married to her naval officer, had just sent the news of her separation—her new husband had been unbearable![99] Uncle Camilo could lend her the money for the ticket, Manuel wrote, scolding them all: "Get out of that putrid 'Queen of the Plata' . . . Live it up a little. What are you waiting for, the hearse!?"[100]

In Madrid this time he found the people not only provincial but, in contrast with his relatives in the provinces, unfriendly. Franco's board of censors made sure there was nothing in the movie theaters that he had not already seen in Buenos Aires, and what there was was dubbed in thick Spanish accents. Despite having new acquaintances in the film business (director George Cahan, his lively wife, Alix, and that glamorous duo, Fernando Lamas and Esther Williams), Manuel found backward Madrid even less receptive than Rome or Buenos Aires.

He took the train to Barcelona, where he could stay with easygoing Germán Puig, who had recently moved there with Dora and Adrián, and where a typewriter awaited. Here he relaxed for a couple of weeks, but no longer, he wrote Malé, because the crowded apartment in a "Gaudí castle" was too chaotic for serious work. Adrián remembers his surprise, coming home from school one day, when the door opened and Manuel, who had been typing, appeared draped in Germán's red silk robe (which was much too long) and warmly engaged the eight-year-old boy in a conversation about school and his friends. Germán, with his decadent John Barrymore air—he still has his profile, but hair and mustache are blatantly tinted—remembers what Manuel said to him then, in a tone both ironic and confident, or at least determined: "Since I'm not going to be a great director, I will be a great writer."

the saga of *rita hayworth*: 1962–67

"movie city" once more with feeling

By May 1961 Manuel was back in Rome. The weather was sunny and mild, flowers were everywhere, and Mario had found him a room with a working-class family on Via Amerigo Vespucci in the old Testaccio quarter, down the hill from his own little attic apartment overlooking Piazza Sant'-Anselmo in the elegant Aventino. The Testaccio was picturesque but Manuel's room was drab and tiny; he embellished its charm in a letter home: "a beautiful place with lots of light, like Ferzetti's apartment in Antonioni's *L'Avventura*, overlooking the Tiber; being near water always makes me especially happy, and I've already begun to swim—there are floating pools nearby—but not much because I have lots of work."[1] The only true part was that the Testaccio bordered the Tiber and there were municipal pools along the river. For health as much as for pleasure—"boring" Esther Williams was his model—Manuel always preferred to live near a pool, if not a natural body of water, where he could swim regularly. Across the bridge in the Trastevere, picturesque with its old narrow streets and intimate *tavolas*, lived "Anita Ekberg with Franco Silva—inseparable . . . Sometimes she looked good, other times like a scarecrow—with her body sticking out all over the place." In this latest bulletin to Malé, Manuel added the "glamour touch" that he was

> going to the same hairdresser as Mastroianni! He costs a fortune, but he massages my hair with Pantene, and he taught me to do it myself. The point is, it keeps my hair from falling out quite a lot—it was getting so that every time I'd comb my hair it came out in bushels—so I go every other week.[2]

He and Mario were very busy translating scripts together, at least one a week; he was back to giving Spanish lessons to Margherita Muzi twice a week; and he had wangled a modest scholarship extension by signing up for an art history course at the Dante Institute.

"This time I'm seeing Rome through rose-colored glasses," he wrote to Malé, adding in capital letters that he was VERY HAPPY, because there was now plenty of work and also many "promises" of Italo-Argentine co-productions on the horizon through his widening circle of film acquaintances: "Even if nothing comes of it, one always has to try and feed one's hopes."[3] He would return to Buenos Aires in the new year only if the Argentine director Martínez Suárez, who had liked some of the dialogue in his third script, "The Cut," showed real interest.

The VERY HAPPY was also a signal that Romance was in the air. "In those years the Eternal City was brimming with lustful adventures everywhere and for everyone," Mario reminisces. "All of us were very young, very poor, but very vital and joyful, innocent in a way, not like the jaded youth of later generations." In a neighborhood café on Via Sant'Alessio, Manuel often ran into Bruno, a good-looking young butcher, and made a date for love in the afternoon. Summertime—as in the eponymous movie about spinster Katharine Hepburn kicking up her heels with Latin lover Rossano Brazzi in amorous Venice—meant café life, furtive love on steamy Roman nights, and excursions to Ostia, Rome's Coney Island, where Mario settled a few years later. Another heartthrob which began during his last year in Rome was an American, Peter.

Strolling around chic Aventino together and inspired by Antonioni's brooding frames, Mario and Manuel took many photographs of each other. From a brief tour with a student group to Warsaw and Moscow, where Manuel got a glimpse of life behind the Iron Curtain, he had brought back a Leica for Mario. Mario took most of the pictures and Manuel posed, often in profile, displaying his noble Roman features, leaning dreamily against doorways like Jeanne Moreau, or, with the entranced expression of a creature from outer space, making fun of *cursi* sci-fi acting. The backdrop was a park with the somber aura of an ancient cemetery, as Mario recalls:

> One day I suggested we go to a hidden part of the park I had
> just discovered, a damp, mildewed place with overgrown ivy
> winding around the ruins of old statues. But a fashion pho-

tographer had beat us to the spot, snapping shots of Sandra
Dee just in Rome making *Come September*![4]

A moody photo from these sessions of the handsome young author-to-be
would appear in the first Dutton edition of *Betrayed by Rita Hayworth*.
Against a palatial wrought-iron gate to the park, Manuel gazes with dark
intensity at the camera's eye.

In the fall of 1961, Manuel was again taking long bus rides out to
Cinecittà, where "the girls in the acting class arrive with false eyelashes and
a pound of mascara on each eye at 9 in the morning!" In the directing course
there were only eleven students and they were able to form a close-
knit group, "even the five Italian students who were very nice and well-
educated." The foreigners were "a Bolivian I knew from Architecture in
B.A., an Egyptian, a Frenchman, a Greek girl . . . and a Brazilian . . . and
two chicks studying to be 'script girls'—one sits behind me and is always
tempting."[5] Buoyed by the playful camaraderie and classroom flirting, he
felt more engaged by the courses at the Centro this time around. Alessandro
Blassetti, "a clown but very nice," taught them that a director has to loosen
up, as if he were one of the actors. To do this, the students practiced imitating the gestures of persons they knew from real life. In another exercise, he
got to direct for the first time, selecting a scene between two actors from the
latest Visconti film—a love scene played by exquisite Alida Valli in *Senso*
(*The Wanton Contessa*). In the screenwriting course the instructor "taught us
to tell a plot first in half an hour, then to make it even shorter," an excellent
exercise for learning the art of narrative.[6]

By December it was "freezing cold" in Rome and a big snowstorm had
paralyzed the trains, which made it too bothersome to go to Cremona for
Christmas. A holiday with his Italian family would be sweet but not worth
fighting crowds and delays for; Manuel would spend Christmas Eve with
Mario and the Muzis. Christmas Day he lunched at the ritzy Carlton with
an "Argentine girl, a painter, quite nice"—the sort of news which, back
home, raised false hopes about "Miss Right"—and on his birthday he
planned to see "*Judgment at Nuremberg* (something light!) with Dietrich,
Lancaster, Tracy, and Judy Garland!" Fellini was filming *8½* with Mastroianni, and Dino Risi was filming *Il Sorpasso* (*The Easy Life*) with Vittorio
Gassman and Jean-Louis Trintignant, but the truth was, Manuel and Mario
were getting nowhere in Hollywood on the Tiber. Annoyed by the popular-

ity of the latest star, Sophia Loren, Manuel complained to Malé that he never liked Rome's "spiritual climate." Everyone was in love with Loren, so earthy and authentic, but she didn't fool Manuel: "So phony!" he exclaimed indignantly.[7] How upsetting to see De Sica, master of drawing room comedies and sex farces, devoting his talent to those "awful Ponti-Loren productions"; rumor had it that to keep her happy, "Ponti was paying for all the prizes Sophia won in Italy, and even in Cannes."[8]

Manuel was jobless, and almost thirty—and, as he later declared, "By thirty, a woman had to have her life together!" Neither "happily married" nor settled in his career, he was still trying to write scripts for the thirties in 1962; he liked writing them but hated the finished product. And yet he persisted, almost desperately, plugging away at another screenplay:

> I try to fight depression by working . . . I've gotten very in-
> volved in the first (positive) part, in which the protagonists be-
> gin to understand each other, but now I'm into his destruction
> (at her hands) and it makes me feel bad. Trying to concentrate
> is a big strain; every afternoon I try for more than an hour to
> concentrate, to then write barely two or three hours . . . I
> think the plot is starting to shape up: it's about a guy who's
> had a nervous breakdown which he's barely survived, and he
> begins to adapt to the world around him. He's at the point
> when it turns out he has to change both job and city. Despite
> everything, he manages to stay sane and strong but that
> doesn't last long. He meets a fascinating woman who's a
> wreck, and partly out of pity as well as attraction, he opens up
> to her and lets her see his weaknesses, to establish real com-
> munication with her (she's a mess) by also showing that he too
> is a mess, to make her more comfortable. At first she reacts
> well, but when she realizes he doesn't consider her as some-
> thing definitive in his life, she begins to undermine his self-
> confidence, his strength; she does it unconsciously, like a form
> of spite since she can't have him, and destroys him. The
> tremendous thing is that sometime after he's disappeared off
> the face of the map, his efforts to give her support have suc-
> ceeded and she survives, that's the story.[9]

He was trying to deal with painful material—emotional turmoil, self-destructive relationships—through writing. When he reread the script a few weeks later, he wasn't satisfied; it was "different from what I intended."[10] The woman appears to be a wreck, but survives; the man manages to survive on his own, but when he attempts to relate to her, it means sacrificing himself. A decade later, in *The Buenos Aires Affair*, he succeeded in developing this theme about a problematic couple: Gladys, a hopeless neurotic, manages to survive; Leo succumbs to psychosis and destroys himself in a car crash.

Manuel was more determined than ever to make a fresh start in New York—but he needed a green card, hence assured employment. He also needed to return first to Buenos Aires to resolve the matter of a visa. An acquaintance of Mario's at Alitalia was trying to get him a ticket-counter job in Rome to give him a steady income and also facilitate his travels, but, again, there were more such opportunities in New York. Nestor Almendros knew the city well (he had studied film briefly at City College before his stint at the Centro), and, after returning to New York in 1959, he wrote Manuel encouraging letters about the certainty of finding a job there to support his writing. Bravely facing the great unknown, Manuel hoped he could convince Mario to come along. But Mario was "not ready" yet; if anything, he yearned to return to Argentina, which he also postponed indefinitely. Involved in making documentaries, he still felt all roads led to and from Rome and remained enthralled, unlike Manuel, with the "magical moment" in Italian cinema: *La Dolce Vita*, *Il Gattopardo*, *L'Avventura*.

When funds from the Dante Institute were delayed, Manuel feared someone was intercepting his letters, that they somehow found out he wanted the money to get to the United States. To the school secretary he had written the white lie that he was an "honorary" assistant, doing documentary films on art (painting, sculpture, architecture) as a follow-up of the art history course he had taken at the Dante Institute in Rome. A month later (he injects ironic levity by acknowledging in his heading "Ash Wednesday"), he was still worrying about money in a letter to Malé, who was urging him to come home: "I went to the most important dermatological clinic in Rome for my hair, and they massaged my scalp with a special shampoo and gave me two types of pills for my nerves. The doctor found me very nervous, and the blame is mostly the trip to Buenos Aires."[11] Upon their insistence, he accepted a loan from Baldo and Malé to cover his travel and visa expenses.

Amid this turbulence, Mario helped him explore "the anecdotal possibilities of my own life," but Manuel was still groping, almost halfheartedly. His talks with Mario, as well as his brief therapy in Buenos Aires in 1960, had helped him recognize a frustrating pattern that stemmed from childhood: he would feel enthusiastic while writing his imitations of old Hollywood movies only to have the good feeling vanish "once I had finished them." In the first months of 1962, he had a new idea for a screenplay:

> I had always been submerged in the movies, but at age twenty-three, when the movies stopped being so good, the dream faded. What was left that was sacred? Memories of childhood films. I took refuge there . . . I was fascinated by the possibility of re-creating moments of being a child cocooned in his cinema seat, and how awakening from that brought no pleasure. The dream itself did, but not the waking.[12]

Manuel first mentioned this new project to Malé that February, calling it "the work on Villegas, but don't tell anybody, especially Papa and El Gordo [his father's nephew]. It has nothing to do with the family but I don't want people to worry." He didn't want to let the cat out of the bag yet.

mario, mentor

When Manuel had returned to Rome from Buenos Aires in the spring of 1961 he was surprised, and a little jealous, to find Mario feverishly immersed in writing. "I'd spend an entire day," Mario recalls,

> filling pages with "automatic writing," going from one idea to another in a disorderly fashion, impelled by the urgency to transport to paper the torrent, with the intention of eventually

developing the ideas further. This second stage, for mysterious neurotic reasons (or neurotic mysterious reasons) was put off indefinitely. But I gradually filled a suitcase with almost always fragmentary texts, strange unfinished stories similar to dreams, almost always dealing with my childhood in a now faraway Buenos Aires, about my women neighbors, school, movies . . . and the neighborhood, particularly the neighborhood. I'd tell Manuel about these things, and he seemed fascinated, and doubtless contaminated by that creative frenzy.[13]

Manuel praised four stories (three in Spanish, one in Italian) Mario wrote over the next two years, the first being "The Blood Rose," about a boy in Buenos Aires who "lives" with so much intensity the stories from the afternoon radio soap opera that he ends up intruding on and conversing with the characters. In "The Wedding of the Painted Doll," a boy falls in love with a doll, but she marries a soldier-doll and abandons him. He finds consolation by going to the movies with a neighborhood girl, but one evening the Vampire Man comes down from the screen and kidnaps the girl. The boy "enters" the movie to save her but he can't, and neither can he return from the fiction of the movie to the real world.

While Mario's first two stories combined fantasy life and popular culture in ways that may have stimulated Manuel, the title of the third story (inspired by the recent death of Clark Gable), "Dialogue with Jean Harlow in Her Winter Garden," could have planted the seed of Manuel's risky decision to use Rita Hayworth in the title of his first book. In this story Mario, who loved Jean Harlow in *Red Dust* with Clark Gable, brings the legendary blonde back to life, chatting with a "freak" in a mysterious mansion where the corpse of Gable lies in one of the rooms. What this may have shown Manuel is how the movies could be a valid literary theme, how screen stars could be fictional characters. Cinephilia, as Nestor Almendros later observed, was a new subject in literature: "There had been movies about moviemakers, but not about the spectator."[14] The fourth story Manuel urged Mario to publish was written in Italian, "Le Orme"—called in English "Footsteps on the Moon," in a film version Mario tried to peddle to Agnès Varda and Alain Resnais upon Manuel's insistence—in which the main character obsessively remembers a movie he has seen about a landing on the moon. The character's real life and the movie become one, a film within a film, condemning him to quixotic madness. When Mario first read the manuscript of *Kiss of the Spider Woman*, he thought it might have been inspired by his story, which was finally made into an art film in Italy in 1975, starring Klaus Kinski and the Brazilian Florinda Balkan.

Mario will never forget the summer night of 1962 when Manuel first mentioned his own fiction writing: it was August 5 and the two friends had just found out that Marilyn Monroe had taken her life.

> One night we went out to eat at our usual *tavola* in Trastevere. It was August 5, 1962. A fellow sat down at the table next to ours with the latest newspaper and we saw the headline that announced the suicide of Marilyn Monroe. The news upset us so much that I'm not sure we were able to finish dinner. We were so identified with the mythical figures of the screen that a star's "mortality" affected us profoundly, as had happened in my childhood with Jean Harlow (1937) and in his with Carole Lombard (1942). We walked around the Trastevere for a while discussing the tragedy. Suddenly Manuel told me he was writing something he wasn't sure yet what it was. It had started as a screenplay but was developing into something else, some *Spoon River* type monologues (by some key characters from his childhood) which he was dealing with in a literary way but which could serve as the basis for a screenplay.[15]

Manuel had not yet realized that this was not a screenplay:

> In order to put some distance between me and the autobiographical stuff, I planned to write a description (for my exclusive use) of each leading character. Learning from past mistakes. I wrote in Spanish, but I didn't know how to do the description. One day in March I was roughing out a scene in the script in which the offscreen voice of my aunt was introducing the action in the laundry room of a typical Argentine house. Suddenly her voice, in the first person, came out quite clearly, talking about my cousin's triumphs with girls.

Tough yet vulnerable Jorge had become Manuel's first character:

> I began to write a kind of voice-over. I could remember ex-
> actly what she had been saying twenty years before, and I took
> note of it . . . Though her voice was supposed to take up at
> most three lines of dialogue, she went on without stopping for
> almost thirty pages. There was no way I could shut her up.
> Everything she said was banal, but I couldn't cut a lot because
> it seemed to me that the sum of the banalities lent a special
> meaning to what she was saying . . . It was my desire for more
> narrative space . . . I could play with it all I wanted . . . By the
> second day it was clearly a novel. I had stories that needed
> more space than the two hours a movie gives you. I needed to
> explain my childhood and why I was in Rome, thirty years
> old, without a career, without money and discovering that the
> vocation of my life—movies—had been a mistake.[16]

He first called these pages "Birds in the Head," a self-mocking title connoting "bats in the belfry."[17] To maintain distance from this explosive material he could not use his own voice, the voice that still embarrassed him in
public, but he felt he could handle dialogue or, as he said, "voice-over." He
discovered fiction writing by pure accident, as a game or an expediency, as if
the "voices," maternal Aunt Carmen's gossip, helped him revive his own
feelings toward the town where, like his mother, he had felt like an outsider.
Happily, and not so innocently, both his hunch and his "insecurity" coincided with modernist poetics: Joycean stream-of-consciousness gave the unconscious a voice; the postwar French *nouveau roman* (Nathalie Sarraute,
Robbe-Grillet) confirmed conversely—with self-conscious objectivity—that
the omniscient narrator was dead.

Manuel began by sketching each character's angle. These sketches for a
screenplay became portraits in a "gallery of voices," where diverse narrators
tell the same story that can never be the whole truth, as in Akira Kurosawa's
1950 film masterpiece *Rashomon*, an open-ended detective story, an ambiguous tale of desire and treachery.[18] With so many voices it would be impossible to reconstruct a linear, rational, sense-making story; with so many voices
he could oblige his reader to connect with the complexities of the human
heart.

He accumulated features and details as before Coco had pasted together images of actresses, but now with another purpose:

> Ninety percent of the novel is real. Sometimes for the sake of economy two characters from films [that Toto relives or reworks into fantasies in his monologues] became one; but it was about me, and the people close to me. The characters were the family that didn't have time for me as a child, as well as the people who had shared something with me in that era, relatives, neighbors, people who had time to listen to me. I wanted them to give me their secrets, their intimacy. Letting them talk or write a letter, they would reveal things to me.[19]

Exploring childhood memories, Manuel was covering ground similar to Mario's. But while Mario had been trying to mold this material into *fantastic literature*, following Argentine masters like Borges and Cortázar, Manuel had stumbled upon a refreshing *new realism* that Mario could only admire. He was amazed when a few days after the "Marilyn" night Manuel

> came to see me at the apartment I shared with Bazzoni in Monteverde Vecchio . . . It was very hot and since it was siesta time I lay down on my bed, and he was resting on Bazzoni's (who wasn't there). We were chatting and suddenly he told me he had brought the writing he was doing and he wanted to read it to me. It was Toto's monologue: I couldn't believe my ears: it was original, authentic, suggestive, beautiful. "Did you really write this?" He smiled like a mischievous little boy. Manuel was adorable but, I had thought, too frivolous and superficial for the role of a serious writer.[20]

After that, Manuel showed up every afternoon: he read out loud and Mario applauded his ingenious spontaneity while helping him style the raw material; sometimes they spent entire evenings lying on the twin beds in Mario's pied-à-terre amid the noises and aromas of the piazza.

Mario and Manuel referred to Mario's writing as *cuento criada* (housemaid story) and Manuel's as *novela sirvienta* (maidservant novel). They played down their creative work as humble housecleaning—the author as

charwoman—but in Manuel's grammatical scheme, where the dominant
gender was feminine, these labels were not dismissive. Through Manuel's
looking glass, "to be *augmented*" to female was a compliment, not an insult.
On the margins of his first draft, he made notes to himself in "kitchen sink"
terms, using cooking metaphors such as *mechar* (to chop up or stuff a piece
of meat)—"*mechar* 'Clara' with constant returns to present"—as a reminder
to insert and orchestrate associative strands in a narrative collage. He scribbled also, in the margins of his first draft, "dejar descansar composición,"
that is, let the manuscript cool off—as if he were baking a pie. Mario, who
never succeeded as a writer, was the midwife of Manuel's literary career,
whose nurturing collaboration helped Coco to become Manuel Puig.[21]
Manuel later recapped this breakthrough period of his life:

> I began writing narrative at age twenty-nine. During the pre-
> vious years I tried not to see reality, which impoverished me
> in the same way as when one doesn't dream. In our dreams
> we confront and question reality. I felt the need to tell stories
> to understand myself . . . My characters have a hard time ac-
> cepting reality; at some moment they manage to escape, but
> the dialogue between dream and reality keeps them alive. The
> solution: accept both dimensions. Without madness, nothing
> changes. For any change, social, political, etc., you have to be
> in that apparently useless territory. Total acceptance of reality
> is tantamount to paralysis.[22]

That "apparently useless territory" was the battleground of creation. He had
been sleepwalking for years, but now, through writing, he felt he was awakening, or keeping both territories alive.

Manuel was insecure about how to write descriptive narrative in "packaged" literary Spanish without making mistakes or, again, sounding *cursi*.
As if by default, he found a way to avert the judgmental "Argentine eye" by
copying the tone of others, by allowing real people, including himself, to
speak or write in their own voices. Third person was "dangerous"—because
the point was to explain without explaining—and would be "suspicious—or
at least old-fashioned." He could now use those wonderful clichés uttered
by Malé or Carmen with impunity.

He began writing fiction on the defensive, as it were. The original draft of *Betrayed by Rita Hayworth* contained many allusions to high culture which he gradually removed like scaffolding, leaving what really mattered to his characters: the movies. Defying the elitism of his fellow Argentines, he would have to assert his marginality, affirm his heartfelt populism, promote his nonliterariness as a positive new value.

Meanwhile, in October 1962, a few days before he left Italy for Buenos Aires, Manuel met in the Trastevere one of the handsomest men he would ever know, a cabinetmaker. This sturdy young man was, in Manuel's eyes, even more gorgeous than the young Sean Connery. They went on an "outing" in the nearby hills one evening, and Manuel returned to Mario the next day in a state of bliss. The romance lasted only three more nights; when he left Rome for Buenos Aires, he was, understandably, reluctant. "I can't believe I'm leaving," he says in a letter to Malé, merely hinting: "I'm going to miss Rome because this time I had gotten into the swing of things." When he revisited Rome a year later, Manuel found his way back to the furniture shop in the Trastevere, but the fellow was nowhere to be found; he asked all around the neighborhood, but had no luck. On trips to Rome over the next several years he searched in vain, always stopping to peek into any furniture shop he ran across. Total frustration. According to Mario, Manuel always remembered the mythical cabinetmaker as the most sensational lover he had ever encountered.

from "queen" to queens

In the fall of 1962, the Puigs bought a large apartment in a new building a block away from Bulnes, on the corner of Charcas and Vidt; Baldo could now give the smaller Bulnes apartment to his two sons. Preparing hastily for his ocean voyage at the end of October 1962—at the eleventh hour, in Naples, he picked up, with great relief, his U.S. entry visa—Manuel made time to buy "rags" for Malé, but pleaded with the family to put off their move from Bulnes to Charcas until he got a chance to recover from the exhaustion of the trip. Despite the double fatigue of travel and arriving in the

midst of a household move, not to mention national crises, he was glad to be
back home. After the Puigs were settled on Charcas Street, in late November, he wrote Mario: "The Queen is supreme, people are *alive, oh so alive*,
and much sharper, maybe all the crises have given them a larger sense of reality."[23] Frondizi's foundering government, supported by the Radical Party,
had devalued the peso and failed to appease the Peronists, who had just won
the largest share of seats in Congress. Manuel was returning on the eve of a
military coup that ousted Frondizi and placed another Radical, Arturo Illia,
at the head of a newly formed civilian government; disruptive workers'
strikes and a wildly fluctuating peso held the country in abeyance. And yet
everyday life in the Queen of the Plata was infused with the modes and
sounds of the swinging sixties.

The Cuban revolution had put Latin America in the international limelight; the publishing boom of Latin American literature, spearheaded by
prolific bard Pablo Neruda in Chile, Octavio Paz and Carlos Fuentes in
Mexico, and Jorge Luis Borges, Ernesto Sábato, and Julio Cortázar in Argentina, was on the rise. Buenos Aires, the Berlin of South America in the
Peronist years, was still also its Paris and Athens, teeming with bookstores
and café intellectuals. Art galleries, publishers, and periodicals seemed to
multiply. *Primera Plana* (Front Page), a trendy new magazine, along with
the more widely read *Panorama*, tracked the latest in art, literature, and politics; *Sur* (South), the cosmopolitan avant-garde literary journal founded by
Victoria Ocampo and Borges in the early thirties, also flourished. Reviews
and interviews gave voice and shape to new literature in these magazines,
which would have healthy competition from *Casa de las Américas* in Cuba to
Imagen in Venezuela, and especially from *Mundo Nuevo* in Paris.

Radical social and cultural change was in the air, fomented by the Di
Tella Institute in Buenos Aires, founded in 1958 by two brothers, economist
Guido Di Tella and sociologist Torcuato Di Tella, wealthy entrepreneurs
who set out to promote artistic, intellectual, and technological innovation.
Located in the heart of the city of fashionable Florida Street, the institute's
Galería del Este dominated the most exclusive shopping stretch, the 900
block that opened onto stately Plaza San Martín, and became a vortex of
mod fashion and pop art. Vernissages—art openings, book signings, fashion
shows put on by chic clothing stores—and "happenings" staged by experimental performance groups all thrilled young hipsters and ruffled the feath-

ers of Argentinc decorum, casting a flashy veneer over the more serious endeavors of poets, novelists, visual artists, and filmmakers.

Manuel's initial enthusiasm to be home in time for the holidays subsided
by the new year, however: "Here sensitive, intelligent people, not directly
linked to literature, have liked my manuscript," Manuel wrote Mario, alluding to friends like Alfredo Gialdini. "On the other hand, three publishing
types, one horrified, another indifferent, the other totally uninterested:
SOBs!" These rejections cemented Manuel's indignation against the "resentful, envious Argentine pseudo-intellectuals," especially after he met, accompanied by loyal Alfredo, with a local critic to whom he had sent the
manuscript of his still unfinished novel. As the three of them sat in a café on
Florida Street, the fellow pronounced: "Your writing is very interesting, as a
preliterary experiment."[24] For years to come this blunt remark would stick
in Manuel's memory as the classic *porteño* response to his first manuscript.
Alfredo claims that on the bus ride home he was even more disheartened
than Manuel, who earlier that week had booked a flight to New York.

On February 6, 1963, Manuel boarded a night plane, with a stop the next
morning in Miami, where he changed planes and flew directly to Idlewild
Airport: as the aircraft landed he took in, for the first time in three dimensions, the fabulous New York skyline. The airport bus deposited him and
his huge suitcase in the heart of midtown, from where he walked, suitcase in
hand, a few long blocks to his destination: the 42nd Street YMCA.

A step away from Broadway's theaters and sleazy Eighth Avenue with
its hustlers, this beehive for transient men had fairly clean cheap rooms and
served his needs from A to Z, as he told Mario in his first, exuberant letter
from New York:

> Salla [Sally] writes to you from the land where she went to
> look for a husband. Will she find him? For the moment I see
> only legions of fags, blacks, and Central Americans who all
> leave me in a state of terror. Where to begin? This city is *fia-
> beschissima* [fablelustissimo], you would go nuts, the people
> seem straight out of Dickens. Those exaggerated toughs from
> the Damon Runyon movies are no exaggeration. And the
> beauty and poetry of the skyscrapers . . .[25]

Mario knew that terror also meant excitement, as Molina in *Kiss of the Spider Woman* would explain to scandalized Valentín: "The thrill is that when a man embraces you, you're a little bit afraid."[26] It amazed Manuel to see so many Latins in Manhattan, though at the same time he expressed Argentine chagrin at the negative image they projected: "Those eccentric people seem to like dirt," and the Puerto Ricans "don't learn English and so it takes them years to assimilate!"[27] Equally jolting were the contrasts between one street and the next, or between neighborhoods, from the depressing slums of Harlem to the sumptuous elegance of Sutton Place.

But during his first months in the city in 1963, New York electrified all his senses with its sights, sounds, and smells, and the most everyday experience was pure magic. One could eat a whole steak dinner with baked potato and a large Coke for only $1.25 at Tad's Steak in midtown—a self-service cafeteria where you didn't have to pay a tip! He drew the line at Horn & Hardart's Automat, however: "I went twice to the ones you put the money in. It comes out a little cheaper, but it's a big pain (getting your change, handling twenty things at the same time), they're always filled with people, and I got depressed—I don't go anymore." At the YMCA he set up a daily routine to feel more at home: "At night I almost always go to bed early because I'm up at 8, bathe and shave, and until 5 do the round of agencies looking for movie work."

He had no close friends or family in New York—Nestor Almendros was back in Europe—and there were many lonely moments that first cold winter. He sent frequent aerograms to Argentina as well as to Italy, Spain (the gallegos in Carballino), London, and even Stockholm, though he confided hardships to only a few intimates, wary in particular of certain acquaintances in Argentina who were prone to rivalry and gossip. March 3 was the first day the temperature rose above freezing, he wrote Malé, explaining how people have to keep undressing and putting things back on because indoors it's hot while outside it's cold. His solution was to wear not heavy sweaters but rather layers: his daily winter uniform in the land of central heating was a green velveteen jacket, green overcoat, and thin long-sleeved brown sweater.

Although he was lavish when it came to dressing Malé, Manuel would always spend minimal time and expense on his own appearance, tending toward almost unattractive colors. Over the years this blind spot for his own wardrobe struck some of his sophisticated friends as odd, considering his

aesthetic sensibility. It was almost as if he were trying discreetly to camou-
flage his effeminacy, or to emulate some Argentine standard of taste which
at the same time he considered ridiculous.

Because the YMCA was cheap and conveniently located for the two
temp jobs he had taken in midtown—translating in the afternoons at a New
York film lab and waiting on tables at night at an Italian restaurant—he was
"in no hurry to find an apartment." Midtown was also convenient because
he was actively seeking employment: subtitle jobs were unreliable; two
weeks or even a month could go by without an assignment. While the subway was "amazingly" fast, it was. tedious if you had to change to another
train; the noise was "deafening" and the "shaking rattles my skull!" he
wrote, apologizing for his handwriting. He often scribbled his letters in
transit, determined not to waste a minute.

New Yorkers seemed friendlier and more relaxed than Romans and
Parisians, and also more generous, as people had been in London. Through
his father's cousin Cuquín, who had business contacts in New York, he connected with a young Cuban architect who needed to share his rent with a
roommate. The Cuban's apartment was a mere subway ride away from
downtown, on upper Riverside Drive in Harlem: "The boy is ideal, a calm
nature, hates noise, orderly, respectful, in a word, a saint! . . . He even lent
me a typewriter to work on the maidservant novel." In March, Manuel
wrote Malé that he had finally bought his own typewriter, a portable
Olivetti. He had only one slight "aesthetic" objection to his otherwise peer-
less roommate, who was also an aspiring artist:

> He does bland abstract paintings . . . I told him I liked two of
> them (the least awful, I didn't know what to say) so now
> they're hanging in my room and I have to put up with them!!
> Next time I'll keep my mouth shut. But this is an incredibly
> good deal, better than London, with great heating all the
> time.

The view of the New Jersey Palisades from his room on Riverside Drive
was "majestic . . . a rocky cliff, with roads and trees, reminds me of the place
in Stockholm, a lake where I used to go swimming." He visited the Cloisters
in Fort Tryon Park and, except for the splendid Unicorn tapestries, dis-

missed this branch of the Metropolitan Museum as "a *cursi*, artificial pastiche by one of those crazy Rockefellers." He was happy with his surroundings, bubbling with news, and as winter thawed he rushed to see every play, musical, movie, whether good, bad, or indifferent.

"This morning going down to that park [Riverside]," he wrote Malé that he felt pleased, as he took his walk, to have "resolved the living problem" so perfectly:

> In the fridge I have a big bottle of grapefruit juice, a lifetime supply! And I make myself tea—the tea season seems to be back, because it's cold, I guess. I still haven't bought groceries, no time to shop; I'm still eating out. The first weeks it seemed I was losing weight because of all the goings-on but now I've gained again; I have to loosen my belt in the movies, and also when I sit down to eat. That's my sign, always. Last night I invited Cuquín's friend and my roommate to the theater because I again got three free orchestra tickets (they're usually eight dollars each, cheap, no?) through that contact in Rome. We saw *Mother Courage* with Anne Bancroft, just opened; she's a new superstar in the theater (*Two for the Seesaw* and *The Miracle Worker*) but she's not so good in this, and the play is cut so drastically (the original is five hours long) that it has no flavor.[28]

Twenty-five years later Anne Bancroft would perform the role of a manipulative invalid in a play written by Manuel, *Mystery of the Rose Bouquet*.

The modest uptown neighborhood provided unexpected perks: art deco movie palaces where the "projection is impeccable." These grand old theaters from the thirties showed double bills for only 75 cents to $1.25, compared with $1.50 to two dollars downtown ("big, boring" movies like *Ben-Hur* cost $3), and new releases opened "the same time as downtown!" This meant not having to take the subway again every night; meanwhile he arranged his weekly fix of Broadway plays and musicals by attending Wednesday matinees when the orchestra tickets cost only four to five dollars.

A highpoint at an uptown movie palace was Joan Crawford on a promotional tour of her latest horror flick. Coming home one evening late in March, he noticed a billboard on the subway announcing "Tonight Joan Crawford in person at 10:30":

> And I sat in the first row! DIVINE, prettier than in the movies, without that hardness, very friendly, she's a redhead now, with a fabulous profile. The upper arms are the weak point—loose flesh hanging like an old lady of seventy—she must be very old—the audience asked about her boyfriends and she named three: John Barrymore (*Grand Hotel*), Franchot Tone (the best companion), and Clark Gable, "who was and always will be the King," said with great emotion and damp eyes; one can see she's quite a show-off.[29]

Chancing upon a diva on the street was even more momentous: "I saw Ava! [Gardner] . . . Quite young looking . . . Her hairstyle was off but a beautiful complexion and perfect legs." Manuel's remarks were frequently unflattering: Joanne Woodward, sighted entering a theater, looked offensively "drab" considering "all the money she earns"; Carroll Baker looked "rather ugly." Whether savoring star quality or scanning their defects, Manuel was always on the alert, a meticulous star-gazer.

He quickly settled into a routine:

> My schedule is UNSHAKABLE: I get up late, around 9:30— my roommate leaves at 8:30, I never hear him—half asleep I shave, bathe, have my tea, and sit down to work from 11 to 2; I give my best and freshest hours to my work; then I go out to lunch and get to the laboratory by 4 (before the woman leaves who gives me the subtitle work) and I stay there working till 8 or 9 till I drop, and then I sometimes stay downtown to see theater or whatever, or come back to the apartment directly.[30]

This routine was about to suffer minor alterations. Through Mario's Irish-American friend Mary Haberdeen (Mario was then renting a room in Mary's splendid apartment near the Piazza Navona), who ran a translation agency in Rome, Manuel had contacts in the New York offices of both Alitalia and Air France. He took a qualifying exam—he knew the four languages required—and while waiting for the verdict, considered a part-time receptionist job at Alitalia's Fifth Avenue office. But when he passed with flying colors, he decided on the full-time Air France job as a ticket clerk at Idlewild—soon to be John F. Kennedy International. Because Manuel was a charming, young, good-looking polyglot—a "classy guy," as an airport co-worker described him—Air France shuttled him between several assignments as interpreter: at customs, at Lost and Found, and principally at the VIP counter.[31] The job was "perfect because it didn't require concentration" and he got to spend most of the day among lively European travelers, emigrating Latinos, and glamorous celebrities:

> When I return home to *my* work I've already seen so many people all day long . . . that I'm totally pleased to submerge myself in the silence of the beautiful Hudson. I'm very happy because I've made an important step in my writing: as I return to the first chapters to correct, I see very clearly what needs to be changed. There's nothing better than leaving something for a few months to let it settle, then you can see it with complete objectivity. There's still a lot left to do; the last three [chapters] aren't yet written.[32]

Besides Malé and Mario, Manuel was corresponding regularly with Nestor Almendros while writing *Betrayed by Rita Hayworth*. Nestor was now residing in Paris, in a tiny apartment on rue Roussellet on the Left Bank. Until the spring of 1963, both friends had feared their careers were hopeless, Nestor thinking he'd end up a Spanish teacher and Manuel, an airline ticket clerk. Around that time, when Nestor received his first real career break working with Barbet Schroeder and Eric Rohmer on *Paris Vu Par* (1964), he also glimpsed a new light in Manuel's letters. The budding novelist was getting up at six every morning, writing one hour a day before going to work, and "the novel was growing."[33] Despite employee blues at the time, years later Manuel remembered 1963–65 as the happiest period of his life, along with 1940–43, when he was best pupil at school and saw a great movie every day. Aside from the thrills of "Gotham" (Manuel's euphemism for the 42nd Street Y), he was enjoying his daily creative progress and "there were no worries about publishers, reviews and sales."[34]

By May Manuel obtained the green card he had so anxiously awaited and took a temporary sublet in Richmond Hills, Long Island, until he found an inexpensive apartment not far from Idlewild, in Kew Gardens, Queens: 8352 Talbot Street. He was sorry to leave scenic Riverside Drive, but the long daily subway ride with its rattling, or "electroshock!!!," was daunting. The bland blue-collar residential Queens neighborhood with tidy little gardens evoked, Manuel wrote Malé, Greer Garson's *Mrs. Miniver*, a dull Hollywood fable about the impact of the Second World War on ordinary English people.

Manuel's upstairs neighbor, a young Cuban woman named María Barceló (now a retired customs officer living in Miami), remembers her neighbor and co-worker at the airport as a friendly, handsome fellow who casually mentioned his writing as if it were a hobby. She was shocked, years later, to learn that this simple, compassionate friend was a famous writer. María met Manuel in 1965, shortly after beginning her new job as a ticket clerk at Iberia. She was catching the bus from Kew Gardens to the airport; at the bus stop she realized she didn't have her wallet, and it was too late to run home. In a panic she scanned the line of people and noticed a "nice-looking guy with beautiful eyes" in an Air France uniform, who looked Latin or Italian, hence approachable. Manuel said very simply, "Why not?" and paid her fare. On the bus to the airport, Manuel told María, who was also looking for an apartment, that there was one available in his building.

He was beautiful "inside and out," and what really touched María was his love for his mother; she was glad to courier packages for him (Manuel charmed other airline buddies into this useful service as well)—clothes for Malé, whiskey for Baldo—on Iberia flights to Buenos Aires. María and Manuel were like family to each other, often making last-minute dinner dates: Maria usually cooked at her place, though Manuel sometimes cooked "something simple, usually pasta" in his "modest little apartment . . . in good taste." Manuel's place was neat, clean, in brief, austere, with a few plants—not many because there wasn't much light—and María noticed "lots of books."

She feared for her friend's safety, though. A fellow movie fan, María compared Manuel with Ray Milland in *The Lost Weekend*, an alcoholic with a split personality—or at least a double life. (The original script for *The Lost Weekend* was actually about an alcoholic homosexual, but got "scrambled" by the Hays Code censors, who eliminated the homosexual component—alcoholism being infinitely more acceptable.[35]) Her decent, honest, caring friend had a "tidy" apartment and was a sweet, handsome boy at the ticket counter; but then he would disappear on mysterious weekend sprees to Gotham or, worse, to Harlem in search of rough trade.

The main attraction at the Kennedy Air France counter was the frequent transit of glamorous celebrities: Mr. and Mrs. Alfred Hitchcock disembarking in 1964, back from the European premiere of *The Birds*; Brigitte Bardot and Jeanne Moreau on their way from Mexico to Paris, back from filming *¡Viva María!*—"Bardot looked superb, very different from how she looks in movies, very tall, radiant, very friendly and joking, she and Moreau were looking playfully at each other."[36]

These and other sightings were epiphanies, but the most momentous was when he looked up one afternoon at the VIP counter and saw, less than two feet away, the exquisite face of Greta Garbo. Even before he saw her, he heard her, or rather a familiar cavernous contralto voice requesting a ticket to Paris, France. Manuel's seamless impersonation of Garbo was no doubt enhanced by this visitation; Guillermo Cabrera Infante describes how Manuel's imitations forever changed the experience of seeing Garbo in dazzling black and white: she became a mere copy of Manuel's imitation.[37] That afternoon as he watched her turn around and walk away, he was discreetly ecstatic at every oblique move of her long limbs. But the show wasn't over. Minutes later she returned to the counter: "Are you sure this plane is going to Paris, France?" Manuel offered to carry her suitcases, and was further impressed when he heard her speak about herself in the third person: "The woman is tired," she said suddenly, handing him the tip and inspiring a lifelong mannerism of referring to himself as "la woman." Then she disappeared into the bowels of the plane, and "the myth became human, vulnerable and anonymous at the same time, Garbo eclipsed by the masses, the gestures of countless individuals also vanishing in a similar airport, or railway station."[38]

Manuel sighted Garbo once more, in New York a few years later, on the Upper East Side; she was taking her daily walk, disguised in shabby trench coat and sunglasses. He ran back to pass her again, dared to stop in front of her, and said: "Thank you for all the beauty you've given the world." Flipping her head back slightly in a famous gesture Manuel mimicked to perfection, she uttered a breathless "Oh!" and continued walking. He was left wondering if it was an "Oh" of modesty, of pleasure, or simply of annoy-ance.

No sooner did he receive his first salary check than he began paying off his debt to the family. When they received the first installment, Malé, ever practical, told him to buy clothes instead of sending money. "Mama, I too was thinking of sending you things instead of the rest of the money," wrote Manuel, on Malé's wavelength.[39] Their letters were filled with details about jackets for Carli and Papa, dresses and accessories for Malé—Manuel would always shower not only his mother but his father and brother with useful gifts from his travels.

A veritable gypsy of the modern age, Manuel took full advantage of his airline employee benefits to travel in every possible direction. Starting in the mid-sixties Malé became his regular traveling companion, and, over the years, they would tour Europe—Western and Eastern—as well as Asia, the United States, the Caribbean, and the South Pacific. He took his first Air France vacation in March 1964: "four delicious days in Puerto Rico . . . in paradise (siestas at all hours!) . . . a mere three-hour flight from New York."[40] As an employee, he could get a 90 percent discount on travel for family as well, he wrote Malé, noting the sensual trivia of his brief tropical interlude with a novelist's pen:

> One day I went to another beach farther away, a bay thick with palm trees where you can eat coconuts fresh off the tree: you dig a hole in the sand filled with cold seawater, you put the coconut in there till it's cold, then slice it open with a ma-chete and drink the milk from inside, and eat a little of the white pulp, and you're all set.[41]

Just back from Puerto Rico in March, he was plotting Malé's first trip to Europe in the fall, with her sister Carmen signed on for part of the itinerary to keep her company. Malé wanted to meet up with her son in Paris, but Manuel preferred to stick to their long-awaited plan to meet in Rome, mainly because he knew he could count on Mario to help him squire his mother and aunt around. Manuel explained to Malé, however, that by now Paris was "more or less like New York," and the only friend left from his student days was Nestor, and Manuel had plans to travel to Europe in April anyway for work reasons. Mother and son were both willful; Manuel convinced her—or himself—with yet another motive, that he was worried about Fenelli.[42]

He was going through a great period, he hastened to assure her, "dating very little" in New York but happy working every day on "Illegible Mess Without Precedent!"—a droll title he gave the novel-to-be, invented for a companion at work whom he "subjected" to daily readings of what had been written that morning or the day before. In the midst of this joyful writing he already feared the emptiness that would follow the completion of his novel. He shared his fears most freely with Mario, who, in a letter written on the first anniversary of Marilyn Monroe's death, had half joked about suicide, which in their private shorthand was DeepBlueSea—alluding to a drama starring Vivien Leigh: "But what matters is that I keep up my enthusiasm imperturbably 100 percent and if I'm going through a bad spell, better times will come, and I'll forget all the bad stuff, that's what you taught me."[43]

He urged Mario to spend a few months in New York, to try it out: "It's up to us together to rescue Argentine literature! . . . Be faithful to your ideas; don't let the envy of others discourage you." Manuel goaded him: "Drop the unhealthy movie business; publish your stories." He even circulated a rumor about a mysterious suitcase under Mario's bed, filled with fabulous texts, so that mutual friends would ask Mario to produce the suitcase. To raise Mario's spirits, Manuel also kept reminding him how much he was needed, and that thoughts of suicide were unthinkable:

> . . . Ay . . . I'm going to tell you about something that occurred to me, I'm terrified of finishing the "servant novel" and not knowing what to do and totally terrified of Mother dying because then there's nothing left to keep me from deepbluesea. But if I know that [you] would suffer if I did deepbluesea-marilyning then I can't do it and you too, think how badly I'd feel if you did such a thing. So, don't you dare, not only for your mother's sake, but for mine.[44]

To Malé he expressed not only concern about Mario, but also impatience: "[Mario] is very neurotic, wants to rewrite everything he's written, for which he has taken off two months from subtitle work to go to a friend's house in the country: hope it goes well for him."[45] Manuel urged Mario to create, but to Malé he stressed his friend's paralysis. Though he was sympathetic, Manuel needed to distance himself from the contagion of his friend's chronic writer's block; he too feared the blank page and needed to feel positive. Manuel countered this fear in part by writing on the backs of used pages, to economize but especially to reduce the anxiety of performance, as if his "scribblings" were tentative and didn't deserve brand-new paper. Later, when he became a recognized novelist and had no need to save on paper, he continued this diffident custom as a ritual, a superstition, as if it were a recipe for success.

Manuel sent Malé frequent news-filled letters, including new jargon to prepare her for her future visit to Yankee land; he had just learned the word *bullshit*, and translated it for her as "ox manure," commenting, "So apropos . . . I plan to use it often." Malé acquired not only a wardrobe of imported clothing but an ever-expanding inventory of nicknames: the "She-Wolf" was a demanding mistress; "Bette" was stern, spunky, imperious, and, like the roles Bette Davis often played, a woman hard to please: "B.A.– N.Y.–Paris–Rome–Venice (Rome-Venice train) Nice–Madrid–B.A. any objections, Bette?"

Mother was Bette, especially when she fussed about clothes he sent, or when he had to fight with her over details such as how to wear her sleeves— "not rolled up, you're too busty"—or question her requests—"You already have fur and suede coats, why do you want so many?"[46] When she was being spoiled with gifts and attentions she was also "la Buschiazzo"—a *cursi* Argentine actress of the fifties who played the mother of equally schmaltzy Luis Sandrini in a forgettable comedy titled, in literal translation, *When Elves Hunt Partridges*.[47] In this film, after the mother has an eye operation, Sandrini runs out of the hospital shouting, "The old lady sees colors!!"— which is what Manuel joked to Mario in a letter about Malé's rapturous reaction to a recent gift.

Despite her youthful vitality at age fifty-six, Malé had just had a hysterectomy; at this juncture, and in the future, her health alarms often had the effect of setting off Manuel's worries about his own fears of aging, of not finding a "husband." Peeved about his "sudden aging" (*golpe de vejez*) at the venerable age of thirty-one, he hopped down to Puerto Rico in April—a fleeting romance in San Juan had begun in March—a trip timed so that he could show up in Europe with a suntan. "Well, be ready for the horror of Falconetti," he wrote Mario. "My hair's short and combed forward—revolting—and my face swollen."[48] For the first anniversary of his employment, Air France was rewarding him with a "free passage to wherever"; he flew to Rome on April 22, 1964, stopping in Paris on the way back. He was already planning his second Air France anniversary trip, to Hawaii in April 1965.

For Mario and Manuel, it was "you and me against the world." Not only did each want success for the other, they also very much wanted "to please our parents: they'll see that we're happy, and they'll be happy for us too, even though it's not the traditional form of happiness," Manuel wrote, a tad wistfully.[49] He encouraged Mario to hold on to their shared illusion to return home in triumph to Buenos Aires:

> When we're back in Reina [Queen] we'll feel very good. Isn't it good to have something to fight for, the return to Reina . . . Swear to me that you'll be my sister forever in Reina and that we'll protect each other and live together in our country . . . The only *way out* is to do something. You scold me for silence on your stories when I keep telling you you're a genius; send me the long ones—if you send them "Printed Matter" it won't cost much; write to me. YOU'RE THE ONLY THING I HAVE IN THE WORLD.

He wrote this letter from New York on a cold day in January 1965, after an early December holiday in Argentina, which had been an "utter nightmare." While Mario tended to succumb to distance and stop corresponding, Manuel's survival seemed to depend on a bimonthly exchange of letters, at least: "Or else! . . . Don't say we've become distanced, because I've never been closer to you than I am now, you're like my second nature; I discuss everything with you." It was the Christmas season, which Manuel hated, the holiday that celebrated most extravagantly the family, and, by extension, made those without family feel more alone; those who were gay or eccentric, more marginal.

It was also his birthday, and he was another year older. In April, Mario sent him sad news: their pretty Irish friend Mary Haberdeen, Mario's land-lady, had died at the young age of fifty-nine. Mary had been an actress in the late twenties and played opposite the ingenue Katharine Hepburn onstage in *The Philadelphia Story*. Besides running a translation agency, which en-abled her to live as an expatriate in Rome, this adventurous woman also wrote detective stories. Manuel consoled his grieving comrade: "Let's fight for a niche together in this world. I don't want to die alone." Around the time of Mary's death, Manuel realized that his on-again, off-again heart-throb, Peter, whom he had met in Rome and whom he had been seeing in-termittently, had dropped him definitively. He was sure of it this time, he told Mario, because no more postcards or letters arrived; he called it, rue-fully, the "latest drama of Bergman," alluding to *The Silence*, a film he found "too contrived"—his honeymoon with Bergman had also ended by the mid-sixties. In May he took a short trip to Acapulco to dispel the blues, but, over the next year, his letters to Mario obsessed over this loss, one of his "great erotic dreams."

Losing Peter was a blow, making Manuel feel even more insecure about his receding hairline; he always attributed the early loss of his youthful looks to his northern Italian ancestry. He had never been totally confident of his physical appearance, even in his early twenties, when he was much sought after, a period that was beginning to seem like a hiatus between awkward childhood and unwelcome maturity:

> I had a more or less passable physique, and sometimes people would turn around on the street and look at me. And more or less at age thirty-two it was as if a light had gone out. My hair started to recede and fall out, my body changed, bent over, and . . . I went on to be not a monster but a person without that physical power to which I was accustomed. I lost that very very soon. It was over, I felt stripped of a lot. That was one of the key losses, among the many in life.[50]

(When I met him four years later, in 1969, I found him strikingly handsome, but, it must be remembered, the standards in homosexual circles were high, and youth was worshiped no less than it is today.) Unable to speak to Malé frankly about his melancholy, he wrote to her in May that he had gotten the "sudden urge" to read romantic poetry from Spain: Gustavo Bécquer, Amado Nervo, Espronceda. These once-popular, florid late-nineteenth-century poets, still respected, wrote verses that average literate readers considered refined, but which were rather sugary: "For every nice bit there are seventy boring parts," he wrote to Malé. He would later use a Bécquer poem for kitsch effect in *The Buenos Aires Affair,* in a recitation by Gladys's mother, Clara Evelia.

birds in the head

By September 1963 Manuel had written three new chapters of *Betrayed by Rita Hayworth* and corrected one "from head to toe." He already had fourteen chapters sketched out: except for three "written" texts, a school composition by Toto, a diary by a poor Peronist girl, and a more introspective journal by the "spinster piano teacher," the rest of the chapters were monologues—by Toto, his mother, his cousins, his friends (and an enemy at school)—or conversations, written in screenplay format. Writing every day, he struggled through successive drafts toward a colloquial style that was emotive but not intrusive, that was both his own and his characters', stylizing the vernacular so that it would sound natural. For instance, working on a monologue of Toto's friend Paqui, the daughter of a poor Spanish immigrant, he made a note to "make everything more *cursi*, à la Delly."[51] Delly—a pseudonym—was a gushy French writer read by Argentine women and children in the forties, in translations even cornier than the originals. In Italy he had read aloud to Mario to check that he wasn't "exaggerating"; in order to "know the enemy" he was now following Mario's advice to study the errors and virtues of lauded Argentine writers, and was finding their spoken language stilted or patronizing. As a child he had almost always read foreign literature, as did many Anglo- and Francophile middle- and upper-class Argentines who tended to distrust the quality of local writers. It was only in New York, when in the midst of writing what was now plainly a novel, in which he needed to keep alive his own language, that he showed some interest in the "pretentious crap" produced in his own country. He spent several afternoons at the main branch of the New York Public Library, where he "discovered a section of Argentine literature . . . I read a novel by [Eduardo] Mallea, *La ciudad junto al río inmóvil* [The City Beside the Still River]; it's so bad that it's interesting, like a treatise on how not to write a novel."[52] He also discovered Roberto Arlt (1900–42), the populist novelist and dramatist of social corruption championed by the left as a more "authentic" Argentine writer than Borges. Arlt was noted for his "realistic" use of *lunfardo*, urban immigrant slang strongly peppered with Italian.[53] Reading Arlt's *Aguafuertes porteñas* (Watercolor Sketches of Buenos Aires), from the thirties, was "very useful":

> [Arlt] makes a special use of *lunfardo* that is disastrous, because he overdoes it. I had my doubts about that [in my own writing], and decided to correct a number of expressions. I think one has to limit it to what's absolutely necessary, when there is no other word the character can use—according to his or her psychology—except for the *lunfardo* word; it's the same with colloquial language—only to be used when it's truly "expressive" but if not, then not![54]

Manuel had no patience for Argentine poetry either, after reading an anthology at the library: "disastrous, Norah Lange, Murat, Silvina Ocampo, all catastrophic; the only one I liked was Alfonsina Storni, more sincere, at least." (Silvina Ocampo became his friend some years later.) Gushy poetry recitals that he had attended in Buenos Aires as a boy with his mother had already cast a dubious shadow over the genre, which he would treat with broad irony in *The Buenos Aires Affair*, drawing parallels between Gladys's mother and a famous national *recitadora*.[55] At the library Manuel read, or reread, not only his compatriots but the canonized modernist Hispanic poets: Neruda had "wonderful moments" when he was "simple"; Antonio Machado was a "jewel" amid the "mush" (which included consecrated poet Juan Ramón Jiménez). He was particularly fascinated to discover "familiar rhythms" in the Gypsy ballads of Federico García Lorca, who dared to be not only antifascist but homosexual; Lorca, like Picasso and Neruda, had produced "indiscriminately," but the ill-fated Andalusian, brutally assassinated during the Spanish Civil War, "also had a grand personality and some wonderful poems."[56] By the time Manuel was a well-known novelist, he would often espouse the opinion that poets, by merely labeling themselves as such, were, except for a few young talents and a few greats, *cursi* and pretentious. He would always be generous, though, in supporting struggling writer friends and admirers, among them some poets. The poetry Manuel sought, writing at his little desk in Kew Gardens, thousands of miles from Argentina, lay in the tone of each episode of his novel, of the "birds in his head." The thrust of what his characters said was the way they said it.

If boarding school in the big city had represented for adolescent Coco a jolting initiation into Argentine class snobbery and ethnic prejudice, Manuel also remembered making his single most important intellectual discovery at Ward: Freud, whom a schoolmate urged him to read. Again a movie, *Spellbound* (1945), with its campy reduction of the "talking cure," compelled him perhaps more than his readings of Freud and became one of the three pivotal movies in *Betrayed by Rita Hayworth* (the other two were *The Great Ziegfeld* and *Blood and Sand*). While Manuel appreciated Freud's "nonjudgmental, often sympathetic spirit" of inquiry, he made light of Freud's Victorian views of homosexuality. But he also found the obvious truths and campiness of those same "simplifications" irresistible. Pop psychoanalysis, as Hitchcock had shown, was an excellent narrative device, but Manuel would amplify his critique of clinical reductiveness in *Kiss of the Spider Woman*, a kind of *Reader's Digest* pseudo-scientific jargon in his didactic footnotes on homosexuality.

Equally important during this period was his discovery of Herbert Marcuse's *One-Dimensional Man* and *Eros and Civilization*, radical treatises that ushered in the sexual revolution of the sixties. Marcuse in particular helped him articulate his intuition that the "medium was the message" and that media and technology manipulated and reduced the individual, dulling the shock and transcendance of revolutionary art and politics. If communism betrayed its own revolutionary principles by reducing the individual to a cipher, the patriarchal capitalist system repressed eros and sexuality. For Manuel, the ideas of Marcuse, Norman O. Brown, and other psychoanalytical sociologists supported his views that sex goddesses like Rita Hayworth and Marilyn Monroe, while exploited by the system and tragically self-destructive, were more revolutionary in their erotic defiance than radical Marxists.

By May of 1964, greatly stimulated by the positive reactions of Nestor and his friends in Paris, Manuel was determined to finish the first draft by September. By July he had completed chapters 3 to 16 and was feeling enormously accomplished, with only the first two chapters to rewrite. The novel—now he was calling it "Desencuentros" (Misencounters), another unsatisfactory working title—would close chronologically in 1948, the year Coco turned sixteen.

Manuel chose not to deal directly with the boy's sexual coming-of-age. Instead he would end the novel, again inspired by the psychoanalytical method, at the beginning, shortly after Toto is born, in 1933. An unsent letter from Toto's father, Berto, to Berto's older brother Jaime, accuses Jaime of letting Berto down. It is here that Manuel becomes the voice of his father, "full of bile":

> I don't know why I write you when you don't care about me . . . It doesn't matter if you don't hear from me, right? Why should it, if it didn't matter whether or not you took me out of school when I was a boy, which I can never forgive you for, and then you closed the factory anyway—an inspired move— and there I was, out in the rain. I repeat to myself that you're the only one I have, my big brother . . . but no matter how hard I try I can't forgive you, Jaime, I cannot forgive you.[57]

By the end of Berto's letter, the story was complete and Manuel now knew how to begin the book too. As if overheard by a child eavesdropping behind the kitchen door, a banal family conversation would introduce the threads that the novel would embroider gradually into a complex portrait of the artist as a boy. After exposing the "truth" (which was what he called Berto's letter, the final chapter, in his preliminary draft), he admitted to Malé for the first time that the book was coming out well but was also "very dark." Dark in mood but illuminating in content: the etymology of *betray* is, after all, to reveal involuntarily. The novel embraces with humor and pathos a vicious circle of betrayals: Jaime betrays Berto who betrays Toto. Coco betrayed father, mother, and even himself as the manipulated spectator who, in turn, would grow up to manipulate fictions and readers.

With the novel near completion, Manuel gave himself a treat: his first trip to Los Angeles, *"grace à* Air France." Los Angeles was a welcome change, a thrill for this lover of old Hollywood. "Stunning, it has so much legend to it," he wrote Malé. "It's the place where I could feel the Roaring Twenties most tangibly."[58] In August he took a second trip to Paris, and by the end of October, he had redone the first and second chapters, attempting to confine the action to two arenas: "the first my grandmother's house in La Plata, a house of women, homey gossip, and scorn for my grandfather, the only man in the house; the man for them was Charles Boyer, remote and marvelous. The second chapter is the house in Villegas, dominated by a man, *papún* (papa)."[59] These two arenas, his mother's parents' house and his father's house, were conveyed by contrasting tones: "I. Mita's Parents House: gentle, tame atmosphere, absence of aggressivity. II. Berto's House: aggressive atmosphere." Thinking in filmic or visual terms, in 1964, he wanted not to explain but to *suggest* atmospheres or ambiences, as he wrote to Mario, flattering his friend's "influence":

> Rereading after months of not reading them was useful. Chapter 3, me at age six fluctuating between the two ambiences, needs to be completely thrown in the garbage and that was the most Fenellian; these matters of influence are so dangerous . . . ; also 4 is weak I think, "Hebe" [MF] must tell me how to fix . . . 5 through 10 just a bit of polishing, I think.[60]

Scolding Mario for sending letters via "the slow boat to China," Manuel announced that all the chapters he hadn't seen, except the first two, were coming his way air mail despite "horror expense." Malé and her sister Carmen were arriving in Rome around the same time, the last week in September, and Manuel wouldn't join them until early October, hence Mario had his work cut out for him—not only as literary agent but as tour guide. Malé, Carmen, and Mario became a mutually adoring trio, which turned into a blithe quartet when Manuel joined them in early October for a long weekend. Together they all visited exquisite Padua and sent bubbly postcards to family and friends in Buenos Aires, La Plata, and Villegas.

Manuel brought in tow the first two chapters—"Voices La Plata" and "Voices Villegas," as he explained, preparing Mario, Malé, and Carmen, his first readers, for the challenge of bare, uncontextualized dialogue that changed the "physiognomy" of the novel. In these dialogued sections he didn't want to reveal too much directly. The first chapters, in effect, would force the reader to take a more active role without a narrator's guidance. While this risky strategy gave the book a decidedly avant-garde makeshift look, Manuel later admitted that if he were to do it all over again, he would have begun it in a more inviting manner. Over the next three years (1965–67) he would be horrified by the resistance of publishers like Mortiz in Mexico, Hamish Hamilton in London, and "even Knopf" in the United States: "According to them the novel is unbearable because it's so confused, filled with characters impossible to follow, since 'you never know if the characters are talking or thinking.' "[61]

Gathered in the sisters' hotel room on Via della Fontanella, Mario, Malé, and Carmen listened, almost holding their breath, as Manuel read his manuscript to its first audience, bringing each phrase to life. When he stopped reading they applauded wildly. Malé, however, couldn't help asking pointedly: "But why so negative?" "Mama, it all ends well," he reassured her. For the future there would be a tacit understanding that Malé would not read his books—even if she did. They were too gloomy or perverse for her; Manuel didn't want to burden her, if he could help it, with his "dark" side. Malé, and even Baldo, would be proud of their son's accomplishments, but also ambivalent, especially Baldo. They were his parents, after all, and they embodied Argentine bourgeois propriety; even Malé, with her devotion to ideas and the arts, was more a resource than a reliable critic. Mario was his mainstay: "How reassuring to receive your praise," Manuel wrote on a flight that November to Acapulco, Mexico. Fearing that he might become permanently sewn into the Air France uniform he put on every morning, Manuel regarded Mario's faith in him as a life buoy.

manuscript to market

"Today I expect to finish correcting," he wrote Malé on February 13, 1965. "Tomorrow I'll send the pages to Paris and Rome, and CHAU." To celebrate, and to escape New York's "worst month," he was giving himself a present, a $755 trip to Tahiti; from New York the trip to Papeete was normally $1,061, but Air France gave him the New York–Los Angeles leg gratis:

> A few days after being there [in Tahiti], at my leisure, I read the novel from the beginning (I couldn't finish it all at once because diversions and excursions got in the way) and it produced an AMAZING impression, all modesty aside; I think I was touched by the magic wand. I'm sure it's going to have a huge impact, but when? I want it to be soon. I'm filled with desire to write new things and yet it doesn't seem possible to repeat the tour de force of the last two years. This March marks three years exactly since I began the novel.[62]

To move on, he needed the confirmation that publication would bring. But even after he read the manuscript from beginning to end, he could not let it be: "I may add a chapter to the end, but it's something that has nothing to do with the plot. It's a little embellishment at the end; let's see when I can write it."[63] This embellishment was a two-page "anonymous" letter written clumsily to the school dean by Cobito, the lower-class ruffian who tried to rape Toto (chapter 11) out of frustrated rage. As a Jew discharged for misconduct—with this character Manuel flashed the spotlight on Ward's anti-Semitism—Cobito (Jacobo) brutally claims that Toto is a lying "faggot" who pretends to be interested in "the Cossack girl" but is really in love with the boy she's dating.[64] If on the one hand Toto was a victim, Manuel subtly stressed in the novel's final chapters an avenging, conflicted Toto who was also a manipulative teller of tales.

Mario meticulously went over every page he received, and Manuel impatiently awaited his reaction: "I can't work on the new 'hostess novel' until I hear from you." He goaded Mario to send the chapters on to Nestor's editor friend in Paris, repeating the address sardonically: "Severo Sarduy, rue Lakanal, Sceaux (Seine), France, Europe, Northern Hemisphere, Planet Earth."[65] The manuscript did not reach Severo until April 1965. Manuel complained: "I don't know how Fenelli sent the papers from Rome to Paris so that they took over a month.[66]

Around this time, Manuel began writing a sequel to *Betrayed by Rita Hayworth* in which he attempted to retrace his adolescence and youth in

Buenos Aires. He never finished this sequel, which he titled "Relative Humidity 95%," alluding to the humid summers in the port city which the Puigs, like many *porteños*, escaped by vacationing at a popular seaside resort, Mar del Plata—and also to another kind of heat. In the only completed chapter, a boy lies in bed worrying about his studies after a night of insomnia and masturbation while in the next room his parents fret. Manuel tried to capture here, perhaps, his (and his younger brother's) malaise as a wayward student living at home in close quarters. He continued with the same montage device he had used for the monologues in *Betrayed by Rita Hayworth*, inspired by films but also by the novels of modernists like John Dos Passos, to portray the agitated synchronicity of real life. The following passage weaves a terse parental conversation, the father's stream of thought, news items about the corrupt government from a daily the father reads in bed, and the thoughts and nocturnal fantasies of the boy in the next room:

> "What's the lazy bum waiting for to get out of that bed?" . . . .
> "I heard him tossing and turning last night. He couldn't get to sleep, the kid always has trouble getting to sleep, like me, like you" . . . "Once he gets his degree, life'll be a lot easier, he won't have your troubles, for god's sake" . . . "If he doesn't get it, he'll be putting a noose around his own neck" . . . "I can't imagine what time he went to bed . . . When's his exam?" . . .
> "Then they send some engineer to the plant, some inspector who knows less than any experienced worker there, and my son studies architecture instead of engineering so he can give his father a hand some day" . . . The strange style of Art Nouveau, Gaudí the Spaniard, the photographs of Art Nouveau houses, . . . the park full of mad Gaudí houses, ugly, a failure, architecture . . . "If this kid gets his degree in architecture and then goes to work for some company for a measly salary, I'll kill him" . . ."It's the same in every profession—the guy with connections, the guy with social standing gets ahead" . . .
> "We're going to have to tie his hands, I'm telling you, because every night I hear the noise he makes against the sheets."[67]

Autobiographical threads from *Betrayed by Rita Hayworth* reappear here in the mother's remarks about the father—"he won't have your troubles"—

and in the father's frustration with his son. Whether Manuel found it difficult to distance himself from the raw material, was too preoccupied with
selling the "housemaid" novel, or simply lost interest in this project, he
forged ahead with a new "hostess novel"—a notch classier than the "housemaid novel"—which would become his second published book, *Boquitas
pintadas*, or *Heartbreak Tango*.

Nestor had by now shown seven chapters of *Betrayed by Rita Hayworth*
to his Cuban "lady editor friend" at Editions du Seuil, who, Manuel wrote
Mario, "was wildly enthusiastic, and instantly gave it a repulsive title: *Characters*."[68] The editor, Severo Sarduy, was a young writer who had already
written two hallucinatory novellas about Cuba. The community of exiled
Latin American gay writers and artists in Paris in the sixties and seventies
came mostly from Argentina and Cuba, in part because Buenos Aires and
Havana were among the most vibrant cosmopolitan centers of Spanish
America. These urban strongholds posed a moral threat to the repressive
autocratic societies governing Cuba and Argentina—geographic and political opposites—which upheld strict laws against homosexuals. Fidel's totalitarian "rehabilitation" policies and concentration work camps were even
more systematic than Perón's nationalist reforms; both leaders were nicknamed "el caballo," or "the horse," patriotic emblems of masculinity. Ironies
abounded, as many observers, including Manuel, noted, in Perón's cultiva-
tion of a Carlos Gardel look with his slicked-back hair: the image of the
national hero was so masculine that it had an effeminate edge, befitting
Gardel's real-life polymorphous sexuality. The Argentine expatriates in
Paris included writers Julio Cortázar and Hector Bianciotti (then a reader
for Gallimard), Edgardo Cozarinsky (filmmaker and critic), and Di Tella
theater directors Jorge Lavelli and Rodolfo Arias. The Cuban group was
equally diverse and accomplished: novelist Alejo Carpentier, then ambassador to France, film critic Carlos Clarens, playwright Irene Fornés,
painters Wifredo Lam and Ramón Alejandro. National boundaries were
erased in this Latin and largely gay network of artists and writers, but competing egos, aesthetic camps, and political views, given the narrow arena of
high culture where one writer (like García Márquez or Borges) could mo-
nopolize the Latin American slot, would inevitably provoke rivalries and
shift alliances.

Sarduy's first book, a daring statement titled *Gestures* (1963), was inspired by the "action painters"—one could see why he would suggest to

Manuel a minimalist title like "Characters." Not only formally risky, *Gestures* was a parody of *The Pursuit*, a political novella by Cuba's premier novelist at the time, Carpentier. Sarduy had arrived in Paris in 1960 on a scholarship from the new revolutionary Cuban government to earn a degree at the Louvre as museum curator. The cultural enrichment and relative freedoms of Europe, weighed against the persecution of homosexuals in Cuba, shaped his decision to remain in Paris, but the clincher was a chance meeting in Rome. Gazing upward at the dome in the Sistine Chapel where God's finger touches Adam's, bestowing the gift of life, Severo sensed the proximity of a fellow gazer, a tall, somber-looking intellectual with piercing blue eyes named François Wahl.

Through his domestic partnership with this respected French-Jewish scholar, who was also the wealthy publisher of Editions du Seuil, Severo became Seuil's Spanish-language acquisitions editor and an exotic member of the charmed *Tel Quel* circle, the avant-garde French "structuralist" cultural elite. Roland Barthes and Philippe Sollers were his new mentors and friends, and France's most famous and controversial psychiatrist and interpreter of Freud, Jacques Lacan, was (Severo claimed) his "personal" therapist.

Manuel arrived in Paris at the end of April, and had a joyful reunion with Nestor, whom he hadn't seen since 1957. Hoping his fellow Cuban would help publish Manuel, who had just arrived from Rome to pick up the manuscript, Nestor arranged a drink with Severo at the chic Café Flore on St.-Germain-des-Prés, two blocks from Editions du Seuil. Upon shaking hands, Severo declared himself Manuel's instant new fan, while Manuel found Severo *mona*, Argentine for cute: a few years younger than Manuel, Severo was slim and oozed Caribbean sensuality with his lively round face, puckish full lips, and slanty dark eyes. Manuel, fresh from Rome, baptized him "Chelo Alonso," after a Cuban dancer/actress who had moved to Rome in the fifties, where she had a brief career in the soft porn of Cinecittà's schlock epics, from slave girl to Theodora the empress, all feathers and kitsch.

Severo, both as a person and as a writer, was a delightful brew of baroque Cuban wit and French sophistication, with a cultural breadth akin to that of his good friend Roland Barthes. Arguably the most influential French literary intellectual of the sixties, Barthes embraced Severo's third novel, *Cobra*, as an exemplar of his latest theory, elaborated in *The Pleasure of the Text*. What Manuel loved most about Severo was the equal pleasure that he seemed to take in sex and his *jeux de mots* and joie de vivre, his blend of *mulata rumbera* and avant-garde poet. During the first years of their friendship, whenever Manuel was in Paris, he and Severo, along with Nestor and others, were Latin revellers by night, cruising sleazy Place Pigalle and dancing the mambo and cha-cha. They and their friends amused each other with their mimicries of solemn literati as well as their favorite divas, from Carmen Miranda to la Callas. Although Manuel and Severo occasionally played "lesbian games" (in *ars combinatoria* with "real men" like immigrant waiters or workers), they quickly became confidants (and at times squabbling adversaries). When Severo suggested a threesome with Nestor, Manuel drew the line: "I couldn't do that with a sister!"[69]

In June 1965, now back in New York and waiting for news, nervous because he wasn't writing, Manuel took off from his job at the airport for a few days to a tropical paradise—Kingston, Jamaica—for sun, sea, and sex. He still couldn't get going on "Relative Humidity." He wrote to Malé, "I'm working afternoons and writing in the morning . . . but you can't force it, you can't write if you don't feel the inner urge."[70] On the other hand, if one project wasn't working, another might. That summer, still without a contract for *Betrayed by Rita Hayworth*, Manuel was trying to work on the "hostess novel," which became "novela hister" because he was feeling hysterical: Malé was coming to "Niu" (New York), together they were going to Paris on July 24, and then he had to return to Niu so could he send her on to Italy, and would Mario please take "Mele" to Calabria and Sicily in "torrid August"? The problem was partially solved: Carlitos came to join Malé on this trip, stopping in New York en route to Europe. While family and friends were his couriers, Manuel was their personalized travel agent: Malé, Carlos, cousin Ernesto and his wife Nelva and daughters, all trooped through the little apartment in Kew Gardens. When Carlos reached Rome, Mario told Manuel later, the tall, good-looking boy left Malé almost entirely in Mario's care, more eager to see Roman girls than Roman ruins. Mario was recompensed, however, by his visit to New York in October 1965, on his way back to Rome from Buenos Aires.

Mario read the first pages of Manuel's new project with his customary zeal, and the two friends enjoyed fall season to the fullest—*Funny Girl* with la Streisand, *Golden Boy* with Sammy Davis, *Hello, Dolly!* with the "divine Miss Channing." In close quarters again for the first time in years, Mario and Manuel had their first real fight. It began on Fifth Avenue (and "luckily ended before they reached Macy's") as a tiff over a new play, *Who's Afraid of Virginia Woolf?* Mario had liked the Italian production, while Manuel thought that Albee—"that lucky bitch"—used rather than empathized with human suffering, unlike Tennessee Williams. *Who's Afraid of Virginia Woolf?* struck him as "forced" because he saw the drama of the sterile couple George and Martha as a cowardly disguise for the tribulations of a gay couple. Manuel tended to be adamant about his opinions, but beneath this argument festered a deeper discord: he was trying to convince Mario to believe in his own fiction writing, and Mario had come to the conclusion that he was not an artist but an intellectual. "Nonsense," Manuel said, insisting that both of them had been "touched by a magic wand," that Mario's problem was his fear—and not of Virginia Woolf. Mario was hopeless, Manuel wrote Malé: "With Fenelli the subject is always the same: the definitive return to Buenos Aires."[71] Mario seemed ever-ready to return to *la patria* but never did; Manuel was determined to return only when he had made it.

Before leaving Rome for Buenos Aires, Mario had passed the manuscript of *Betrayed by Rita Hayworth* to Coco Krimer, who had influential friends in Italy: a wealthy woman (Laura González) from Naples, who acquired Spanish books for Einaudi, and Blanca, Italo Calvino's Argentine wife. Manuel had been skeptical: "I don't think an Italian can appreciate my thing, it's the exact opposite of theirs." But the *napolitana* liked it, which encouraged him because she was a communist, that is, "anti-romantic . . . the complete opposite of the novel," so the book might appeal to "everybody" after all. Calvino knew a little Spanish, having spent part of his childhood in Cuba, but his cerebral style was more *simpático* with the work of older Argentine writers Silvina Ocampo, Borges, or Cortázar.

Through mutual friends, Calvino had also met Severo Sarduy, with whom he shared his Cuban memories; Severo urged him to put in a good word at Gallimard, and Calvino also assured him that he would help publish the book in Italy as soon as it was accepted for publication in Spanish. Manuel exulted at this news, but several months later it seemed as if Calvino had dropped the ball. The distinguished writer transformed, in Manuel's lexicon, into an "old witch"—a category he would later apply to Borges and a few others as well. Mario and Manuel soon parted ways with Krimer (whom they would remember, on the positive side, for his excellent imitations of Bette Davis): too much bitchery, especially when Krimer met Malé, and then said that she was the real Manuel Puig because she gave a better performance.

In Barcelona in the early sixties, Carlos Barral, a poet from an upper-crust Catalan family, had founded with editor Victor Seix the literary press Seix Barral. The first publisher in Spain to promote the new Latin American writers, Barral initiated a stellar list in 1962 with the young Mario Vargas Llosa's first novel, *La ciudad y los perros* (*Time and the Hero*), a savagely realist but at the same time allegorical portrayal of a military academy in Lima, Peru, as the corrupt microcosm of a fascist state. Seix Barral quickly became the most prestigious publisher in the Spanish language, and Barral, "lean, birdlike, throaty-voiced, and given to infectious enthusiasms," as Alastair Reid described him, vigorously supported the Cuban revolution like many engagé intellectuals in Europe and the Americas.[72] Barral was a "champagne Marxist"—as Manuel dubbed the most zealous radicals he knew in Buenos Aires, who were invariably among the most privileged members of society.

In the spring of 1965, after Severo failed to convince Seuil (François, that is) to publish Manuel's manuscript, Nestor had taken it to his friend the young Spanish writer Juan Goytisolo, a reader for Gallimard. As *catalanes*, Juan and Nestor shared a dry northern Spanish temperament. They were both in Parisian exile, both anti-Franco, and both had ties with Cuba. The Goytisolos had owned a Cuban sugar mill since the nineteenth century, which, to their good fortune, was sold before the revolution. A Fidelista until the early seventies, when many intellectuals—including Jean-Paul Sartre and Susan Sontag—became disillusioned, Juan later credited Nestor as the first pro-revolution intellectual to catch wind of Fidel's Stalinist streak, as early as 1961.[73]

Juan's reaction to the manuscript was immediate and enthusiastic; he good-naturedly scolded Nestor for showing it first to Sarduy at Seuil. Gallimard would publish the book in French, and Goytisolo phoned Barral in

Barcelona, too, urging him to nominate the manuscript for the Biblioteca Breve prize, whose jury would meet in December. As Juan later wrote:

> In the mid-sixties, when I had my modest job as Spanish reader for Gallimard, I received a visit from the filmmaker Nestor Almendros. He carried under his arm a typed manuscript and placed it in my hands saying: "It's the novel of an Argentine friend who works as a steward for Air France. Read it. I'm sure you'll like it." Nestor, as always, was right. Few times in my life have I dipped into the literary text of someone I didn't know with such surprise and delight. After reading the manuscript, caught as a reader in the web of a highly original and personal world, I felt totally convinced of having found an authentic novelist. I wrote immediately to the author to communicate my opinion and to give him the good news that Gallimard would publish the book.[74]

The ardent support from Nestor and Severo, whose opinion "everyone trusted," had been a tremendous ego boost, and now the news about Gallimard made Manuel feel reborn "out of my ashes, an Ava Fenix Gardner Fenix."[75] He went to Paris to meet Goytisolo. His first impression of this serious, thin, quiet fellow with piercing blue eyes and nervous tics—who pronounced Puig in Catalan as "Puch" even though "his family is actually Basque . . . but they've been in Barcelona for a generation"—was mixed.[76] Nestor had warned him that Juan was timid, and Manuel pegged him as the kind of *loca* ("queen," like the French *folle*) who, despite his pursuit of stalwart Arabs, suppressed his feminine side. He was also one of those naive communists who were anti-Franco but not anti-Castro, even though both ran repressive regimes. But Manuel trusted Nestor's council: Juan was a good person, one of great integrity, and would be very helpful.[77]

    Their conversations that November determined the title, *La traición de Rita Hayworth* (*Betrayed by Rita Hayworth*), as Goytisolo recalls:

> [Manuel], who would afterward come up with brilliant and sometimes fabulous ideas for titles, had given Nestor the manuscript with a dozen provisional and not terribly substantial ones. In his response to my notes—which, unfortunately, I

have not kept—the novelist summarized for me the sentimental education of his protagonist and mentioned the impression caused by "the betrayal of Rita Hayworth," a phrase
the little boy keeps repeating. The phrase captivated me: this
should be, perhaps, the title. Thus it was Manuel Puig's invention, but my discovery.[78]

Manuel remembered differently: the title was on his list, but he didn't like
it, because he thought it would cause the book to be judged as too frivolous;
Juan insisted that it was the best option.[79] Whatever had transpired, both
were right: the title was risky, but it fit like Gilda's sleeve-length glove, en-
capsulating the book's humor, language, cinematic and camp homage, and,
again, its driving theme of paternal and filial betrayal. The Cuban writer
Guillermo Cabrera Infante in London had been hearing about "Sally" from
Nestor for some time and when Nestor finally explained that Sally was the
author of a fascinating new novel called *Betrayed by Rita Hayworth*, Cabrera
Infante instantly thought it deserved a prize for the title alone.

After it had been settled that Gallimard would publish the French edition, Goytisolo, on one of his trips to Barcelona, delivered the manuscript to
Barral. Manuel's fate was now in "the hands of those Catalans," as he wrote
Malé, "whom we Argentines think of as peasants"; but they were at least
more supportive than his fellow Argentines. Meanwhile Manuel returned to
Paris to sign the contract with Gallimard, a "glamour touch that helped me
endure three years of publishing frustration."[80]

It was indeed a glamour touch: only once before had Gallimard accepted
for its Du Monde Entier series (which included Faulkner) an unpublished
manuscript in Spanish. "It's totally unusual," Manuel was told by a prestigious art critic he had met through Severo, Damian Bayón, a natty Argentine in Paris who vaguely resembled, with his handlebar mustache, Salvador
Dalí: "He knows about many who tried and failed . . . This Bayón is from
the *Sur* clique (Ocampo, Murena, etc.) and I'm eager for him to see the manuscript and pass on the news to those other vipers. He was strange, had to be
Argentine."[81] Even before signing the contract with Gallimard, Manuel had
been on the lookout for possible translators.[82] The editors at Gallimard soon
had more good news: Laure Bataillon, the daughter-in-law of a well-known
French Hispanist, had agreed to translate *La traición de Rita Hayworth*. She
was supposed to be a meticulous translator, had translated the "best" writ-

ers—that is, Borges and Cortázar, including the latter's sensational new novel *Hopscotch* (1964)—and so was certainly acquainted with Argentine Spanish.

Back from Paris, gloomy about putting up with the Air France job for another year, Manuel began "to see blackness everywhere" when news didn't arrive. Around this time he scribbled a morbid note (on an Air France schedule printout) for a script: "A person dreams that he's going to have a horrible life and a worse end, which then happens in real life; another sees that someone just like him is condemned by his circumstances to have a horrible life and has it, and laughs at the other who dreamed it and had it."[83] He looked again to the movies for inspiration, spending his days off revisiting Josef von Sternberg's stylishly erotic dramas and Ernst Lubitsch's sophisticated comedies at the Museum of Modern Art. Lubitsch's sympathetic European humor, his earnest characters, and the homey neighborhood atmosphere of *The Shop Around the Corner* (1940) reminded Manuel of his own homespun human comedy about General Villegas. After a von Sternberg retrospective in December, he was intrigued to realize that this great director had been ahead of his time, "the first poet of underground cinema" (as one critic aptly notes) for his "total absorption in style, remorseless interest in sexual existence [and] subtle conviction of hopelessness and amorality."[84] Manuel reminded Malé that they weren't very enthusiastic when von Sternberg's Marlene Dietrich films came out in the thirties, beginning with *Blue Angel* (1931), because these weren't like the typical soap operas they listened to on the radio. But after seeing *Dishonored* (1931) again, in which Marlene plays a sort of Mata Hari in World War I, he notes: "It's SUBLIME, an adventure comedy on the surface but so beautifully told and with such bitter and lucid hidden depths."[85]

Two weeks later, on his thirty-third birthday, Manuel received a bittersweet letter from Barral: the Biblioteca Breve prize had been awarded on December 20 to the Spanish writer Juan Marsé, but all six readers had liked his book; it had been the last finalist to be dropped, which was apparently a big deal. "My book is a reality thanks to Air France and to my connections in Rome and Paris . . . thanks to the gallegos whom everybody thinks are so backward, and to Almendros (Spanish) and Sarduy (Cuban)," he wrote home, and "no thanks to Argentina, land of envy."[86] Far from home and close friends, and with the holiday season and his birthday tolling another year gone by, Manuel felt despondent.

Cine Teatro Español, General Villegas (courtesy of Biblioteca Municipal General Villegas)

Coco and Malé, 1933 (courtesy of Carlos Puig)

Coco in school uniform, General Villegas, 1939 (courtesy of Carlos Puig)

The men, c. 1942: Coco; his maternal
grandfather, Ernesto; cousin Jorge Puig; Baldo
(courtesy of Carlos Puig)

Manuel with Laura Kacs, Buenos
Aires, 1947 (courtesy of Carlos Puig)

Malé, holding Carlitos, and the Delledonne family, in La Plata (courtesy of Carlos Puig)

Carlitos, Malé, Manuel, and
Baldo in La Plata, 1948
(courtesy of Carlos Puig)

Mar del Plata, 1950: Baldo, Carlos, Malé, Manuel (courtesy of Carlos Puig)

Manuel, at right (in a typical pose, à la Rosalind
Russell), and Mario Fenelli in Rome, 1958
(courtesy of Mario Fenelli)

Buenos Aires port: Manuel
leaving for Europe in 1956
(courtesy of Carlos Puig)

Nestor Almendros in dark glasses, Manuel across the table, and schoolmates at Centro Sperimentale di Cinematografia (courtesy of Carlos Puig)

Manuel in a park in the Aventino, Rome, 1962 (courtesy of Mario Fenelli)

Elena Muzi, Pety Delledonne, Margherita Muzi, Carmen, Malé, Manuel, and Mario in Rome, 1964 (courtesy of Carlos Puig)

Malé and Carlos Puig in Rome,
1966 (courtesy of Carlos Puig)

Manuel in Argentina, 1967 (photograph by
J. Lamarca, courtesy of Carlos Puig)

Severo Sarduy at a café in
rue Bonaparte, Paris, 1970
(photograph by D. Roche, Editions du
Seuil)

Manuel at a cocktail party, New York, 1975
(photograph by Layle Silbert, courtesy of Layle Silbert)

Manuel, Raul Julia,
and Sonia Braga in
Los Angeles, 1985
(courtesy of Carlos Puig)

Manuel in Turin, Italy, 1986
(photograph by Angelo Morino)

He was "poisoned" against Argentina. Even before his first novel was published, Manuel thought he saw how Argentine literary politics could affect his career. If he stayed in Argentina, he'd be buried alive. There was a "rivalry in the air" that filled people with malice: the old writers were wary of new blood; his contemporaries, envious rivals, were worse.[87] He had a definite idea about how he (and Mario) would save Argentine literature, seeing himself as an intuitive woman struggling against the patriarchal establishment:

> You and I are the only ones on the true path, the only contemporaries I've read who express themselves in poetic, irrational terms. Look at when la Borges tries to deal with Argentine things straight on, it's a horror, but when he manages to lose himself in fascination for something foreign/strange, then it's good because he expresses the CAPACITY TO BE FASCINATED that is so Argentine.[88]

La Borges had said as much thirty years earlier: that the Argentine was only true to himself when he liberated his imagination.[89] But Manuel saw himself (and Mario) as having gone beyond Borges with a new generation's "capacity to be fascinated."

From New York that winter, Manuel sent a formal permissions letter in his charming broken English to the real Rita Hayworth, in care of her lawyer. Carlos Barral had asked him to contact the star to avoid legal complications, and to assure her that her name in his title did not reflect on her as a real person but was rather an homage to her image.[90] The lawyer acknowledged receipt of the letter but, to Manuel's disappointment, Miss Hayworth did not reply.

After signing the Gallimard contract, Manuel had also flown to Barcelona to meet Carlos Barral:

> . . . a disaster, first of all our personal styles clashed, he was dressed to the teeth, I was merely covered. He was rich and a bon viveur and a communist; I was poor, of frugal habits and only a socialist. But I must admit I was not too tactful. I ac-

cused some intellectuals of touring Cuba for free and giving
Castro adulation instead of constructive criticism. He was just
back from Cuba, which I didn't know, and took offence at my
apparent criticism of Fidel.[91]

Despite his proven literary instinct, Barral had decided, even before he met
Manuel, Goytisolo realized, that this "effeminate, vulnerable and fragile Argentine was not worthy of appearing in the prestigious catalogue of the
press." Manuel was not only a "movie queen" but middle-class too: Barral,
with the elitist attitude of affluent leftists, could not openly admit his disapproval of the book's kitsch populism and the author's gay sensibility. When
Goytisolo visited Barral and spoke about *Betrayed by Rita Hayworth* with the
certainty that it would win the prize, "Barral's face, normally friendly, had
the unpleasant semblance of someone who has just received some bad news.
His attitude—the least possible enthusiasm over my discovery—became
clear to me weeks later when the prize was awarded."[92] Barral praised the
writer out of one side of his mouth, but ridiculed him on the other. As literary editor at *Primera Plana* in the sixties, Tomás Eloy Martínez first heard of
this "prodigious Argentine writer"—who had missed winning the Biblioteca Breve prize by a margin of two votes—from Barral. Recommending
that *Primera Plana* interview Manuel in New York, Barral quipped:
"They'll find him in the Air France office at Kennedy. His name is Juan
Puig and there he is, at the reception desk, waiting for a movie star to appear."[93]

Initially *Betrayed by Rita Hayworth* was ahead of Marsé's novel, *Afternoons with Teresa*, by one vote. The novelist Luis Goytisolo, who shared his
brother Juan's enthusiasm for Puig's novel, was on the committee and had
convinced most of the other jurists to vote in favor. Thus, Juan felt confident
that Puig would win, despite the fact that the principal competition was a
native Catalan author (except for the young Peruvian prizewinner Vargas
Llosa, who had just moved to Barcelona, all the judges were Spaniards:
writer Juan García Hortelano; critic José María Castellet; Salvador Clotas, a
rich young Catalan playboy, influential in local cultural politics; and Barral's
co-publisher, Victor Seix). However, Barral pressured his friend Salvador
Clotas to turn the vote in favor of the local author, who was also a fellow
Marxist. *Betrayed by Rita Hayworth* not only lost the contest but Barral de-

cided not to publish it. He claimed that it would probably be censored any-way under Franco's regime, and that he had already had enough problems with the censors. This was true and the embattled publisher's assessment was probably correct, but left- as well as right-wing—and, indeed, gen-der—politics ultimately prevailed. Machismo, whether swinging its big stick from the left or the right wing, condemned the novel's sexual radical-ism.

Nonetheless, considering that Marsé belonged to Barral's clique, even the fact that "dark horse" Juan Manuel Puig was nominated and endorsed with such enthusiasm caused quite a stir. During this controversy Guillermo Cabrera Infante, like his fellow exile Severo Sarduy, became an ally of Manuel's. If Sally and Chelo shared an exquisite *rumbera* sisterhood, Ma-nuel and Guillermo's mutual passion—and one that spilled over into their writing—was Hollywood and the cinema. Manuel focused on actresses, "women's pictures," and the silent screen, while Cabrera Infante placed more emphasis on great directors or auteurs and, like Nestor, appreciated a broader range of genres. He favored, aside from François Truffaut, of whom Manuel was also fond, Howard Hawks, John Ford, Orson Welles (as boy genius), and, above all, the "Cock"—Hitchcock—whom Manuel also idolized. They parted ways on westerns: Manuel had grown up in a west-ern—General Villegas—which he felt no need to revisit. The unremittingly straight Guillermo had a penchant for the blondes of the fifties and sixties (like Angie Dickinson) which, except for la Marilyn, Manuel didn't share. From Manuel, Guillermo learned to pay more attention to actors/actresses and their personalities, presence, and appearance.[94]

Manuel first contacted Guillermo when he sent him the manuscript of *Betrayed by Rita Hayworth*, along with the following letter written in a mix-ture of Spanish and English, from Queen of the Plata, in June 1967, and prefaced with jokes about their "rivals" Carlos Fuentes—a.k.a. Ava Gard-ner—and Mario Vargas Llosa—a.k.a. Esther Williams:

> Guillermo My Sultan: (Please don't show this letter to Ava, or
> to the terrifyingly gymnastic Esther): I'm a beautiful odalisk,
> (girl)friend of la Sarduy and la Almendros, I'm la Sally, re-
> member? la Manuel Puig. How are you? Are we going to be
> friends or something more? I'm dying to meet you after hear-

ing so much about you, and after reading your unforgettable book (1). And now I want to be la witty but a strange force blocks the course of my thoughts: are you already dominating me? I'm thrashing, kicking and screaming mentally but it's all useless. I'm a weak female and I give in; but what if you don't want me? Well, in the next few days I'll send you a copy of Margarita Cansino's betrayal. I don't know what you'll think of it. If you want to show it to some English publisher, please do it. Of course you'll get your commission. Am I offending you? Far am I from wanting to offend you (2) . . . Let me talk a little about your novel, which *fascinated* me. Favorite part: Ella cantaba boleros ["She sang boleros," translated as "I heard her sing" in the English version].

Manuel's casual critique was unerring: the most compelling, heartfelt section of *Tres tristes tigres* is "Ella cantaba boleros." This anecdote is the seed of the novel, which Cabrera Infante had begun to draft in nostalgic homage to a great Havana nightclub bolero singer, Fredy Rodríguez, whose death occurred during his first months of exile in 1964. Manuel diplomatically but pointedly indicates the most frivolous section as well:

What least impressed me was "The Story of a Stick." But great GLAMOUR & true WITT and fundamental necessity to communicate an experience, are qualities missing in so many famous starlets, lost as they are in the labyrinths of narcissism. Here they liked your book a lot. The literary crowd treasures it (and will probably be copying you; soon we'll find out). They all read it, but it can't be a best-seller because of the price: 1700 pesos, in a country where the median salary is 30,000 pesos . . . How I'd like to form with you [and Sarduy] the trinity of talent. Well, darling, write me and if you need something, ask me for it. I want you to be in debt to me for favors. That way I'll conquer you and you'll protect me, since I'm so weak; and I want to show you my new work "B.P." [*Heartbreak Tango*], a "serial" in 16 episodes, and the musical comedy I'm working on right now "Tango versus Bolero." I do it all so that one day I can tell the man of my choice, "Look what I'm capable of, but I'd leave it all for you, my man, to wash your shirts and make your food, everything in exchange for your fucking." Because that's how I am, make a note of it . . .

Sally

(1) This I really mean (2) That's the real me: *Cursi* and truthful.[95]

A tour de farce, as Guillermo would pun, of satire and prophetic acumen; with coquettish wit Manuel speaks to their affinities, as he plays at seducing his prey, in the campy role of "Mata Harry" to allure Guillermo into his camp. Guillermo Cabrera Infante joined the campaign in defense of *Betrayed by Rita Hayworth*, motivated as well by his own problems with censorship and the publication of *Tres tristes tigres* at Seix Barral, where the "Francocensors" had clipped away at the "crude" language in his carnivalesque fresco of sex, streetwalking odalisques, and nightlife in Havana on the eve of the revolution.

In response to the dismay of the Goytisolos and others when Manuel lost the prize, Barral promised to exert his influence to publish the book in Mexico City, where, because of frequent problems with censorship under Franco, he often farmed out books to Joaquín Mortiz—a press run by a Spanish compatriot, Joaquín Mortiz Diez Canedo. Among Manuel's new literary peers, Pere Gimferrer, a respected young Catalan poet and critic, assured him that Barral was doing the right thing. Drawn to Gimferrer's intelligence and eccentricity—the poet fancied himself a sort of long-haired, maniacal dandy, and always wore white gloves and a long scarf, even in midsummer—Manuel trusted his advice that *Betrayed by Rita Hayworth* would fare better outside Franco's Spain.

In the fall of 1966, after he ran off to Honolulu to rest "a few days on these islands after the typhoon of censorship in Spain," Manuel learned that he had a new defender (his original "golden five" were Mario, Nestor, Severo, Juan Goytisolo, and Cabrera Infante): the Uruguayan critic Emir

Rodríguez Monegal, then the editor of the Paris-based *Mundo Nuevo*, the first cosmopolitan Latin American magazine published outside the Spanish-speaking world.[96] "Maximum prestige," Manuel wrote Mario, ". . . he publishes la Borges, la Sábato, la NERUDA, la Fuentes; big sensation in B.A."[97] In August 1966 Goytisolo had passed the manuscript to Monegal, who immediately wrote to Manuel, requesting permission to publish a chapter in *Mundo Nuevo* and sketching out the ideas he would later develop in his first article about Manuel's work: "As an Uruguayan I appreciate your profound portrayal of our alienated Río de la Plata in the novel . . . and greatly value your subtle parodical re-creation of a mentality and a language."[98] Manuel chuckled to Mario at Monegal's "our alienated Río de la Plata" remark, but was elated by the appreciation.

When Mortiz finally turned the novel down for reasons similar to Barral's, Manuel suspected the latter's "black hand"; this dismissal of his work, on what Manuel surmised were ideological grounds, reminded him of his experience at Cinecittà. He suggested that Mario take advantage of the contact with Barral, who might want to publish "Footsteps on the Moon" because he's "neorealist and Marxist," which was up Mario's alley. Having just read "horrible Carlos Fuentes, *Where the Air Is Clear*, exalted by the critics," Manuel exclaimed he couldn't understand where he fit in "between Air France, Latino-Americanitis, Argentinitis." What he was writing had "nothing to do with what seems to be acceptable."[99] When a year later his novel still had not been published, Manuel wrote to Emir: "I sometimes wonder what would have become of me, with all these publishing obstacles, without your support and Goytisolo's (operation Gallimard), and I tremble (*in the best Luise Rainer tradition, of course*)." And he proceeded to give Emir a blow-by-blow account of the *Rita* saga—much like the impersonalized memorandum format he was using in an episode of his new novel, *Heart-break Tango*, to impart the significance underlying a barrage of multifarious trivia:

Oct. 65: J. Goytisolo reads ms and hands it to Barral for Dec. contest.

Jan. 66: Barral informs MP that he's interested in publishing it.

Feb. 9, 66: MP passes thru Barcelona, they sign a contract

(promise to pub in Oct.) and Barral sets him up with Carmen as agent. Barral promised to send in a week a copy of the only complete ms for him to make final corrections, but takes over a month and a half. A series of delays occur, and

Aug. 66, Barral writes him a personal letter saying the publishing house's censorship department advises against, and that's why he sends it to Mortiz.

Oct. 66: A friend of Manuel's passes through Mexico and talks to Mortiz: the ms still hasn't arrived.

Jan. 67: No news from Mortiz, the contract w. Carmen terminates Feb. 67: she responds that both Barral & Mortiz still considering. Negotiations pending with Mortiz in Mex (Diez Canedo) and Paco Porrúa in B.A. Finally Mortiz doesn't want it if he can't have B.A. market. Meanwhile, Manuel loses his advance which has been going back and forth bet. Barral and Mortiz, after a year and a half waiting plus 2 trips to Barcelona, 1 to Mexico.

Aug. 67: He finds out Gallimard has sent advance to [Carmen] Balcells, but he has seen neither hide nor hair of it. (B.A. Aug. 28, '68)

To negotiate the Gallimard contract and the excerpt in *Mundo Nuevo*, as well as the possibility of his own edition, Barral had obliged a reluctant but obedient Manuel to enter into a contract with the energetic Barcelona agent, Carmen Balcells, who handled all of Barral's authors. A year later Manuel would "disengage" from Carmen—a hefty Catalan woman, genial yet imperious, who became the Big Mama of the Boom after the grand success of her client García Márquez—because she was doing "absolutely nothing" for him. This was not just his impression: forceful, charismatic Carmen had a "meat and potatoes" attitude about the business. Unless she saw large pecuniary potential in a writer like Gabo, her less commercial clients, among them superb writers like Juan Carlos Onetti, always felt neglected and that (to extend the metaphor) she had "bigger fish to fry." José Donoso's novel *The Garden Next Door*, a roman à clef about a disaffected Latin American writer (himself) in Spain in the seventies, sketched her—broadly—in the character of the "formidable Nuria Monclus."[100]

When in 1970 Seix Barral requested the rights to publish a Spanish edition of *Betrayed by Rita Hayworth*, by that point circulating in two Argentine editions and acclaimed as one of the year's best books in *Le Monde*, Manuel wrote Emir, "Isn't that hilarious . . . I feel like Gale Sondergaard in 'Return of the Spider Woman.' "[101] The return of the repressed, and the triumph of a ferocious femme fatale! Though his fourth and most famous novel had not yet been conceived, the spider woman seemed to be in his thoughts.

Manuel would never quite forgive Barral: when last he saw him, in 1980 at a bookfest in Caracas, the publisher was gravely ill, gaunt, with "wrinkles on her wrinkles." Alluding to *The Picture of Dorian Gray*, Manuel remarked to a friend: "She's such an evil woman that she's gotten old!"

romance perchance?

Not all was work or worries in Manuel's last year in New York: in the summer of 1966, before joining Malé in Europe, he met a sailor in steamy Port Antonio, Jamaica. Handsome, tall, with even-featured Sidney Poitier looks, Kendrick St. John was sweet, simple, and passionate. Responding in early August to the first letter from Manuel in Paris, Kendrick wrote to him from Kingston: "I still remember with estacy [sic] the short time we had together in Port Antonio. Our meeting was so incidental but the memories are still indelible. I trust that in October we will relive those memories." The Jamaican gently advised Manuel to be careful (with rough trade) if he "can't be good" (faithful); Manuel wrote him back immediately, expressing frustration that in romantic Paris with its balmy August nights he wasn't with Kendrick but, instead, with his aunt and mother (in Nestor's spacious new apartment on Boulevard Jourdan, near Les Invalides). As fellow travelers, Manuel and Malé were "Sebastian and Violet," Manuel would say, but, whenever possible, Manuel tried to arrange for her to be accompanied by another traveler, often her sister Carmen (until Carmen's death in 1987) or Mario. As time went on, it became more apparent that Mama was the only constant center of his affective life, but he needed a certain balance: travels with Mama, work, romance. These three parts of his life required deliberate, often frantically byzantine arrangements.

Kendrick again replied eagerly: "It's wonderful to read your letter. I honestly feel something special about you."[102] For the next three months Manuel corresponded with the sailor, mostly about plans to visit each other which circumstances kept foiling—to their mutual disappointment when an October rendezvous never occurred. By October's end Kendrick was expressing slight jealousy as well as pangs of longing: "You have a friend in Rome who obviously means a lot to you . . . On the other hand you have not had a chance to know me well enough to decide if you would be happy living here in Jamaica."[103]

The two had already discussed living together in Jamaica, but Manuel had also expressed his desire to be near his "friend in Rome." Whether he meant soul mate Mario or the disappeared Adonis E.M., the cabinetmaker, Manuel's choice of lovers—usually working-class, usually heterosexual—made it impossible to have sexual partner and soul mate in one package, and this dichotomy also made it difficult for him to sustain an affair. In the same letter Kendrick happily informs him, "My vacation is all set for Dec. 3 and I had planned to spend most of the two weeks in NY with you. How would you like that?" but also adds, "When I called tonight you seemed surprised, but not too excited." Whether because Manuel was already settled in his ritual of compartmentalizing work and play, friends and romance, or because Kendrick's call interrupted another engagement, the forecast was cloudy.

After Kendrick's vacation to New York had to be postponed because he was on duty, Manuel managed to spend Christmas Eve and Day with him in Jamaica before taking off for Paris, but by then they were not getting along, as Kendrick wrote in a letter after the holidays: Manuel had "seemed disappointed" and would have preferred going directly to Paris. Manuel arrived in Paris on the twenty-seventh, called Nestor from the airport to make arrangements to stay overnight at his apartment, and the next afternoon boarded a plane to Rome, arriving in time to spend his birthday with Mario and to dine on a fabulous osso buco at the Muzis'. For "las Margas" he had hastily bought a gift of duty-free cognac, while for Mario, movie posters and tapes from New York Public Library theater records—"Tallulah Bankhead, etc." He saw a "lousy" Italian movie, "the second one directed by Alberto

Sordi, with [Silvana] Mangano, [Anita] Ekberg, and [Giulietta] Masina. I don't know which of them was worst," he wrote Malé, and it didn't help that there was no "career" news in Rome.

Back in Paris, staying at Nestor's comfortable apartment, he dined with Juan Goytisolo and his wife, the writer Monique Lange, a pleasant and "straightforward" woman who put him at ease. Because the next day he was flying to Marrakech—a place dear to Juan—he had a perfect excuse to leave dinner early, so that he could go to the theater: an "awful" play but *she*, Danielle Darrieux, was wonderful. He and Nestor as always talked into the wee hours, and, after a few hours' sleep, Manuel left on an early flight. Finding the Arab city "tiny and lovely, easy to see in little time," he enjoyed spending the New Year's weekend alone—or at least not with anyone he cared to mention to Malé—and "happy with all I've accomplished."[104]

Manuel had by now exchanged several letters with Emir Rodríguez Monegal, and they were on a first-name basis before meeting in Paris the morning after he returned from Morocco. Thanking Emir for recommending him to Scribner's, Manuel had briefed him on his publishing woes with Hamish Hamilton in London and Knopf in New York:

> The Spanish reader reports were devastating: according to them the novel was unbearably confusing, filled with characters who are impossible to follow because you can't tell if they're speaking or thinking . . . What sort of divine donkeys are these people who are in charge?[105]

Emir had already requested permission to publish a chapter of Manuel's novel for *Mundo Nuevo* and was actively seeking a publisher in Spanish for the book as well. Manuel spent all Monday morning in Paris with the Monegals. Emir spoke about the writers with whom Manuel appeared to share affinities, like the Uruguayan Onetti, who also incorporated *lunfardo* in his novels. (Back in New York, Manuel read Onetti's *Shipyard*: "Qué plato," or "Fancy that," was his tepid comment.) A note by Mary McCarthy in *Encounter* (the British magazine *Mundo Nuevo* was modeled after) sent him to the pages of Ivy Compton-Burnett. "To my great surprise . . . I found my incognito dialogues had been done twenty years ago—and here I thought I had invented something new," he reported with sly humor.[106]

Manuel felt at home with this fellow *ríoplatense* in Paris, drawn to Emir's warmth, cheerful wit, literary clout, and, at first, fatherly concern. He was also amused by Emir's wife, Magdalena Gerona, a glamorous upper-crust society lady from Montevideo who faintly resembled Jeanne Moreau. Over tea and pastries at the couple's elegant apartment in Proust's *quartier* on Boulevard de Courcelles near Parc Monceau, they launched into movie talk: the latest Truffaut film, Nestor's innovative cinematography, the glorious Garbo. Emir had been a film critic in Uruguay and had collaborated with Homero Alsina Thevenet, his colleague at the newspaper *Marcha*, on an early book on Ingmar Bergman. Uruguay, much smaller than its dominant neighbors Argentina and Brazil, was more liberal, church and state more clearly separated, and it was also the first Latin American nation to have a welfare system. The *orientales*, as they're called because Uruguay is situated on the east bank of the river, have always been considered Argentina's country cousins, a bit provincial. Born in the town of Melo, near the Brazilian border, Emir was an earthy *criollo* despite his vast erudition. Tall and heavyset, with a long face, bushy dark eyebrows, and straight dark Indian hair, Emir had a commanding presence, and, while he put Manuel at ease as a fellow provincial, Manuel also saw in him a powerful ally. (Manuel later pinpointed the forties actor his new benefactor resembled: George Brent, a "mildly sinister leading man," who co-starred with Bette Davis in the grand-style melodramas *Jezebel* and *Dark Victory*.)

What most interested Manuel was the current "gossip" that he and Sarduy were "the two best new writers in Spanish"—Emir's firm opinion. Emir's was not just any opinion; it was a respected critical assessment. This man of letters by age forty-five had already produced a considerable opus as literary critic, biographer, and scholar, and at the early age of fifteen he had been among the happy few first readers, outside a small inner circle, to recognize Borges's genius. By the late sixties he had gained a reputation analogous to Edmund Wilson's in Anglo-American letters and, judged in retrospect, perhaps did more than any other individual to launch the worldwide recognition of the new Latin American writers in the 1960s.

The *mundo nuevo*, or "new world," his literary journal alluded to was not only the southern hemisphere but a vital, innovative Latin American culture at the center of the international community. The chapter published from *Betrayed by Rita Hayworth* would precede an excerpt from *La Vida: A Puerto Rican Family in the Culture of Poverty—San Juan and New York* (1965) by Oscar Lewis, which, as a treatise of the sixties consciousness-raising war on worldwide poverty, was one of the year's most significant books. Emir had resolved that they should highlight Toto, whose "texts" were the most lyrical and who was, after all, the central character and Manuel's "alter ego," and they decided on the 1942 monologue, appropriately introducing the key moment of "Rita Hayworth's betrayal." A meticulous reader of Manuel's manuscripts from then on (indeed, until his death in 1985), Emir returned the chapter to Manuel, who revised it that afternoon, then met with Severo, and dined with Nestor. On Tuesday Severo and Manuel went to lunch at the Monegals', and Manuel brought a Libertad Lamarque record for Magda—an amateur chanteuse—along with the chapter for Emir. Magda, who was Emir's second wife, had something of the *pituca* (an upper-crust bourgeois lady) about her, and Manuel indulged freely in chatter with her about ballad singers, from Edith Piaf to Libertad Lamarque to Marlene Dietrich.

To Emir as well as to his "golden five" he could confide how desperate he was to leave Air France. Both Goytisolo and Emir advised patience, but Manuel felt he couldn't go on writing and working an eight-hour day; in a whole year he had produced only three chapters of his new novel because of the tension of waiting to hear if *Betrayed by Rita Hayworth* would finally be accepted for publication. To create a bigger splash around the publication in *Mundo Nuevo* and to help get the novel published, Emir suggested that he interview Manuel, but Manuel hedged. To Mario he wrote: "I think interviews all come out looking like pure bullshit; what the writer has to say is already written in his book, or will be in the next."[107] This demure reluctance was also a cover-up: not only nervous, like many artists, about sounding inarticulate, he was also concerned about being mistaken for one of his characters, afraid that he might reveal his effeminacy as when he intruded, over fifteen years ago, upon that movie set in Buenos Aires: "Because I know my limits (I am not a theoretician, I am not articulate, nor is it good for me to analyze too much what I do (!)) I'm planning to avoid the ambushes of literary circles, all the radio, TV, and newspaper interviews in general."[108] He explained to Emir that he had already turned down two radio interviews (despite "my love of the glamour") in Buenos Aires when he returned home briefly in February, after news of his being a finalist for the Seix Barral prize had rippled across the Atlantic. "I think in my case, oh rainbow plumes of the bird of paradise, the most sensible thing is to disap-

pear behind the work, let it impose itself by itself (I cede exclusivity in making a fool of oneself to T[ruman] Capote)."[109] After reading other interviews
by Emir, however, as well as the first issues of the magazine, which introduced new writers alongside established figures, Manuel felt more assured
of a "rational, historical" support for his own work:

> The interview with Sábato in the November issue you gave
> me, with the theory about "peripheral cultures," makes me
> feel that my convictions are shared and understood . . . The
> most important aspect of the magazine is the example it sets, a
> consistent tone of liberalism, desire for dialogue, distrust of all
> extremist positions . . . just what the doctor ordered for us
> Latin Americans with Catholicism on one side and left-wing
> delirium on the other . . . You might just be the drop of water
> that wears down the stone.[110]

By the spring of 1967 Manuel had not only had it with Air France and
his life in New York, but with Kendrick, as he confided to Severo in late
January; it was "a purely sexual thing," with which, after a few months, he
would be "fed up." Again Manuel seems almost unaware of the compart-
mentalization of his affections: unlike Severo, who slept with stevedores and
fellow intellectuals alike, Manuel did not mix friendship with sex; friendship belonged in one sphere, sex another. Sending Severo a photo of Kendrick, he coquettishly asked what Chelo Alonso thought of his man, but also
quipped: "A woman doesn't live on prick alone."

Kendrick continued to seek ways to be with Manuel; denied a visa for
the United States, he suggested they try Canada, but Manuel seemed to
want more than anything to move back to Argentina, where he could focus
on his writing. "I'm ready to move to Buenos Aires," replied Kendrick in
March, "to find a way to make a living there to be with you." Kendrick's letters, at once rudimentary and lyrical, revealed a vulnerable virility which
Manuel would invoke, perhaps unconsciously, in the love letters of the character he was then creating, the doomed Juan Carlos. Years later Manuel
would speak of Kendrick as one of his great loves, but the romance was, as
with the ill-fated affairs in *Heartbreak Tango*, ephemeral at best.

twilight of the sixties:

his brilliant career: 1968–73

front page in swinging buenos aires

"Writing is my idea of happiness"—Juan Manuel Puig was quoted as saying in his first interview, titled "An Unknown Novelist." This was the last time "Juan" appeared in his name in print—it could be translated as Jean or John, creating confusion, and he had never liked being called Gianni or Johnny, a nickname Baldo gave him. While Toto was making his debut in *Mundo Nuevo*, *Primera Plana*'s New York correspondent, an economist named Borrini, had interviewed Manuel at the Air France VIP reception desk at JFK Airport. Featured prominently as the first story in the Arts and Shows section—followed by a review of Juan Goytisolo's novel *Marks of Identity*—the interview was framed by Mario's striking photos of Manuel standing behind a glass-topped counter, right palm poised as if about to vault him over the counter to catch the next plane to Argentina, where he could devote himself full-time to writing.[1]

Primera Plana also competed with *Betrayed by Rita Hayworth*'s April 1967 debut in *Mundo Nuevo* by running another excerpt from the unpublished novel, prefaced by the statement "No text by Puig has been disseminated in Argentina till now." "Esther's Diary: 1947" was chosen for this "family magazine" because, as Borrini explained to Manuel, it was the only chapter "that your father could read without any problem."[2] The editors at *Primera Plana* also chose this chapter because it was explicitly political; Esther was a Peronist girl from a working-class neighborhood, a girl with a political conscience.

Even though *Primera Plana*'s spread meant that *Mundo Nuevo* shared the glory, Emir supported all efforts to introduce Manuel to the public, and particularly to readers in his own country. As Manuel wrote Emir, "I suppose *Primera Plana* . . . puts one in circulation."[3] But excerpts from "Esther's Diary" might be understood as "too close to the real thing," Emir warned, and he "was doubly right," Manuel lamented a month later. Without permission to do so, and limited by the magazine's format, the editors had printed only the second part of the chapter. Without the mushy beginning ("Sunday the seventh—I should be happy and I am not. Sorrow, not deep but still sorrow, wishes to nest in my bosom. Could it be the fading light of this Sunday . . .") where, as Manuel put it: "I laid it on thick so that the reader would get it; how the devil else could the reader realize that it was the character who was *cursi*, and not the author?"[4] As it ran in *Primera Plana* the excerpt invited high-handed misreadings and surly dismissals, such as "I know how Puig's characters speak; what I don't know is how he writes."[5]

Manuel also worried about Emir's *Mundo Nuevo* introduction, which seemed reserved in contrast with the usual hype of publicity and journalism. Emir assured him that the tone was merely a critical convention and that "actions speak louder than words": the first entry in the tenth issue was Toto's monologue.[6] And the introduction was hardly reserved, presenting the new author as a bold innovator within the rich tradition of Argentine writers, both experimental (Nestor Sánchez) and consecrated (Arlt, Borges, Cortázar), as someone shaping a new narrative language out of the raw material of spoken Argentine.[7] It placed him, furthermore, among the emerging literary talents of the hemisphere: previous issues of *Mundo Nuevo* had featured Carlos Fuentes (*Change of Skin*), future Nobel Prize winner Gabriel García Márquez (*One Hundred Years of Solitude*), Chilean José Donoso (*This Sunday*), and Severo Sarduy (*From Cuba with a Song*).[8] Describing *Betrayed by Rita Hayworth,* Emir explained the narrative technique used in the chapter that followed: the "stream of consciousness of a child, Toto, which sketches a cluster of people alienated by the movies (they go every day, only speak of films, imagine their own movies, turn daily life into a sad parody of their films)."[9]

Sartrian existentialism—"alienation"—still held sway over *ríoplatense* intellectual discourse through the sixties; upon reading Emir's introduction, Manuel wrote promptly to both Emir and Severo after he was told by art critic Damian Bayón that it gave the impression that the whole novel was this one character's monologue, making it sound tedious, "à la Robbe-

Grillet." Coupling Manuel with "experimental novelist" Nestor Sánchez didn't help, as Manuel wrote Severo, whom he now called Empress of the Belles Lettres: "Sánchez is a horrible bore, don't you think?"[10]

The label "parody" would become a sore point for Manuel, especially upon the publication of his second novel, *Heartbreak Tango*. In Emir's first interview with him, Manuel tried to clarify that he wasn't mocking his characters' feelings and sufferings:

> I don't condemn affectation, I sympathize . . . If I see a check-out girl at the supermarket imitating the hairdo of some diva, with ridiculous results, rather than laugh I feel sad or embarrassed, especially if she arches her pinky as she gives me the change. See how good-hearted I am. My characters are portraits, not caricatures.[11]

If readers laughed it was because he was mimicking the speech real people used, already a parody, if you will. The term *alienation* was not his, because for him those old movies were not alienating. He wrote about the Argentina he knew, the Argentina that needed to compensate for its cultural void by copying more glamorous, acceptable models.

Despite Manuel's protest, *Heartbreak Tango* would be both praised and condemned as parody, and, as he feared, it scandalized the inhabitants of General Villegas, many of whom felt he had trashed the lives of the local people, "merely imitating" the way girls in town wrote letters. A radio announcer from La Plata published a review in the Villegas newspaper with a subhead that read literally (and incongruently) "Gossip in a Useless and Perfect Book": How dare this son of our province make fun of our grandfathers, who had no choice but to read novels in serial form?[12] Even more than the offensive content, Manuel's defiance of literary conventions was a slap in the face of bourgeois propriety. To this day his brand of parody remains enigmatic: like mischievous filmmaker Ernst Lubitsch, Manuel had "a miraculous ability to mock *and* celebrate both at once and to such perfection that it was never quite possible to tell where the satirizing ended and the glorification began."[13]

Manuel's beeline approach to his career was beginning to gain him the reputation of "professional" novelist in Argentina—an impropriety in the eyes of those peers who were supported by family money, or who worked as journalists, editors, professors, or psychiatrists. "Manuel was a professional novelist who wrote every day and who even knew the birthdays of the directors of *Panorama* and *Primera Plana*, the two principal cultural magazines," quipped Germán García, a psychiatrist whose autobiographical novel, *Nanina*, competed with *Betrayed by Rita Hayworth* for the local limelight when both were published by Jorge Alvarez in 1968.[14] While snobbery toward a professional writer made a certain sense among authors of Borges's "gentleman" class and generation, Manuel considered it hypocritical of the politically committed younger writers of the fifties and sixties—who claimed to be opposed to elitist entitlement—or simply sour grapes, since they wanted fame and remuneration as much as he did.

Emir continued to bolster Manuel, and it was his contacts in New York who were instrumental in finding Manuel his first publisher in English, E. P. Dutton—but the focus of their transatlantic correspondence soon turned to broader issues. *Mundo Nuevo*'s moderate liberal stance, seen by the left as apolitical at best, was already coming under fire in a campaign led by *Casa de las Américas* (House of the Americas), the official cultural organ of the new Cuba. *Mundo Nuevo* was funded by the Ford Foundation, which, in 1966, had taken over the financing of the Congress for Cultural Freedom, which had been founded by the CIA in 1950 to promote cultural relations between the United States and Latin America. Exposés of CIA financing had started as early as 1964: an editorial in *The Nation* questioned whether or not the CIA should be financing "congresses, colloquia, cultural assemblies."[15] By the time the second issue came out, Emir was receiving letters from his increasingly suspicious old friend, the Uruguayan film critic and journalist Homero Alsina Thevenet, who, among other friends and contributors, urged Emir to defend his independent position. In the third issue Emir published an editorial, "Cultural Commissaries," addressed to his "inquisitors" and then, in August 1967, a longer response titled "The CIA and the Intellectuals."

If the fifties had been sullied by witch-hunts for Communist screenwriters, paranoia in the revolutionary sixties invented a new label for politically inconvenient artists and intellectuals: CIA agents. Manuel joined Severo Sarduy, Cabrera Infante, and others, like Goytisolo and Argentine poet César Fernández Moreno, in support of *Mundo Nuevo*.[16] Trying to dispel

Emir's anxiety over the controversy, Manuel declared, "If anyone has any doubts, he should take the trouble to proofread your magazine page by page; he'd have to be a magician to find some trace of the CIA."[17] Fuentes and Vargas Llosa were pro-Fidel but also supported the merits of *Mundo Nuevo*, while García Márquez, a close friend of Fidel's, and Cortázar, a well-meaning idealist, refused to contribute after the scandal broke out. The pro-Fidelistas cast aspersions on some of *Mundo Nuevo*'s contributors, like Cabrera Infante, whom Fidel and his followers were now calling a *gusano* (worm); it seemed to Emir and his friends that even natural allies like Cortázar and García Márquez were capitalizing on political issues to suppress new literary talents who had made their debut in *Mundo Nuevo*. The most heavily attacked, Cabrera Infante, especially empathized with Emir Monegal's plight, caught as *Mundo Nuevo* was in the left-right crossfire. Cabrera Infante, whose father had been a founder of the Cuban Communist Party, had directed the literary supplement *Lunes de Revolución* in Havana until 1961, when, after protesting censorship, he was forced into exile.[18] Refused a residence visa in Franco's Spain for having been a Cuban revolutionary, he settled in London in 1965 with his wife, Miriam Gómez. Sarduy could not return to Cuba, either, in his case because of the persecution of homosexuals.

Facing his accusers in a polemic that lasted until his resignation in 1968, Monegal argued that he—and not the CIA—had editorial control over *Mundo Nuevo*, that Paris was the home of the magazine to situate it in neutral territory—where, he emphasized, dialogue was possible—and that all perspectives were tolerated. The position fomented by Cuba, however, was what Fidel had spelled out to the Cuban intellectuals in 1961: within the revolution, everything was permitted; outside the revolution, nothing. The ideological battle between *Mundo Nuevo* and *Casa de las Américas*, which played out partly as marketplace competition, spanned the hemisphere: Argentine contributors to the Parisian magazine, many of them the writers clustered around *Primera Plana* and *Sur*, broke into factions, and several *Primera Plana* writers joined the defamatory campaign against *Mundo Nuevo* so as not to betray the *Casa de las Américas*.

After Emir resigned from *Mundo Nuevo*, some of its former contributors (notably Goytisolo, Vargas Llosa, Cortázar, García Márquez, and Fuentes) joined forces (with funding from the granddaughter of a Bolivian mining entrepreneur) and founded, in 1970, another even more transitory Parisian journal, *Libre* (Free), believing that they could maintain an independent stance and uncompromised loyalty to the Cuban revolution. *Libre* collapsed in 1972 after the "caso Padilla"—staged trials in Havana of the poet Heberto Padilla and several other writers—precipitated a historical confrontation between Castro and the international community of intellectuals. Cabrera Infante updated Manuel on the fate of *Libre*:

> the magazine in Paris, directed by Goytisolo and financed by Patiño's granddaughter—Albina du Bois-Bouvray, who has just democratized her name into du Boisrouvray—, began as a club of exquisite *fidelistas* led by Cortázar and has become a band of "shameless pro-imperialist intellectuals"—according to Fidel Castro—led by Cortázar![19]

There was a further exodus of writers from Fidel's camp—from Sartre and Sontag to Goytisolo and Vargas Llosa—while others, like García Márquez and Cortázar (although the latter protested the staged trials), remained loyal. Meanwhile, right-wing pressures in Argentina closed down *Primera Plana* and sent *porteño* intellectuals into exile in Europe, the United States, Mexico, and Venezuela.

By late May 1967 the "unknown novelist" was back in the parental home on Charcas Street, armed with his definitive nom de plume and three chapters of the new novel he had begun in New York. Nervous about Buenos Aires "re-entry," Manuel had been encouraged by Emir to look up fellow *porteño* contributors to *Mundo Nuevo*, who would be on his wavelength. Among these acquaintances, Manuel would especially hit it off with Edgardo Cozarinsky and novelist Beatriz Guido. Cozarinsky, who made experimental films, lived mostly in Paris from the sixties on, but maintained a home base in Buenos Aires, where he shared an apartment with his companion, local film critic Alberto Tabbia. A short *porteño* who slightly resembled character actor Martin Balsam, Alberto appreciated Manuel's fondness for obscure actresses and his theory that the actress was the *auteur*; whenever Manuel was in town, Alberto invited him to press screenings. Youngish, balding, light-eyed Edgardo was a sophisticated fellow campster with a dry worldly wit, sweet-tempered, and, despite his noteworthy erudition, humbler than most *porteño* intellectuals. He had written a doctoral thesis on Henry James, but had learned his literary ABCs, like many young Argentine writers, in the discerning company of Borges and the *Sur* group. Manuel first visited the offices of *Sur* with Edgardo, and nearly fainted upon seeing the blown-up photograph of Adolfo Bioy Casares over the receptionist's desk. Bioy, Borges's closest collaborator, was, aside from being an important writer, breathtakingly handsome. (Manuel would get along better with Bioy's wife, the brilliantly witty Silvina Ocampo.)

Beatriz, plump, scatterbrained, but enormously intelligent, gave Manuel moral support during his fight to publish *Betrayed by Rita Hayworth* in Argentina, and became a close confidant. Married to Leopoldo (or "Bapsi") Torre Nilsson, Argentina's premier film director (and a compulsive gambler who looked like a cross between Fritz Lang and Raymond Burr), Beatriz would co-author with Manuel the Argentine screenplay of *Boquitas pintadas*.

Manuel's new vocation was exhilarating; the only gnawing uncertainty was the still unpublished *Betrayed by Rita Hayworth*. *Primera Plana* announced that it would be published by Mortiz in Mexico, Einaudi in Italy, and Gallimard in France, but only the last would come true. After the Mortiz deal fell through, "brave Paco Porrúa," editor in chief at Editorial Sudamericana in Buenos Aires, was less cautious than Diez Canedo and signed up *Rita* in September 1967. Now Manuel could return more confidently to the hostess novel in progress—which was turning out to be "an old-fashioned serial"—and face the terror of the blank page, typing, as usual, with two fingers on the backs of used pages.

In December, *Mundo Nuevo* published Toto's other monologue; along with Emir's mention of Manuel in the November issue, it couldn't have come at a better moment. Malé had just suffered her first episode of heart failure and was very down—as was the rest of the family, accustomed to her bubbly energy. It was Christmas, which, to Manuel's dread, they were going to spend at the *quinta* (country house). In thanks for the *Mundo Nuevo* piece, Manuel wrote Emir: "It completely changed the family atmosphere, helped us through the hateful 31st and 1st, and brought joy, and hope for the fucked-up Onganized future," referring to the Onganiato, the military regime (1966–70) under the oppressive leadership of General Juan Carlos Onganía.[20]

Manuel had just sent Guillermo Cabrera Infante, for Christmas, a map or chart of the Latin American Boom writers cross-dressed as MGM movie stars:

METRO-GOLDWYN-MAYER!
(by special arrangement with Emir Rodríguez Monegal)
PRESENTS

Line I
1) Norma Shearer
   (Borges)
   Oh so refined!
2) Joan Crawford
   (Carpentier)
   So fiery and stilted
3) Greta Garbo
   (Asturias)
   All they have in common is that Nobel
4) Jeanette MacDonald
   (Marechal)
   Oh so lyrical and tiresome
5) Luise Rainer
   (Onetti)
   Oh so sad

Line II
1) Hedy Lamarr
   (Cortázar)
   Beautiful but icy and remote
2) Greer Garson
   (Rulfo)
   Oh so warm
3) Lana Turner
   (Lezama)
   She's got curls everywhere

4) Vivien Leigh
  (Sábato)
  Temperamental and sick, sick, sick . . .

Line III
1) Ava Gardner
  (Fuentes)
  Glamour surrounds her but can she act?
2) Esther Williams
  (Vargas Llosa)
  Oh so disciplined (and boring)
3) Deborah Kerr
  (Donoso)
  She never received an Oscar but still she waits
4) Liz Taylor
  (García Márquez)
  Beautiful face but such short legs . . .
5) Kay Kendall
  (Cabrera Infante)
  Lively, witty, and glamorous. I expect big things from her

Line IV
1) Vanessa Redgrave
  (Sarduy)
  A divinity!
2) Julie Christie
  (Puig)
  A great actress, but since she has found the right man for
  her (Warren Beatty) she doesn't act anymore. Her luck in
  love matters is the envy of all the other MGM stars
3) Connie Francis
  (Nestor Sánchez)
  Miss Christie's contract doesn't allow any starlets under
  thirty to be signed by Metro Goldwyn Mayer!
4) Paula Prentiss
  (Gustavo Sainz)
  No more starlets under thirty!!!

These outrageous comparisons (considered by Cabrera Infante the most brilliant literary criticism of the era) played on the anxiety of the three "starlets" discovered by Emir—Guillermo, Severo, and Manuel—who were breaking into the ranks of the literary establishment. "A star is born," Manuel wrote Emir that December. "It's Metro and it's eternal glamour. *I'm shining before my first film is out in the movie houses, but the previews were great . . . unless the Olympe Bradna case repeats itself: today a triumph and tomorrow OUT, finished, washed out . . . (Is this new star here to stay?)*"[21] Politely thanking Emir for publishing another installment from *Rita* in *Mundo Nuevo*, Manuel feared too much exposure of the text might ruin its chances of ever being published, noting only half-jokingly that "Severo and I were remarking in Paris that we're both your inventions. I hope you're not thinking of uninventing me for some mysterious reason?"[22]

Meanwhile, Buenos Aires was in full swing: the city's myriad bookstores and cafés were humming with intellectual fervor over Marx and Althusser, Roland Barthes and structuralism, and especially Freud and Lacan: near the Villa Freud in the classy Barrio Norte, a bakery sold Erich Fromm tarts and Melanie Klein croissants. No one artist embodied the sixties more wholly, even in engagé anti-*yanqui* Buenos Aires, than Andy Warhol, and the most enduring legacy of his art would be its liberating elision of the boundaries between high art and mass culture. The late thirties and the forties—when Coco had been pasting pictures of Rita Hayworth in his cutout book, composing (unwittingly) a portrait of the pop artist as a child—were the same years that, in a small, ugly mining town in Pennsylvania, the sickly youngster Andrew Warhola also immersed himself vicariously in the glamour of Hollywood. Both had found in those larger-than-life images nothing less than freedom. Manuel Puig would blast similar boundaries with a well-honed sense of the put-on too, but by recycling the debris of mass culture in a creative effort to recuperate a buried authenticity.

Everyone (Ernesto Schoo recalls) was charmed when Manuel first walked into the offices of *Primera Plana*, wearing a sexy black leather jacket, flashing his wide mischievous smile, and carrying a manuscript under his arm. His acquaintances there—Schoo, Tomás Eloy Martínez, Homero Alsina Thevenet, and others—contributed to *Panorama*, a general interest magazine for a mass readership, and the liberal newspaper *La Opinión*, as well as *Primera Plana*. In the seventies, faced with the threat of imprisonment or even torture, as in the case of editor in chief Jacobo Timmerman, many of these writers would choose exile. The clique also included fashion columnist Felisa Pinto (married to Gato Barbieri's brother, jazz trumpeter Rubén Barbieri) and Silvia Rudni, a young political journalist. Manuel was a lively presence at the Di Tella vernissages; the circle of friends who showed up at these gallery and boutique events on Florida encompassed intellectuals and—more fun—the fashion crowd, performance artists, and cineastes, among them Luzbel González, Marcial Berro (fashion reporter and jewelry designer), set designer Kado Kotzer, and installation artist Renata Schussheim: artisans who shared his eclecticism, from curiosity about the variations of embroidery stitches or silent films to appreciation of all forms of music, from boleros to Arnold Schönberg. A young admirer of the newly famous author then, Renata, with straight proto-punk-red hair and big blue eyes, cut a striking figure at Di Tella, where she modeled her latest sartorial inventions. Though mere acquaintances then, Renata and Manuel reconnected in the eighties to collaborate on experimental theater in Brazil.

Manuel preferred social playmates with whom he could work—Felisa, for example, was his fashion consultant for *Heartbreak Tango* and she contributed authentic illustrations from women's magazines of the thirties and forties (*Maribel, Para Ti*) for the covers of the Sudamericana editions of *Betrayed by Rita Hayworth* and *Heartbreak Tango*. Felisa and sexy actresses Marcela López Rey and Libertad LeBlanc—a buxom blonde à la Mamie Van Doren—were fun, chic companions, even willing bait on erotic forays. After movie outings Manuel and Felisa, or sometimes Libertad, would go for a drink at a particular beer garden on 9 de Julio—the avenue Buenos Aires boasts is the widest in the world—where he fancied a waiter whose work schedule he seemed to know by heart. "Just an ordinary-looking straight guy," remarked Felisa; Libertad remembers that Manuel took notes as they sat at the café, and, after reading *Kiss of the Spider Woman* some years later, both Felisa and Libertad realized that this obscure object of desire at the beer garden could have been a model for the waiter Molina had a crush on.[23]

During the last months of 1967, happy months of intense writing, journalists Tomás Eloy Martínez and Silvia Rudni were close to Manuel, bonding over their concern about the worsening economic and political situation in Argentina and its effect on cultural life. Every Saturday during November and December Manuel would visit Tomás at his place downtown, to go over drafts of *Heartbreak Tango*. Another cohort was firebrand Susana "Piri" Lugones, a pivotal figure in Manuel's nascent literary career. Manuel had been introduced to Piri at Jorge Alvarez's bookstore/press on Talcahuano in downtown Buenos Aires, between bustling Corrientes and Lavalle. In the late sixties and early seventies, Jorge Alvarez was a meeting place for young writers, including Luis Gusmán, Osvaldo Lamborghini, and Piri's friend Rodolfo Walsh. Though she was petite, almost frail-looking with a conspicuous limp, Piri Lugones, an enthusiastic advocate of revolutionary art, seemed a dominatrix to Manuel, with her imperious Bette Davis air and penetrating eyes. From a distinguished Argentine family, she introduced herself with defiant sarcasm as "granddaughter of the poet, daughter of the torturer." Her grandfather, one of Argentina's greatest poets, Leopoldo Lugones, had committed suicide over an unhappy love affair, and her father, a torturer for the police during the "infamous decade" of the thirties, had invented the deadly instrument of torture called the *picana eléctrica,* or electric prod—cruelly applied to prisoners' genitals to force confessions. Piri, who had many affairs and was married several times, lived up to her flamboyant heritage. In the end, she and her sometime lover Rodolfo Walsh were counted among the 30,000 "disappeared": she met a violent end, beaten to death in 1977 by Jorge Videla's secret police for her support of guerrilla activities during the "Dirty Wars."

Piri made it her duty to *épater le bourgeois* and would sometimes go slumming with Manuel on nocturnal excursions in the Boca, flirting with sailors along the southside docks. These adventures, mostly voyeuristic or imaginary, as if Coco were still playing hide-and-seek with Elenita, were particularly kinky for Manuel because of Piri's limp. Germán García and Daniel Divinsky, a young avant-garde editor who collaborated with Jorge Alvarez in those years, consider Piri the inspiration for the principal characters in *The Buenos Aires Affair*: the artist Gladys, with a physical defect—a missing eye—and her menacing lover Leo, an art critic and cultural czar with a political past.[24]

A month after Manuel signed the contract with Sudamericana *"me voilá emmerdé encore une fois,"* he wrote Emir:

Sometime in September, the book already in galleys, a scandalized linotypist (!) informed the editorial board that the verb *coger* [literally, in Spanish, "to grab," but "to fuck" in colloquial Argentine] was used more than thirty times, and not precisely to mean "grab"—for fear of censorship they're postponing publication.[25]

Censorship was the rule under General Juan Carlos Onganía, who had "grabbed" the reins of government in 1966 from his liberal predecessor, President Arturo Illia. Political fervor, sexual liberation, and Di Tella's experimental foment in artistic and intellectual circles had to be curbed before they spread to the working classes. After a week of strikes by students and workers culminated in a violent clash in Córdoba (called the *Cordobazo*) in May 1969, censorship and other restrictive measures made the atmosphere increasingly tense. Ernesto Schoo recalls Manuel's almost reckless indignation at that time. They had gone to see the last showing of a movie; it was a national holiday and, following the custom, the theater played the national anthem, a signal for the audience to stand up. Everyone stood except Manuel, who remained seated. When Schoo tried in vain to pull him up from his seat, fearful that someone in the audience might come over and pick a fight, Manuel protested: "Why should I show respect for this horrible government?"

By merely letting ordinary people speak in their own way about an oppressive reality, that is, by portraying the Argentina beyond the glittering pavement of Florida Street, *Betrayed by Rita Hayworth* was political as well as avant-garde art. Piri Lugones, a fierce promoter of Rodolfo Walsh and other young left-wing writers, urged Jorge Alvarez to publish this book, with its subversively frivolous title. Alvarez's first (and ongoing) project, cartoonist Quino's radical political comic strip serial, *Mafalda*, was also a risky enterprise; though a bad businessman, Alvarez had good instincts and would be inclined to support Manuel.[26]

In June 1968, at a moment when the arts and the press were both under close scrutiny, *La traición de Rita Hayworth* was finally published. Manuel rushed over to see the first edition hot off the press. A thrill and a horror: the edition was riddled with typos which, for months, he would hasten to correct in every copy he could lay his hands on, whether in a bookstore or on a friend's bookshelf. In a tense atmosphere that promoted discord—Martínez and Ramiro de Casasbellas, the magazine's editors, hated Alvarez, Manuel wrote Emir—*Primera Plana* not only did not advertise the book but almost would not have reviewed it had it not been for Edgardo Cozarinsky, who wrote the first review, "An Apprenticeship of Life."[27]

Cozarinsky retraced the book's underground career before its publication, and he underscored its timely invocation of the movies—"the only possible mythology of this century." Assuring the reader (to dispel Manuel's concern) that only three chapters were narrated by Toto, Cozarinsky addressed the book's pathos and lyrical power: "The movies of the 1930s remain like an uncorrupted Eden; the most ridiculous illusions preserve the nobility of the simple emotions that engendered them." Anticipating the exigencies of the intelligentsia, he advanced the notion that Manuel was a pop novelist and an incisive analyst of "mass culture, urban folklore or the opiate of the masses: let the sociologists choose." At the same time he asserted that Manuel Puig was a modernist—Toto reincarnating daydreamer Emma Bovary and Proust's frail young Marcel. *Betrayed by Rita Hayworth* was the classic demonstration of what French critic René Girard called "triangular desire."[28] The inhabitants of Colonel Vallejos did not relate to each other directly but, as Don Quixote followed the example of a chivalrous knight, and Emma Bovary, a romantic heroine, they modeled their lives after the stars of the screen.

Cozarinsky astutely noted how the book fit, unobtrusively, the tenets of Russian formalism, French structuralism, and Bakhtin's concept of the novel as a "dialogue of languages." A positive review in *Sur* (written by Luis Justo) stressed further the novel's battle with censorship and the delicate matter of Toto as a "protohomosexual" protagonist. *Sur* editor in chief Pepe Bianco, a leading critic, novelist, and translator, and his elegant younger partner, Enrique Pezzoni, a discerning critic and later an editor at Sudamericana, instantly realized that Manuel was an authentic new talent.

Like Cozarinsky's review, Emir Monegal's article, "A Literary Myth Exploded," also blazed a trail for future Puig scholars.[29] Along with Cabrera Infante, Emir distinguished Manuel as a creator of the "novel of language," in which the author's role and other traditional literary conventions are subverted. Like the Cuban's recent, highly acclaimed *Tres tristes tigres* (*Three Trapped Tigers*), set in Havana in 1959 on the eve of revolution, *Betrayed by Rita Hayworth* was a spoken book, a gallery of voices. Emir was the first to articulate Manuel's humorous yet nonjudgmental attitude toward his characters and, Manuel declared, to make him feel that his intuitions and his conscious efforts were in perfect harmony.[30] Even though he had felt such harmony in the trance of writing, it was reassuring to be understood in print by a reader.

Though encouraged by the recognition he was receiving, Manuel felt generally ill-treated by the fatherland, as he reported to Emir: "They've all read your DIVINE SPREAD on [sic] *Imagen* but nobody mentions it, how generous of them." Most "critics were lukewarm. After more than three years of waiting, that came as a big disappointment."[31] Good reviews in widely read magazines like *Panorama* and *Siete Días* were not given prominent placement, and the only two major newspapers to review the book, the liberal-left *Clarín* and moderate-conservative *La Nación*, considered it "minor" with "cinematic tics in the dialogue." (The ultra-conservative *La Prensa* ignored it.) In *La Nación* the critic disapproved, polemically, of the author's use of spoken Argentine: "the experiment is interesting but undermines the writer's effective participation in a form of language which is not his own code and whose legitimate user is the common people." "Can you believe this!?" Manuel exclaimed to Emir.[32] Political posturing determined what qualified as literature: the writer could not use the language of the common people, a language which was not—or rather should not be—his code.

Prudishly censorial, *La Nación* pegged Puig's "thin" stories about frustrated housewives and insecure adolescents as "depraved" and narrated with "defiant crudeness . . . [as] the ill-humored chronicle of a social milieu and an era, with few variations in his portrayals of people's lives." Even "Borges's people" had begun to attack; Manuel was upset by a slur uttered in public by Carlos Mastronardi, a *Sur* poet and critic, and a dear friend of the maestro. (As Borges's biographer, Emir lamented but excused the blind master's lack of interest in the younger generations.) The Argentine bourgeoisie perceived it as a Peronist novel:

> My novel presented a problem: it dealt with children and housewives in a small pampa town: it had no explicit political ideology, but its implicit criticism of the system was unpleasant to the censors. Worse than that, some of those children spoke the type of foul language that usually hides a fear of sexual initiation, and that really irked them.[33]

Manuel would always insist that he was neither for nor against any political party. There were Peronist traces in his work, beginning with his early screenplay, "La tajada"; many of his friends and acquaintances were Peronists, among them the actress Fanny Navarro. He identified with anyone marginalized, whether by class, sex, race, or age—and he sympathized with the desire for a Peronism that would *really* work for everyday people. His work was politically engaged in the sense that he wrote for his reader. Unlike certain engagé pundits, he did not presume to give voice to "those who don't have a voice." This was a messianic populist slogan he pooh-poohed by insisting that "everyone has a voice, but not everyone writes."

By trying to explain rather than taking a clear political position, he was inevitably embarking on a thorny path on the eve of the decade when military regimes would take over not only Argentina but its neighboring countries Chile and Uruguay. For some Argentines who had lived through the forties and fifties, it felt as if the country were reliving not only the Perón era but the fascist thirties in Europe. If under Onganía *Betrayed by Rita Hayworth* was labeled a Peronist novel, in the seventies *The Buenos Aires Affair* would be accused of anti-Peronism and censored during Hector Cámpora's presidency for juxtaposing obscenity with the name of Perón; even more damaging would be references in the novel to the use of torture by the secret police, and to the Socialist Party's initial "misunderstanding" of Peronism in the fifties. By the seventies, the guerrilla activity of the new Peronist left had accelerated into the tensions building up to the infamous Dirty Wars when military extremist groups "disappeared" 30,000 fellow Argentines. The horrors of this era would be the subject of many novels by writers of Manuel's generation, such as Luisa Valenzuela and Osvaldo Soriano. When in 1982 (the year he was nominated for the Nobel Prize) Manuel heard from Roberto Fernández Retamar, the director of *Casa de las Américas*, that *Heartbreak Tango* would be published in an edition in Cuba, his comment was "Better late than never."[34] By then a veteran of the ideological wars, he had learned to suspect behind most "literary" criticism the dynamics of cultural power struggles.

Wary of the poor distribution in Latin America and its damper on sales, Manuel compulsively visited bookstores to find out the number of books sold: "disorganized" Alvarez couldn't tell him how many copies had actually been printed in the first edition. They claimed six thousand, but he didn't believe them, and a year later (August 1969) there was still no mention of a second edition. In Buenos Aires Manuel reported with dismay that "some bookstores took it out of the display window and hid it in the back because parents were complaining" about the explicit sex and shocking street language.[35] Radio Nacional broadcast a negative critique by popular radio announcer Antonio Carrizo, a fellow Villegan and an unsuccessful writer. As Manuel wrote to Emir:

> Here things are not going so well: two major bookstores have rejected the book as pornographic; on Radio Nacional, there was a 15-minute harangue; in the [popular women's] magazine *Claudia* Olga Orozco [a respected poet] did a review stating that the book was horrendous; two interviews, for *Atlántida* and *Siete Días*, were canceled without any explanation. I'm seeing, after a good stream of reviews, a hard-line second wave of reactions. Meanwhile *Primera Plana* completely ignores me while endorsing Germán García's *Nanina*, a dumb little product typical of our underdevelopment. Luckily I'm going to Europe to have a little fun because this is getting nasty. I think it's going to be difficult for me to live here; I need to find excuses to travel to detoxify from time to time.[36]

(As a "consolation prize" for canceling its contract, after ceding the rights to Jorge Alvarez, Sudamericana had agreed, reluctantly, to pay for his airfare to Paris to work on *Betrayed by Rita Hayworth* with his French translator, Laure Bataillon.)

Emir had left Paris to visit family in Montevideo before taking up his teaching post at Yale in October, and he wrote back to Manuel from Caracas, Venezuela, where he was visiting a friend. Incensed by the "antipornography or antiliterary campaign against the best novel produced by an Argentine since Cortázar's *Rayuela*," Emir stressed that what was "obscenely" unacceptable to Manuel's fellow citizens was "the exposure of underdevelopment"; "our Libertad Lamarques want to continue believing that they are Bette Davis."[37]

Having just been in Paris revising Laure "la magnifique" Bataillon's translation of *Rita*, Manuel was excited by the prospect of being read by non-Argentines.[38] Manuel already keenly felt that aggressive Argentine insecurity and prudish machismo would always keep him at bay; he would never receive the love or acceptance he craved:

I cannot communicate with people who know nothing of the world and think they know everything, lacking real sophistication . . . And the last straw is their sick joy in tearing down a fellow Argentine who has something valid to contribute— and not only the writers, but businessmen, workers, office employees.[39]

He wrote these words to Emir from Rome, where he was staying with Mario, covering expenses with a subtitle job.[40] On this occasion Mario asked him, "With all these new super-interesting friends that you have, will anyone replace your gorgeous 'Daniel Denis'?" Manuel asked him about those stories in the famous suitcase, and if he had definitively thrown them into the fire. Mario remembers that Manuel comforted him with these words, more or less:

I know you have something to say, and you'll say it. You don't need to say it now, but maybe when you're eighty years old with a few flawless pages, you'll do it. To be a writer one doesn't need to have a career or fill many pages, sometimes only one little book will do, one of those paperbacks that fit in one's pocket.

those little painted lips

Most people are other people. Their thoughts are someone else's opinions, their lives a mimicry, their passions a quotation.

—Oscar Wilde, *De Profundis*

Betrayed by Rita Hayworth had unmasked more literally than Manuel ever would again the life within; it remains (particularly in Toto's guileless soliloquies) his most lyrical novel. He needed new "tricks" so as not to repeat himself, he told Mario, when he first mentioned the second, or hostess, novel in 1965. He claimed, afterward, that *Heartbreak Tango* had come to him during a visit to Villegas, after an absence of eleven years, when he returned to Buenos Aires briefly in February 1967, and he

> met up again with some of the characters from my childhood. I was struck by an overwhelming disenchantment in those whose lives fitted into the social system of the period and who had never made any attempt to rebel. They had accepted all that world of sexual repression, had accepted its rules, the hypocrisy of the myth of female virginity and, needless to say, they had accepted authority. They struck me as disillusioned, now that they were growing older . . . It wasn't that they were conscious of being let down, just that they gave off an air of frustration and unhappiness . . . These people had believed in the rhetoric of irresistible love, irresistible passion, but their lives had not reflected this in any way.[41]

These people had married and produced children, had gone the normal bourgeois route, like Elenita and Raquel, whose harmonious home life he had longed for as a child, and which a part of him would always envy. They were the ones who, in Coco's childhood, seemed to be the winners, like cousin Jorge, the darling of all the girls, still, as an adult, an adolescent Don Juan. Manuel knew this character so well in part because his own love life was, after all, a succession of affairs. Jorge had been both Manuel's model and antithesis, and now was a model for his *Heartbreak Tango* creation, Juan Carlos.[42] Manuel had been molded in that remote town, but, unlike the others, he had resisted its strictures. Stimulated by backward glances, which confirmed his good fortune in having left that world behind, he recaptured the past once again, but this time in an even more distanced frame.

Manuel saw Villegas as an ongoing melodrama or, translated to radio, a soap opera like the ones people used to listen to every afternoon in Villegas. The Villegan "unconscious was inhabited" by the soap operas or women's pictures they attended regularly; their feelings were the feelings of characters in a melodrama, and they spoke the language of those old songs, radio plays, and movies to which they were addicted.[43] Manuel's image of Villegas as a soap opera led to a friend's suggestion that he write a *folletín*, or "serial novel," in the popular style of the best-selling Spanish author Corín Tellado.[44] "Impossible," Manuel at first responded, "I couldn't even write a letter of condolence." But *Heartbreak Tango* would begin with an ending, an obituary notice, followed by the standard *folletín*-style letter of condolence. His characters, comatose consumers of soap operas and tangos, were social conformists who needed to "act," who resisted self-knowledge and honest self-expression; they saw themselves as romantic heroines or the star-crossed lovers in popular songs. The book took the shape of a radio drama, subtitled *Folletín*, and, like *Betrayed by Rita Hayworth,* it had sixteen chapters, or episodes—sixteen would become the magic number of chapters in nearly all of Manuel's books.

Tangos spoke of "poor spinsters" who had been left in the dust because women (unlike men) gave "everything" when they loved; of men who had been abandoned by their women; and, ultimately, of the burden of being a man. Pitched in the nasal, whining tones of Libertad Lamarque or Carlos Gardel, tangos were not exotic, like their exported image, but as homespun as the delta blues—music about loneliness, nostalgia, and love lost. The tango originated in the 1890s as a lascivious dance in the brothels of Buenos Aires, in the dockside settlements teeming with new immigrants from Italy, Spain, and Eastern Europe. Of remote African origin, and in its original form a duel of sexuality and violence, domination and submission, it showed (as Borges put it) that "a fight could be a celebration."[45] At first its lyrics were improvised and obscene, and then they began to tell rustic sentimental stories about gauchos and their women. Finally, the lonely, seamy side of life and love became its main subject, tinged almost always with bitter recrimination.

A reflection of the "half breed" culture of Argentina, by the twenties the tango was popularized beyond the banks of the Boca by slick-haired idol Carlos Gardel, the illegitimate son of a French prostitute. He had begun his singing career in the house where his mother worked, where whores and hoodlums would bump and grind, thigh against pelvis, "cutting" or pausing suggestively[46]: in the brothels men also danced with men, crossing the line between machismo and buggery, and women danced with women, to excite their clients but also because many prostitutes were, or became, lesbians. Just as the forbidden waltz at first caused a scandal in Johann Strauss's Vienna, so the lumpen tango, straight from the lower depths inhabited by harlots, thieves, and foreigners, was too lewd for polite *criollo* society, where it struck both a xenophobic and homophobic nerve. Many prostitutes were Jewish, sold into white slavery from Eastern Europe; the petty thieves or *lunfardos* were often Italian. After 1910 the National Council of Education (presided over by educator Ramos Mejía) "nationalized" the tango, or cleansed it of its association with Jews and homosexuals. The tango was tied up in a nostalgia for its own past, not only for its former festivity but for "homosexual desire lost in the sanitization of a forbidden dance."[47] Only after it was adopted by the sophisticated "gay Paris" of the "lost generation" between the wars did this racy rite of arousal gain legitimate cachet. But it lost something in translation, now refined into a stylized ballroom dance for the elegant international set; or, in Borges's words, "a devilish orgy had become a way of walking." For the lower-class provincials in Argentina, however, the sizzling lyrics of seduction and abandonment remained their language of love.

Gardel was an Argentine hero with whom Manuel could identify: a talented musician and a bisexual celebrity who necessarily cast a veil of discretion over his private life; a man of modest origins, known to be kind and generous, a true man of the people. Gardel not only sang but composed, and his lyricist was Alfred LePera, whose tangos Manuel preferred and quoted almost exclusively in *Boquitas pintadas*. So as not to disillusion his fans all over South America and in Europe, it was never disclosed that Gardel and LePera were probably lovers. The duo died together, on tour, in a plane crash over Medellín, Colombia, in 1937; it was a national tragedy. Manuel would one day write a musical in honor of this universally mourned Argentine tango star who lived a double life. Called *Gardel, uma Lembrança* (Remembering Gardel), it depicted the life of a man whose "universe is inhabited by defeated creatures, forgiven betrayals, and the idealism of one's first love. Resentments do not last in his world because he understands and empathizes with all people. He never looks down upon them but rather sees them as equals."[48] Manuel could identify with Gardel's stoic discretion about his love life. While embroidering on the idiosyncrasies of his own sexual adventures, Manuel—like Gardel—did not divulge actual names except when confiding in his most intimate friends; Manuel had to imagine, mostly from the work, the details of the hero's brief existence. In July 1987 *Gardel, uma*

Lembrança would be performed in Rio, but it was a mediocre production as well as a minor work.[49]

Heartbreak Tango traces overlapping love triangles in Colonel Vallejos: Nélida, nicknamed Nené, a naive lower-middle-class blonde, and Mabel, a proper upper-middle-class girl who's really a vixen, vie for the handsome, consumptive Juan Carlos. Nené longs to marry him, while Mabel secretly has an affair with him. Mabel has mixed feelings about marrying him not only because of his illness but because, though from a good family, Juan Carlos is from old money gone downhill: his father had died leaving his wife and two children in debt.

Marina Calavera's brother Danilo, a tall, thin, handsome, suave young man, very popular with the girls in General Villegas, died in 1943 of tuberculosis. As a child, Manuel met him once at a ladies' tea, and remembers that because he shook hands with Danilo, Malé washed his hands thoroughly when they got home, for fear of contagion. Danilo had apparently contracted TB from his older brother Vicente, who had returned home with the disease after traveling around the region on an electoral campaign. Danilo Caravera, his brother Vicente, and perhaps Baldo were the composite model of the consumptive Juan Carlos in *Heartbreak Tango,* who is resentful because his once prosperous family has come down in the world. TB, the industrial age's plague—followed in the twentieth century by cancer and AIDS—that had killed many a romantic hero or heroine in the latter nineteenth century, was not uncommon in the Argentine backlands before hygienic conditions were modernized. Manuel's backwater vision of Villegas in his first two novels would remain a vision petrified in time. When he received a visit in Rio in 1986 from one of his childhood friends, José Luis Chavarri, he was surprised to learn that they finally had running water and electricity.

A subplot introduces Raba (Fanny), a servant girl, and her romance with Juan Carlos's drinking buddy Pancho, a bricklayer, who moves up in the world and becomes a policeman, abandoning Fanny for a clandestine affair with Mabel after her family has been disgraced by a lawsuit over the sale of diseased cattle. Episode 11 records Fanny's thoughts as she cleans house, feeling abandoned by Pancho. Composed of tango lyrics as they play in Fanny's mind, the episode builds from a folksy tale about a gaucho and his gal, to the bitter "Aquel Maldito Tango" (That Damn Tango) about a girl in a sweatshop who is seduced and abandoned, to a sad tale about a forlorn blind girl, and, finally, to a brutal lament about the "cruel lonely night." At this point, Fanny catches Pancho leaving Mabel's bedroom and kills him in a fit of rage.[50]

Manuel used tango lyrics (mostly LePera's) as epigraphs for each installment of *Boquitas* "because they're pretty but especially because they immediately evoke a melody, create a very efficient nostalgic effect." In the first episode, "He was my whole life" prefaces the news of Juan Carlos's death, which is followed by grief-stricken Nené's condolences to his widowed mother.[51] When Nené, at the novel's end, dreams of being reunited in heaven—and in the flesh!—with Juan Carlos, Manuel felt that her naive romanticism was best expressed in the words of the bolero "Nosotros" (The Two of Us), written by Pedro Junco and sung by Agustín Lara. Nené takes the lyric "in the name of this love and for your good I bid you farewell" and makes it her own: "in the name of Juan Carlos who for my good bids me farewell."[52]

Significantly the original book's final title, *Boquitas pintadas* (Little Painted Lips), came not from a tango but a dulcet fox trot, "Blondes of New York," with lyrics by LePera. It was sung by the great Gardel in *The Tango on Broadway*, an arcane Argentine flick in which the star visits New York in 1934 and finds himself pursued by and pursuing the "blondes of New York." If *Betrayed by Rita Hayworth* was a screenplay manqué, the new novel paid tribute to Manuel's earliest movie love, the American musical, and was a tongue-in-cheek homage to the tango.

When Manuel first mentioned he was writing a *folletín*, Tomás Eloy Martínez immediately suggested running it in weekly episodes in *Primera Plana*. Manuel was thrilled, as he wrote Emir:

> For me it's a very interesting experiment. I want to combine the avant-garde with popular appeal, the latter being very important to me. I want to send you something soon to get your opinion. It's very risky material, but the good part is that I got out of the autobiographical mode for a while. The second novel [here he refers to *Humedad*] is stuck because I needed to breathe other air; I was fed up with "totismo" [Totoism]. Besides, the second one is a bit abstruse, more difficult than *Betrayed by Margarita Cansino* and I'm concerned about leaving the reader behind.[53]

He wanted readers to be drawn to his next book; he didn't want it to take three years to get published. Literary kitsch could be a didactic tool, Manuel felt: while kitsch was the schlock that passed for art in fascist states, it could teach something to people who did not have access to more privileged forms of education.[54] He had hit on an idea, Emir assured him, that others would envy: innovative fiction that was also entertaining. His novel was a good tragicomic soap opera that also revealed how melodramas undermined the social values they appeared to uphold.

Buoyed by *Primera Plana*'s promise to start his serial in January, Manuel forged ahead, determined to finish by the new year. And he did, completing in a few months—"record time," he told Mario—the best-seller he would consider, in retrospect, his most effortless novel. He wrote it with "iron discipline," working a couple of hours in the morning and four or five more in the afternoon and evening; on the final chapters he worked till eight or nine at night and then went swimming (at an indoor pool where, according to Tomás Eloy, he was having an affair with a swimming instructor).

To accentuate his own distance and, at the same time, his characters' lack of self-awareness, for the first time Manuel risked using the third person. Still apprehensive about handling standard Spanish, he played with a supposed objectivity by overdoing it, inventing an affectless "weather report" third person which followed meticulously the course of one day in the life of his characters. He used this deliberately flat voice to interpolate brief impersonal descriptions between letters: the contrast between the tone of the letters and the affectless description of the letter writer's actions dramatizes how disconnected the character is from her feelings; at the same time, by leaving out everything but the trivia of everyday activity, Manuel joked to the reader about how limited the supposedly omniscient point of view really was. He continued perfecting narrative devices from *Betrayed by Rita Hayworth*—using each new chapter or section to spotlight a different character, or using dialogue to provide the immediacy of the real. In *Heartbreak Tango* he used dialogue (with the character's inner thoughts running alongside) to provide also the immediacy of improvised theater, highlighting the dramatic effect of veiling truth with lies.

Manuel set most of the action of the novel between 1937 and 1939, years when Malé and Baldo were struggling newlyweds in Villegas, when his mother was the outsider who had married the local Don Juan, stepping inevitably into a rivalrous situation with other women in town, and seeking solace in her little son. Using letters, newspaper articles, police reports, and other supposed "documents," he began the novel with dramatic news, Juan Carlos's funeral in 1947, and ended with a coda in the present, 1968, announcing Nené's funeral. Juan Carlos's death marks the boundary between the characters' past and present, corresponding chronologically to Manuel's adolescence and the closure of his childhood in Villegas. Manuel paid obsessive attention to dates in *Heartbreak Tango*—he paid the same consistent attention in real life to birthdays. Almost all of the novel's significant events occur in the months of his parents' birthdays, beginning with Juan Carlos's death in April (fall), Baldo's month, and ending with Nené's demise in September (spring), Malé's month.[55] If stream-of-consciousness was a dominant device in the first novel, he mounted his episodic serial, with its complex and yet precise plot, mostly upon an edifice of letters—his own lifeline to loved ones, one might recall, in recent years. At Johns Hopkins in Baltimore, on an academic tour in 1976, Manuel met John Barth, the honored writer in residence. Barth asked: "Manuel, when you wrote your epistolary novel, were you trying to return to the roots of fiction, as I was with my novel *Letters?*" Edmund White, who had introduced the two novelists, stood by, amused at Manuel's reply: "I'd been living in Paris and elsewhere so many years that I have the characters do the writing; that way, if they make a mistake, it's their fault."[56]

Broadly speaking, letters are literature, with the exception that letters—to the chagrin of inquisitive biographers—are intended for certain eyes only. Normally a private mode of disclosure, letters become fodder for gossip when made public, and are always potentially dangerous.[57] In the eyes of former neighbors in Villegas, Manuel went too far when he aired their dirty linen under the guise of fiction, mischievously revealing their secrets while they looked on, indignant and helpless. For the first time he had sculpted a perfect plot, carved out of town gossip, about ostracized women who dared to act as free agents, about maligned outsiders—an implied defense of those who were "different." Writing was a playful, perhaps vengeful way to make sense of the past. The people he was "analyzing" were still himself and his family; Villegas was a family too, a family whose betrayals he now betrayed.

a best-seller

Sentimental about love, driven by ambition.

—José Ortega y Gasset

Manuel had finished *Heartbreak Tango* by the last week of December 1967 when he received the disappointing news that Casasbellas, the editor at *Primera Plana*, decided the book was too long to publish in serial form; the other magazines and newspapers he approached over the next months, from the conservative daily *La Nación* to *Panorama*, all said the same thing.[58] Manuel thought that, more than its length, the novel's fragmented structure made it difficult to sell. Still stuck with Jorge Alvarez as publisher—and with no income in sight—he dispatched a last-minute application to the Guggenheim Foundation, to which he would apply again two years later, both times to no avail.[59] Now at Yale University, and still recuperating from the bitter battle over *Mundo Nuevo*, Emir explained to Manuel that his failure to win the fellowship had nothing to do with his talent and everything to do with politics:

> Caro Tenuto:
>   . . . Through a friend at the Guggenheim I found out that as long as one of the judges [for fellowships to Latin Americans] Juan Marichal of Harvard University remains on the committee, you should not even bother to apply. This Spanish gentleman (educated in Mexico, and the brother-in-law of Pedro Salinas, an illustrious mafioso) thinks your books are bad. The fact that his specialization is the "History of Ideas" in nineteenth-century Spain (if such a thing exists) should placate your vanity.[60]

Writing to Severo about his "drama of suspense and love, in two acts, titled . . . Ay, I don't dare, I will bring it to you so that you can confirm my folly, the *folletín* in 16 episodes," Manuel announced his upcoming trip to Paris in late spring 1968.[61] With Severo's helpful suggestions about some final structural problems, he penciled in the last touches in the wake of the

May student riots in Paris, which would reverberate in Argentina exactly one year later. "If I show what I write it's because I'm insecure about the results," Manuel would admit freely. He always involved his close friends of the moment, if only to confirm an intuition or dispel a doubt, or as sources for "raw material": Nino, who in his cluttered apartment on Place d'Italie in Paris hoarded Argentine movie magazines and other memorabilia from the thirties, helped Manuel find song lyrics for *Heartbreak Tango* and, later, film dialogues for *The Buenos Aires Affair*.[62]

When he returned to Buenos Aires at the end of June, good news awaited him: at Sudamericana, Enrique Pezzoni had reversed the publishing house's previous veto. As Alvarez did not "bother" to pay royalties (Manuel was not his only author to complain), Pezzoni obliged the lax publisher to release the option for a second novel which Manuel had been pressed to grant. With Pezzoni's supportive presence, Manuel was able to follow every detail of production, including the design of the jacket; the image was a genuine illustration of two tailored ladies from *Bon Ton*, a haute couture magazine of the thirties, which Felisa had procured. Whenever possible, and certainly for all the original editions of his works, Manuel would select (in consultation with those in the know) the cover art. Always on the lookout for materials in travels over the years with Malé, he gradually acquired a small but valuable collection of illustrations, mostly art deco prints or arcane film posters. He was particularly fond of two white Russians who had fled to Paris in the twenties: Erté, designer of *le style Ritz*, a refined commercial art whose artificiality was an effect of "color, jewels, movement . . . the triumph of detail over age, place, gender," and the glamorous Tamara de Lempicka, who painted kitschily stylized, pseudo-cubist nudes.[63]

In May 1969, Gallimard finally published *La trahison de Rita Hayworth*, and by June *Le Monde* had lauded it as one of the best novels of 1968–69 to be published in France: "The immense richness of its language, spoken language, natural and wise . . . makes Puig and his work a completely original phenomenon in Latin American literature."[64] *Heartbreak Tango* was published four months later in Buenos Aires, in September, and it was an instant best-seller: "Already 100,000 copies!" Manuel wrote Emir:

> Severo, Nestor Almendros, Pepe Bianco, María Rosa Oliver and others believe "Heartbreak Tango" is better than

"Rita"—I think they're nuts but if they all think that, better
for me. "Rita" was much more carefully written, but I think
"B.P." is impressive for the structure.[65]

Its structure did impress certain literati, but, most important, *Heartbreak
Tango* appealed to many readers; with its tragicomic plot about characters
presented both as private individuals and members of their social class, it
was social realism made fun. The novel had something for everyone: romance, sex, humor, suspense, nostalgia, all as experienced by real people,
consumers of soap operas and *cursi* love songs. It was almost "hyperrealist"
in its reproduction of an era and a place, in its mimicry of the way people,
especially women, think and feel.

It opened the gates to Colonel Vallejos, providing the reader with a
guide to the even richer emotional content of the first novel. Reviews and
interviews appeared in quick succession, and Sudamericana rushed to bring
out its edition of *Betrayed by Rita Hayworth*, which became a best-seller in
Argentina in 1970. Manuel appeared on the cover of magazines all over
town: in one photo he was wearing his leather jacket, imagining (he told a
friend) that motorcyclists would find him sexy as they stopped for the light
at a busy corner and caught a glimpse of his photo at a kiosk. Rosita "Frou
Frou" Bailón, a fashion designer at the Galería del Este who was almost as
campy as the characters in the novel, named a line of forties-style platform
shoes "Boquitas pintadas"; the "hottest" Argentine media celebrities clamored to star in the film version planned by Leopoldo Torre Nilsson and
Beatriz Guido. Manuel's peers envied his ability to invent a novel about the
people, for the people, and, in a sense, by the people. "There are two elements that need to coincide for me to write a book," as Manuel later ana-
lyzed his writerly urges:

> I have to feel a need to exorcise certain personal obsessions.
> There are others I have no need to exorcise. Each of us has his
> own little masochistic game, and wants to continue with cer-
> tain tortures until death, but there are some tortures of which
> I do say "enough of this already." But I don't write a novel—
> since for me it's not only about writing but about communi-
> cating—if I have the sensation that that problem is not

shared. That is, I'm interested in situating myself as one more victim of the collective unconscious . . . Yes, I'm very interested in clarifying certain things for myself and achieving certain stylistic [aesthetic] goals, but the book has to be read too; if not, it lacks a certain sexiness. Writing is a dialogue with another person. On the other hand, I go alone to see a movie: that's an act in which the other person is for me the movie.[66]

Moviegoing was easy, passive play: something to sit back and enjoy; writing, on the other hand, was an active testament of love, an ongoing relationship, hard work, often painfully confrontational.

Now that there was money to keep him going, he had "the strength" to start a new novel in a new genre, a "sort of thriller." His own intuitions and the reactions of those he trusted, like Emir, seemed right, and he would continue to combine "innovation with popular appeal":

Well, the Puig bulletin is completed with the announcement of his next novel, along detective story lines, now shooting on location in perverted Buenos Aires. It's a sort of thriller. Do you remember the slogan MGM used to launch *I'll Cry To-morrow* with Susan Hayward? It went like this: "A film shot on location inside a woman's soul!" Well the same can be said about my thriller.[67]

The debut of *Heartbreak Tango* coincided with holiday festivities and the collapse of the Onganía regime, and the book was nominated as a finalist for the *Primera Plana* literary prize. On New Year's Eve, Felipe del Canto, a wealthy playboy and advertising entrepreneur who owned a fabulous wrap-around penthouse in the heart of Buenos Aires's elegant Barrio Norte, threw one of his extravagant dinner parties for seventy-five guests in honor of the author. Everybody who was anybody at the Galería del Este or in Buenos Aires's high society was invited, as well as international luminaries like Severo Sarduy, who was passing through on a book tour. It was a hot summer night, and all the windows and French doors were thrown open onto an ample terrace with a spectacular view of the harbor and the delta of the Río de la Plata. Champagne bottles popped and poured, huge joints were passed, everyone danced rumbas, sambas, and rock 'n' roll, and, at one or two in the morning, Severo leapt onto the long dining table, pants tight front and back, and began to strip. Manuel immediately followed suit and joined *la rumbera* for a striptease à duo, imitating Rita's "Put the Blame on Mame" in *Gilda*. All the revelers were ordered to join in: except for Felisa, the few women at this bacchanalia hightailed it.[68] Though he could be sexually enterprising, Manuel was almost a puritan when it came to drugs; at the same party, Felisa remembers, Manuel would not smoke pot for "hygienic" reasons, he didn't want to come into contact with any germs. He claimed another practical pretext, as a writer: he never drank in excess or took mind-bending drugs, because memory was his most valuable tool. "It was as if he were from an older generation," Renata Schussheim remarked; "he wouldn't take drugs or smoke pot even at intimate gatherings of a few close friends." These friends, like writers Luisa Valenzuela, Tamara Kamenszain, Hector Libertella, were doubtless more "sixties" but still enjoyed Manuel's witty, flirtatious company.

Among the *Primera Plana* judges that year were María Rosa Oliver (whom Manuel called one of those "funny millionaire communists" common among the Argentine cultural elite) and Paraguayan novelist Roa Bastos. They arrived at the same decision as the Biblioteca Breve judges four years earlier: Manuel's writing was too frivolous. During his visit that May to Buenos Aires, Severo tried to defend *Heartbreak Tango* before some of the committee members who, like María Rosa, were good friends of his, but to no avail. "La Chelo was very brave," Manuel wrote to Cabrera Infante. "She fought tooth and nail even though her position as my friend and a fag was uncomfortable."[69] While some critics claimed the book was too gimmicky—its many narrative devices do produce a cluttered effect—Manuel felt their conclusions were influenced by their homophobia.

From his desk on Gloucester Road in London, Cabrera Infante sympathized with Manuel's desire to escape to Europe; Manuel, like himself and other "unhappy few," was caught between the "Castradoradores" (pun on Castro worshipers and castrators) and a reign of mediocrity.[70] In a recent letter from Queen of the Plata, Manuel reported to Cabrera Infante that even the hard-line "bolches"—left-wing intellectual snobs or poseurs—were forced to praise his controversial novel *Tres tristes tigres*, in "all conversations about the boom of LL; not Libertad Lamarque whom we love so much, but

Latin American Literature."[71] That is, with this new institution came power struggles and hegemonies. "Everything is very sad and flat," Cabrera Infante wrote him, "and I can understand that you are drawn to Europe; after all, Argentina belongs to the Alvarezes!" Unfortunately, as Manuel had already learned in Rome, and Cabrera Infante reminded him, Europe was not a free port. "The scourge has spread to England too."

To help fund his travels Manuel accepted an offer from the magazine *Siete Días* to serve as film and theater chronicler at large in New York, London, and Paris; the pay was minimal but at least covered his airfare. At the time (1969–70) intellectual peers on the home front looked upon these "Letters from Manuel Puig" (published as *Bye-Bye Babilonia*) as unadulterated kitsch. Full of digressions, the bulletins sound occasionally like Mabel or Nené's letters in *Heartbreak Tango*, coyly humorous, but Manuel's hunches about culture and fashion were fresh, shaped by common sense as well as sensibility. He turned his reader's attention to revivals and the latest productions, and to the disjunctions and continuities between past glories and current successes.[72] Reflecting the foment of the late sixties. Manuel's chronicles, for all their camp are filled with lucid glimpses, and chart concerns and materials he was fleshing out in his novel-in-progress, *The Buenos Aires Affair*.

London in early 1970 was cold, people's faces inexpressive compared to the greater joie de vivre on faces in New York, now his favorite city. Argentine friends, newlyweds Delia Cancela and Pablo Mesejean, felt the same way; Delia and Pablo, both visual artists, had just come from New York to do a special issue on fashion and color for *Vogue*. Swinging London, they assured Manuel, was no more: "It's like arriving late at a party where the few remaining guests look tired. You can't tell if it's a party or a wake."[73] The only friendly faces in London were Latin ones (Italian, Spanish), which all seemed to say: "The places one has to go to make a living!"[74] Comparing this visit with his trip to London in 1958, Manuel realized that on the earlier occasion he had been in the hands of friends like Paul "007" Dehn—now a sought-after screenwriter—who took good care of him. He concluded that, as usual, memory was selective; the British had been as nasty then as they were now but he remembered only the good parts. He saw Paul and other friends: everybody was busy but, with the "cult of friendship" in London, there were constant lunches, dinners, banquets. Manuel left London that

winter on a sour note, as he reports in his *Bye-Bye Babylon*, Argentine jour-
nalese:

> London gem: I have a plane to catch at 10 a.m. In the hotel
> they forget to call me at 7. I wake up at 8:10. Panic. Without
> thinking I put the typewriter in my suitcase, instead of my
> bag (which doesn't get weighed). I get to the airport at the last
> minute. They charge me for excess luggage because of the
> typewriter, a fortune. I argue, there's no time to move the ma-
> chine to the bag. The employee, a kind of Flora Robson,
> seems to derive sadistic joy from the incident . . . I've had it!
>
> Good-bye London: It seems I stepped in and then out with
> my left foot forward. To boot, I'm leaving with the flu. On the
> plane now, I have a fever.[75]

Manuel began to see enemies everywhere on the British front, including in a
sympathetic critic, David Gallagher. Guillermo, burdened with his own
Cuban paranoias, thought Manuel was overdoing his Argentine ones: "Our
mutual Sally became quite historical all of a sudden and wanted to find a
British publisher, a lover, two lorry drivers, and Lord Snowdon all in one
day. It was not impossible, but difficult, yes."[76]

British publishers were resistant to American translations, and even after *Betrayed by Rita Hayworth* received great reviews in the United States, an
edition did not come out in the United Kingdom until a few years later.
Guillermo began urging Manuel to employ an agent, to which Manuel
replied on the spot: "But my dear, I'm a career woman; that's *my* job."

After stops in Paris and Milan, Manuel went on to Rome, where, win-
tering chez Mario, he nursed the flu he had caught in London. Milan had
been a ball, Manuel wrote Emir: Feltrinelli beat Einaudi to the punch and
signed first *Heartbreak Tango* and then *Betrayed by Rita Hayworth*, and
Manuel had reveled with old and new friends like Inge Feltrinelli, the
buxom German widow of the publisher, who had a Tallulah Bankhead flair
for bars and bartenders. Feltrinelli, a staunch and dapper Marxist deeply en-
trenched in Italian politics, had blown himself up a year earlier by mistake
with a homemade bomb, and Inge was now living with a prestigious Argentine architect at her townhouse on Via Andegari, which over the years

would be open to Manuel on his flights through Milan.[77] *Heartbreak Tango* was a hit in Spain; Seix Barral wanted to publish an "emergency edition" in Barcelona, and invited Manuel "to make personal appearances." Seix Barral was expanding its horizons and also wanted to publish *Betrayed by Rita Hayworth*, Manuel noted in triumph, making a playful allusion: "I feel like Gale Sondergaard in *Return of the Spider Woman*." He continued:

> And also it seems "forever Kay" [Guillermo] and "darling Vanessa" [Severo] are returning, which means the new Seix Barral is trying to imitate Universal and its well-remembered superproduction "Three Wise Girls Smart Up." Or was it "Three Smart Girls Wise Up"? (The three of us are taking singing lessons so that they'll give us the role of Durbin!!!)[78]

In New York, Emir's new friend José Guillermo Castillo, the director of the newly founded Center for Inter-American Relations, couched in a stately Park Avenue town house donated by the Rockefeller family, was about to land an American publisher for Manuel.[79] Castillo, a cherub-faced Venezuelan artist (and owner of a gallery in Caracas) who gave lavish receptions in the late sixties for writers, publishers, translators, literary agents, and society patrons, also promised Manuel a translator for both novels. Jack Macrae, editor at E. P. Dutton, and his associate, Marian Skedgell, enthused by their success with Norman Thomas Di Giovanni's translations of Borges, were willing to take a chance on this risky new foreign author—but only if "Di Gi" would undertake the translation. For a variety of reasons, including the difficulty of the text and the payment he was offered, Di Gi decided against the project.

For Manuel, as for many polyglot writers (and publishers), translators were necessary evils. "I'm tired of nursing translations and dealing with translators," Guillermo Cabrera Infante remarked in agreement, "who in the best of cases are pathetic people who earn their living betraying."[80] For both Manuel and Guillermo, translations were rough drafts which they had to alter and refine into literature. Upon finishing *Betrayed by Rita Hayworth* in 1965, Manuel already knew he needed to publish beyond national borders to survive. He was an Argentine, after all, for whom Paris and New York were the capitals of the civilized world. Translations were generally pale

clones, and the original would always be best understood in its own language, but, having done subtitle work in film, an industry that depended
upon global marketing, Manuel was preconditioned to think of the Spanish
version as a small cog in a vast publishing apparatus. As it turned out, for
most of his career he would feel more appreciated outside his own country,
if not outside his own language. Because of this destiny, which Guillermo
experienced much more radically as a Cuban outcast, he kept urging
Manuel to take on an agent, because "in these countries [outside of Latin
America] it doesn't work without."[81]

When Manuel returned to Buenos Aires from Europe in April 1970, in
time for a sunny Argentine autumn, he was an international literary figure.
He had been invited as an honored writer to the Frankfurt Book Fair coming up in September, where European and even Asian publishers and literary agents would pay him court. *Betrayed by Rita Hayworth* would be
nominated as one of 1971's most notable books by the American Library Association at the same time (March 1972) that *Una frase, un rigo appena*
(*Heartbreak Tango*) came out in Italy (with 65 errata, Manuel noted) in a
prestigious Club degli Editori edition of 80,000 copies. Now Manuel was
mentor to aspiring young writers, like Luis Gusmán, who were filled with
genuine admiration for *Betrayed by Rita Hayworth* and *Heartbreak Tango*.
The tall, thin, soft-spoken Luis, with his almost archetypal Argentine
melancholy, had met Manuel through their high-strung mutual friend, Osvaldo Lamborghini. Osvaldo, Luis, and Luis's wife and fellow psychologist
Beatriz Castillo, an energetic woman who complemented her husband's lan-
guid presence, were among the few Argentines whom Manuel felt were his
sincere advocates, and he gratefully reciprocated by connecting them with
critics, academics, or publishers who might promote their work in the
United States and Europe.

Since the Di Gi deal had fallen through by the end of March 1970, I entered the picture at the age of twenty-three. I had already cut my baby teeth
on excerpts from Severo Sarduy's latest arabesque-in-progress (*Cobra*, 1972)
and had collaborated with Cabrera Infante on his Joycean *Tres tristes tigres*.
With Emir as my close consultant, I seemed a reasonable candidate, but the
publisher would have to see samples in English before the book was accepted. Manuel chose a few scattered dialogues, monologues, and Herminia's journal: "Not difficult and rather seductive," he said.[82] Only the

latter was true, but he worked with me, led me by the hand, encouraging my first awkward attempts, and by May 1970 we both had a written agreement with Dutton. I was to be paid a flat fee of $1,500, and the author, an advance of $2,500. By December 1970, we had turned in the manuscript. *Betrayed by Rita Hayworth* was an immediate success, in September 1971, thanks largely to the exuberant *New York Times* reviewer John Alexander Coleman, who gave Señor Puig—"full of literary allure, magnetic glower, smouldering good looks and plenty of plain panache and strut"—a grand head start.[83] Manuel even discovered, on a trip to Mexico, that his fans now included the real Rita Hayworth.

He met her in Mexico City at her suite in the Camino Real Hotel during the filming of *Wrath of God* with Robert Mitchum.[84] When he returned to Buenos Aires for New Year's 1971 (after a whirlwind "career woman" tour from "frenetic" New York to "relaxing" Mexico), he described the occasion:

> Arriving in Mexico was wonderful; what healthy people. There's no rush-rush and I saw a lot of sweetness; I think I'm going to spend some time there toward the end of '72. Rita, Mrs. Hayworth, was there and I phoned her. She was divine, very warm; we spoke for about an hour and later I went to see her at the hotel. She was so old that she frightened me. She must be around sixty but the tiny wrinkles on the cheeks make her seem more like seventy, so sinister . . . She knew all about the book from the reviews and was DELIGHTED with "Betrayed by Herself"; she asked me to send her an autographed copy.[85]

Ms. Hayworth had not read the book, but she was grateful for the publicity. Manuel told her that he was glad to return at the very least "a fraction of the pleasure she had given him" and the world. Manuel had brought her the *New York Times* review, illustrated with the glamorous photo of her as Gilda, which he asked her to autograph. She wrote demurely: "I don't really believe you were betrayed by me." She was so moved to be remembered in this way, Manuel said, that tears rolled down her cheeks, though Mexican playwright Vicente Leñero, who helped arrange the meeting, remembers that his Argentine friend had been sadly disappointed by her vague indifference.[86] A few months later Manuel visited her once more, at her home in Beverly Hills; this time the ravages of Alzheimer's, the disease that would eventually kill her, were evident. Whatever transpired when Manuel met her, to be acknowledged by an ex-goddess of the silver screen was both a dream come true and a disillusionment.

Manuel clearly suspected that *Heartbreak Tango* would shock people in Villegas: while he had promised Malé it was "harmless," he warned her, in the same breath, not to discuss it with her acquaintances there. He told Elenita, when she came to visit him in Buenos Aires, to explain to the people in town, especially the older folks who would recognize the sources, that his aim was not to expose real persons but to create characters by capturing the strong, admirable "spirit" of certain individuals. Having read the book, Elenita thought otherwise but, like his teacher Ana María Ladaga and others who were fond of him, dismissed the controversy by saying "he was so imaginative": even his friends were jolted by the dissonance between their image of Coco as "delicate, refined" and the crude language in his first books. Many townspeople felt mocked to see their speech in print, particularly certain conservative Spanish Catholics who reduced the two novels to "the product of resentment" against the upper-class landowners; the Puigs, after all, were a nouveau-riche mercantile family. While the romances "our grandparents" read had their "laws" and required a certain sentimentality, this "son of Villegas" had constructed a "long hair," "baroque," trashy novel that misrepresented "respectable people" and at the same time was so photographic that it left little to the imagination.[87] These contradictions in the review published by the local newspaper did not seem to bother its readers, evidently undecided as to whether the distortions or the accuracies were worse. Intolerance and the absence of cultural sophistication conspired with a justifiable sense of betrayal and exposure. Years later in Brazil, an Argentine friend in exile, Patricio Bisso, told Manuel he had lent his signed copy of *Heartbreak Tango* to his grandmother, thinking she would be fascinated by this re-creation of her era. She was shocked—"Muy fuerte" (strong stuff), she said—and hastened to throw it out with the garbage.

Felisa Pinto was going to interview Manuel for a television program called *Identikit*, in General Villegas in 1970, with Aída Bortnik, a journalist and screenwriter who later wrote the script for *Official Story*. After the censorious review "Gossip . . ." came out in the local paper, however, Manuel decided against this plan: "I was afraid I'd be lynched." Felisa did the interview in Buenos Aires in 1972—Manuel's first appearance before a camera as celebrated author—but already there were strong feelings against him and it was not aired; the military government was steadily taking over the media, and censorship was flaring up.[88]

Did Manuel ever return to Villegas? Some townspeople claimed that he did return on at least two occasions, once in 1971 and the last time in 1984.[89] After the Puigs left Villegas, and especially after Manuel left Argentina in 1974, never to live there again, he sometimes fancied returning to the town like "eyes without a body, like a camera, to that point on the pampa equal to all other points."[90] He was curious to see how the lives of his schoolmates and others had turned out; perhaps, too, it was a way to be close again to the Villegans without feeling exposed. Every so often he claimed to experience a tinge of nostalgia, especially on rainy nights: "the smell of wet earth, the rain wetting the trees and the roofs of houses bring back a whole life I thought buried forever."[91] Whether or not he revisited Villegas, after *Heartbreak Tango* he never returned to the town as a subject, as if the place had finally been laid to rest and the novel was an elegy to a time that no longer existed.

"that tango made my heart break"

In October 1971, Malé joined Manuel for nearly three months on a tour of three continents: it was mostly "career" travel. Though the tensions between Malé and Baldo, who fought like cat and dog, seemed to grow worse as time went on, Baldo resented these absences, referring to mother and son, acidly, as the *novios* (fiancés). Carlos, recently married, and Malé's sister Carmen, who sometimes accompanied her on her trips, supported Malé's escapades with Coco, in hopes that with Malé away from home, tensions would be eased. On shopping sprees in New York and the capitals of Europe, Manuel spared no expense to dress his attractive, youthful-looking mother.

Guillermo Cabrera Infante and his wife, Miriam, remember when Manuel first brought Malé to their flat in London: "She was dressed all in white, gloves, hat, everything, and sat there so properly, almost like a doll."[92] Similarly, in the late seventies, when Nestor had moved to New York, Manuel and Malé met him at a restaurant. Before they sat down, Manuel noticed something "off" about his mother's makeup and said quietly: "Mama, don't you think you need to go to the ladies' room?" When she didn't react to his suggestion, he stared at her furiously and repeated: "Mama, you'd better go to the ladies' room." This time he nearly shouted, and she got the message. She was his mirror—or as Coco Krimer carped after a falling-out with Manuel—"the real Manuel Puig." She was now in her mid-sixties, her health required vigilance, and, while she was his most intimate friend, she also exacted a performance.

Early in 1970 Manuel had begun his "sort of" thriller, which he first called "Black Pearls," and then "Yeta" (slang for "Evil Eye").[93] Superstitious, he decided not to test fate, and came up with *The Buenos Aires Affair* by 1971, teasing that he chose the title with the English translation already in mind, to circumvent the hassles we suffered until settling on the compromise of *Heartbreak Tango*.[94] "I like the American title of *Boquitas* a lot," Guillermo had reassured him, more or less: "Of course [it's] not as brilliant as *Boquitas pintadas,* in which the author himself seems present, as occurs with good titles."[95] Manuel's campy titles underscored his subversive frivolity and rebellion against literary propriety; *The Buenos Aires Affair*—in imperial English—pressed a sensitive political button.

Mario believes Manuel was thinking of both of them when he constructed the character of Gladys Hebe D'Onofrio, a depressed aspiring artist with a typically Argentine-Italian surname. Her bag-ladyish collage–performance art—she gathers and communes with beach debris and litter—can be seen as a play on Mario's crumpled pages in the mysterious suitcase, Manuel's risky revivals of trashy culture, and, of course, the "anything goes" pop esprit of those installations in vogue at the Galería del Este. Gladys's close relationship with her narcissistic mother, an amateur poet who nurtures an artistic rivalry with her daughter, was pure Manuel and Malé too.

Back in "torrid B.A." in January 1972, Manuel was confronted with "a small scandal": suddenly slang, frank sexual talk, and tango lyrics were fashionable among the new writers, in books like

> Juan José Hernández's novel, *The City of Dreams,* and another
> by some guy named [Mario] Sexer or something called *La
> perinola* [The Top]. Acquaintances stop me on the street to tell
> me what disgraceful copies they are of *Boquitas*. La Hernán-
> dez gave me her book and it's really a scandal; what an idiotic
> woman. I don't care about these women but it does alarm me
> that the critics say nothing. On the contrary la Hernández has
> been treated very well in *La Opinión* by la Urondo, *Cortázar's
> pimp.*[96]

The critics praised his imitators without acknowledging his influence. According to Manuel's own rules of grammar, they were all one catty gender,
from journalist Paco Urondo to Hernández, a young pretty boy and the protégé of Pepe Bianco, editor of the prestigious journal *Sur.*

While no review matched the bells and whistles with which *The New
York Times* had ushered in *Betrayed by Rita Hayworth*—"a triumph . . . a
masterpiece"—*Heartbreak Tango* would be hailed in English translation by
responsive readers who praised its "tangy universality," and Manuel Puig
would once again be honored by the American Library Association as the
author of a Notable Book of the Year (1973).[97] By discovering the implicit
social critique buried within the banal *roman-feuilleton,* Manuel Puig had
created the most avant-garde Latin American fiction to date.[98] As Borges
had transformed the popular detective story into metaphysical fable, so had
Manuel given the trashy sentimental novel a new life. Now he took up the
genre Borges had redefined, but would depart radically from the cerebral
sphere of those Borgesian labyrinths, daring, "in a country known for its in-
sufferable snobbishness in matters of culture," not to imitate Borges or any
of the "existentialist crew [like Sábato or Cortázar] that has plagued the
River Plate for so long."[99]

While Paris and New York received this newcomer with enthusiasm,
Buenos Aires ignored his impact on local literati. Typical of the snubbing he
received in Argentina was Borges's dismissal of the Spanish title: "Imagine a
book that has lipstick on its cover." Even though Manuel already knew how
"nasty" that "old woman" was, this was yet another blow on the home front,
from the Argentine intelligentsia. Borges had apparently given Jack Macrae
(the American editor of both writers at the time) a different version of his
response to the title, however. As a lover of the tango, the old maestro ad-

mired the prosody of Gardel's lyrics *boquitas pintadas*: the title was a brilliant one which, he also agreed, could not be translated literally into English. Upon Borges's death in 1986, in the obituary he was invited to write, Manuel excused the elderly blind man, who reportedly refused to read anything published after 1950, but not without a bit of chastisement:

> When Borges was passing through New York in 1973, a journalist from *Newsweek* asked him what he thought of my books and he gave the same answer he always gave: that he hadn't read anything that had been written less than fifty years ago, but he added that in my case the titles were so horrible that he wouldn't even read them after such a period of time had passed. This was my last encounter with him, at a distance. Now I am asked to write something in his memory and all I can think to say is that his relationship with literature is a beautiful story of requited love. There are few who have loved books as he did, and literature embraced him as a privileged lover. But into this company of two there came a third presence. In his last years of blindness, the voice of a woman begins to be heard, a voice transmitting poetry to him, becoming poetry itself, the voice of one with whom he cannot avoid falling in love. A story too romantic for his propriety to permit him to tell. If he heard me, he would blush. It's my revenge for that comment about the horrible titles.[100]

Wistful, perhaps, about Borges's requited love affair with literature, Manuel wanted to be embraced, or at least understood, by his compatriots. To add insult to injury, he had found out that while Dutton provided lodging (Mr. Macrae's town house in the West Village) for Borges on his visits, they made no such provision for Manuel.

In the shadow of Borges, García Márquez, Cortázar, Fuentes, and Vargas Llosa—the principal writers of the Boom—Guillermo Cabrera Infante identified with Manuel's sense of neglect and marginality in Latin America. The Cuban's *View of Dawn in the Tropics* (1973), written as he was convalescing from a nervous breakdown induced, in part, by the stress of persecution and isolation, was rejected by the left because the book's depiction of power and violence throughout Cuban history included Fidel Castro's human rights violations. Noting the economy and delicacy of Guillermo's writing in this work, Manuel was irate, in contrast, about the critical prestige of "la Gaba" (García Márquez), whose *Autumn of the Patriarch* fulfilled Manuel's "darkest pronouncements" that "she" was ruined by her critics, believing everything they said. Now, to read her, one needed only to skim: "Every sentence pretends to be the maximum phrase of all of literature, and each one ends by weighing a ton." And la Cortázar—each new book worse than the last—she was becoming "another fixture of Latin American underdevelopment, along with fleas and demagoguery."[101] Manuel had a more personal bone to pick with Cortázar and also with Vargas Llosa, both of whom had initially dismissed Puig as a lightweight, only to follow his lead. Cortázar came out with a volume of stories, *We Love Glenda So Much*, the title story referring to actress Glenda Jackson. Vargas Llosa, known for long, somber political novels like *Conversation in the Cathedral*, suddenly decided that he too could be humorous and even wrote about a radio soap opera writer in *Aunt Julia and the Scriptwriter*; later, his *Real Life of Alejandro Mayta*, about a homosexual revolutionary, would follow on the heels of *Kiss of the Spider Woman*. The mere existence of rivals or imitators signaled, nonetheless, that Manuel had made his mark.

The backbiting on the home front, and disappointing book sales in Europe despite excellent reviews, aggravated Manuel's impatience to launch the Dutton edition of his best-seller, *Heartbreak Tango*. Manuel revised translations into the languages he knew—English, Italian, French, and Portuguese—very painstakingly. If the solutions he proposed to me ("writers dare where translators fear to tread," as Cabrera Infante said) sometimes imposed an awkward literalism, they produced, for the most part, positive results.[102] Elsewhere I have spelled out the creative variations he came up with to adjust *Heartbreak Tango*—our most difficult project together—for an American reader unacquainted with tangos, boleros, and other regionalisms.

Around this time Manuel realized that the academic lecture circuit was a source of supplementary income. Now that *Betrayed by Rita Hayworth* had come out in English, Emir initiated Manuel into the lecture circuit of North American academe. Manuel was at first shy and insecure about speaking in public because he was not an intellectual like Octavio Paz or a suave orator like Carlos Fuentes. Emir encouraged him to say whatever came to mind. At Yale University in the autumn of 1971, Manuel inaugurated the speech he would repeat with variations, on campuses throughout the country, which began more or less with these words: "When I was a little boy on the pampa . . ." With Emir there asking questions, he felt more at ease, but when he went alone to give talks, he at first found it stressful, as this description of Manuel at the University of Missouri in 1977 seems to indicate:

> The small, dark, middle-aged man with a receding hairline sprawls back in his uncomfortably straight chair, and nervously tries to light a cigarette. One, two, three flicks of the lighter and finally it's lit. His blue-gray sweater is pulled haphazardly over a green turtleneck, and no adornments except for a watch strapped around his left wrist. In a small high voice he asks if the audience can hear him, and with a nervous little sigh he begins to speak, making a joke about himself, that he was here "to reveal the insecurities behind the novels . . . that he lived simply on royalties, no expensive vices."[103]

In part this timorous performance was an act, or, rather, Manuel was simply putting his jitters to good use. Over the years, a growing number of North American professors and critics—among them fellow Argentines Alicia Borinsky, Alfredo Roggiano, Saul Sosnowski, as well as gringos Ronald Christ, Frank MacShane, John Coleman, or *beau ténébreux* (as Emir called) Alfred Mac Adam—would squire Manuel through these necessary exercises; Christ would establish (first as director of *Review* magazine for several years, then as editor of Lumen Books and as a translator) a professional friendship with Manuel most significantly in the late seventies, when Manuel's relationship with Emir was rocky.

Manuel and I were headed for rough waters too. In order to give the translator a fraction of royalties, Dutton reduced the author's percentage in the agreement Manuel and I had signed for *Heartbreak Tango*—as Jack Macrae put it, there was not enough of the pie to go around. Manuel's Dutton frustrations peaked after *The Buenos Aires Affair* came out in 1976, and he left Dutton.[104] Since early 1972, tensions had begun also to build between Emir and Manuel, culminating in a spat over Susan Hayward. Over dinner, after watching a Hayward movie on TV, Emir made the mistake of criticizing her *cursi* acting; Manuel flared up like a tantrum-throwing Coco, genuinely upset by Emir's sarcasm about an actress who had struggled her way up from a humble childhood and who was now dying of a brain tumor. And yet, in December 1958, when he saw *Soldier of Fortune* with Clark Gable and Hayward, he wrote Malé joking that: "It's been a while since I've seen such American trash, worthy of a Monday in the Spanish theater in Villegas." Emir's quip provoked Manuel to defend Hayward as if she were a member of his family (which in many ways his actresses were): he was allowed to berate his ladies, but no one else could, at least when they, intentionally or not, made him feel vulnerable about *cursilería*.

Sparks between these two friends had already been struck between Emir's predicament as a Latin American man of letters adrift in the petty politics of North American academe and Manuel's occasional "career woman" alliances with some of Emir's (usually Argentine-born) professorial foes.[105] Emir's fatherly demeanor was also wearing on Manuel, who was now not only a "grown-up" but also a well-known author. Their correspondence, when Manuel was back in Buenos Aires in April, smacked of psychoanalytical crossfire: "Dear Jill and Emir," he addressed us both, in a self-conscious or "straight" style (in Spanish) with, as usual, occasional terms in English (my italics): while avoiding affectionate nicknames like "Jillemires" (except for "Susana" to me) and gender games, he could not suppress an occasional Mabelism. After thanking Emir for his hospitality and expressing confusion that hostility should have crept into what was in many ways a pleasant visit, Manuel cut to the chase:

> Your attitude toward me can be summed up as follows: you always make me seem wrong, no matter what I say, contradicting or disregarding me. You even got to the point of attacking my anti-cultural thing as a weakness, when you were the first to discover that that's what was interesting about my work! And what's more unforgivable is that you attacked Susan Hayward, the poor thing sick as she is right now! What a weight on your conscience if she dies . . . So, what is the intention of this letter then? Well, in short, nothing more than to state that I don't like the direction our relationship has taken

and to give you my advice, to you who have given so much of
it to so many: control, little sheik! *See what temperament did to
Mario Lanza!* Let's change roles and let me play daddy a little
. . . Well, I say all this with the sacred purpose of getting
closer, not further away. Love to Susana and for you a hug
from Manuel.[106]

Emir's reply, two months later, was to send Manuel a supportive review of
The Buenos Aires Affair he had written for Octavio Paz's journal *Plural* in
Mexico, titled "The Dreams of Evita," in which the critic praised Manuel's
campy quotations from unforgettable scenes of female heroism in the cinema.[107] Along with his article, Emir sent a note imploring Manuel not to be
so "emotive": the most important thing was that we loved him, and "everything else (being a star, all of us asking the mirror who is the fairest of them
all) is pure ego nonsense."[108]

loss of a readership

Heartbreak Tango had flowed but "Yeta" crawled; Manuel was writing
about the problematic present, and he needed to find a narrative mode that
would help establish distance. The obvious solution was third person, but
how to use it? He saw the book as a "story of contained violence"—in tune
with the narrative conventions of detective fiction, a popular genre among
urban Argentines as producers as well as consumers of detective novels since
the twenties, when Borges compared Buenos Aires to Chicago as a corrupt
city of mythic gangsters. The detective genre—both as social satire and entertainment—was especially effective on screen, translated into film noir.
Attempting his own *roman noir* now, Manuel was guided also by another
Argentine obsession—Freud; and there was a connection: the Viennese doctor himself spoke of crime detection as a model for his own analytical
method. The narrative voice could thus be a kind of schizoid observer, or
disembodied third person, a conscious self gradually unmasking the clan-

destine contents of the unconscious. Again, Manuel's most significant source of inspiration was not literary but cinematic, in this case Alfred Hitchcock, the master of the psychological thriller, and perhaps the first Hollywood filmmaker to handle explicitly such unpleasant subjects as sexual dysfunction and misogyny.

Pepe Bianco and Enrique Pezzoni were among Manuel's consultants who read drafts and chapters of his new manuscript; Luis Gusmán and Beatriz Castillo helped him clarify his views on the Oedipus complex, Freud's interpretation of dreams, and Lacan's "mirror stage" in terms of "the mechanisms of anguish in the child, when he sees himself reflected in the gaze of the other, the adult."[109] Manuel knew more about Marcuse, Norman O. Brown, and Freud, Luis Gusmán recalls, than his friends suspected. Another novelist who was also a therapist, Osvaldo Lamborghini's wife, Paula, who specialized in treating guerrillas and terrorists and drawing out their guilt about killing, was Manuel's most fertile source of Freudian and Peronist rhetoric, which was prevalent in the cocktail chatter of local intellectual circles.

Manuel had done his stint with therapy in 1960 to deal with what he feared was a pent-up, unresolved, violent, almost criminal side, as if he were a kind of Dr. Jekyll and Mr. Hyde. Through hypnosis, he claimed he gained access to his "unconscious motives" and felt more at ease with his sexuality, but, mostly, therapy had helped him harness his "other" to serve his writing. His character Leo's progress in the local cultural scene would appear to parallel Manuel's own epiphany: "To fully assume the responsibility that this prestige implied, Leo decided to initiate psychotherapeutic treatment, for the sake of the magazine rather than for his own benefit."[110] Psychobabbling Buenos Aires gave Manuel license to X-ray himself, and he projected onto the screen of his fictional characters those emotions too turbulent to approach head-on.[111] As Manuel would mischievously remind academic interlocutors over the years, Freud was the "inventor" of the twentieth-century novel; if we are ruled by the unconscious, no narrator can be omniscient. But Manuel was also tired, bored with his own voice; he had already taken the psychological route with Toto. In *The Buenos Aires Affair,* he would narrate more extensively in the third person, while continuing with his cinematic montages of dialogue, dream imagery, and inner monologues. He also introduced a new device to mock objectivity, which he would expand upon in

Kiss of the Spider Woman: footnotes. To describe Gladys Hebe D'Onofrio's masturbations in *The Buenos Aires Affair*—Manuel claimed that conversations with women friends helped him articulate precise descriptions of the "mechanics" of a woman's masturbation—he placed explicit captions in footnotes to Glady's sexual daydreams in the text. *The Buenos Aires Affair* unfolds in a cultural milieu which obeyed the "terrorism" of psychoanalytical formulae and Marxist theory and yet bought into Peronist slogans like *táctica* (strategy)—a euphemism justifying lies and dishonesty. Argentina's schizophrenic condition was, as Manuel summarized it, "culturally evolved, politically underdeveloped."

The left, or analytical, side of the Argentine brain is extremely sophisticated, Manuel would joke: when Ingmar Bergman's films were the latest rage, in the fifties and early sixties, they appeared in Buenos Aires even before they opened in Paris; by 1970 there were more Lacanian psychoanalysts in Buenos Aires than in Paris.[112] The right, intuitive side, on the other hand, submitted to an old feudal tradition of authority, or "verticality"—blind faith in the (now decrepit) macho, in Perón. Manuel used "vertical" in his graphic portrayal of Leo's fornications with Gladys in *The Buenos Aires Affair* with a cocked eyebrow, as he would say, alluding to *verticalista*, another political euphemism, denoting an authoritarian, hierarchical (vertical) structure of power and social values.

His analysis of Argentina's split self began with *Betrayed by Rita Hayworth* and the little boy torn by confusing gender messages at home, confirmed and legislated by the omnipotent bourgeoisie to the north. Sexual conflict was the core of this new story: the (perfectly) ill-matched lovers Leo and Gladys personified two Latin prototypes, a male sadist and a female masochist. Leo Druscovich, who in his youth, during Perón's first presidency, had raped and killed a homosexual, has become an influential art critic. Gladys is an unappreciated artist who has returned to Argentina from a long stay in Washington, D.C., where she had sexual experiences in a more liberated environment but was unable to find either personal or professional satisfaction. And one night, in Washington, unable to appease her chronic insomnia and acute depression by watching romantic old movies on TV, she goes out walking in the city, is attacked by a demented rapist, and loses an eye while resisting. Playing with Hollywood clichés, Manuel set up a first encounter between Leo and Gladys at a wintry deserted beach resort, not far from Buenos Aires. (Turbulent passion at the beach or on the shores of idyllic waters was a romantic commonplace at the movies—from sluttish Joan Bennett and Robert Ryan in *The Woman on the Beach* (1947) to strident Joan Crawford and Jeff Chandler in *Female on the Beach* (1955), she in spiked sandals and silken shorts.) Leo threatens to kill Gladys up until the novel's climax—Manuel employed eerie "Hitchcockian" suspense—but kills himself instead, by accident. Guillermo's wife, Miriam, who read *The Buenos Aires Affair* in one afternoon, couldn't put it down; it is a sexy book filled with perverse eroticism. Miriam gave the book a pithy summing-up: "The killer is not a man, but sex itself."[113]

Despite the hopes of the Peronist left, the economic and political situation in the country continued to deteriorate when President Hector Cámpora stepped down in 1973, the same year

> Perón returned to Argentina, brought back by an alliance of the left with the old, mostly right-wing Peronist party. I didn't like this merge, but my friends on the left who were joining up believed firmly that Perón's charisma would give strength and cohesion to the Argentinian left, and they believed also that Perón's populist but vague dogma was, deep down, a socialist one. I never thought so: to me he was skillful but too self-centered to create something bigger than himself, such as a real socialist movement. When he was ousted from government in 1955 he chose Franco's Spain for a residence, and he was on the best of terms with the Spanish dictator. That was one of the many evidences of his real political tendencies. As history tells, the moment he came back to power he eliminated the leftist members of his cabinet.[114]

The Buenos Aires Affair's mixture of sex and politics was explosive: the affair between Leo and Gladys takes place in May 1969, the same month as the *Cordobazo*, the massive Argentine student uprising in solidarity with striking workers that was brutally suppressed by military forces. As Manuel said, "The return of Perón brought with it the renewal of censorship. My attitude toward Perón wasn't reverential and that was seen as sacrilege. I wrote about the good and bad sides of the man, through my characters, but that was a sin."[115] Peronist critics rejected his depiction of leftist Leo as a pathological aggressor, for example; Manuel was damning, indirectly, not only the country's militaristic buffoons but also left-wing intellectuals:

> The main male character had been a college student during Perón's first term, '46 to '52; he had then been in a leftist student movement and that had meant harassment by the Peronist police. I couldn't eliminate that from the novel; it would have been unfair to the character, to history, to the truth I try to find by means of my novels. My left-wing friends thought that was most inopportune. In 1973 Perón was the choice of the left and to criticize him was reactionary ... In my novel there was mention also of Perón's good points, the creation of labor laws, for instance. But in 1973 there was room only for praise of him; criticism was blasphemous.[116]

In spite of the few, mostly negative reviews that appeared, the book sold 15,000 copies in its first three weeks. Important reviews and scheduled interviews with Manuel on television were suddenly canceled, however, and in January the book was withdrawn from circulation and in April re-released in censored form: entire paragraphs with references to Perón, or to police and military brutality during the first Peronist era, were whited out, as were "obscene" or "perverse" sexual details.

The situation grew worse and the book was banned as pornography. Words became actions when the Morality Division of the Federal Police sequestered all copies of the novel in January 1974, and booksellers at several principal bookstores in downtown Buenos Aires spent a "symbolic" night in jail. Roberto Sala, head of the Unit of Criminal Investigations, explained that action had been taken upon "verifying that these books had been declared pornographic, and that these procedures had been initiated by a complaint lodged by the League of Family Mothers of the Parish of Mercy."[117] It was a municipal, not state, ordinance, prohibiting sale only in Buenos Aires, but this meant that the book was unavailable in the rest of Argentina. Manuel's novel was placed on a blacklist of *prohibidos*, which included Luis Gusmán's novel *El frasquito* and books by fellow writers Marcelo Pichón-Riviere, Enrique Medina, and Hector Lastra. Upon Perón's death in 1974, followed by the brief precarious presidency of his wife Isabel (a quasi-clone of Evita), the government fell into the hands of a right-wing military coalition. During this nightmarish transition,

> the emerging Triple A faction, the Anticommunist Argentine Alliance, began calling people on the telephone at home, telling them they had to leave the country. You didn't have to be a communist; they called anyone who was inconvenient to them in some way . . . I thought that when Isabel was replaced by the Junta in 1976, the prohibition of the book which had been considered anti-Peronist would be lifted, but the Junta, totally anti-Peronist, renewed the prohibition.[118]

Kiss of the Spider Woman would join the list of prohibited books in 1976, and the ban would not be lifted until the fall of the junta in 1983. Even though *The Buenos Aires Affair* was censored, Sudamericana wanted to continue publishing him, but Manuel, overreactive even in the best of circumstances to adverse criticism, did not want to be at the mercy of regional politics; his desire to reach out to a wider market led to his move to Seix Barral in Spain. Symptomatic of the "erasure" of Puig in the Argentine cultural sphere of the seventies after his initial runaway success with *Heartbreak Tango* was the absence of his name in *Crisis*, the most important intellectual and political journal from May 1973 to August 1976, which cited new and established writers of all political and aesthetic persuasions, from Borges and Bioy Casares to David Viñas, Sábato, Cortázar, Ricardo Piglia, Osvaldo Soriano, and Jorge Asís. In 1989, César Aira, a young novelist who admired Manuel Puig's work enormously, commented that at the time Puig provoked "a tremendous anxiety, rejection, repulsion."[119]

Whether or not his book supported or condemned Perón, Puig was under siege: on the one hand, by the left-wing Peronists; on the other, by the right-wing military with which Perón's widow had become allied. It was time to get out of town. From 1973, when he escaped to Mexico for two years, until his final decision to leave Argentina permanently in 1976, when at home with his parents, Manuel received death threats on the phone from Triple A. The absurd, frightening situation was Kafkaesque, unbearable:

In December 1974 it had been more than a year since I had
left Argentina, but the Triple A, a Nazi organization protected by Isabel Perón, called my parents' house to ask me to
leave the country in 24 hours . . . or else. I was on a long list
with left-wing people who had endorsed Peronism.[120]

The last straw for Manuel, as for many Argentines, was political destabi-
lization, especially when he became aware that he was being followed on the
street, and not by an admirer. He had noticed the same man with the same
umbrella several times, and had once been pushed, on a crowded sidewalk,
into oncoming traffic, at first, he thought, by mistake. He had already heard
similar stories from other writers and friends—like journalist Aída Bortnik,
who would write the screenplay for the Oscar-winning *The Official Story*
(1985), a moving feminist denouncement of the disappearance of citizens. In
September 1973, Manuel left Argentina for Mexico.

exile: 1974 –79

adiós, buenos aires querido

The tango is the devil's dance.
He uses it to cool off.

—Erik Satie

Manuel had more than one reason for choosing to flee to Mexico: in October
1972, at a Mexican embassy party in Buenos Aires which he attended with a
new friend, film critic Carlos Monsiváis, he was instantly smitten with
Miguel Vélez, a young Mexican intellectual. Vélez was flattered to be pursued by a literary celebrity, but was also heterosexual or, at most, sexually
ambivalent. Manuel immediately invited him to a formal dinner party at
Felipe del Canto's, where the young man felt both proud to be Manuel
Puig's companion and embarrassed. Manuel, eager to turn fantasy into reality, rambled on about the affair in a letter, brimming with literary gossip, to
Guillermo and Miriam:

> Well, meanwhile . . . I fell in love . . . [with a] Mexican, friend
> of la Monsiváis, SWEET, etc. Here until December . . . I'm
> going nuts because finally there's a good man in my life. But
> . . . it seems that in his life I'm only one more adventure. What
> a destiny mine is, what a whore's life, for me who deep down
> is a one-man woman, like Helen Morgan . . .
>
> Oh, I'm dying of suspense. In one week my fiancé returns
> from his trip (three weeks). What will he bring me as a gift?
> A ring? I assure you he's so charming . . . Love to you, and

wishes for Darnell and Sondergaard to have handsome and
good boyfriends like Vélez, who doesn't love me, who's going
to leave me . . . What do I do if he leaves me? I'm dying of
fear. In December he returns to Mexico for good—should I go
with him? Yes, but he doesn't want me to go. Because I'm
ugly! and old! He's only thirty-three.[1]

Early in the new year, after Christmas in New York, Manuel flew off to
Mexico to pursue and, after persistence, seduce the "Mexican gentleman."
He had finished *The Buenos Aires Affair* but was unsure as well as tired of it.
He had also just turned forty, which made the Mexican obsession all the
more intense.

Among the faraway lands he had first visited as an Air France employee,
Mexico had been an unexpected discovery, an exotic place where he spoke
the language, so close to Hollywood and yet still a Latin country. Mexico
City itself was ugly, he had written Malé from New York in 1964, but full of
beauty, with its mural art and its architecture—Aztec monuments, colonial
cathedrals, "marvelous" modern buildings like the art deco Palace of Fine
Arts filled with pictorial treasures, or María Félix's moderne spiral-
staircased apartment house in Colonia Roma. And everywhere music, mariachis singing rancheras, and sentimental songs like "María Bonita"
dedicated to María Félix by the smitten Agustín Lara.

Though in April 1973 the romance was already on the rocks because the
Mexican had gone back to women ("those tramps"), a year later the affair
still had life in it. From New York in May 1974, Manuel wrote to
Guillermo:

> And now . . . let the church bells ring; the Mexican came [to
> New York] for Easter! He was lovely, and little by little he
> proposed that I go to Mexico with him in his car from the
> 18th to the 3rd of June, Yucatán, etc. and afterward very little
> by little he came to propose that I stay at his house "indefi-
> nitely" to see "how you like Mexico." In brief, I, after ~~hours~~
> ~~minutes~~ ~~seconds~~ tenths of a second of profound and total re-
> flection said Yes! I'm so happy, because I really love him so
> much and I can't live w/out him. Not all the problems are
> solved, but I think it will all turn out well. I conquered him

with patience, cooking, washing, and ironing; he thought I'd
be an egocentric, dizzy ~~starlet~~ dame, and found a little mama.
Ay, may it all turn out well because if not I'll end up an old
maid. My address will be c/o Vélez [etc.]. Well, I'm wild with
joy.

Manuel's Vélez fantasies helped offset real worries: his parents' health and
his confiscated book, now being disputed in court. His family needed him,
and yet this was no time to return to Buenos Aires, as he reports in the same
letter: "Then came a horrid episode; it seems that Papa was dying of cancer,
a horror, they called me urgently from B.A. I didn't go because of the trial
matter, and when they opened him up it was only ulcers. But I spent six days
of horror, thinking that Mama would be left alone."

Manuel's honeymoon with Mexico would turn sour, but in his never-
ending quest to find a home away from Argentina, Mexico then loomed as a
welcoming mirage. The Mexican film industry was more professional and
prolific than Argentina's, which had limited production resources.[2] In June
of 1974 (a few days before Perón died), settled in the house of his friend Ricardo Regazzoni, a handsome painter from a wealthy family, in Coyoacán,
the most fashionable neighborhood of Mexico City, Manuel was invited to
participate in a roundtable colloquium at the Universidad Nacional
Autónoma with the Italian novelist Alberto Moravia, whom Manuel had
met in the fifties in Rome. At the colloquium Manuel discussed movies with
Moravia, a seasoned cineaste whose acerbic novel *The Conformist* had been
filmed by Bertolucci in 1971. A luxurious reproduction of the thirties in
Mussolini's Italy, featuring top European stars Jean-Louis Trintignant and
Dominique Sanda, the movie was an international success. But with all its
self-conscious aestheticism, Manuel found the film superficial and hypocritical: unlike the novel, it glamorized fascism; armed with radical pretensions,
Bertolucci reinforced bourgeois values. Curious about Moravia's opinion of
The Conformist and other cinematic versions of his novels, Manuel asked the
famed Italian author how the stars' presence affected the interpretation,
wondering "if the inclusion of popular actors/actresses in a cast can either
strengthen or weaken a character?"

The success of *Heartbreak Tango* began opening portals to the world he
most wanted to enter, indeed had been trying to enter for the past decade.
Leading Latin actors wanted to play his characters, and young Argentine

filmmakers bombarded him with offers and projects. The adaptation of his work by the film industry began to be a reality for Manuel in the early seventies, but, absorbed in his writing and skeptical about the quality of the aspirants, he didn't accept, until in 1973 he was approached by Beatriz Guido and her husband, the distinguished director Leopoldo Torre Nilsson, an energetic and charismatic figure in Argentine cultural life in the sixties and seventies.

Closer stylistically to European than to Hollywood directors, with an earnest commitment to literature as well as to cinema, Torre Nilsson (son of pioneer Argentine filmmaker Leopoldo Torres Ríos) tended toward a sententious realism. A writer as well as a director, he had made several films based on literary works, most notably *The Seven Madmen* (1929), Roberto Arlt's seminal novel about social and existential angst. Unlike the warm, loquacious Beatriz, Bapsi (as Torre Nilsson was called by friends and family) had a sinister air: tall, portly, almost always wearing dark glasses. Bapsi was a man of letters with a sharp Anglo-Argentine wit, a compulsive gambler, and a socialist all in one, and had been admonished by an Argentine judicial court in 1967 for publishing a story called "Seduction" because it was filled with sexual slang from the streets of Buenos Aires. Along with fast-talking Beatriz, known for her surrealist bons mots and conversation-stoppers, Bapsi was so enthusiastic about *Boquitas pintadas* that when the book came out he and Beatriz fought over it as they read it one night together in bed, Beatriz tearing out each page as she finished to pass it on to Bapsi, impatient to devour those "little painted lips." They were on the same wavelength as Manuel when it came to the idea that sexual taboos were the root of Argentina's problems, as Bapsi declared with his customary esprit:

> Latin American violence, Borges, the decreasing population in the northern province, and the Argentine military . . . All those things have the same origin, a lack of sex education. If Borges, the Argentine military officers, and the northern folk made love better, we'd have worse literature, more inhabitants, and a better army.[3]

Manuel didn't believe that the novel would work as a film. He felt that without its written, literary structure, the story would fall flat: what had

made the novel a success with a wider audience was the whole package, and
it would be difficult to bend this material to fit conventions and the limitations of the Argentine cinema. Torre Nilsson insisted that he was interested
in experimentation and in following the form; he bought the rights for *Boquitas* from Sudamericana, and invited Manuel to write the script. Hoping
"to prevent someone else from butchering it," Manuel agreed to accept the
job only if Beatriz would share the screenplay credits with him and Bapsi
would promise to get Manuel's (and Malé's) beloved Argentine star Mecha
Ortiz to play a bit role as the lecherous Gypsy whose mouth waters for luscious Juan Carlos, who comes to her to have his fortune read. Manuel insisted that Torre Nilsson create a good scene for her, which he did, in the
style of Marlene Dietrich's sassy foretune-teller in Orson Welles's *Touch of
Evil*. Since the elderly Ortiz couldn't remember her lines anymore, Manuel
even invented a simpler version where she had to say only a few words. In
the end, the scene was one and a half minutes long, very kitschy; Ortiz repeatedly caresses a crystal ball, instead of the desirable young Juan Carlos.
Manuel later said of this script and his first filmed project:

> I produced a kind of condensed version which preserved
> some of the original moments. I wasn't comfortable with it.
> The film wasn't without interest, but I disagreed with the di-
> rector. He pretended to listen to me and then did his own
> thing. The film is very uneven.

The valid aspect was, surprisingly, the vision Torre Nilsson had of the characters: more severe, less humorous and conciliatory than Manuel's more em-
pathic view of them as victims of circumstance. When he followed his
intuition Torre Nilsson made them look grotesque, which Manuel felt was
better than his attempts to be faithful to the novel's more gentle parody—
unsure ground for Torre Nilsson and hence the movie. While Torre Nilsson
had chosen and directed the actors well, the film was a literal translation: it
captured the soap opera plot, but not its subtle satire. Manuel had portrayed
his characters' foibles with a poignant levity, too evanescent for Torre Nilsson's style.

Nonetheless, in September 1974 *Heartbreak Tango*, by "acerbic young
novelist" Manuel Puig, won high praise at the San Sebastián Film Festival,

where Manuel was received as a celebrity and awarded best-script prize, the Pluma de Oro (Golden Pen).[4] The movie was a hit in Buenos Aires, with only one negative review in *La Opinión,* "where they insult me," Manuel wrote from Mexico. "In the B.A. newspapers *my* prize didn't appear, they just say the movie received the Pluma de Oro prize. Only *La Prensa* mentions it was best-script prize but doesn't mention my name."[5] Manuel was very proud of the prize—"I'd never won a prize in my life." But his joy was mitigated by the fact that in Buenos Aires no mention was made of it—"because I'm on the blacklist, what do you think of that?" he wrote to Guillermo Cabrera Infante.[6]

Again he was disheartened by the visible lack of appreciation for him in Buenos Aires, and also because "Torre Nilsson has not even called me about the prize, or paid me!"[7] Manuel was frantic about the falling peso: "Each day the money earned from the film is less and less." He was also convinced that Bapsi had squandered the profits at the casino.

Fearing for his family's safety in Buenos Aires as well as his own life, as soon as Manuel could establish himself elsewhere, he planned to get his mother out of Argentina. On July 1, 1974, Perón died, unleashing the Argentine nightmare that would last for almost a decade. That same month the Vélez affair ended, Manuel wrote Guillermo from Mexico, recounting the episode of the failed romance as if it were a pastiche of *Suddenly, Last Summer* (Manuel had his reader in mind as usual: Guillermo was a fellow fan of Tennessee Williams):

> Let me tell you: I'm still alive but I don't know how. I arrived
> May 15 and my fiancé was waiting for me in the airport, cra-
> zier than ever w. joy. I thought everything would be divine.
> After 2 days we went off in his car: Veracruz, Yucatán,
> Cozumel, a little over 2 weeks. Little by little the veil was
> lifted and I discovered the truth: he was a total schizophrenic,
> 2 persons in one. One of the two loved me and was charming,
> but the happiest moments (there were several, ecstasy of total
> communication) were followed unfailingly by an abysmal fall,
> and Mr. Hyde would appear: atrocious, a reactionary, a fairy-

killer. I had never thought such cases existed, they seemed like '40s movie inventions. BUT THEY EXIST. In Buenos Aires when he got bad he disappeared; he hid, and the same here on another trip I took and in N. York. But on a trip together, spending the whole day together, it was impossible for him to hide it. One can see that in him the homosexual thing is frightfully conflictive; one part of him accepts it and the other rejects it. The point is he pulled so much shit on me, and I saw that he was so sick that MY LOVE DIED: a true salvation.

Back from the trip I went to a friend's house, and have been here since; what a liberation I felt! The important thing is I saw the light: I had not deceived myself; he is an adorable being, but unfortunately has a twin inside. During this whole romance I felt that strange things were happening, and I was knocking myself out trying to understand it. The good part is that upon seeing the truth I was cured; really, love went out the window. And months have passed and I don't even think of seeing or calling him.[8]

Fifteen years later, the Argentine female psychiatrist in Manuel's final novel *Tropical Night Falling* relates in similar kitsch Freudian terms her torrid affair with an elusive Mexican. Vélez's split personality was not the only thing straight out of a forties movie; Manuel embroidered the affair with harlequin excess, humorously, but also with pain. He realized he'd better break off the affair when they were out driving in Mexico City one day and Vélez cursed an effeminate *maricón* on the street, exclaiming angrily that he would have liked to run him over. Right then and there Manuel decided that Vélez was a closet queen who projected his own self-hatred onto others. Manuel told Guillermo that his episode of "Velezitis" was over, and that on this occasion "St. Joan saved me." He meant the mature Joan Crawford in *Autumn Leaves*, who flees her young lover (Cliff Robertson) when he loses his temper and throws a typewriter at her.

After the plan to live with Vélez failed, Manuel packed up his own Olivetti typewriter in the fall and took refuge with Ricardo Regazzoni. Charming and intelligent, Ricardo was a "lucky girl" who lived with a "steady husband" at Violeta 8, an elegant three-story white stucco house adorned with celestial blue-framed glass blocks, nicely situated on a narrow, shady cobblestoned street. But the quarters became too close for comfort after a few months; Manuel had spats with the steady husband and Ricardo had to ask him to leave. By May he had moved in with a fan, Televisa film acquisitions manager Javier Labrada, young and enthusiastic, also living in Coyoacán. Round-faced, good-natured Javier made Manuel feel at home and was soon christened Rebecca, the daughter of Rita Hayworth and Orson Welles, that is, Manuel's "daughter." Javier's friend Agustín García Gil, a slim young playwright who would author some scripts with Manuel, became "Yasmin," Rita's daughter with Aly Khan. Like other acolytes, these two would become rivalrous, and "Becky" also "acted out" when he met Mario Fenelli a year later, on a visit to Rome. Mario had produced *Betrayed by Maria Callas,* an Italian TV documentary, and Javier remarked to Mario, "Mommy doesn't like the fact that you used her title." Mario was doubly hurt. Not only had his triumphant "sister," whose first novel—and title—he had helped engender, left him in the dust of obscurity, but he was insulted by this callow new admirer. Manuel eventually smoothed things over, but Mario would always resent "that nothing, Becky." After Manuel died, and the *New York Times* obituary came out with a mention of Manuel's "sons" Javier and Agustín, Mario suspected with outrage that, to boot, Manuel had left a fortune to "las mexicanas."

Manuel took refuge in the beautiful Coyoacán homes of his friends and immersed himself in the "marvelous" melodramatic Mexican movies he saw on television or at the Televisa studios, courtesy of Becky. Javier, in charge of the Televisa budget, ordered many films for the Televisa archives that were of little interest to Televisa's audiences but of great interest to "Rita." "I'm seeing lots of old Mexican movies; there are marvels," Manuel wrote to Guillermo:

> I discovered la [Juan] Orol, la Ninón, and lots more. I'm doing my doctorate in Dolores Del Rio and my Master's in María [Félix]. Besides, I've found the man of my dreams, identical to a Basque boy [Danilo Cortari] who looked like Errol Flynn from my town and who inspired *Boquitas*—his name is Miguel Torrucos, male lead in *Acapulco*. He died in a plane crash years ago—divine!

l, onward: upon detaching myself from my torment I
: of flirts [flirtations], one DIVINE, with a psychiatrist
.econd gay psychiatrist I've had in my life; the other one
was a Spaniard). It turns out he has another (stable) relationship with a very neurotic folle, and with me it was love at first
sight, and it seemed to be working, but one day he said we
had to separate, because the other one was totally dependent
on him. It was all *Now, Voyager*, the same ambience; he was
Claude Rains and Paul Henreid all wrapped up in one, and
the damn faggot was Tina, Paul's daughter. And I Bette, of
course, with my eyes eternally swollen from crying. The thing
made me suffer quite a lot but luckily I hadn't gotten too used
to his company. He had a huge one and was very protective, a
marvel, but destiny said . . . no. I've been collecting those no's.
I wish they were pearls so I could make myself a fabulous
necklace. My consolation is writing: I'm making good
progress on the novel.

Manuel camps it up in the role of disillusioned spinster Bette Davis in *Now,
Voyager* at the moment her lover leaves to go back to his wife. But was he really Spider Woman, like Barbara Stanwyck in the film noir classic *Double
Indemnity,* a strong, "treacherous" female with an assertive, aggressive sexuality—a bad woman who in the end receives the punishment she deserves?
Whether to amuse his friends or to disguise sadness, Manuel tended to
frame his life's episodes as revivals of classic women's pictures, with himself
in the leading role.

spinning the spider woman

In November 1973 Feltrinelli published *Fattaccio a Buenos Aires* (roughly,
"Sex Crime in Buenos Aires") with an over-the-top jacket design depicting
a man's hand down his unzipped fly, from which the surreal appendage of a

miniature female nude emerges. In the Italy of the seventies, with feminism and the Communist Party riding high, there was an openness to the sex and politics of films like Lina Wertmuller's *Love and Anarchy* (1973) or Liliana Cavani's more eccentric *The Night Porter* (about an S-and-M love affair that begins in a Nazi concentration camp), which came out in 1974. Manuel was hailed by an Italian critic as a "literary alchemist" who had invented a new concept of culture, a fusion of high and low.[9] By early 1974, he was working on a new idea for the novel that would become *Kiss of the Spider Woman*: exploring the romantic woman who idealized the perfect man. He was having difficulty finding a believable model, he explained coyly, in the age of feminism.

Manuel's women friends like Aída Bortnik, Felisa Pinto, and others were liberated urbanites. The only romantic "woman" left was the character Manuel would create in *Kiss of the Spider Woman*, Molina, a certain kind of old-fashioned queen who worked in beauty salons or show windows, in some ways an uneducated version of himself or, as Manuel put it, "a type I knew very well":

> I wanted to work with an unsophisticated type, a reactionary in a certain way—the type of homosexual who rejects all experimentation, all new trends. They've accepted the models of behavior from the Forties—you know, the subdued woman and the dashing male—and they have, of course, identified with the subdued though heroic woman. And they don't want to change that fantasy, or can't. These types, although they're film crazy, would even reject the new movie heroines and heroes. They're still attached to the prototypes of *One Way Passage* and *Now, Voyager*. I think one of the main questions of my novel is: Can people change their eroticism after a certain age? I believe it's almost impossible; sexual fantasies crystallize during adolescence and imprison you forever. I'm saying this with a Claude Rains cocked eyebrow.[10]

For "Molina" types, movies and actors went downhill after 1950, when a hypocritically artificial realism and the "empty technique" of method acting took over. Gone were the twenties and thirties, when women were glamorous, and love conquered all. Manuel called the top American actresses of the "confused eighties," who reacted against the glamour girl/sexpot niche and represented a new womanhood (Ellen Burstyn, Jill Clayburgh, Meryl Streep, and Glenn Close), "The Four Horsewomen of the Apocalypse."

The slow pace of warm Mexico City was still good for his nerves after humid, jittery Buenos Aires, as was his new circle of friends. Javier's luxurious new flat on Avenida Universidad became home from the spring of 1975 until Manuel's move to New York the following winter; Agustín collaborated with Manuel on prospective film and TV scripts, helping him in particular with local Mexican slang. Avila Camacho, the wealthy nephew of a famous Mexican politician and, as poet Manuel Ulacia recalls, "an extravagant queen" who often appeared in public dressed in a velvet cape and top hat, would sweep Manuel from one party to the next. A high point at one of these gatherings was meeting legendary screen star Dolores Del Rio— "divine, young in body and mind: she remembers everything!" Through Camacho, who dabbled (between parties) in filmmaking and nude photography (of his friends, including Severo), Manuel met luminaries of the Mexican film industry such as paunchy Barbachano Ponce, the cigar-smoking "fat cat" producer of Luis Buñuel's *Nazarin*. "Here I will soon be crowned Miss Showbiz," Manuel wrote to me, referring to various movie, theater, and television offers that spread before him like a magic carpet. Miguel Sabido, dapper and sharp-tongued, was a talented theater director who remained one of Manuel's closest friends in Mexico, and collaborated on Manuel's last produced play, *The Mystery of the Rose Bouquet* (1988).

Mexico's literary, academic, and publishing world received Manuel with open arms, from Onda (New Wave) writers and film buffs Gustavo Sainz and Carlos Monsiváis to playwright/journalist Vicente Leñero, novelists Sergio Pitol and Julieta Campos (a Cuban married to a Mexican political scientist who later become the governor of the state of Tabasco), and the elegant society lady/journalist Elena Urrutia. Manuel bonded with two exiled Uruguayans—journalist Danubio Torres Fierro, and poet Ulalume González de León, who offered Manuel her house as haven for a month. Built by her Mexican architect husband Teodoro, this luxurious home with swimming pool was nestled in exclusive San Angel. The daughter of poets Roberto and Sara de Ibáñez, Ulalume was a slight, attractive, almost birdlike woman, with intensely staring eyes, aptly described by Manuel as being in a permanent state of poetic erection. She was charmed when Manuel taught her young daughters Sophie and Berenice to dance like Carmen Miranda. Notwithstanding her sumptuous circumstances, Ulalume shared Manuel's parsimony, perhaps carrying it a degree further—when serving cocktails to visitors, for example, Ulalume would put out a tiny dish of three or maybe five olives—but Manuel could swim every day in her pool, which was good for his health.

Manuel was diagnosed with high blood pressure and advised by doctors to swim daily and to watch his diet; for him the downside of Mexico City was its altitude, almost seven thousand feet above sea level. "Health," he wrote to Guillermo, who could empathize,

> I am noticing the transit to the half century, I've had little problems (high blood pressure, things on the skin) and all because of nerves, poor things that we abuse so much. I resisted tranquillizers for months, but then I accepted reality and every night I take marvelous little pills, resolving everything.[11]

He was only forty-three but felt the half century looming. Escaping grim Buenos Aires meant confronting the alienation of exile, where, in Mexico, he was surrounded by Argentine intellectuals who raged against authoritarian rule but, as Marxist Peronists, ignored the fascist components of Perón's first presidency. The conjunction of the political nightmare and his personal search for happiness inspired the initial notes for *Kiss of the Spider Woman*, but the seed needed to sprout; it was by way of a personal fantasy that he came up with his first idea for a story in which "these two guys would meet through a mediator—movies; otherwise they couldn't talk to each other. One is heterosexual, the other one isn't; they're both defensive. The gay one doesn't have much education, but a *great* fantasy life." Manuel could not control the world or his own emotions, but he could control his inventions. By placing these two men together in a cell, he was taking a big leap out of the literary closet.[12] If his sexual preference could be inferred by cultivated readers of his first novel, he was making an unambiguous statement in his fourth by placing a homosexual, not diminished by gross caricature, on center stage; it would also be his only novel to portray a love affair between two men. Despite the fact that Peronists had kicked the left out of government, intellectuals were promoting a Peronist left and accusing Manuel of being reactionary. Manuel later commented that

> history hadn't taken place, nobody had acknowledged reality, Perón hadn't kicked the leftists in the pants, I was still a reactionary for not having joined the movement. Worst of all my book had been banned by the right wing and the Argentinian left didn't care.[13]

Manuel felt obliged to walk a tightrope of diplomacy between left and right, which, on the one hand, upset his friends Emir and Guillermo when he appeared to be courting the left, and, on the other hand, branded him a reactionary for trying to stay out of controversies.

In spite of his protestations, Manuel was genuinely, intuitively political in his writing—and most explicitly in *Kiss of The Spider Woman*, though he was not a public spokesperson like other writers. His novels can also be regarded as feminist in that his constant subject was the political nature of our sexual lives, or the sexual dynamic of the body politic. At least in the seventies, feminism defined itself as pluralist, not only focused on women but on seeing human issues *differently*. No matter what sexual orientation or identity one embraces or writes about, the respect for difference, or recognition of being different, is what makes one's approach feminist in this light. "It's not who you are"—since you never have one unmovable identity—"but how you are," as the Daughter would say in Manuel's play, *Under a Mantle of Stars*. Manuel consistently spoke for difference, not so much for groups as for the individual, in all his works, though nowhere so openly as in *Kiss of the Spider Woman*.[14]

He realized that he needed the reader—and he was thinking first of the Argentine or Spanish-speaking reader—to understand and to care about homosexuality in order to be drawn into the story. The reader needed, in a way, to replay his own life and attempt to understand himself by examining not only feelings but theories, beginning with Freud on the Oedipal complex. At first Manuel thought all this information could seep through the characters' conversations. But then he realized that they couldn't have books about homosexuality in the cell, and besides, the gay character was uneducated, almost illiterate. Since homosexuality was such a violently repressed topic in his own culture, what better way to represent the marginalized than by inserting it in the margins, or, in this case, at the bottom of the page? Wherever the character's lack of information created dramatic tension, Manuel inserted footnotes—explaining to the average reader the theories, controversies, and misconceptions surrounding homosexuality to date (1975)—which grow and grow until at one point they nearly take over the whole page, at the same time pushing the (didactic) author down to the bottom of the page. By exposing the kitsch of scientific rhetoric by way of the footnote (a comic device he had used already for Gladys's masturbations in *The Buenos Aires Affair*), Manuel would reduce Freud to an almost Hitchcockian simplicity. A few years later, when his friend René Jordan suggested that Manuel eliminate the footnotes in the English translation, Manuel insisted on keeping them; they were "for all my sisters. I want them to know about Hirschfeld, etc."[15] Despite his ever-present mischievous irony, Manuel did have a political mission: to educate both the victims and the perpetrators of homophobia in Latin America.

The novel's first audience actually turned out to be readers in Spain, the only country that would publish the book. Even though it received lukewarm reviews, the timing couldn't have been better. Spain had just been liberated from almost forty years of Franco, and a younger generation of readers, which included the young gay filmmaker Pedro Almodóvar, was ready for a public forum on sexuality. Manuel would deliver it with humor, and would even satirize the analyst's couch by turning it into a prison cot and by taking the talking cure to its ultimate mutual transference: Valentín and Molina become, through verbal as well as sexual intercourse, each other. (Not to lean too heavily on the writer's choice of names, but Valentín is Molina's Valentino, and Molina is a quasi-anagram of Manuel and Malé combined.)

The footnotes, expanding into mini-essays on homosexuality, culminated in Manuel's own thinly disguised invented "theory"—voiced by a nonexistent Swiss female psychoanalyst named Dr. Anneli Taube—toward a bisexual utopia. Her theory exhorted men and women to embrace the feminine and masculine within each of them, suppressing neither, in order to avoid rigid homosexual or heterosexual roles. This manifesto was really a condensed autobiography.

The rejection which a highly sensitive boy experiences toward an oppressive father—as symbol of the violently authoritarian, masculine attitude—is a conscious one. The boy, at the moment when he decides not to adhere to the world proposed by such a father—use of weapons, violently competitive sports, disdain for sensitivity as a feminine attribute, etc.—is actually exercising a free and even revolutionary choice inasmuch as he is rejecting the role of the stronger, the exploitative one. Of course, such a boy could not suspect, on the other hand, that Western civilization, apart from the world of the father, will not present him with any alternative model of conduct in those first dangerously decisive years . . . other than his mother. And the world of the mother—tenderness, tolerance, and even the arts—will turn out to be much more attractive to him, especially because of the absence of aggressivity: but the world of the mother, and here is where his intuition would fail him, is also the world of submission, since the mother is coupled with an authoritarian male, who only conceives of conjugal union as subordination of the woman to the man.[16]

Manuel claimed at times that he yearned to be "normal" so as not to suffer so much, and, unlike Molina, Manuel did explore his bisexual nature; he did have sex with women, if infrequently—as long as they were not "motherly" but, rather, young and girlish. But women had no real role in his love life. As his name suggests, Molina is Manuel in his sexual preference, while Valentín, a caricature of a Marxist guerrilla fighter, fulfills not only Manuel's wish for a straight lover but also embodies Manuel's questioning consciousness. Valentín mouths Manuel's oft-repeated remark that sex is the most innocent thing in the world, and has been corrupted by the roles and meanings assigned to it by social systems. Molina and Valentín, like Gladys and Leo, represent two sides of Manuel. Together, they even inherit his real-life technique for dealing with insomnia by seeking refuge in movies. In the prison cell Molina at first narrates films at night (three of them real films, the other three, inventions) to help Valentín fall asleep, as Manuel would lull himself to sleep on many nights, watching those comforting old flicks. The imprisoned men "can't face certain subjects directly. Slowly, unconsciously, they reveal themselves," like the repressed characters in *Heartbreak Tango*. Manuel (like most human beings) could not confront "certain subjects" ei-

ther. The principal characters in his novels never seem to sustain relationships, to integrate as adults their sexual and emotional lives—the region of
personality that perhaps most concerned (and eluded) Manuel.

Kiss of the Spider Woman begins in *media res*, like a dream—like Hitchcock's classic *Vertigo*—with Molina's narration to Valentín of the plot of *Cat
People*, a classic horror film about sexual repression. Because his characters
could only express themselves metaphorically, Manuel was first going to use
the Victorian camp classic *Dracula*, about the famous vampire whose blood-
sucking serves as the perfect euphemism for oral sex. While in New York in
1974, however, he saw *Cat People* on late-night TV and thought that "this
was the film Molina would have chosen." Its metaphor for sexual repression
was more specific to the heterosexual prisoner's unconscious fears about
sharing a cell with his queer companion: fulfilling a prophecy from the Ser-
bian village where she was born, Irena (Simone Simon) turns into a ferocious panther when a man arouses her. Not only is this strange female's
sexuality a source of terror, but she ends up killing the psychiatrist who
thinks he can cure her "frigidity" by seducing her, thus dramatizing the failure of psychoanalysis to deal with "female sexuality and all that is beyond
conscious reason."[17]

If Toto in *Betrayed by Rita Hayworth* manipulated the plots of movies to
unfold his feminine or passive sides, revealing both the voyeur he is and the
artist he is becoming, Molina narrates his films to work through his and
Valentín's hang-ups toward some kind of metamorphosis. "The whole
novel is a reflection on roles. The two characters are oppressed, prisoners of
their roles, and what's interesting is that at a certain moment they manage to
flee from the characters they imposed on themselves."[18] Rereading *Kiss of
the Spider Woman* as he worked with translators on various versions, Manuel
felt it told the story of "a person with noble ideals, isolated in a cell with a
weak person with whom he sets up, without wanting to, an exploitational
relationship and then begins his effort to avoid roles, to avoid hiding behind
a mask."[19] *Kiss*, then, brought to life a utopian ideal of sex and gender: to be
oneself beyond gender, to be able to "enjoy experiences that are not within
an accepted pre-established model, something very difficult to achieve."

> In that cell there are only two men, but that's just on the sur-
> face. There are really two men and two women. I agree with

Theodor Roszak when he says that the woman most desperately in need of liberation is the woman every man has locked up in the dungeons of his own psyche.[20]

Manuel preferred the label *loca* to "homosexual." Only half in jest, he insisted that the noun *homosexual* was irrelevant:

> For me [homosexuality] doesn't exist. Heterosexuality doesn't exist either. Sex isn't transcendental—it's as necessary as eating and sleeping, an activity of the vegetative life. What's transcendental for me is affection. Sex doesn't define anything. Our sick old society one day decided that sex had a meaning and a weight, with guilt and who knows what. Sex is a toy that's been given to people to have fun with, to help them forget about diseases and death and bad weather. Sex has no meaning beyond the fun that it is. I don't think there's a difference between men and women, except for what they have between their legs. The distinction between masculinity and femininity, the whole notion of role playing, isn't natural. I remember in the 1940s, people were seriously talking about the difference between the cortex in women and men! With a straight face too! It's terrible that, to enjoy sex, people have to assume a role that would give them and their partners a kick. It all becomes a big masquerade. Of course, I'm talking in utopian terms. But you must have such an attitude if you don't want to perpetrate all that.
>
> When people ask me, "Are you gay?" I say, "I'm a person." I'm not defined by what I eat for breakfast, which, for me, is as important as the kind of sex I have. Sex is innocence, a toy—and we shouldn't let it get spoiled by associating it with such heavy meaning.[21]

As Manuel said, "For me the only natural sexuality is total sexuality, with a person of your own gender, with a person of the opposite gender, with an animal, with a plant, with anything."[22]

For younger gay Latins like Roberto Echevarren, a Uruguayan poet and professor at NYU at the time, the politics of *Kiss* were "in" but Manuel's portrayal of a gay man was anachronistic, belonging to another era. (Manuel purred to Roberto, whom he had met through Monsiváis some years earlier: "You're *so* moderne . . .") Manuel resisted politicizing his own sexual preference as an identity, and his stance on this matter still counters identity politics. When the play version premiered in Brazil, Manuel was branded reactionary by a militant gay critic; Manuel denounced this stance as another form of censorship in his remarks at an international forum on censorship in 1985. In his commentary "El error gay" (The Gay Error) he briefly rebutted the critic's charge that he had not portrayed "homosexuals in a heroic light" in the figure of Molina, and defended the value of showing "gays as unexceptional human beings, in this case gentle and muddled, but at the same time courageous and loving."[23] "The Stalinist queens," as Manuel called them, wanted him to be more political and less a woman. They never understood that to be a woman was already political, or as Allan Baker, his translator in Britain, remarked with quiet wit: "It was never his ambition to be a second Eva Perón."[24]

The almost Aristotelian unity of *Kiss of the Spider Woman*—one restricted space, a narrow time frame, two protagonists—came out of Manuel's years of striving to be a storyteller, to ensnare his reader in a tightly knit web, to produce effects akin to Sidney Lumet's court drama *12 Angry Men* (1957)—innovative, when he saw it in London in 1958, in having the action all occur in one room, ending when the jurors exit to present their verdict to the court—or to the musical comedy *How to Succeed in Business without Really Trying*, which made a strong impression on him in New York in 1963: "something brilliant, a musical comedy . . . which all takes place in an office, and it's all choreography, I mean even in the moments without dances, just comedy, the slightest gesture or step is marked. It has an incredible harmony."[25] The theme of this musical, the quest for power in the corporate world, is achieved by the mere manipulation of image. In *Kiss of the Spider Woman*, Manuel would be the first writer to explicitly link the Broadway-Hollywood manipulation of images with that of the Third Reich. He had recognized that the German National Socialists were perhaps the first political force to use the tools of the studio system—charismatic stars and technological extravaganzas—toward a political end, the first government to make cinema into a propaganda machine.[26]

As has often been said, censorship and state control force writers to be creative. *Kiss of the Spider Woman* began as a dialogue which then continued until the last page, because what else could these two men do in a cell but talk? Telling stories was their only active escape from the impotent passivity of imprisonment. Manuel's characters could at least ask each other questions, simulating the Socratic give-and-take. In a bare prison cell, "all they have are words," and the only possible drama is conversation.

Like Toto in his daydreams, Manuel was about to make an elusive fantasy real. In fiction he would liberate the woman—in the way a real-life lover like Vélez refused to accept—in Valentín, who allows himself to make love to a man; Molina, out of love for Valentín, opens himself to political action, though Manuel warns, "It's not that they go beyond all limits; Molina is still the romantic heroine who chooses a beautiful death, sacrifice for her man." The novel's title is drawn from Valentín's words to Molina—"You are the spider woman"—when Molina finally succeeds in seducing his man, though we are not sure if the spider woman might not really be Valentín, kissing (seducing) Molina so that he can manipulate him. From tragic Greek heroine Ariadne to Gale Sondergaard, *spider woman* is another word for femme fatale. Joan Crawford is certainly one as the beautiful society woman in *Humoresque* (1946) who can have any man she wants. Molina is the last romantic woman, loyal only to Crawford's creed: "What good is a woman if she's no use to anyone"—a pithy line quoted in *The Buenos Aires Affair* from *Humoresque*, in which Joan's beloved tormentor, the virtuous violinist John Garfield, plays the famous Liebestod, or love/death, theme from *Tristan und Isolde* while Joan, now saint, resolves to cast herself into the ocean, sacrificing her life for her lover's art. Molina plays a similar role as heroine for Valentín when he bravely, or foolishly, delivers a message to the *guerrilleros*, surrendering his life for the cause. The sexually aggressive Joan, or Molina, the spider woman, needs to be punished for asserting personal power.

In June 1973, before Manuel left Argentina, a lawyer friend introduced him to a couple of ex–political prisoners; the conversations he had with them, along with input from friends involved in the political scene, helped him shape the figure of the militant *guerrillero*—a much sketchier character than Molina. Manuel would strain credibility in his prison setting by placing a common prisoner, sentenced on a morals charge, in the same cell as a political prisoner. If in previous eras political prisoners had been treated more respectfully than common criminals, the Nazi influence on the Argentine punitive system had turned the tables. Common prisoners received relatively better treatment than political prisoners, and special buildings, such as the Naval School of Mechanics in Buenos Aires, as well as concentration camps, were set aside for the torture of political prisoners. Manuel would take into account, however, a popular macho assumption that even the most noble political prisoner was still a male animal who needed sex at any price, in any form, and could therefore be manipulated by a homosexual informant. After all, homosexuals were despicable and deserved exploitation; a window dresser like Molina could have been thrown in as a decoy. Releasing him also followed the practice of allowing certain prisoners to "reinfiltrate" among their colleagues as unwitting bait. While it may seem farfetched that the prison warden obtains food for Molina and that the two prisoners spend their time talking about movies, these fictional strategies reflected the nightmare atmosphere of the mid-seventies, when military officials exploited their power as rapists and torturers of their victims but also used female captives, usually "Montoneras" (left-wing Peronist guerrillas), as cultivated geishas. Instead of dining at home with their wives, who were the uneducated daughters of other officers, the officers would take these highly literate ex-citizens out to dinner, to "discuss books, movies, politics."[27] Hearsay about gays in prison would also inform the novel, providing the circumstance of Molina's imprisonment, for reasons similar to that of a friend of Manuel's, Patricio Bisso. From his conversations with fellow Argentine exile Silvia Rudni, not a Peronist but a radical leftist, Manuel had gathered data about the left-wing Peronists as well as background on the debates between the Peronists and the radicals.

On a fleeting trip in the fall of 1973 to Europe, revising translations and visiting editors, Manuel arrived in Rome for the publishing debut of *Fattaccio*, and to visit, for the last time, his dear friend Enrico Cicogna. The premier Italian translator of Latin American literature was dying of cancer—*Fattaccio a Buenos Aires* was among his last translations. Manuel brought pages from his work in progress about the *guerrillero* and the window dresser, and read them to Mario as they sat in the Caffe Rosati, a famous literary hangout, on Via del'Oca near the Piazza del Popolo. Mario was excited about this new manuscript but also concerned for Manuel and, like Manuel, concerned for the safety of the Puig family in Buenos Aires.[28]

At the same café Manuel interviewed, over several mornings, an ex-*montonero* living in Rome, a former schoolmate of Mario's, who helped Manuel flesh out the political setting of the novel.

In Rome on this occasion he met Alberto Arbasino, Italy's most prestigious gay writer of the moment, who would not only hail *Bacio della Donna Ragno* with a superlative review (1979) but would become Manuel's most ardent literary advocate in Italy. The introduction had been arranged by Angelo Morino, who helped the cancer-stricken Cicogna finish *Fattaccio*.

Manuel spent the spring of 1974 in New York, residing at the apartment of Norberto González (an Argentine whom he had met through Regazzoni) at 21 West 58th Street, glamorously around the corner from the Plaza Hotel. Norberto was away, and Manuel had the place to himself, a situation he preferred so that he wouldn't have to disturb anyone if he wanted to watch a movie on TV at 3 or 5 a.m. At Norberto's we worked intensely for a month, two afternoons each week, revising the translation of *The Buenos Aires Affair*. During this time Manuel continued his Nazi film research: for over two weeks at the Public Library he listened to the speeches of Goebbels and Hitler to grasp the rhetorical tone of the international publicity for Nazi propaganda films. (He would reproduce this verbal kitsch in long-winded footnotes to the Nazi film Molina naively recounts to Valentín.) He also viewed German Nazi films in special collections at the Museum of Modern Art and in SoHo, from Leni Riefenstahl's grandiose documentaries *Olympia* and *Triumph of the Will* to more obscure curios.

Among the curios was *HitlerJunge Quex* (1933), a sugary fascist melodrama about the epiphany of a German boy who leaves his drunken abusive Communist father and kindly but submissive mother for the noble (subliminally homoerotic) family life of the Hitler Youth, sponsored by the Fatherland.[29] The film applauds the boy's rejection of his parents for the Hitler Youth, a true family that deserves his loyalty. Male beauty and bonding are equated with order and cleanliness in the fascist aesthetic; the feminine is chaotic; women are dirty. The Germans parodied and in certain ways surpassed the America cinema; the National Socialists understood that to compete on a global scale, politically and economically, they had to dominate the media, and their cinema was already the most avant-garde in Europe both technologically and aesthetically, with its expressionist, stylized, innovative use of the camera.

While Manuel was repelled by paternalism and saw communism as the other side of the same coin, he would push the fantasy that Molina and Valentín form a new utopian family, like the Hitler Youth, in the magical space of their cell, where together they seek an alternative to Valentín's trite communism. In prison, though the state is a dictatorial father, the two men are free, or cut off, from all other familial and intimate ties. During this transformative experience Molina, apparently devoted to his mother, utters a bitter statement that echoes what Manuel sometimes felt about Malé: "She already lived her life."

Uptown at MoMA and downtown in SoHo, Manuel searched for an outrageous Nazi film for Molina to relate to Valentín, one that would provoke the Marxist to give the window dresser a political education. At one point he considered *La Habañera* (1937), Douglas Sirk's last movie made in Germany (filmed in Spain's Canary Islands), which touted prejudice against corrupt, underdeveloped South Americans: an idealistic German doctor saves Zarah Leander from the claws of a tyrannical Hispanic husband.[30] All these melodramas were so exquisitely bad that Manuel ended up creating a composite, "Destino" (Destiny), mixing in bits of several Third Reich productions as well as parts from the Hollywood war flick *Paris Underground* (1945), which starred Constance Bennett (usually cast as a vixen) as a British heroine who works with her American lover for the Resistance even after they are both imprisoned by the Nazis. From conversations with Nino about esoteric German cinema, especially musical melodramas, Manuel would shape Molina's zealous narration in his invented Nazi propaganda film, but the film which most inspired Manuel's invented "Destino"—translated into English as "Her Real Glory"—was *Die grosse Liebe* (The Great Love, 1942) with Leander.[31] The deep-voiced Swedish chanteuse, who became the best-paid film star in Germany after Marlene Dietrich left in protest, plays here a cabaret singer in love with a noble German officer. Because the lovers are separated by the trials of war, she falls momentarily for another man but ultimately sacrifices this "lesser" love to wait patiently, like other good German women, for her war hero to return. With her undying loyalty, this cardboard figure was a model for Molina's beloved Leni, named in homage to Hitler's star filmmaker Riefenstahl, whose aesthetic Manuel revered.

There was a double edge to Manuel's fascination with kitsch films like

HitlerJunge Quex which glorified national folk culture and appealed to his populist bent, just as his eros was polarized around idealized male power and female submission. As he uncovered films from Axis countries Germany, Spain, and Italy, the products of culture seemed to confirm, time and again, the disjunction between merit and morality, ethics and aesthetics.[32] During Perón's embargo on Hollywood movies during Manuel's formative adolescent years, the only foreign movies he could see were German, Italian, or Spanish. This early fascination with a largely fascist cinema blossoms in full force in *Kiss of the Spider Woman*, and Manuel clearly connects Perón and Hitler by playfully using Perón's nickname, the Conductor, to designate Hitler in the rhetorical footnotes to Molina's account of the Nazi film "Destino."[33] "Not everybody is born in a big country with access to other forms of culture, education," Manuel rationalized:

> There are many people who live in the sticks and have nothing. They are soaking in machismo, in a hostile environment. What do they do? They have no choice. The movies provide an alternative. They help you to not go crazy. You witness another way of life. It doesn't matter that the way of life shown by Hollywood was phony. It helped you hope.[34]

There's hope and there's pessimism, and Manuel's *Kiss of the Spider Woman* landed somewhere in between.

Though fiercely critical of authoritarianism, Manuel would probably have yielded to the golden-haired Nazi hero whose noble profile makes his character Leni quiver in "Her Real Glory." Manuel often spoke of the gorgeous blond German officer who, during the Occupation of France, was film star Arletty's lover. Disgraced by her liaison, Arletty is still remembered for her line in the classic *Children of Paradise* (1945) "C'est si simple l'amour" (Love is so simple), which she uttered to besotted Jean-Louis Barrault, so in love with her, and so visibly effeminate.

In Mexico Manuel continued to immerse himself in the "cabaretera" movies from the thirties through the fifties—"poor quality but meaty!"— and the rancheras and boleros which were then popular. In all this sensuality he encountered contradictory messages about machismo, as he told Tununa Mercado, a fellow Argentine writer then in Mexico:

He wanted to include a Mexican cabaret movie in the narrative of *Kiss*. He saw dozens, "so as not to disdain any of them," and invented one which, in his opinion, was the common denominator of them all. He was fascinated by the songs in those movies, particularly the work of José Alfredo Jiménez, the Mexican Discépolo [great Argentine composer of tangos] . . . in whose songs Manuel saw "a rejection of machismo and at the same time the impossibility of renouncing the mystique of the dominant macho."[35]

A common thread in the cabaret movies was the sexual fear and fascination surrounding the cliché of "hot-blooded Latins" and the dangers of "south of the border" romance. Films like *Aventurera* (*Adventuress*, 1949) or Manuel's other favorite, the trailblazing *Mujer del puerto* (*Woman of the Port,* 1933) were extravagant melodramas about corruption, betrayal, rape, incest, white slavery, with either redemptive or suicidal endings—or both. Every possible melodramatic plot twist has its place in *Aventurera*, which was titled after a bolero by Agustín Lara. Other "cabaret" gems include *Salón México* and the classic *María Candelaria*, with the haughty, fine-featured Dolores Del Rio playing an improbable Indian girl—always a camp favorite for today's San Francisco audiences. The cabaret flick heroines have gay appeal not only because they are excessively female, but also because of the "fallen" woman's need to maintain a double identity, to hide her true identity out of shame and as a strategy for wreaking revenge on the society that wronged her.

These outrageous tragedies were at the same time musicals: the sordid brothel would swivel suddenly into a lively cabaret with dancing sirens. The elaborate tropical numbers, à la "Tutti Frutti Chiquita Banana," could have been conceived by Busby Berkeley, but the choreographer was the dancer: narrow-waisted blond bombshell Ninón Sevilla. Manuel first discovered this Cuban dancer in Mexico, and in New York he was "shocked" that his Cuban friends didn't seem to know her. A delirious cross between Carmen Miranda and Betty Grable, Ninón became a major star in Mexico in the late forties and early fifties—and she was also a darling of the French existentialists. In *Sensualidad* (1950), one of Manuel's favorite scenes is Ninón sitting in court—like Jane Russell three years later in *Gentlemen Prefer Blondes*—exhibiting her legs to the judge to justify her cabaret career: "With these legs, what else could I do?"[36] Kitsch personified. "Ninón Sevilla does not make one truthful gesture," Manuel explained, both amused and amazed:

> It's all imitation, nothing rooted in her own real-life emotions. Ninón mimics the gestures she's seen made by great tragic actresses of the movies. She's ridiculous in that she makes it all excessive and false, but there's such intensity in her attempt, she seems to believe so much in those gestures she admired in her childhood, that she's no longer ridiculous but rather pathetic, and from pathos she moves on to the sublime. The intense sincerity of her false belief redeems her.[37]

Ninón's most perfect monument to kitsch is her "Persian Market" dance number in *Aventurera*, "not only for its mélange of 'styles,' but also for its intention to copy classical ballet." The "exotic, sensual" setting, a supposed Persian marketplace, was Ninón's earnest creation: "I like to go to the root of things, and I went to the Arab neighborhood and told them I wanted to stage a Persian market, as authentic as possible. They helped me by lending me rugs and explaining how to arrange things on the set."[38]

Manuel's taste in movies was eclectic, but all the films he loved were essentially Hollywood-style melodramas. He always fell for the same movie, whether it was made in Germany in the twenties, Argentina in the thirties, Mexico in the forties, or Japan in the fifties. Suffering women, betrayals, abandonment: the stuff of melodrama was universal truth.

Encouraged by Barbachano Ponce, Manuel interrupted *Kiss of the Spider Woman* in the fall of 1974 to begin work on a "kind of musical comedy"—or musical drama. While even as a respected novelist he would not have complete creative control in the media of film and theater, working with others was an escape from the solitary tension of the writer's desk, his preoccupation with the critics, and, especially, those stressful emotions that nourished the world of his fiction but poisoned everyday life. Having achieved distinction as a novelist, he felt confident enough to abandon the solitary task of novel writing for this teamwork, which, he already knew, would be fraught with anxieties of another nature.

He wrote a script in three weeks, in "record time," he exclaimed proudly, though he always worked single-mindedly and could crank out dialogue with great speed. "It's a full-steam melodrama," he wrote to Guillermo, "without any distance from the material; the author cries along with the heroine and we hope with the audience." He called it "Amor del bueno" (Good Love) from a song by José Alfredo Jiménez, the Mexican *charro* (cowboy) star who had died a year earlier. It was a love story about two singers, and a dramatization of Jiménez's songs, so in a sense it was an imagined biography of Jiménez—the real author, Manuel the "copyist" claimed, with his usual self-effacing irony. Some years later he would use the same formula, an imagined biography based on music, to write a play about legendary tango singer Carlos Gardel.

He wrote "Amor del bueno" for Lucha Villa, a tempestuous ranchera singer: if his novels took their shape from real people or film characters, he wrote plays always with certain actors in mind. This was particularly true for their adaptations into the languages of "glamour" like French or English, as when he first conceived of *Mystery of the Rose Bouquet* in French because he imagined it as performed by two *monstres sacrés*, the grandes dames Edwige Feuillère and Danielle Darrieux.

Barbachano Ponce was very enthusiastic and promised to stage "Amor del bueno" in April 1975. With the exciting anticipation of a stage production, Manuel felt less pressure: "Now I'll continue with the novel, but there's no hurry."[39] He had other concerns: Nestor was very down because his father had just died; the Argentine government was blackballing Torre Nilsson's latest films; and Mexico was more and more inundated with Argentines. At the moment things were fortunately "tranquil on the sentimental front . . . a new, autumnal boyfriend with graying temples who fucks in silence: does he think he's at Mass?" Televisa had also commissioned him to write a program about American movie stars, a "sort of collage-presentation of my favorite stars and directors." And Barbachano Ponce suggested he create another theater piece, which became *Muy señor mío*, a bedroom comedy, written for Mexican parodist Carmen Salinas.

But the actors in Mexico were, as they had been for Luis Buñuel in the fifties, a source of keen frustration. Lucha Villa, who was supposed to star in the musical, was a moody alcoholic and didn't want to play the part. *Muy señor mío* was a flop because the director, Nancy Cárdenas, "a tough-looking woman with her heart in the right place," as Renata Schussheim described her, was a fierce feminist and defender of gay rights and wanted to combine mariachis with high moral content. Aside from Miguel Sabido, Manuel claimed there was no one in Mexico who could understand his "border crossings," his love for minor genres (as he called them), and his desire to make theater both popular and sophisticated. "Amor del bueno" was never staged, and it would have been better if *Muy señor mío* hadn't been. Manuel attributed these failures, in part, to a "disturbing" parallel between macho attitudes toward women and the intelligentsia's opinion of "minor" genres: "Everybody enjoys them, but nobody respects them."[40]

What he may not have been able to accept was that these other endeavors were inferior to his novels. By the summer of 1975 he felt enervated by the slow pace he had liked so much at first: "mortal for my nerves"; mostly he feared for his health, especially his heart, living in Mexico City. In August, he took up with his novel again, still at Javier's place where, in November, he finished writing the book. He felt he needed to get out of Mexico for his health, but also to shake off career frustrations. He moved on, this time back to an old love, New York, and from New York, in the summer of 1976, Manuel recounted to Cabrera Infante the end of his honeymoon with Mexico's cultural "mafias":

> Let me tell you my adventures: Mexico turned out to be DEATHLY . . . I recognized the existing mafias and their firm decision to close their doors on me. All aggravated because they're the biggest liars: they smile and never show their real faces . . . The two theater projects and the movie (with Ripstein: *Hell* . . .) were indefinitely postponed. Everything got worse in November when an Argentine friend, semi-refugee, journalist, Silvia Rudni—did you ever meet her?— twenty-nine years old, died of a very weird meningitis. The year before I had already had a little heart trouble, and it came back, except stronger. My blood pressure dropped to the lowest point, in December, and went up to the highest, horrible. Well, big specialists looked me over and luckily there were no lesions on the heart. It was all a product of my nerves, aggravated by the altitude.

new york, new york

Manuel arrived in early January on a snowy winter night at the apartment I was sharing with friends on King Street, where he stayed for a few months until he found a reasonable rental nearby, a tiny studio apartment on the corner of Carmine and Bedford, one block down from a bell-ringing Catholic church. He felt at home in this noisy, picturesque Italian neighborhood, vaguely reminiscent of scenes from neorealist movies; he could almost see it in lyrical black and white. And he was especially exhilarated to be living two steps from Christopher Street, the main gay artery of the West Village. In his corner aerie on the second floor of the small gray building, he created a tidy white-and-beige ambience. With two wicker chairs, a jute rug, a settee, and a miniature kitchen/writing table, he replicated the monkish austerity of his room in Buenos Aires. In the windows facing south and west, he hung plants to add a touch of the tropics. A reporter from Eastern Europe naively interviewed Manuel that summer as an exemplar of the Latin American writer in exile, and said solemnly, "You must be so relieved to breathe the free air, having fled tyranny in Argentina." Manuel, suppressing a laugh, was reminded of Jack Benny, acting as a stern Nazi in Lubitsch's *To Be or Not to Be* (1942) and revealing the frivolous twit beneath his uniform when he daintily articulated, rubbing his hands: "How nice it is to breathe the fresh air of the Gestapo again." When Manuel met the Scottish writer and translator Alastair Reid for a cup of coffee on Seventh Avenue, he told him that he had to spell it out for the ideological reporter: "It wasn't so much that I was fleeing . . . you've got to understand," pointing in the direction of two young men kissing on the corner of Christopher Street and Sheridan Square. "This for me is Mecca; why would I want to be anywhere else?"

Even so he found the city less welcoming than in 1963, though now he could enjoy the paradise of multiple movie channels. Unfazed by the dangers of New York City's streets, he amused friends with sex talk about "four Turks" in the baths and encounters in alleys, often inventing Hollywood-coded euphemisms, such as: "It was a Clark Gable double bill: *Key to the City* [anal intercourse] and *To Please a Lady* [masturbation]." But in a West Side bar when a fellow came up to him and said, "I want to fuck you in the ass," Manuel replied—à la Vivien Leigh in *The Roman Spring of Mrs. Stone,* the story of a disenchanted woman with diminishing options—"What you say is not only vulgar but redundant." Now almost forty-five, he was beginning to feel too old for a city with such a "youth cult."

For him, 1976 was a "black year, frightening . . . The country had come out of its *hippie* euphoria (which had failed, had ended); I had come to a defeated city."[41] Rock music, which he found jarring, was a symptom of alienation; no more Fred and Ginger and sensual rumbas: instead of dancing together, the young people danced alone, disjointedly. The sixties had liberated, more than joy, people's neuroses. Manuel's gloomy vision of a climate of "asexuality," in which his women friends complained of not finding Mr. Right, was shaded too by his own diminishing prospects for romance in the midst of plenty, because New York in the seventies and early eighties was probably more sexual than ever—until the plague of AIDS descended.

Manuel's "baby-boomer" devotees, like Bruce Benderson and Howard Mandelbaum, felt the same way about the unhealthy atmosphere. Manuel met Howard through Carlos Clarens, a Cuban movie critic and friend of Nestor Almendros. Upstairs from Cinemaphilia, a rare books and magazine shop that he managed on Cornelia Street, Howard had a private movie club where he began inviting Manuel to special showings. Carlos, together with film historian John Kobal, had amassed a valuable collection of film posters and publicity photos—and convinced Howard to co-manage a rental business which they relocated to 23rd Street and called Phototeque. After a falling-out with Carlos, Howard renamed the firm Photofest: this vast archive of the famous and the arcane still busily rents out and traffics in art photos and publicity shots of stars and secondary figures from the history of cinema, television, and the theater.

With friends came rivalries, some playful, others ferocious. Manuel had a falling out with Carlos too. Carlos (whom Manuel called Gail Patrick, a minor actress who played bitchy roles) was very handsome, would never admit his age, and had to be the center of attention; when Manuel teased this class-conscious white Cuban by suggesting that he had black ancestry, that was the last straw. Howard would often come over to Manuel's little studio on Carmine Street to watch a movie on television; Manuel would sometimes "go overboard" and invite Howard to dinner before or after the movie. The menu was usually spaghetti with ketchup but, according to Howard, "Manuel felt his charm would compensate."

La Bruce, an aspiring East Village writer, joined Manuel's growing network of "daughters" after I introduced the two in the mid-seventies. Bruce, a dilettante Francophile devoted to Roland Barthes, the fin de siècle decadent Joris-Karl Huysmans, Colette, and the *precieux* Pierre Louÿs, was engaged in a novel he called "The Slaves of Fashion." Together, Manuel and Bruce called Howard Flora Dora—after an old-fashioned dance-hall girl from the gay nineties, a "good girl who obeys Mama"—especially after Howard became Manuel's dependable "video slave" in New York. When the VCR emerged as a household necessity in the eighties, Howard would record movies on television for "Mommie dearest." The slight, green-eyed Howard was named after an assortment of pretty actresses, and when Manuel's Mexican daughter Yasmin (Agustín) stayed at Howard's place in New York, he called Howard Miss Linda because posters of Linda Darnell covered every wall.

Howard felt uncomfortable with the female nomenclature and pronouns, but Bruce, the other New York daughter, matched Manuel's campy wit, egocentrism, and notes on rough trade; Manuel often found Bruce's notions inspiring.[42] If Manuel's model was Garbo, Bruce's era was the fifties, and his model, John Waters's retro, trailer-park prima donna, Divine. A hefty frizzy-haired bohemian with demonic, close-set blue eyes, Bruce Benderson shared with his ex-college chum Camille Paglia a mission: *épater le bourgeois*, jolt the yuppies. In the seventies and eighties this meant knee-jerk liberals as well as conservatives. Bruce's punk novel *User* would come out of his nocturnal excursions to Times Square; Manuel's spin on la Benderson's unholy crusade was that "she" was "such a flapper."

Bruce and Manuel had decided that the macho or unisex leather scene—which they both agreed was emotionally frigid, misogynist, and repressive of the inner woman, or, in any case, of femininity and femaleness—was not a new wave but, as Bruce said, a cold wave. The Reaganite eighties threatened a regression to the stifling social and cultural life of the fifties. Manuel's instincts went against the current wave; if anything, he would hide his masculinity and, more precisely, his member between his legs, a kind of "pubis angelical" disappearing act; if his romantic life didn't improve, he often declared in mock despair, then he would have a sex-change operation.

Manuel responded to Bruce's "wave" wisdom with a wistful bon mot, coining the new breed of gay men "Cold Wave Queens." He explained the phenomenon, for a *Christopher Street* interview, with psycho-anthropological irony: "In the States nobody punishes homosexuals any more, so they have to punish themselves. It's just a fad, the exploitation of the sicker side of the homosexual's condition." He considered it silly and hoped it would pass. It was good that roles were changing, that women were "no longer submissive" nor men "dominant," but he also kept hearing from his friends how hard it was to communicate with the objects of one's affections.[43]

Manuel agreed with the flapper that the only people in New York with erotic vitality or "a fire in the eyes" were the Puerto Ricans—a complete turnaround from his adverse reaction to the slums of Washington Heights in the early sixties. During his time in New York in the late seventies Manuel was invited to write a series of impressions on sexual mores in New York for *Bazaar*, a hip new magazine coming out of post-Franco Spain. The Latins he encountered in Manhattan provided him with raw material, as in this monologue by a Mexican exterminator which Manuel structured as an interview and called "Erotic Cockroaches":

> It's easy to talk about the sexual revolution with my Latin women friends who live in New York. They're the ones who are gaining ground, so any mention of the subject plunges them into a heated debate. My Latin male friends too, but they're all intellectuals and I'm less certain about them; in a way they're losing ground and all their noble generosity makes me suspicious. That's why, when an unwary and probably Mexican exterminator entered my apartment—like the plagues of Ms. Venus, cockroaches are the permanent residents of this modern city—I proposed an immediate discussion of the matter.
>
> "No way," he said, "I have no time for that, I don't go out with women. Even if they pay their own way, I don't get busy with that. Why would I, when in my country anybody can eat a whole lunch with the seventy cents for a lousy small glass of Coca-Cola, mostly filled with ice cubes? I don't go out with them; after my eight-hour shift, I'm beat. Well, I don't do a hell of a lot, and in almost every building there's an elevator. Why am I laughing? Well, nothing really . . . That it's true

what they say about the milkmen bringing home the milk? Well, I don't know about them, but I know a thing or two about exterminators . . . What am I laughing at? Well it's not always the same for all of us. I have a pal—we always work together—who never gets any. And one day I was fed up and the maid was alone in a big house, and my pal was dying to say something to her and he didn't dare, and right there and then I told the pussycat that the big ox wanted her and right there and then the matter was settled. And what do you know? He's still with her and it looks like he's going to get married. What do I know if the damn ox is ugly or not? Well I guess so, he must be, I don't notice guys. No, handsome I'm not, it's the mustache . . . Oh, come off it . . ."[44]

The following year, when Manuel abandoned New York for a more erotic cockroach-infested city, Rio de Janeiro, he would continue to explore this form of spontaneous reportage as fiction, in a novel based on taped dialogues with a Brazilian bricklayer. *Blood of Requited Love,* an obsessive, confessional work, simmering with misogyny, class resentment, and closeted homosexuality, would expand upon the destructive insecurity that festers beneath macho bravado.

Manuel was less sanguine about the East Village Nuyorican Café scene in 1979: "The Puerto Rican is the 'great hope' though it may be just for the moment: those people have fabulous stories to tell, their lives are true dramas, operatic. But so far all I see is a group of poets supporting each other."[45] Out of solidarity (and so as not to disappoint his young devotees), Manuel endorsed certain poets, like José Kozer, a Cuban friend; however, he was not convinced by most of what was labeled poetry.

Manuel went regularly to MoMA's film archives—and became close friends with film curator Stephen Harvey—as well as to Theater 80 on St. Marks Place, always in search of rare old films he had never seen before. When Malé visited New York in these years (between 1976 and 1979), she was a regular too. A great convenience for Manuel was that Theater 80 was right across from Bruce's apartment, which meant the flapper could chaperon Malé to the theater for a Garbo double bill, which gave Manuel a few hours respite in the afternoon. Manuel would watch movies he'd seen countless times before on television, but his forays to theaters and archives were reserved mostly for unexplored territory. His most impassioned friendships were, more than ever, with other cineastes—"not critics," he clarified pointedly, but with people like Stephen Harvey.

Other comfortable acquaintances in New York were novelist Mark Mirsky and his wife, Inger Gryttig. While Mark and Manuel had little in common (a tenured professor at the City University of New York, Mark, once a motorcycle hipster, was converting to Orthodox Judaism), Manuel appreciated his warmth and earthy humor. Mark helped arrange teaching gigs for Manuel at the university, and Manuel helped Mark publish one of his books in Argentina, through his publisher friend Daniel Divinsky. As editor of *Fiction* magazine, Mark had published an episode of *Heartbreak Tango* in 1973, in an issue with stories by Peter Handke, Raymond Carver, and Günter Grass. The Fiction Collective, a CUNY-based group of younger writers, quickly adopted Manuel as honorary member, and brought him to CUNY in the seventies as a creative writer-in-residence.

At a party one night in 1977 at Mark's newly acquired Bowery loft, round-faced, cheery Brazilian novelist Nélida Piñón and Manuel had their hands read by a tall, sensuous young blonde, Nina Straus, Roger and Dorothea Straus's daughter-in-law. According to Nélida, Nina said to her: "You have many loves in your life, and you will have glory but it will come late." And to Manuel: "Your love life is so-so, and you have your glory now. About the length of your life I'm not sure, but there's some fuzziness; perhaps not so long." Manuel apparently laughed, but did ask Nélida in jest, "Would you like to exchange fortunes?" Reality mimics fiction: Manuel had created a similar scene in *Heartbreak Tango* in which the handsome Juan Carlos goes to a Gypsy who reads his cards and his eyes, torn between her attraction for him and the certain death she sees inscribed. Nélida's memory now seems like a foreshadowing, although Manuel had his own "astrological" method, based on the conjunction of the year of one's birth and the Oscar-winning actress of that year (in his case the "sign" was Greta Garbo, in *The Grand Hotel*).

In 1976, even before it was published in Spanish, Manuel had begun arranging for the translation of *Kiss of the Spider Woman* into English. Finally convinced by Jack Macrae to take on an agent, Lynn Nesbitt at ICM, he eventually disengaged from Dutton and moved to Knopf. He offered me a flat fee to do the translation, without a royalty agreement (which would be handled "later"). I insisted on a proper publishing contract, and Manuel, who wanted to do it his way, found my attitude dismissive—familiarity and money are often uneasy partners. We parted on a bitter note, several months passed, and by the following spring in New York, we met again and were reconciled with an alacrity that was characteristic of Manuel's friendships and long collaborations. I still regret not translating *Kiss of the Spider Woman* (though the footnotes would have been tedious).

Manuel approached other friends, among them René Jordan, a Cuban film critic living in New York who wrote subtitles for Columbia Pictures, and whom he knew through Nestor and Guillermo. With his finely chiseled features and a somewhat formal manner, René was Merle (after china doll–like Merle Oberon, Cathy in William Wyler's *Wuthering Heights*). Telling René, "I don't want Jill to do it; she wants points," he offered him the same magical fee of $2,000. René was reluctant to get involved because of the footnotes; the rest of the book was mostly dialogue, which René, experienced in film dialogue, felt he could have handled expeditiously. Manuel refused to eliminate his footnotes, however, even though they were less relevant to his reader in English, and he eventually landed Emir's friend Tom Colchie, a translator of Portuguese works. Manuel liked his gentle manner, and Tom, on his way to becoming a successful literary agent, mainly for Brazilian writers, would later come to represent Manuel.

pubis angelical

When Manuel had arrived in New York in January 1976, overwhelmed by the details of entry papers, lodging, and his sick parents in Buenos Aires, he also had the idea for a new novel, which "boosted my morale, because in November I finished my previous novel, *Kiss of the Spider Woman*, and I always feel empty after finishing." By spring, set up in his new little Village apartment, he had brought Malé to spend a few weeks to get better, and was looking forward to a European trip in early fall thanks to an invitation to

the Frankfurt Book Fair. "About movies: nothing new, it's all so boring I
don't see anything," he wrote to Guillermo Cabrera Infante. "On the other
hand, I'm crazy about Pickford! I see a lot of silent movies [at MoMA]. But
my current infatuation is Hedy, from 1938 to 1945, no further."[46]

A film actress in Central and Eastern Europe in the thirties, Hedwig
Kiesler grew up in a wealthy Jewish Viennese home. After her infamous
movie debut at age twenty, running nude like an Aphrodite in the Czech
film *Extase* (released in 1932, the year of Manuel's birth), she caught the attention of Viennese ammunitions mogul Fritz Mandl, who married her.
Mandl turned into a jealous husband almost immediately and tried to buy
or ban every copy of the film. In her ghost-written autobiography, *Ecstasy
and Me: My Life as a Woman*, she states: "I had everything I wanted, clothes,
jewelry, seven cars. Every luxury except freedom. For Mandl actually held
me a prisoner! . . . He had not married me, he had collected me, exactly like
a business prize."[47] By means of drugging a maid who closely resembled her,
she made a dramatic escape to Paris, then to London and on to Hollywood.
Exuding an exotic, sultry sexuality, Hedy was grabbed up by Louis B.
Mayer and renamed Lamarr—from across the sea (*la mar*) perhaps? At
twenty-five she would take over as sex symbol from Greta and Marlene,
now in their thirties. With her high cheekbones, she had the extraordinary,
disturbing beauty of the mythical Jewess. For Manuel, too, she was the archetypal dark-haired, light-eyed Argentine girl of the forties. She was never
more perfect than as the seductive siren to Charles Boyer's Pepe Le Moko in
her 1938 Hollywood debut, *Algiers*. In Manuel's favorite scene, Pepe, a condemned thief, decides to leave the safe haven of the Casbah for her, knowing it means certain death, and he speaks, as he beholds her, of their mutual
nostalgia for home, for Paris: "You know what you are to me? Paris! That's
you . . . The whole town!"[48] (Boyer's French-accented pronunciation of
"town" strikes a deliciously kitsch note in this heightened moment of
supreme devotion and sacrifice.)

For Manuel an important key to Hedy's mystique was that she was not
understood in her own time. She had begun working in the sophisticated
capitals of Eastern Europe with the likes of Max Reinhardt, but after the
war, when conventional realism took over, her appeal waned. In films she
made in 1943–44 she tried to be more conventional, but came off as stilted
and cold, and, after 1945, her perfect beauty began to fade. *The Strange*

Woman (1946) marked the demise of the world's most exquisite face—though its owner lived well into old age to tell her tale. A pathetic decline too: there were sightings of Hedy in cheap delis in the seventies (in the eighties she would be caught shoplifting).

As a group of us dined one icy January evening in 1976, in a Japanese restaurant on West 4th Street, Manuel listened to the conversation in patient silence, contributing only occasional smiles and mischievous winks. Suspicious of sushi, he ate almost nothing. He often disguised his parsimony by declaring that he would eat only in flea-bitten delis, "where the real New Yorkers eat" (just as he eschewed taxis because, he insisted, "The drivers are so reckless"). Manuel stared into space as we local New Yorkers chatted. Finally, when the check came, we heard him exhale, dreamily, "La Hedy." More than an utterance, it was an emanation. The novelist at work.

The new novel of which he spoke was "La Hedy" and would become *Pubis Angelical*, motivated, Manuel felt, by the death of his friend Silvia Rudni in Mexico but also by his own health fears, the apocalyptical ending of Cámpora's government, and, last but not least, the ephemeral, misunderstood Hedy. Told in three sections, which stretch from World War II into the future (Manuel's one attempt at science fiction), the novel concerns Ana, a beautiful Argentine woman, who lies dying of uterine cancer in a hospital in Mexico. The novel begins with what appear to be scenes from the past but are really Ana's hallucinations about her past life as a stunning Hedy-like actress called Ama (Mistress of the House), who is held captive by her jealous millionaire Viennese husband, who (like the real Mandl) collaborates with the Nazis, then escapes to Argentina. Based on Hedy's *Ecstasy and Me*, this subplot is a spy thriller with a Nazi touch.

Hedy is reincarnated in Ana's dream about a totalitarian future (the novel's third part) in which her avatar, W218, is a sort of sexual social worker, as one scholar described her: Manuel delves into sci-fi to imagine a world in which the desires of sexual rejects could be fulfilled, a fantasy alluding to his own sense of physical decline. Nightmares past, present, and future fill this shadowy novel. Silvia Rudni's tragic premature death and her political activities provided a model for Ana and her ex-lover Pozzi: in a hospital bed, awaiting the results of her tests for a malignancy, Ana is visited by Pozzi, a fellow middle-class intellectual who pressures her to support the Peronist cause. The theories of Lacan and Marx occupy the couple's argumentative dialogue. Ana is also, like all of Manuel's heroines, himself. She is not only an Argentine pining away in Mexico, but a daughter longing for her father, who died when she was a child: "Papa, I have to ask you something: is it true that the dead can see what's going on with the living? I think they can, something tells me yes, but then why don't I get any word from you?"[49] Even though Baldo Puig lived, Manuel had lost hope of communication with him at an early age.

Peronism became an explicit subject in *Pubis Angelical*, discussed at length by Ana and Pozzi. Manuel often explained in public that he didn't have a clear political vision, that he wanted to allow his characters who have divergent points of view—in this case, Ana and Pozzi—to spell out the issues. Was Manuel too cagey to pass judgment or was Peronism too complex for anyone to give the movement a definitive assessment? *Pubis Angelical* continued *Kiss of the Spider Woman*'s questionings about "the clash between political ideals and personal needs . . . the Peronist puzzle": was Peronism left or right, fascist or popular? At the same time, Ana's filial ambivalence and guilt reflect Manuel's own festering frustrations with Malé:

> If Mama isn't here with me it's because I don't want that, because I can't put up with her, she gets on my nerves. And it's shameful to tell Beatriz that Mama couldn't come to Mexico because of the altitude, because of her heart, when hers is far stronger than mine. Why don't I tell the truth? . . . It's shameful to have invented that heart ailment.[50]

After *The Buenos Aires Affair,* this was the novel he had the most difficulty writing.

During the summer of 1976—*Kiss of the Spider Woman* was about to be published in Spanish—Manuel wrote forty pages, which he threw out in August.[51] He had exhausted what was perhaps his most authentic vein, the language of his first two novels, which were grounded in pop culture and Argentine speech. It seemed as if his prolonged exile obliged him to speak from a language in which he was not fully at home. Manuel's camp spirit and inventions continued to flourish in new forms in the seventies—in *Kiss*, *Pubis*, and *Eternal Curse on the Reader of These Pages*—but these novels feel driven by an overtly political or didactic purpose, as if he were responding to the critical pressures he had so vehemently resisted, and to his inevitable entanglement in politics as a Latin American writer.

Seix Barral published *Kiss of the Spider Woman* in time for the Frankfurt Book Fair in September of 1976, after Manuel tried to hold back the publication some months. Terrified of the possible repercussions for his family in Buenos Aires, he had been having nightmares all summer long about the apartment on Charcas being bombed. In Germany, at the fair, Manuel tried to lie low politically while maintaining a high literary profile: a difficult balance to strike amid dueling publishers and ambitious writers, especially considering Latin America's political significance to radical European academics and intellectuals.

The Chilean José Donoso, on a panel of writers discussing current politics and literature, noticed Manuel sitting in the front row of the audience with a blank expression on his face. Pepe, as he was called, exchanged glances with Manuel, and surmised that Manuel did not want to be dragged into the heated argument that had just exploded between German academics in the audience and the panelists.

Returning from the fair at the end of September, Manuel took up the writing seminar at Columbia University he had debuted that spring. When first introduced to the students in Frank MacShane's plush Victorian office in Dodge Hall, Manuel seduced the room of aspiring writers with camp charm, batting his lashes like languorous butterflies. "This is Columbia *University*? I thought it was Columbia Pictures, the studio, of course, that made Rita Hayworth a star."[52] The "script" was more like *All About Eve*, with novices from all over Latin America—Enrique Giordano (Chilean), Adelaida López (Chicana), Vicki Slavuski (Argentine), Jaime Manrique (Colombian), and Ilan Stavans (Mexican-born)—all yearning to step into Bette's shoes. Manrique's obituary of Manuel, "The Writer as Diva," reflects an infatuated (or fatuous) fan's disappointment that Manuel no longer looked like "an Italian movie star—a young, but more refined, Marcello Mastroianni":

> In his mid-40s . . . the classical, Mediterranean features were
> unchanged, but he was now a bit overweight and his hairline
> had begun to recede . . . Like Garbo's his eyes were a tool, a
> weapon, not just organs for seeing, but for expressing what he

saw. Like the great diva, he raised his eyebrow (the left one) to indicate pain, disdain, despair.[53]

Manuel was very supportive of Manrique and other young gay writers. In an attempt to avoid student confessionals (the usual fare of creative writing courses), he chose another easy but more useful teaching method. Using techniques he remembered from the Centro Sperimentale, he had them rewrite their own work or a film they all knew, like *Carrie* (1976), to get them "inside the structure of things," or scrutinize the nuts and bolts of his own work-in-progress. Vicki Slavuski remembers that Manuel could enter into what each person wrote, and in the exercises with *Carrie*, in which they tried to imitate the Hitchcockian technique of building suspense out of the manipulation of point of view, he would make each student insert his own story. These informal weekly meetings with students relieved the solitude of work at his typewriter, and provided a relatively painless way to pay the rent.

Malé visited during high season at the Met and on Broadway, and Manuel recruited friends to "baby-sit," among them Merle Kaufman, the owner of the apartment I shared at King Street, and a close confidant of Manuel's until he left New York in 1980. Like Bruce and Howard, Merle, a social worker, unwittingly provided Manuel with psychobabble and New York Yiddish for the next novel brewing, one that he would write in English.

Determined not to spend another summer in New York, the following spring Manuel accepted invitations to Europe, as well as to Venezuela. Caracas, a two-hour drive from the Caribbean, was the seat of the most prestigious literary prize at that time in Latin America, the Premio Rómulo Gallegos; it was a publishing hot spot and cocktail-party town. Manuel visited with Isaac Chocrón and entourage; then, after talks at the university, he took a brief Caribbean vacation, as he wrote Howard later in the summer from Athens:

> Venezuela was a dream, a wet one. They couldn't find me an apartment so they (the University) sent me to a luxurious hotel on the beach, far from town. It was by a deserted beach and jungle. Occasional loafers would show up and the aver-

---

age was 1½ men a day—It was at least one, mostly two, and some days three and four—I'll tell you all about it in person—I was treated not too gently, just like Bijou in that Seven Sinners bar—There was even a Homolka type who threatened me. I had a great time but now I can't believe that men don't look at me in repressed Gotham.[54]

(Bijou was Marlene Dietrich's impersonation of a South Sea harlot in *Seven Sinners* (1940), one of Manuel's all-time favorites; with his wall-to-wall thick eyebrows, Oscar Homolka played the heavy.)

Before Athens he rested a few days with Malé at Mario's new place in Ostia; while Malé chatted endlessly with Mario or went to the beach, Manuel returned to writing *Pubis Angelical* on the terrace overlooking the sea. Admiring Manuel's ability to throw out drafts and rewrite from scratch, Mario recalls:

> I still see him typing on his portable typewriter under the umbrella, shaded from the strong sun. At midday he ran off to consummate his sacred half-hour swim (a custom he always followed, especially in Rio, even on autumn mornings) and he seemed not to care about leaving the papers he was writing scattered on the table in complete chaos. In his absence the wind often spread them around and I was in charge of picking them up off the floor (or gathering them from the garden below).[55]

As always when Malé and Manuel returned to Rome, they had dinner chez las Margas, and, on this occasion, they went to see old French and Italian movies—including Max Ophüls' *La Ronde* with "super" Isa Miranda—at the Centro Sperimentale, which Manuel translated for Howard as MoMA. Writing to Guillermo to reserve rooms for Malé and himself at the Strand Palace, Regent's, or on Cromwell Road, he reported his recent vertiginous itinerary: "Caracas: May 23–June 6: then Madrid, Rome (June 10; chez Fenelli); June 15: Athens, Cairo, Eastern Europe; London July 18–20." At this point Guillermo and Manuel hadn't seen each other for four years, and Manuel joked anxiously: "Will we find each other 'fané'?" (a gallicism in a famous tango, meaning "faded").

Underneath the compulsive political discussions in *Pubis* ("the episodes told by those characters who need to discuss politics")[56] lie what were, for Manuel, the inescapable problems of aging, loneliness, erotic rejection. "Even if there were a perfect Marxist society, where everything was shared in the best human spirit, there would still be one capital—physical beauty, sexual beauty. That wouldn't be shared."[57] "Ana's story typifies the dilemma of the beautiful, superior, subordinated women of the thirties and forties as well as Manuel's sense of himself as a displaced writer and a sexual being. Ana and W218 (her past and future selves) can read minds but, at the same time, are the slaves of men. Manuel situates Ana at the crossroads of past, present, and future, where "her repressed fantasies, her fears, her uncontrolled desires" reflect both Manuel's view of his own unconscious sources as a writer and the self-conscious effort he makes to re-create himself as a woman. The futuristic story about W218 is both a joke and a grave commentary on what Manuel needs or at least seeks—and perhaps the sexual role he plays in middle age when he services anonymous, unsavory types. Through the three stories he weaves his ever-steady questioning of sexual stereotypes, pleading for the importance of communication and equality between men and women, whether born or self-created: "Sexism is as serious, perhaps more so, than economic corruption and workers' struggles. The battle of social freedom must begin there. The foundation of exploitation is in the relationship between men and women."[58]

Pubis Angelical was not finished until 1978 in New York, but in the meantime Manuel again set aside fiction for another project, a film.

hell has no limits

Almost any man may, like the Spider, spin from his own innards his own airy Citadel.
                                                                        —John Keats

Arturo Ripstein, a slight, intense man whose father had been a commercial producer of Mexican films, was already an accomplished director when

Manuel met him at a gathering at Barbachano Ponce's house in 1975. Ripstein had collaborated with a number of leading writers, Carlos Fuentes, Gabriel García Márquez, José Emilio Pacheco, and Vicente Leñero. His father gave him an early start in the film world, in his teens, in the fifties—the era of some of Manuel's favorite Mexican movies—as assistant (or, as he clarifies, chauffeur) to Luis Buñuel during the Spaniard's exile in Mexico. Ripstein's films are more realist than surreal, but Buñuel's impact is felt in his bizarre characters and claustrophobic scenarios.[59] Ripstein very much admired the richly autobiographical *Betrayed by Rita Hayworth*, and Manuel gave him autographed copies of his latest books; even more impressed by *Kiss of the Spider Woman*, Ripstein would direct a strong stage version in Mexico, which ran for two years (1979–81) and received a national prize. In Frankfurt in September 1976, Manuel received an urgent telegram from the Mexican director, commissioning him to write a screenplay based on José Donoso's 1965 novella *El lugar sin límites* (*Hell Has No Limits*). After writing the script for *Heartbreak Tango*, Manuel had sworn "Never again!" But he was intrigued by this novel by Donoso, whom he respected, and within two months he handed Ripstein the first version of his script.

In Manuel's "M-G-Monegal" list, Donoso was Deborah Kerr: "She never received an Oscar but still she waits." Pepe Donoso felt pleased and honored when he learned that Manuel had authored the screenplay of his novella, which dealt frankly with the taboo subject of homosexuality. La Manuela, the congenial transvestite who dons a red dress and dances boleros, was a complex, intriguing character in this story about a run-down whorehouse in rural Chile.

For Manuel this was almost a rehearsal, though he didn't realize it then, for his contributions to the film version of *Kiss of the Spider Woman*—the challenge of bringing a believable, sympathetic queen to a wider audience. La Manuela, in love (unrequitedly) with Pancho, a resentful young truck driver, is the gay male madam of the brothel in Estación El Olivo; the major landowner of the district, Don Alejo, is a patriarch who owns everything and virtually everybody in town. In this case, Don Alejo is benevolent, protective of the prostitutes—including La Manuela, who wants, however, to gain complete economic independence from Don Alejo, as does Pancho. Manuel worried about what Ripstein would do with his script, but, as it turned out, Ripstein was in tune with Donoso's unmasking of macho stereotypes—he portrays Pancho as an angry, insecure stud, and benevolent Don Alejo is even more elderly in the film—and gave the grotesque whores and La Manuela the human depth with which Donoso had imbued them. Manuel feared mainly that Ripstein would turn the gay character into a caricature, while Ripstein felt that Manuel was trying to make La Manuela too exaggerated and Pancho super-macho, and believed that his directorial interpretation of Donoso's feelings about machismo and sexual underdogs was more nuanced. As Manuel saw it, Ripstein's psychological realism and expressionist touches—mirrors, dark interiors—tried to reflect an inner life but were oppressive; his camera direction tended toward "artsy" static tedium.

After the script was taken out of his hands and worked over by the Mexican writer José Emilio Pacheco, Manuel asked that his name not be included in the credits. Pacheco and Ripstein had agreed on making it clear to the spectator that Pancho kills La Manuela, whereas Manuel wanted to preserve the original's ambiguous ending—which left La Manuela's fate to the reader's imagination, and also left open the possibility that Pancho's brutality would go unpunished.

Though the film was "overdone, like an El Greco painting," Manuel ultimately regretted withdrawing his name from the credits:

> I liked it, but I had taken my name off it, because of the threat of censorship. At that time, 1978, the Argentine drama was at its worst, so I became hysterical. I was also censored in Spain and Hungary, so I was becoming paranoid. The film was a success.[60]

With the Mexican elections coming up, Manuel was concerned about possible censorship, especially, he implied, if a known homosexual signed a script in which the main character was gay. But Ripstein claims that Manuel feared he would deal with the transvestite in a crass manner. It was the same apprehension Manuel experienced later with Hector Babenco's, or, rather, William Hurt's, interpretation of Molina.

While Ripstein had similar fears about Manuel's "over-the-top" version, he also admits that the best moment of the film was written by Manuel: the fatal dance that poor Manuela, decked out in a red feathery flamenco dress outlining his bony male buttocks, performs for Pancho. La Manuela dances to a wordless Spanish song (by Los Churumbeles de España) titled "La Leyenda del Beso" (Legend of the Kiss), based on the myth of the sleeping princess awakened by a prince's kiss. Manuel added words and inverted the myth: this time the sleeper is a young man awakened to his sexuality by a woman's kiss. La Manuela's dance for Pancho, aggressively seductive, precipitates disaster: when brother-in-law Octavio sees Pancho swept away to the point of kissing La Manuela, Pancho is obliged to defend his masculinity by beating La Manuela to death.[61]

In 1978 this adaptation won the prize for best screenplay at the San Sebastián Film Festival: Manuel had finally arrived as a scriptwriter, and Ripstein asked him to come up with a screenplay of his own choosing. Manuel had worked on a novella by his friend Silvina Ocampo titled originally *El impostor* (The Impostor), which he retitled *La cara del villano* (The Villain's Face), a ghost story or thriller about double identities and about a young writer who commits suicide. (That same year Manuel gave his seminar at Columbia University on this film adaptation.) As an admirer of Silvina Ocampo as well as Borges and Bioy Casares, Ripstein was open to the idea and liked the original novella. Manuel thought it would match Ripstein's dark style, but Ripstein didn't like the script and shelved it. A year later producer Barbachano Ponce asked him for a script and he pulled Manuel's out of his drawer; Ripstein still didn't like it and rewrote it.[62] The film, which finally came out in November 1984 under the title *El Otro*, represented Mexico at the Rio Film Festival and bombed.

Meanwhile, Manuel's closest friend to have successfully broken the Hollywood barrier was Nestor Almendros. Already the acclaimed cinematographer of the New Wave directors François Truffaut and Eric Rohmer, he had just won an Oscar for his North American debut, the visually gorgeous midwestern "mood piece" *Days of Heaven* (1978).[63] Nestor passed through New York (on his way to Paris) after the awards ceremony, and Stephen Harvey, the film curator, organized an Oscar party for him at MoMA; it was the event of the season.

In the summer of 1978, Manuel returned to Mexico for respite from frenetic New York. Barbachano offered him his summer house—for a nominal rental fee—in Cuernavaca, or the City of Eternal Spring. Though there were too many tourists, from the time he first visited in the sixties Manuel was drawn to Cuernavaca's lovely climate, impressive cathedral, and color-ful plazas, its glorious past and luxuriant present. Conveniently close to Mexico City, Cuernavaca was an oasis for bohemians and an ideal second home for the rich and famous, like film star María Félix.

In the Las Delicias residential neighborhood, where he would one day buy his dream house. Manuel stayed at Barbachano's manor—practically empty of furniture, but with a big pool and a beautiful garden. He had just finished *Pubis Angelical* and, encouraged by Barbachano, was contemplating a new "cabaret" story focused on a self-destructive woman, which became a screenplay, *Recuerdo de Tijuana*. Embittered by the Ripstein experiment, Manuel vented his frustration in the prologue to the two screenplays that had been commissioned by Barbachano: *La cara del villano* and *Recuerdo de Tijuana*. (This volume would be published in 1985.) He summarized the dif-ferences he saw between writing scripts and writing novels in the following five points:

> 1. Writing novels permits many stages of elaboration; movies—you can't repeat or try variations, too expensive. A novel can take three years—I like to be left alone, but that's too much solitude!
> 2. Scripts are less difficult than novels, but there are fewer re-wards because the real author is the director—forever the au-thority issue.
> 3. Before writing a script it's always good to first interest a producer in the initial idea.
> 4. In literature you don't need a great or particularly original or profound idea; it's the treatment; whereas with movies, with their demand for condensation, the initial idea is all.
> 5. In terms of rewards: a book, even a manuscript, gets read; but if a play or movie doesn't get produced, it's as if nothing happened.

Beyond practical differences, in "Cinema and the Novel" Manuel described the two genres as incompatible. Manuel saw his novels as a way to commu-nicate shared problems with others: on the other hand, "I go alone to see a movie: that's an act in which the other person is for me the movie." As a spectator who went to the movies to be transported, and as a novelist who wrote to grapple with actuality, Manuel wanted the novel to portray and analyze life, while a film was a dream, condensed, allegorical:

> What did *El lugar sin límites* and *El impostor* have in common? On the surface, only their length: they were both short novels, or long short stories. But once I had finished this third adaptation, I could see another obvious common denominator. Both stories were allegories, poetic in tone, without any claims to realism, even though basically they dealt with well-defined human problems.
>
> My novels, on the other hand, always aim for a direct reconstruction of reality, hence their—for me, essential—analytical nature. Synthesis is best expressed in allegory or dreams. What better example of synthesis is there than our dreams every night? Cinema needs this spirit of synthesis, and so it is ideally suited to allegories and dreams. Which leads me to another hypothesis: can this be why the cinema of the 1930s and 1940s has lasted so well? [The movies] really were dreams displayed in images. To take two examples, both drawn from Hollywood: an unpretentious B-movie like *Seven Sinners*, directed by Tay Garnett, and *The Best Years of Our Lives*, directed by William Wyler, a "serious" blockbuster that won a bunch of Oscars and was seen as an honor for the cinema.
>
> Forty years later, what has happened to these two films? *Seven Sinners* laid no claim to reflect real life. It was an unbiased look at power and established values, a very light-weight allegory on this theme. *The Best Years of Our Lives*, by contrast, was intended as a realistic portrait of U.S. soldiers returning from the Second World War. And as such, it was successful. But, after all these years, all that can be said of this film is that it is a valid period piece, whereas *Seven Sinners* can be seen as a work of art. When I look at what survives in the history of cinema, I find increasing evidence of what little can be salvaged from all the attempts at realism, in which the camera appears to slide across the surface, unable to discover the missing three dimensional photographic realism. This su-

perficiality seems, strangely enough, to coincide with the absence of an *auteur* behind the camera. That is, a director with a personal viewpoint.[64]

For Manuel the current cinema's realism was pure surface and therefore pointless—even when executed by the supposed new *auteurs* like Martin Scorsese. "So much pretension and slowness . . . and they have nothing to say. That's why the studio system worked better," he remarked to Guillermo who, along with René Jordan, agreed, for the most part, with Manuel.[65] At least the "unreal" thirties and forties entertained while they reflected an era, and were formally refined and imaginative. The current scene wasn't "intelligent enough" to produce either entertainment or meaning, and, he predicted, the films would not have a lasting "poetic" value. The new actors were "dead children trying to imitate live people," he said with ferocity.[66] This opinion might have been narrow, but whether it was or not, it reveals something about how he perceived the future. In 1981, when his ten-year-old niece Mara, Carlos's daughter, of whom he was fond, spent Christmas with him and Malé in Rio de Janeiro, not only couldn't he stand how "rebellious and destructive" the new generation was but even "her redeeming feature, her voracity for films" did not bridge the gap:

> She belongs to the new generation, sees TV all day at home and doesn't care for stars, names, anything, just the images in movement. Awful, I can't discuss stars with her at all. She's seen *Superman* four times at movie houses and refuses to notice the actors have a name, an identity of their own. Exactly the opposite of what we loved, the continuity of their identity beyond the films. What's going to happen in the next century?[67]

Manuel returned from his vacation in Cuernavaca to his cozy anonymity in New York, the "protection of a tomb," safe from the judgmental Argentine stare: "Argentines know each other: they only have to speak a few words and they know your class, your level of education, even your sex fantasies."[68] New York was a city where he could be himself, a city that tolerated all eccentrics.

As ever, he followed a routine: "When you write a novel, you can't wait for the moment of inspiration. You have to work every day; if not you'll never finish. The gestation of a novel takes me two or three years." Every morning he sat at the portable Olivetti typewriter on his little table by the window overlooking Carmine Street. At noon, following the doctor's orders, he went to the municipal pool a block away from his apartment, on Seventh Avenue. After his midday swim, he had a frugal lunch, and then, on some afternoons, his creative writing seminar at Columbia University, but always his dates with the movies on television: "For me, New York was, above all, old movies."[69] In order to wake up at 3 a.m. to see a movie, he would sometimes go to bed early in the evening, and frequently saw two or three movies a day. The New York routine also included a stream of visitors, constant telephone calls, and numerous theater and opera events, especially when Malé was around and entertainment was de rigueur. As in every city Manuel inhabited, he gathered friends and admirers.

Among his new pals was Paloma Picasso, whom he had first met in Paris through her "mariage blanc" with Argentine Rafael López Sánchez. Suave, slight, nervous, with *compadrito*, or Valentino, looks, Rafael was a charming dilettante who managed Group TSE in the seventies and briefly discussed a collaboration with Manuel on the Gardel musical that Manuel later realized in Rio. Rafael would find greater rewards in devoting his public relations skills to Ms. Picasso's career as a jewelry designer. With her penchant for vintage forties fashion, fostered by the Cambil-Arroyuelo duo, and her strong, somewhat heavy facial features, a female version of her famous father, la Paloma was up Manuel's camp alley. Manuel socialized with the couple mostly in Paris, but also in New York, where they moved in 1982; eventually the marriage ended in an amicable divorce.

As Manuel acquired fame, he grew more impatient with old friends like Germán Puig who never "made it" and were, in some cases, perhaps envious of Manuel's success; Germán claims they parted company because he didn't read Manuel's novels. Manuel also grew more set in his ways. Shortly after he settled on Carmine Street, Pepe Bianco came to spend a few days in Manuel's minuscule apartment. Pepe was taken ill and found out that he needed to have a gallbladder operation. The day before entering Lenox Hill Hospital he phoned Octavio Paz, who was teaching at Harvard, to notify him; they were good friends, and Pepe needed the comfort of friends. While he was talking, Manuel kept motioning to him to cut the call, finally blurting in a loud whisper: "Expensive!" Paz finally asked: "What's going on there?" And, causing Manuel to blush with embarrassment, Pepe said emphatically in his high nasal voice: "This harpie won't let me talk, it's too expensive."[70]

In the eyes of some of his Argentine acquaintances in New York, Manuel had become selectively reclusive. Raúl Núñez, an Argentine architect who lived in a high-rise apartment on the 23rd Street waterfront, with a spectacular view of the East River, would often invite Manuel to dine with him and his roommate, TV critic Arthur Unger. Manuel called Raúl one day and said he couldn't accept any more invitations because he was unable to reciprocate in his small studio apartment; Raúl replied that it didn't matter, he enjoyed Manuel's company just the same. Whether or not Manuel felt guilty about not reciprocating, or was avoiding social obligations which he found boring, the friendship faded.

Arriving in New York from Paris one night in 1978, Nestor Almendros called "Sally," who, as Nestor had calculated, was still up watching a movie, in this case starring Lana Turner. They hadn't seen each other for months, and even though Nestor was comfortably settled in for the night in his hotel room—and had called to arrange a date for the following evening—Manuel insisted that he come over and talk about movies and about the "latest fashions," that is, the current literary and political gossip. Nestor was tired but also eager to see his friend, and why stay in a hotel when he had a friend in the Village? He arrived with all his suitcases at the apartment, which, he was surprised to find, was "the size of a closet." By around 2 a.m. their conversation drifted to the subject of Lana Turner. Manuel adored "the sweater girl" and her campy splendor. A *cursi* version of the "sensitive woman," she sincerely wanted to be remembered as a real sensitive woman who tried to do her job: the gap between who she was and what she wanted was formidable. Nestor said she was a lousy actress, a whore, and he detested her.

Suddenly Manuel ran to the door, opened it, and ordered his jet-lagged friend, who stared at him speechlessly, to leave: "A person who hates Lana can't remain under my roof. You're like all the other French women, nasty and bitter. You're a veritable Stéphane Audran." At 3 a.m. Nestor found himself with his suitcases out on the street on a cold New York night. They didn't see each other again for quite a while, which made things uncomfortable for mutual friends like René Jordan, Guillermo and Miriam, as well as

Orlando Jiménez Leal, the boyish, buoyant Cuban filmmaker who lived in New York and whose wife at the time edited *Vanidades*. Nestor and Guillermo decided Manuel was in a bad way, and that his friendships were being affected.[71] But Nestor eventually forgave Sally. In letters Manuel wrote to Nestor afterward, this unfortunate memory turned into an ongoing joke as Manuel addressed his friend as "Dear Stéphane . . ."

eternal curse on the reader

Soon after Manuel finished *Pubis Angelical*, in October 1977, he noticed among the swimmers at the municipal pool a rugged gray-haired younger man who was often there at the same hour. Manuel engaged him in conversation and, after a few casual lunch dates, learned that Mark had a Ph.D. in sociology but had lost his professorial position and was teaching part-time as a lecturer at NYU; he was also divorced, and he seemed deeply depressed. Out of this encounter Manuel would write his first and only novel in English, *Eternal Curse on the Reader of These Pages* (1980):

> I tried to get interested in what was going on in the country and make friends, but I felt very isolated . . . I had a violent clash with a fascinating North American character . . . Mark, who was younger, stronger, healthy (could do many more laps than me), handsome, and a citizen. He had none of my problems. I wanted to be him and, it turns out, he wanted to be me . . . I got him to open up to me and found out that he hated being American, wanted to have an accent, was a Marxist and wanted to be a writer. Ultimately he rejected me; I disappointed him because I didn't match his image of author, and it amazed me that he didn't realize how privileged he was.[72]

Mark, who despite Manuel's "fascination," struck most of Manuel's friends as not only taciturn but ordinary-looking, accepted his frequent social invitations reluctantly, but did not reciprocate.[73]

With such an object of desire, whose whole being spoke of an absence of desire, Manuel was on some level seeking absence, rejection. The book's title, a quotation from one of the most corrosive, nihilistic novels about romantic love—Laclos's *Les liaisons dangereuses*—came from the pit of this despair. At the gym Mark looked like a man who had everything, and turned out to be, as Manuel put it, "morally and spiritually bankrupt," just like the empty (North) American dream so coveted by the rest of the world, certainly the world south of the border. Manuel was the successful writer but exiled and isolated, no longer young and desirable; Mark was desirable (to Manuel) but a career failure (he was a blocked writer and failed to achieve tenure at the university); he was at home, but in self-imposed exile and isolation. Each not only had something the other wanted, but also something they didn't want to recognize that they shared: for example Mark's apparently self-indulgent choice of isolation shed light on Manuel's own destiny; Manuel's sexual advances opened fearful gates to Mark's own sexual ambiguity.

Manuel finally gained entrance to Mark's dingy one-room apartment by giving him a television set (Manuel had just bought a new and larger one for himself)—and it was "a great triumph getting him to accept it," Manuel told his neighbor Merle.[74] Mark lived in total austerity: one chair, one cup, one spoon, one fork, one mattress. Though a relatively young man—he was in his late thirties—Mark seemed to have no hope for his future, and blamed an absent father and narcissistic mother for all his problems. When Manuel described Mark's apartment to Merle, a therapist, she gently ironized that Mark "obviously wasn't expecting company." She explained, earnestly, that he was probably living in a reclusive fantasy world, and that such austerity meant "he couldn't visualize the other."

In his relationship with Mark Manuel at first saw himself as the older displaced Latin American who clearly sees through a self-centered younger North American: it was the psychodrama of the critical father and rebellious son; the narcissist is the parental figure, producing a son who is a mere reflection of himself. "Visualizing the other" struck a chord: the patriarchal, critical Argentine eye and now this narcissist (whom he had discovered in the pool's reflection) who could see only himself. Exhausted by his last novel, *Pubis Angelical*, and unable to move ahead with his current efforts, Manuel was feeling that he had said all he had to say in novels.[75] At a safe distance from Argentina, he tried to work on the abandoned "Relative Humidity" manuscript in the seventies, in New York, and a decade later in Rio de Janeiro, but each time, another project intervened, including novels in which he continued to explore similar narrative ideas. He would last attempt to complete this unfinished work after he and Malé settled into their new home in Cuernavaca, early in the summer of 1990.

His chronic insomnia took a greater physical toll as he turned forty-five, in December 1977, and New York was a tough noisy city; it became more and more difficult to concentrate. These were symptoms he had already described in minute and vivid detail in his "case studies" of Leo and Gladys in *The Buenos Aires Affair*, especially Gladys, a depressed, suicidal artist whose creative intuition was not appreciated by critics. The effort and the isolation of writing intricate fiction were too enervating for Manuel, especially if he was only going to be disappointed by reviews and enraged by critics. As he passed through his forties, it was also harder to shrug off unresolved emotional stress. The novel was where he most successfully integrated self and society, and yet this (for him) analytic form was leading more and more to the limitations of analysis, whose findings would always be ambiguous, fragmentary, unreliable. *Pubis Angelical* took up where *Kiss of the Spider Woman* left off, leaving the reader to decide if well-being is achieved through escape or through commitment. In *Pubis Angelical*, the language of feminism Manuel heard everywhere in the western hemisphere permeates Ana's story: the ephemeral dream of glamour, the actress's past, and the futurist hallucination underscore the importance of achieving self-knowledge, of Ana's acceptance of herself as a maturing woman, of the difficult acceptance of reality.[76] But Manuel still leaves interpretation up to the reader, and not only as a postmodern tactic; he, personally, was still seaking a solution or at least to accept resolution.

The only reliable facts were dreams and fantasies, which he felt film and theater were better suited to treat. He was now an authority in the literary world, could work confidently with others, and, potentially, would be much better paid. There were increasing worries about his aging parents and attendant economic pressures: his father would soon retire, there was runaway inflation in Argentina, and his brother could barely provide for his own wife and child. Both Malé and Baldo had recently had serious digestive troubles, but were doing better by January: Baldo's pains were diagnosed as ulcers, and Malé underwent a gallbladder operation, from which she recuperated superbly. Malé was more and more Manuel's dependent—and it was depressing to constantly confront the aging process. Mother and son were one: that is, not only was Malé in some ways the real Manuel Puig, but Manuel had become a "mother," not only to his "daughters," in the camp sense of mother, or drag queen, but also to his own mother.

Illness, particularly in conjunction with failed or lost love, is never absent from Manuel's novels; from Juan Carlos's consumption to Valentín's food poisoning to Ana's uterine cancer. Illness, hypochondria, and the fear of death loom even more prophetically in his later novels, most particularly *Pubis Angelical*, where Ana, the main character, is a bedridden hospital patient, and *Eternal Curse*, where Mr. Ramirez is a wheelchair-bound invalid.[77] Larry John (the fictional Mark) explains in freshman Freudian terms to the older Argentine invalid that the most important thing for a child is how he

> feels he's regarded by his parents, and how he feels they re-
> gard themselves. Whether they're pleased with him. Whether
> he makes them proud. All their feelings about their son and
> themselves . . . are picked up by the child as reflections of him-
> self . . . And he can make mistakes and believe that his own
> image is what he sees when he looks down that sewer.[78]

The Puig patriarchy and the fragility of machismo haunt this adversarial duet of father and son, success and failure, heterosexual and homosexual, and, ultimately, writer and reader. Also included is a dialectic between North and South America, between English and Spanish. Here were two characters for a novel, in a way a variation on Molina and Valentín, who could work through a kind of psychodrama, another "transference" in the form of a dialogue, based on Manuel and Mark's transcribed conversations: "The book started as a kind of exercise: I proposed a dialogue three times a week, paying him. We'd meet two hours each time, with a typewriter in the middle since he didn't want a tape recorder . . . It was a problem lived, and I wanted to write about it, in English."[79] *Eternal Curse* came out as cinema verité or pseudo-documentary, a montage of interviews. Manuel explained, still in midstream:

> I asked his permission to take notes on his life: I took about
> 200 pages of notes in English, and now I'm trying to deal with
> the notes . . . Language used to be a vehicle of psychology and

of characters, a language in which I had all the keys. Now I have all the data in a language to which I don't have the keys. In this novel I am not interested in myself as a character, but rather in the counterpoint of the American who is my papa. The American is a left-wing boy who rejects the whole system he's immersed in and then, in some way, applies in his relationships all the repressive action he criticizes . . . I put myself in the old man's place.

Manuel was not, literally, a character; indeed, except for his first incarnation as Toto, he was never again a character; but it is undeniable that he is present in all his characters, in the way a dreamer is in his dream. Contrary to what Manuel says, his novels were also like dreams. Manuel helped his editor come up with an enticing and sufficiently melodramatic précis of this "collision of two 'solitary fantasy systems' " for his jacket cover:

The late 1970s. Winter. Greenwich Village, New York City. Ramirez, a demanding seventy-four-year-old Argentine exiled to America ostensibly for political reasons, is an invalid, confined to a wheelchair, who lives in a nursing home under the auspices of a human rights group. Larry, a moody, self-absorbed thirty-six-year-old American down on his luck, who occupies a bare, grimy apartment on Carmine Street, is hired to push Ramirez about the neighborhood. As we follow Ramirez and Larry on their jaunts through the Village and overhear them in the old man's nursing home and hospital rooms, their relationship becomes a complex of deceptions. Is Ramirez merely a pathetic hypochondriac/amnesiac who has forgotten his past, knows only the literal meaning of words and feels no emotions? A frightened man marked for murder? A perverse patriarch who terrorized his wife and son? Is Larry a crazed Vietnam veteran? A currently unemployed history professor? A son irremediably damaged by his abusive parents, as he so readily and frequently insists? . . . While both men twist each other up in lies—and Larry slowly deciphers Ramirez's memoirs, encoded in French novels (*Les liaisons*

dangereuses, *La princesse de Clèves*, *Adolphe*)—Ramirez and
Larry come to depend on each other; arrive, more often than
not, at unspoken understandings; are . . . shown to be each
other's shadow.[80]

The old man dies at the end, but it appears as if their bond has helped the
younger man move on with his life. The only way into the younger man's
mind, Manuel rationalized, was through the interview:

> It's a case I couldn't let escape: such an emblematic, interesting
> character. In the novel, my father is exiled to New York,
> comes into contact with this boy who's a sociologist and who,
> dismissed from the universities, works as a waiter, gardener,
> caretaker of old people. He takes my father around in a
> wheelchair. My father's English is defective; the other's isn't
> but the notes are. Then I tried, for the boy, a kind of Spanish
> translatorese, flat, fictional. I realize it's slightly demented un-
> dertaking but . . . there, that's how it came out.[81]

No doubt, in part, Manuel, both a romantic risk-taker and a pragmatist,
branched out into this unexplored territory to avoid the hassle of dealing
with translations—at the same time he was interviewing Mark, he was involved in the exhausting process of translating *Kiss of the Spider Woman* into
English in which several hands had to intervene. As with each novel, *Eternal Curse* was directly connected to a moment in his life: Ramirez suffers a
loss of nationality; he says he knows words in different languages but not
what he should *feel*; he suffers amnesia because of a repression that is psychological but determined in good part by the political. As an Argentine, he
rejected roots in the old country, feeling totally removed from Europe, but
he has also rejected/been rejected by Argentina.

   With Larry's alienation and Ramirez's total sense of displacement,
Manuel was now satirizing in these two Beckettian psychobabblers nothing
less than French, that is, Argentine (pseudo-philosophic), existentialism.
Eternal Curse, beginning with its jinxy title, would be another book the Argentines would "love to hate." A frivolous treatment of their alienation, it
was written in awkward English and translated into a flat Spanish that had

nothing to do with the authentic, vibrant language of Manuel's first novels; in their short memory, the Argentine commentators forgot that they hated that "mockery of the way Argentines speak." The book was the product of linguistic exile and, with the help of his New York "daughters," Manuel incorporated Yiddish slang like *klutz* and *nebbish*. But he got uncomfortable when critics emphasized his linguistic displacement—as when an Argentine academic in Paris attributed Ramirez's linguistic aphasia and illnesses to Manuel's "somatization" of exile or transference of his linguistic limbo into physical disease. Manuel was super-sensitive to Argentine remarks, and said to his French translator, Albert Bensoussan: "A literary investigation should seek meanings, but the Argentine vice is to seek a guilty party, someone to accuse, and that's a police investigation."[82]

The loss of language was a delicate point; if, on the one hand, Manuel himself spoke of somatizations or psychosomatic manifestations, he was worried about a possible impoverishment of his language. Already there seemed to be a general consensus that his writing was a disappointment after *Kiss of the Spider Woman*. *Eternal Curse* reflected not only exile, however: with Mark he felt he was giving up his hopes for "marriage," and the book explores that sense of loss too. He was stuck in the role of voyeur, vicarious "vampire," crippled father, or an aged version of Toto—who once upon a time fantasized that he was a mascot to the handsome father of a schoolmate, a role allowing him to be in the company of a desired man, but at the cost of giving up his sexuality.

Eternal Curse is an American story, but it is also the continuing saga of Manuel's lifelong conflict with his father. Ramirez, in the novel, misses his son and hence has paternal feelings for Larry, but since he's a foreigner, an invalid, and helpless, he finds himself in a weak, or filial, position to the younger Larry. Larry, unable to have a successful relationship with a woman, recounts to Ramirez a string of attractions, including his forbidden thoughts about his mother and his latest failed romance with a nurse named Virgo—Malé's astrological sign. Larry is also Manuel, conscious of his Oedipal relationship with his mother and ashamed on some level of his lack of affection toward his father. When Larry is aroused listening to his wife and her lover, he is still the voyeuristic child witnessing the primal scene.[83] The novel is pop, heavy-handed Freudianism, and didn't go over well with American readers.

The "eternal curse" is not only Manuel's nihilist lashing out at the critics:

it is the eternal curse of being human too, and finally, the eternal curse of knowledge. No matter how much we understand about the whys and how unsuccessful our family or sexual relations are, life goes on, and how do we go on with it? Again, the participation of the reader in Manuel's writing is more than fashionable self-reflection; only one who needed—or thought he needed—the reader would curse him. All Manuel's novels (except *Betrayed by Rita Hayworth*) were planned, but he always allowed the content to decide the form as he went along; in *Heartbreak Tango*, he decided not to include Nené's letters to Juan Carlos, because the reader could intuit her answers on the basis of the information given. The participation of the reader was essential to his constructions; he sought to avoid redundancies so as not to underestimate the reader; for him writing was, apart from a therapeutic puzzle, an engagement with the reader. This novel inflated the real, expressed the inner gloom that New York had come to represent for Manuel.

the kiss of success

Even though Christopher Street was the mecca for gays from all over the repressive globe, the New York publishing establishment still, in the seventies, obeyed occult restraints not dissimilar—though less extreme—to censorship in less liberated societies. An unspoken policy seemed to hold sway at *The New York Times* and other major newspapers: books with overt homosexual content were not highlighted in reviews until Knopf published John Cheever's *Falconer* in 1977. Tom Colchie believes that this event broke the ice because soon after the *Times* review, Knopf opened its doors to *Kiss of the Spider Woman*. Mark Mirsky, at this crucial juncture, had told Bobbie Bristol at Knopf that "it was a disgrace that Manuel Puig had been cast into the outer darkness." She asked to see the book.

Manuel became a momentary celebrity on the New York gay literary scene when, at Edmund White's suggestion, *Christopher Street* ran a cover story and interview that came out in April 1979, right after the publication of *Kiss of the Spider Woman*. Manuel made positive comments about Cuba in this interview, which upset Nestor and Guillermo, who figured Manuel was trying to earn brownie points with the fashionable left on both sides of the Atlantic—which, at the time, didn't work anyway. Fashion luminaries, particularly those with literary aspirations (like Diane von Furstenberg), and New York literati, like White, sparkled in Manuel's social firmament. White remembers a luncheon around that time with Manuel and Christopher Cox in the West Village: they talked endlessly about film, but Cox was scandalized that Puig's only interest seemed to be actresses, not directors or scripts. Unlike Cox, White saw through the irony, and immediately admired the famous Argentine writer's "simplicity and charming lack of pretension." Manuel was refreshingly campy and accessible; White remembers with affection Manuel's manifest indifference to literary life, or at least that his principal obsession seemed to be the "search for a husband." From a slightly younger generation, White belonged to the Violet Quill Reader group, gay writers who wrote for a gay audience and who envied Puig's wider international reputation and his transcendance of the gay ghetto. White was a bit too politically gay for Manuel, but Manuel knew he needed support from sympathetic literary quarters. He much preferred recreation with frivolous glamour queens (of any sex), though, than with heady intellectuals.

Kiss of the Spider Woman had been published in 1976 by Seix Barral, then the most influential literary press in the Hispanic world; the house that had at first rejected *Betrayed by Rita Hayworth* was now Manuel's official Spanish-language publisher, with his prestigious ally, the poet Pere Gimferrer, at its literary helm. At the 1977 International Book Fair in Buenos Aires, *Kiss of the Spider Woman* was included on a distinguished list of books—Vargas Llosa's *Aunt Julia and the Scriptwriter*, Cortázar's *We Love Glenda So Much*, and Alejo Carpentier's *Rites of Spring*—which could not be imported, displayed, or sold.[84] Banned by a right-wing dictatorship, Manuel thought the international leftist publishers would leap to publish his novel, but Gallimard and Feltrinelli, his publishers in France and Italy, resisted, claiming it wasn't well written. Manuel suspected that the main reason was, as Juan Goytisolo later said:

> In an era [the seventies] in which the image of Latin America
> as an embattled continent turned pens into machine guns and
> writers into loudspeakers of revolution, a figure and work

like his [Puig's] produced a reaction of distrust, scorn, and rejection. Julio Cortázar's ex-girlfriend [Carvellis] vetoed the publication of *Kiss of the Spider Woman* [at Gallimard] because it no doubt hurt the clichéd image of the militant Marxist-Leninist upon presenting him as moved and carried away by the cinematic, Scheherazade-like arts of his apolitical and homosexual cell companion. These same moralizing and sectarian suppositions made other left-wing European publishers follow his example. The error couldn't be more gross. Just as two poems about the Spanish Civil War by the least politicized of our poets of 1936—I refer to Luis Cernuda and his admirable Spanish Elegies—are the only ones that can be read today with emotion by virtue of their depth, Manuel Puig is author of the best political novels of the sixties in Latin America because they're the work of a writer who knew no other commitment than the one he had contracted with writing and with himself.[85]

Kiss of the Spider Woman offended the European intelligentsia because of the relationship between a window dresser and a revolutionary, and because of the sexual take on politics and revolution, or, as Manuel put it, his perspective on "two sides of the same struggle for human dignity." In May, Manuel sent a frazzled shorthand note to Guillermo about "horrendous boycotts, Feltrinelli rejected, problems here," and a month later, he was defiantly positive:

> By contract I owed Gallimard another book and I presented *Spider Woman*. The readers' reports (I thought Bianciotti [editor at Gallimard] was a good person) were horrendous. I was content because I was saved from Gallimard, but content only because I was frightened by . . . Bianciotti's reaction.[86]

He had been betrayed once more by a compatriot, and it was even worse in exile, where Argentines had to jockey among themselves for international recognition. In Argentina, while some critics would recognize that he was innovative and transgressive, many others, often with political agendas, would "use my last book to criticize the newest one," Manuel began saying in the early seventies. Bianciotti ("Bianca") had already nixed *The Buenos Aires Affair*, which was rescued by Severo and published by Editions du Seuil as *Les Mystères de Buenos Aires,* an apropos allusion to the first detective serial by Eugène Sue, *Les Mystères de Paris.* Bianciotti, then the Latin American acquisitions editor for Gallimard (a post Severo would assume some years later), was becoming more French than the native Gauls, and is now a respected French writer. Seuil also published *Kiss of the Spider Woman*; Manuel warned Bensoussan that the uneducated Molina speaks in a flat, slightly ungrammatical, colloquial manner, to the point that his language might irritate the reader. He also complained about previous French translators, another form of caveat.[87] The Knopf translation had gone through several revisions, and caused Manuel "terrible headaches," as he confided to Guillermo during the harsh New York winter of 1977: "Now I'm going crazy with the translation into English . . . The kitsch aspect of Molina's voice doesn't come out in direct translation, it has to be completely re-created . . . There's so much to rethink in English it gives me mental cramps."

Despite Manuel's celebrity on Christopher Street, the initial reception of *Kiss of the Spider Woman* in New York was lukewarm. *The New Yorker* was going to publish a section but begged off, and novelist Robert Coover nearly sank the book in *The New York Times* by describing it as a collection of thin devices: "a rather frail little love story," he said, referring to the "unedited dialogue" as a "radio script." While he recognized that "Mr. Puig's fascination with old movies largely provides its substance and ultimately defines its plot, its shape," he didn't find the handling of "these film synopses" notably innovative. Manuel also received flack for the footnotes, which many reviewers claimed were useless; he had made them elementary "on purpose" for a certain reader, and "elitist attitudes" from *Le Monde* and *The New York Times* were upsetting and embarrassing.[88] Manuel undertook, naively, his own publicity campaign, visiting Village bookstores like Three Lives so they would know he was available to give readings. He hoped this effort would induce the publishers to bring out a paperback edition.

In Rome he had felt like an outsider because "the circle of writers and filmmakers was closed: they all thought alike and protected each other, were organized in cliques." In New York the problem was isolation, his own, and that of his intellectual friends, who seemed to him reclusive. There was very little "one-on-one contact."[89] The sales in Spain were, thus far, disappointing, and even flamboyant ally Severo, then the acquisitions adviser at Editions du Seuil, had barely championed the book. Unable to live on the sale of his own books, Severo was very cautious when it came to politics, literary and otherwise; he lived under the protective wing of his companion François Wahl, adopting a French identity and decorum.[90] Over the years he became, in the eyes of some Cuban and Latin American acquaintances, François's puppet, to the detriment of his emotional well-being as well as his editorial freedom. Manuel was now calling Severo—with his round Buddha-like face, serpentine gait, and Gallic verbal arabesques—La Poupée Mécanique, after a transvestite in Severo's novel *Cobra*. When François edited out certain explicit sex scenes in the French edition of *Kiss of the Spider Woman*, Manuel felt betrayed. Severo's rejoinder was to call career-oriented Sally *la hormiga* (the ant): a sad skirmish for both friends.

flying down to rio: 1980–88

kiss, the play

In prison, all of womankind is transformed into one beloved woman and that beloved woman into an impersonal, universal womanhood.

—Milovan Djilas

Vacationing in August 1979 in Cartagena, on the Caribbean coast of Colombia, where he had been invited to a writer's conference, Manuel already planned not to spend another cold winter in New York, and for a moment considered settling in this steamy colonial port city. "Frankly," Manuel wrote Howard Mandelbaum from Cartagena, "last winter in New York was rather insipid. Good friends like you and the flicks kept me alive, but I don't want my babies to see me around with a sour face." He hoped "la Harold," a friend of Howard's, would sublet his little apartment. New York had been demoted from Gotham to "that open sewer," and Cartagena was gorgeous, he wrote to Manrique, his Colombian friend in New York. Greta Garbo, Yoko Ono, and Joan Didion had recently vacationed there, but the cultural life was "too evanescent."[1] What turned him off most was not the squalor of Cartagena but the bland reception given him by the literary establishment in conservative Bogotá, where he had delivered lectures: they "could not forgive a major author for coming out with a gay novel."[2]

While still in Cartagena, he received a telegram from Buenos Aires with sad news—the death of Mario's father. Mario and Manuel had been talking about living together again, with or without lovers; they were family, after all. They wanted peace and glamour in a Mediterranean or tropical setting, where the living was easy and economical. Mexico was out because of the altitude, Malé's heart condition, and Manuel's hypertension. As Carlos Fuentes was quoted as saying: "Only goats and Mexicans dare fornicate in Mexico City." Their new home would have to be convenient; that is, not too third world for Malé. Earlier that summer, in Rome, the friends had decided on Marrakech, of which they both had joyous memories from the sixties; Mario agreed to being part of a threesome, as long as he had separate living quarters. Morocco had the advantage of neighboring Spain, where Manuel had stimulating friends like writers Pere Gimferrer and Terenci Moix. At the time, his principal source of income came from Spain, where his novel *Pubis Angelical* was a best-seller. With such a suggestive title it "sold like hotcakes," Manuel jested.

In October he would return, via Mexico, to teach his seminars at Columbia and CUNY. But by the time October 1980 rolled around, the sales of *Pubis* in Spain and Mexico had saved him from the classroom. Meanwhile, Mario, the sun-worshiper, who was dividing his time between Rome and the beaches of Turkey and Tunisia, was diagnosed with a detached retina and wouldn't be able to travel again until after the operation—to be performed by a specialist in Modena, in northern Italy. This meant they had to postpone Morocco. Malé and Manuel flew to Paris and on to Rome, where they celebrated Christmas with Mario, the Margas, and other friends (Eddie Caviello and "Norby" Fuentes from New York), and where Manuel revised the translation of *Kiss*, the play, with Angelo Morino. Christmas was a happy reunion, and a special treat was the exquisite Christmas Eve Mass in San Anselmo Church, near the shady park in Aventino where Mario had taken photos of Manuel, it now seemed centuries ago to both friends.

Mario's operation was postponed, but with Malé on his hands, Manuel had to move on: royalties awaited them in Spain and he wanted to meet up with Mario after New Year's in Marrakech. By the time Mario recuperated and returned to Rome in mid-January, he was surprised to hear that Manuel had called from Marrakech; he and Malé had gotten sick there, and they had left for Brazil. Soon after, in a letter from Rio de Janeiro, Manuel explained that "because of Mama" they needed to be in a place where they could trust the doctors. "The Moroccan experiment didn't work," Manuel wrote Bensoussan, who was working on the French translation of *Pubis* and had hoped Manuel would remain close by. Moving back to Galtieri's dictatorship in Argentina was out of the question.

Manuel urged Mario to join him in buying an apartment in Rio; it would be a good investment in a city they loved, and it was relatively close to Argentina, so that family and friends could visit. As ever, Manuel was discouraged with Mario's inertia; he could never decide to leave Italy, where he always had to scrounge for work. Of all the middle-class establishments, Italy's was the stuffiest, and, when it came to paying artists, the most tight-fisted. Manuel, anxious to care for his own elderly parents, thought Mario should be near his aging mother. The two friends were no longer spring chickens either, and the frequent, relatively inexpensive flights from Rio to Buenos Aires would be a godsend for periodic medical checkups with family doctors and Argentine specialists.

Manuel's decision to move to Brazil was swift. The Carioca film industry, which had developed later than Mexico's or Argentina's, was booming by the late seventies; in Brazil, though he didn't yet know it, Manuel's biggest movie adventure would begin. Shortly after arriving with Malé in Rio de Janeiro, in February 1980, Manuel was approached by stage designer and director Dina Sfat to do a Brazilian production of *Kiss*. Dina had recently married Paulo José, a popular Carioca actor who was perfect for Valentín, and they began working with Manuel on the project for the "avant-garde" Ipanema theater, with actor Rubens Correa, another star in Rio, who was eager to play Molina. It was as if Fate had decided he was making the right move. Now that he had the means, from continuing royalties, and especially thanks to the success of *Pubis Angelical* in Spain and to the exchange rate, he was able to purchase a luxurious apartment in glamorous Rio. By March, he had closed a deal on a duplex in Leblon—it had belonged to a soap opera star—at a bargain price because he was paying with "ready money" from his Seix Barral royalties. Just as Baldo had arrived in Buenos Aires almost forty years earlier with all his monies in a suitcase, Manuel showed up at the realtor's door with a cash-filled suitcase. (Large cash payments were not uncommon in Brazil, where the currency fluctuated so violently that a bank account worth thousands on Friday could be reduced to hundreds by Monday.)

Rio was perfect: a big city with a cultural life and a beach where Manuel could swim every day. The Cariocas were relaxed, fun-loving, and "tropical but not too tropical"—and the boys were black, beautiful, and available. In February he applied for permanent residency; at the same time, he secured a tourist visa for Mexico, keeping his options open: no one country in Latin America could be trusted completely. Manuel's move distanced him, of course, from New York's multiple movie channels, but Brazil meant the rebirth of his health and sex life, as he wrote to Howard: "Things are very good, romance is better than ever, career is OK."[3] And if he had lost the paradise of movie channels, 1980 ushered in a machine that would come to his rescue: the VCR.

In May 1980, on one of his trips back to New York while still settling into Rio, Manuel invited René Jordan, the film translator and critic, out for a farewell dinner, which, considering Manuel's pecuniary allergy to restaurants, surprised René.[4] His surprise turned to dismay when the restaurant turned out to be a dive in Chinatown where they were confronted, said René, "with a suspicious-looking soup." In the course of the dinner conversation, Manuel leaned over and said confidentially, as if the flyblown walls had ears, "I have something important to talk to you about, but not here." They went to a seedy nearby "park"—a small dusty square with a few sad trees where the occasional lingerer looked either like an addict or a dealer— and Manuel pulled out of his pocket a wad of dollars, an action which jolted René, already uneasy. Then came the mysterious explanation: since René (because of his line of work) was the first person Manuel knew who had a VCR, he was asking if René would record movies on TV, but "only the ones" starring his actresses: Rita Hayworth, Lana Turner, Susan Hayward, Joan Crawford, Hedy Lamarr, Bette Davis, Katharine Hepburn, and so on. The money was for his expenses. René responded with mild humor: "Are you asking me a favor, or offering me a job?"

A few years later, when they met up at the Miami Film Festival, René asked if Manuel had found a source for his tapes. Manuel replied casually: "Oh, I have my *esclavitas*." He meant Howard, Bruce, and others like film buff Bob Gottlieb at Knopf. Indignant but amused too, René quipped: "So, you considered me one of your little slaves?" There were many other *esclavitas*—in Los Angeles, in Mexico (la Becky), in Rome (Mario), in Paris (Nino)—a vast and growing network of adoring friends, acquaintances, and film fans willing to accommodate him or, unlike René, be bribed. In some cases, Manuel purchased VCRs and even television sets as gifts, which of course obliged the recipient to reciprocate. As he enumerated his problems with customs, trying to purchase and ship a machine from New York to Rio, Manuel spoke of these contacts as cogs: "And meanwhile the other machine in Rome is recording." Manuel had ordered Mario early in 1982—by now Mario was "Bette Davis" in her older, ugly phase, or simply "Baby Jane," as in the horror movie *What Ever Happened to Baby Jane?*—to buy a TV and recorder. He would be reimbursed by Manuel, who arrived at Mario's house in Ostia a few months later and left the next day, armed with cassettes. "What's not producing," Manuel complained, "is the one in New York [Bruce or Howard], very little. I can't believe that there aren't frequent cultural programs . . . I'll see what to do about it, maybe pass the machine on to someone else."[5] While this was a hurried shorthand note written to Malé, who, in Buenos Aires, was about to move into the new apartment Manuel had bought for her in Rio, the demotion of persons to their functions is still arresting.

Over the next several years Manuel would amass over 3,000 films (including operas) and film segments contained on approximately 1,260 videocassettes. He insisted upon filling each cassette, so that frequently two full-length features and part of a third were on one tape—Howard was irked by Manuel's rule not to waste an inch. He often recorded or had his friends record over used tapes, and frequently he was only interested in saving a specific film clip, sometimes for a detail such as a hat. Felisa Pinto, who visited Manuel on several occasions in Rio, remembers when he showed her, over and over again, maybe fifteen times, a scene where Hedy Lamarr adjusts her hat in front of a mirror. It was precisely the frame where the first sign of decline, perhaps the shadow of a line at the corner of her mouth, became manifest; of equal interest—hence his insistence that Felisa study the way she adjust the hat—was the forties style which he wished to discuss with a fashion pundit.

For Manuel his video collection was a reference library, an archive of historical details and evocative images. Hence, his first priority was not the quality of the reproduction—which was usually poor—or general accessibility: only Manuel (and to a lesser extent Malé) knew how to locate a movie or find the rest of a film in his idiosyncratic, homemade *videoteca*. By the standards of major film collections, Manuel's capricious, haphazard collection was not that large; also, three different video systems had been used

(Beta, PAL-N, and NTSC), for which he needed the same number of VCRs to view them at home; to simplify mechanical matters, he bought the same number of televisions. In Rio he and Malé rarely went out to a movie theater, and his apartment on Rua Aperana became a permanent "cine club" for the Puigs and their friends.

The search for filmic gems had become, by the time Brazil was home base, a principal motive for travel. Travel kept Manuel from feeling isolated, but it was becoming more and more exhausting. On several occasions he accepted university invitations because they coincided with video conventions—events, as Howard explained, "in which movie lovers bargain with gangsters who pirate reprints." In May, the year after he moved to Brazil, Manuel was not looking forward to "a dreadful lecture tour of German colleges, and not too well payed [sic]," at the University of Göttingen, but what drove him to accept the invitation were "the German films [that] aged better than the French . . . it's just my hope to find cassettes of [Lilian] Harvey, [Anna] Sten, [Brigitte] Helm, [Zarah] Leander, [Elisabeth] Bergner that drives me."[6] The German actresses of the twenties and thirties were the most fascinating, the sexiest: Brigitte Helm, famous for her robotic performance in the classic *Metropolis*, was the absolute symbol of "cool sophistication."[7] Lillian Harvey, on the other hand, was an average, slightly plump star of the twenties and thirties, one of many of Manuel's obscure fetishes which mystified his friends. As Howard commented, "I can't understand why he was so hung up on that one."

Manuel hopped over to France for colloquia honoring him and Mario Vargas Llosa in Orléans, in Toulouse (where he spent a weekend of respite in the country home of professors Milagros Ezquerro and Michelle Ramond, whom Manuel nicknamed "Danielle Darrieux"), and at the Sorbonne. In Paris he stayed at Nino's apartment near Place d'Italie, where he worked with Bensoussan and negotiated film and theater productions. Nino recorded oldies off French television for him to take back to Brazil. In June he was back at the Berlin filmothek, thirsty for more: Berlin Horizonte invited him for the festival of the Cultures of the World, where he gave the lecture "Film and Literature," about his experiences with Ripstein and censorship.[8] Michi Strausfeld, the German literary agent who ushered Manuel around Berlin, remembers that Manuel was his usual sparkling self, never the cerebral intellectual but always lucid, and his paradoxical remarks provoked heated discussions on "committed literature" with politically narrow, literal-minded German academics.

He returned home in June, exhausted but happy to have purchased his first collector's film cassette: *The Congress Dances*, with Lilian Harvey and Conrad Veidt.

With the sale of the dramatic rights to *Kiss* in both Italy and Spain, Manuel bought aside from his own duplex, his parents' apartment, "which started a war with my senile demented daddy who doesn't want to live here, just to antagonize everybody."[9] He had found both apartments in the fashionable beachside neighborhood of Leblon, next to Ipanema. His fifties duplex, a walk-up in a quiet cul-de-sac, was light and airy, with a jungle of plants on the sun-drenched balcony facing the spectacular Os Dos Ermaos mountains. Aside from the plants, he kept the decor in his place predictably minimal— white and wicker—with art deco accessories. Upstairs was his bedroom and study; downstairs, a maid's room, the living room, dining room, and kitchen. Malé's apartment was a mere block away, and, over the next year, Manuel would commandeer the interior design and meticulously retro-glamorize her apartment to look like a middle-class Argentine household from the forties with deco furniture, almost as if it were a set design for an old Argentine movie. For the first time in his life he had the means or gave himself license to live in comfort—and to provide a home for Mama. Loyal to daily routine, he and Malé would go down to the beach at 10 a.m. and take a long leisurely swim; then Manuel would spend a couple of hours re-vising translations and writing until lunchtime. When Malé came back from the beach, where she would linger if friends or family members were present, she prepared lunch. Often leaving guests and Malé to "talk among themselves," Manuel would ascend his "Ziegfeld Follies" spiral staircase to the bedroom to take a nap or continue writing, unless there were errands to run or visitors to whom Manuel enjoyed serving drinks or afternoon tea on the terrace. Seven p.m. was the official "cine club" hour, followed by dinner and, afterward, another movie.

The Olivetti typewriter found its place on his desk in the study, sur-rounded by his "little cloning laboratory," as Alan Pauls, a young Argentine writer who visited in 1987, called it, because the shelves were lined with editions and translations of Manuel's books. The only other books he collected were biographies of producers and actresses—and most of the shelf space in the apartment was devoted to his growing *videoteca*.[10]

Since taxis were a must for getting around busy Rio, especially for Malé, who was not up to jostling in public buses in her mid-seventies, Manuel indulged in yet another luxury, a white Alfa-Romeo sedan complete with a black chauffeur, Aristides, who worked as a handyman for the building in the morning. In the afternoon, after siesta time, Aristides, always smiling, was ready and waiting to take Manuel, Malé and their visitors out, often on shopping errands. A favorite excursion was to the plant nursery. With happy-go-lucky, superficial, affectionate Aristides, they were always joking and laughing. Decked out in his white uniform to match the shiny white sedan, Arístides reminded Manuel of that faraway flick, or his memory of the flick, *Blonde Bombshell* (1933), in which the handsome chauffeur drives up in a Rolls and gallantly opens the shining door for blond bombshell Jean Harlow, whose shapely leg was swiftly followed by a svelte, curvacious body swathed in a skintight gown and luxuriant furs.

Thinner, and with a permanent suntan, Manuel seemed years younger when he returned to New York in the mid-eighties; friends who hadn't seen him since 1980 remarked how trim and healthy he looked.[11] Life in this beachcomber's city of sex and samba was relaxed and informal and the streets buzzed with sensuality—nubile dark bodies undulating in the balmy sunlight, wide smiles on people's faces, the smells and colors of tropical fruit, the singsong of Brazilian speech blending with the sounds of discos and traffic—as Manuel and Malé strolled down to the beach, past the street vendors hawking their wares. While he dressed up for occasional professional events or embassy cocktail parties, for everyday life—running errands or working at home—Manuel didn't have to deal with cumbersome winter clothes and could dress, as he preferred, in torn old shirts and swimming trunks or light cotton pants. Mario teased him about wearing rags in the house, with all his money. (Mario himself tended to do the same.) Wearing rags at home was a comfortable writerly habit, but his friends sometimes thought he was overdoing it. Manuel didn't neglect *el cutis*—his complexion—though; ever since his early thirties he was a great believer in the remedy of his mother's generation, Pond's cream, which he smeared liberally on his face after his daily shower.

Felisa, Mario, Hugo Sottotetti, and Alfredo Gialdini, as well as Carlos and Malé, recall that Manuel was never happier than in those first years in Rio. Aside from the young working-class men available for casual sex, especially for some slight remuneration, he found again and resumed his relationship with Amilcar, the married construction worker he had met years before, as he told Howard:

> Romances—You can't imagine the bad luck that's plaguing me. I had found TWO very nice men, one young and full of life, the other one 38, married, enormous, quiet, a tender bull, the one I told you about, the one I looked for all over Rio and found, after 13 yrs of separation. In June it's our 14th anniversary. Well, just sit there and listen to these horrors: the young one was transferred to the same job in the provinces and the other one got very sick; he has bronchial asthma, suddenly very bad; he had a first attack four years ago and recovered. But now it's serious, especially because it affects its (yes, I wrote "its," I really think of him as an animal, a loving one though) his heart—and I hate it (Garson loses big Pidgeon so soon in *Blossoms in the Dust*). This is a new role for me and I hate it.[12]

In May 1981, good news: Manuel was granted a residency permit, and he was on his way to Italy to pick up a prize. Thanks in part to the attention *Kiss* received from Marco Mattolini's stylish stage production, the Societa di Autori had awarded *Kiss* the Istituto Italo Latino Americano prize for the best Latin American novel of the year.[13] Previously won by canonized writers Jorge Amado, José Lezama Lima, and Juan Carlos Onetti, it meant a considerable amount of money—three million lire, two million for him, one for translator Morino. While Manuel didn't look forward to the pomp and circumstance, the money wasn't bad for Italy, and the event was packed, Argentine ambassador et alia, the dinner very pleasant. He sat next to the distinguished Sicilian writer Leonardo Sciascia and the novelist Natalia Ginzburg, who had reviewed the Italian edition of *Heartbreak Tango*:

> There were speeches and then they asked me questions. I did my simple act; a big success: "there had never been such vivid communication." I can imagine: with those mummies Onetti and Jorge Amado.[14]

In Paris to promote the French edition of *Pubis* a couple of weeks later, Manuel was feted by Severo and Juan Goytisolo, who told Manuel that in Spain he was considered the best writer in the Spanish language in the seventies.[15]

He returned to Buenos Aires in late June for his and Malé's annual medical checkups, and then flew back to Rio with both parents before the onset of the southern winter. To take care of his father, who had been diagnosed with Parkinson's disease, Manuel had hired a nurse. Elderly Baldo, still the ladies' man, flirted with her, as he did customarily with Manuel's female visitors. This was Baldo's charming side, Manuel wrote to Howard, late in July:

> Now my ordeal. The first days with my parents here were hectic but promising. It was the first time they were living at their apartment and there were a thousand details to attend to. I was running all over the place and leaving no time for love which is bad, but anyhow, my mother was recuperating from her backaches and sleeping well. Father came because he feared she would become critically ill after . . . 25 nights in a row without sleeping because of the pains. Well . . . everything seemed ok until he started showing signs of discontent. Suddenly, the 10th evening, he became violent and threatened to kill my mother if she didn't go back with him, cursed me, etc. I had to call 2 psychiatrists that night, one I know socially who lives around the corner, who brought along a colleague. Well, he calmed down and for another 10 days he became a lamb, totally meek and repentant. The day after the attack I decided to put him on a plane back home but due to his change I didn't dare.

Meanwhile, with the tension of settling everyone in, including himself, and trying to get his father to see a psychiatrist, he woke up one morning with "a terrible rush between the legs" (meaning "rash"), an irritation from bathing shorts, he thought. He passed it on to Amilcar, and "only then did I go to the doctor and find out that certain allergic psychosomatic rushes can be infectious . . . The wife got very upset, we itched away, a whole circus."[16] Baldo continued to have temper tantrums, and, because there was concern that he might hurt or even kill Malé, Manuel managed to send him back to Buenos Aires with Carlos, in a sort of commando operation, effectively separating the couple, or as Manuel confided to his friends: "I took her away from him." Manuel convinced Malé to leave Baldo and to stay with him in Brazil. Coco finally had his way, making Baldo's sarcastic remarks to Malé about "tu novio"—your boyfriend—come true, symbolically if not literally.

Baldo declined steadily, and by the mid-eighties was placed in a nursing home in Buenos Aires. Carlos, closely bonded with *el viejo*, took charge of the factory and watched over Baldo until his death.

The move to Brazil was not only a new lease on life. While Manuel had been producing plays and writing scripts in Mexico and New York for the last decade with relatively minimal results, in Brazil he would have his first major success as a playwright, and theatrical productions of *Kiss of the Spider Woman* would begin to crop up all over the globe. Its first adaptation on-stage was in Milan, in 1979:

> *Spider Woman* has been done on stage in Italy; results I don't know yet, but somebody asked for the rights for France after seeing it: I'm doing my own adaptation estimulated [sic] by a brazilian [sic] producer who's staging it here. Since it's just 2 characters I hope it'll be done everywhere.[17]

After his cover-story interview of Manuel in *Christopher Street* in 1979— which spotlighted the author of *Kiss* as a hot celebrity in gay New York— Ronald Christ (then a professor at Rutgers) was eager to write the play directly in English with Manuel for appreciative West Village audiences. Manuel was dubious at the time: the book seemed too unwieldy to adapt to the temporal constraints of a play because the plot development was "too long and splintered," especially the film narrations, the characters' fantasies, and those extensive footnotes.[18] How could one trim what was integral? On the other hand, the novel led its reader from the very birth of a relationship to its final consequence, in the spare form of a dialogue between two characters, unfolding within a tight bubble of time and space.

Kiss played successfully for over a year in Milan. But when Manuel saw it with Mario and Angelo Morino, the Italian translator, he was uneasy because "the word got lost . . . It was modern theater—projections, music, very visual."[19] Too much multi-media, not enough emphasis on the language; it was like a musical and was meant to be a play. But the production, a resourceful, if free, adaptation attuned to the medium of theater, was well received; Marco Mattolini, the director, had tried to respect the dialogue and the setting, with a lavish set made in Cremona.[20] Einaudi, more prestigious than Feltrinelli, published the novel as *Bacio della Donna Ragno*. Manuel, pleased by this move (arranged by agent Tom Colchie) and "the absence of erratas," particularly liked the work of translator Morino, who was more painstaking than Cicogna. *Bacio* won him the award for the best Latin American novel of 1981 and, months later, a nomination for the Nobel Prize. The news reached him in Rio, in early October, but he took it with a grain of salt, as he wrote Malé:

> I think it's a bit premature, but it's 150,000 dollars, not to be sneezed at, but now on to other matters . . . That professor from Scotland wrote to tell me she had recorded one of Janet Gaynor's first sound movies! The first version of *A Star Is Born*, with Fredric March.[21]

Writing from Caracas later that month, he realized how much publicity he was receiving because of the Nobel nomination—a stimulus for the proliferation of productions in theaters "everywhere" from Caracas to Stockholm.[22] From Caracas he flew to San Francisco, at Berkeley's invitation—the men weren't fun: all bodybuilding, no lust—and the university kept him too busy, with no time to escape; thankfully the next stop, after Los Angeles, was Mexico and Televisa, where he recorded a whole slew of Hollywood classics la Becky (Javier) had recently acquired.

Back in 1979, the Italian theater debut had led to a first offer to make *Kiss of the Spider Woman* into a film: In August 1979, from Mario's beach house in Ostia, Manuel wrote film archivist Stephen Harvey at MoMA that he had signed an option with RAI 2, educational TV in Italy, and that top actors were vying for the role of Molina, namely Gian-Maria Volonté, Giuliano Gemma, and even Marcello Mastroianni! But Manuel preferred Volonté, whom he had met at a film festival; Volonté had remarked to him how movie theaters were dying out in Italy because everyone stayed home and watched television.

If France would sign on, they wanted Gérard Depardieu to play the young Marxist, though Manuel again opined, "I prefer Gemma; he's lost weight and looks very noble and stark," adding, "The other menace is Philippe Noiret for the fag . . . If all goes well it'll mean good money and a prestige product."[23] If the abridgment of his novels into movies or plays would always involve disappointing compromises, the rewards were too tempting to pass up: glamour, glory, and, above all, money. Working with others was, again, a relief—from the prolonged solitude and the responsibility of novel writing. When he began work on the theater version of *Kiss*, he was finishing *Eternal Curse* and looked forward to working simultaneously on a team project.

Manuel's version of *Kiss* in Spanish was first produced in Madrid for the Teatro Martín, directed by José Luis García Sánchez, the esteemed Spanish filmmaker who had made *Las truchas*. Actor José "Pepe" Martín played gay Molina with buffoonish excess—"too comical," Manuel put it mildly. Curly-haired Pepe, a tall *madrileño*, compulsively cheerful with a booming voice, usually played the Don Juan type; playing a *folle*, he confided to me, was a risky departure. He wanted to work with Manuel not only because he was excited about the play but because of his equally ebullient wife, Silvia, an Argentine journalist—he had a "soft spot in his heart" for all things Argentine. (The bubbly duo were devoted hosts to Manuel and Malé on their trips to Madrid, and remain in close touch with Malé Puig.) Manuel adored the actor who played the political prisoner, Juan Diego, "a bonbon . . . not handsome but a glorious voice and fascinating personality."[24]

The very first performance, a dry run, was staged in April 1981 in a small theater (Sala Escalante) in the coastal city of Valencia. *El beso* had been published just after Franco's death in 1975, and Spain was open to Manuel after the *destape* in the mid-seventies, the explosion of all that had been repressed by forty years of dictatorship. If initially the friendship between the window dresser and the Marxist had been offensive, it was now a welcome jolt. The play was enthusiastically received; Manuel Puig was politically in tune with the "reality of our times."

> Nobody wants to give up the pleasure due him in life in order to be a revolutionary, and the *hombre ludico*, the hedonist, can only fulfill himself in the community as a revolutionary.[25]

On opening night, May 1, *El País*, the principal newspaper of the new liberated Spain, featured a full-page spread with the headline *"Kiss of the Spider Woman:* Homosexuality & Marxism." The theater was packed with national-art and entertainment bigwigs, among them Fernando Rey, Buñuel's lead actor and a longtime friend of Manuel's, famous in Hollywood for his suave role in *The French Connection*; another admirer of Manuel's was the young trendsetter of the new Spanish cinema, Pedro Almodóvar. Puig was now fully recognized as one of "the few authors capable of popular committed literature," an accessible literature that produced pleasure without compromising artistic originality or political idealism. "Puig likes boleros, not as an intellectual, but sincerely, spontaneously."[26] The Spaniards, sentimentalists under their new racy veneer, went for the play's wishful romanticism; all over town the billboards were papered with Molina's climactic words (echoed onstage in Pepe Martín's soap opera tones) to Valentín: "Ahora yo . . . soy tú" (Now I . . . am you).

Meanwhile Manuel was at work with his translators in Rio, New York, and Paris on theater versions of *Kiss*, as well as on the Italian translations of the novels *Bacio* and *Pubis* with Angelo Morino. The novels had been delayed because of Angelo's previous commitments, about which Manuel quipped: "I hope you're better from your cold, and from translating [Osvaldo] Soriano and [Manuel] Scorza."[27] *Kiss*, and also *Eternal Curse*, seemed ready-made for the stage, but this was deceptive. Mario suggested that Manuel rework *Eternal Curse* as a theater piece, but Manuel discouraged his eager European translators from embarking on its adaptation. The novel was about "revealing and exhausting the subject of certain problems," and not reaching, after all that, a gratifying answer. "The worst pitfall is the subject of the son's desire for the mother," he wrote Bensoussan.

Already, in his own theater adaptation of *Kiss*, Manuel reinstated "the word" but had to pare down the text by reducing Molina's six film narratives to one, about *Cat People*; he managed to eliminate 25 percent of the original dialogue and to condense the rest.[28] The dialogues in the play were livelier, more "natural," but also less ambiguous, more superficial. The Italian production had inspired the minimalist notion of a single set: the prison cell. Molina's interviews with the warden would be projected via a taped voice-over which, at the play's end, like a contrapuntal Greek chorus, vocalizes each character's final monologue. The play, published in various languages, is almost a kind of blueprint, more straightforward than the novel, the characters less reflective.

This abridged version would be the basis of the screenplay, which subordinated the novel's dense and subtle weave of movie plots, fascist politics, sexuality, and the imagination to the spider woman's stratagem, the seduction, the love that conquers all under generic patriarchal oppression. Set in a Latin American prison, *Kiss of the Spider Woman*, one film reviewer would later remark, "is essentially a homosexual wish fantasy about how the love of a real man, however brief, can be transforming—purifying."[29] While *Kiss* reflects more than any other of his novels Manuel's painful realization that such a fantasy could be fulfilled for him only in fiction, the film would leave out the novel's most crucial aspect. When William Hurt masculinized Molina at the end, when he dies heroically for a political cause, he defeated the whole thrust of Manuel's argument: Molina doesn't have to conform to manly manners to be heroic, effeminate doesn't have to mean cowardly.

Of the six film descriptions, Manuel chose to retain *Cat People* because it was the most familiar—hence recognizable to the widest audience—and also because it so vividly illustrated repressed sexuality and its outlet, violence. Simone Simon's enigmatic foreignness stressed, grotesquely, the "flawed" woman, different, possibly dangerous, metaphorically a queer, a man who cannot quite be a woman. Manuel rewrote Molina's commentary with broader irony: "She's a flawed woman . . . All we flawed women come to a sad ending."[30]

Shortly after Manuel had begun work on the staging for the Brazilian production with Dina Sfat, she and Paulo split up; the actor dropped out of the project, and Manuel, though he "felt bad for what Dina was going through," asked her to bow out as well. Iván Albuquerque, who ran the Ipanema theater with his wife Leyla, took over the direction and cast actor José de Abreu in the role of Valentín. Iván and Leyla, along with Rubens Correa, were among Manuel and Malé's closest friends in Rio, and would spend many an evening at the Puig cine club.

Opening night at the Ipanema theater, August 14, 1981, was attended by local and international celebrities, and friends and family who flew in from Buenos Aires for the event.[31] It was a thrilling evening, and the production was the best thus far, Manuel told friends, because the Brazilians had infused it with their eros and humor.

> I met the political prisoner, another dreamboat . . . The direc-
> tor uses him very cleverly, and undresses him slowly, first you
> see legs, then chest, then . . . The queen is played by a sort of
> Patrick Magee who's done all the Magee roles, Marquis de
> Sade etc. . . . excellent, at the beginning he was playing it as a
> sort of Gale Sondergaard [heavy] but I convinced him to be
> more Spring Byington [lighter]. Now he balances it very well.
> Audience response great, but it will take word of mouth for
> audiences to show. The fag is becoming more & more of a
> Beulah Bondi, thank G-d, with dashes of Miriam Hopkins.[32]

The play's sensationalism and political relevance would spur local producer
Flavio Tambellini and director Hector Babenco, another Argentine exile, to
approach Manuel about a film version in Brazil. At the same time, the play
drew negative press from militant gays—"Stalinist queens," as Manuel
called them—politicized by AIDS, which by 1982 was spreading like wild-
fire. (Manuel's first friend to be hit was in the United States, a cultural attaché in Washington, D.C.) Gay critics were particularly offended by
Manuel's portrait of the gay character as a frivolous queen instead of a hero.

By then, in Rio, Manuel was basking in celebrity, and was known across
Latin America. With the theater debut and news of the Nobel nomination
spreading, he was constantly interviewed on Brazilian television and had
become a famous face. People would stop him at the airport or on the streets
and ask for his autograph. In November 1981 he was approached by Argentine director Raúl de la Torre to make a film based on *Pubis Angelical* with
the number-one Argentine soap opera actress (very *cursi*), Graciela Borges,
de la Torre's fiancée. Manuel adored Graciela, a good friend, but was extremely skeptical; the novel was too complex and any reduction would
make it trivial. Nonetheless he encouraged de la Torre, who "seemed devoted to the project and had integrity"; selling film rights meant income,
and an Argentine film, no matter how mediocre, was publicity and an antidote to censorship.[33]

Rio was perfect for life, love, and work. "Love life: for me [Rio is the]
Garden of Eden, more and more Antonio Morenos, Billy Dees, Juano
Hernández . . . revenge after meager New York seasons," he wrote to
Howard. "Something unheard of here is VD, can you imagine?"[34] After the

Argentine military coup in 1974, (relatively) gay-friendly Brazil had become home to many gay Argentines fleeing an intolerant and unstable situation. The African-based "Candomblé" religion appeared to govern sexual mores in Brazil: in Afro-Brazilian folklore, the gods embraced active-passive personae without gender distinctions, and were often transsexual.[35] In the eighties Brazil's booming soap operas and talk shows prominently featured gays and transvestites both as actors and as characters. One Argentine performer and costume designer, Patricio Bisso, played a talk show hostess, Olga on the Volga, "a Russian sexologist of the Soviet liberal line," a kind of transvestite Dr. Ruth whose mission was to raise the Brazilian per capita orgasm index.

Demure and soft-spoken like Manuel, Patricio had been a young admirer of the famous gay novelist since meeting him in Buenos Aires in 1972 through their mutual friend Felisa Pinto. In the mid-seventies, Patricio was nabbed as a "sex offender" and detained for a week in the municipal prison, which had been the ESMA, or Naval School of Mechanics, the same majestic building in Buenos Aires where thousands of dissidents would be tortured and killed. After his release from this traumatic experience, Patricio left the country as soon as he could, following other friends who had already moved to Brazil. In Rio, in the early eighties, he again met up with Manuel, whose daring novel about two men in prison made him a hero for young gay artists. Patricio became a "daughter" in Rio, forming part of a group of young Argentine exiles and Brazilians working in and around the movie industry who regularly gathered at Rua Aperana to watch old movies. Manuel was delighted by the enthusiasm of these young cinephiles as he introduced them to the treasures of MGM. Since Patricio wore a multitude of hats (he would say "feathers in his cap")—as minor character actor (usually a transvestite), costume designer, wardrobe assistant, and imitator of Edith Piaf singing "La vie en rose"—Manuel greeted him with alternating nicknames: "Who's here today: the chorus girl or the seamstress!?"[36] Patricio would handle the wardrobe for both the Brazilian theater production and the film of *Kiss*, as well as play a bit part in the movie as a cabaret performer: Olga on the Volga, of course.

As *Kiss* was making its theater debut in receptive Rio de Janeiro, Manuel was already finishing his first original two-act stage play, a "kind of sex farce" with interlocking Oedipal triangles, deceitful parental figures, and a daughter driven mad, possibly by incest. This "mixture of romance and cruelty," in which he borrowed touches from *A Streetcar Named Desire* as well as from *Desire*, Ernst Lubitsch's romantic comedy about jewel thieves with Marlene Dietrich, was called *Bajo un manto de estrellas*, or *Under a Mantle of Stars*, and was produced, again with Iván Albuquerque and the Ipanema theater troupe, in 1982 as *Quero* (*I Desire*). The original title in English was the ironic "Legitimate Desires" (1983).[37] In this play Manuel brought together soap opera melodrama and drawing room comedy; the characters, with shifting identities and inauthentic emotions, play out literally and parodically Pirandello's motto "I am as you desire me." In *I Desire*—a more bluntly ironic title than the dreamy *Under a Mantle of Stars*, evoking idyllic romance—all passions seem fake, or at least disconnected, as the characters shift identities and collapse into caricatures or archetypes, or paper projections of someone's (Manuel's?) solitary hallucinations. The main theme, Manuel's old obsession, was the gaze of the other, the definition and circumscription of one's identity by the "censoring eye."

After a successful run in Rio, with actor Rubens Correa again, Ivan's wife, Leyla Ribeiro, and a handsome newcomer, Edson Celulari (a courier of videos for Manuel from New York to Rio), *Under a Mantle of Stars* was produced in 1983 in Caracas at the experimental Rajatabla (Clean Slate) theater. In March, Malé and Manuel joined Mario (who was finally committed to the move to Rio) for a trip to Egypt, followed by stops in Paris, Barcelona—to correct the galleys of the Seix Barral publication of *Kiss*, the play—Madrid, and New York. Manuel's visit to New York was the first in two years, a joyful re-encounter with friends, theaters, and especially videomania. Manuel arrived in Caracas in April for the first rehearsals of *Under a Mantle of Stars*. He worked closely with Argentine director Gustavo Tambascio and the results were "as he desired": it was a fun, classy production, the costumes were George Cukor *Camille*, and the decor was fifties salmon. Tambascio had hit the right note, Venezuelan "empty-headed hedonism." Manuel returned in August with Malé for opening night, and again in September. Ronald Christ, who had launched his own small press, Lumen Books, was still lobbying to produce a play with Manuel in English, and now to publish it as well. Manuel was skeptical about possible productions in the United States, as he warned Ronald: "All they want is to camp . . . or to really ACT."[38] He thought the play would work better in Italy—where (he conjectured) the Italians acted all the time without realizing it.

requited love

From 1980 to 1983, Manuel purchased four apartments in Rio: his; Malé's; one with Mario, several blocks away in neighboring Ipanema; and another farther toward downtown, in Copacabana. This meant four properties he had to furnish and manage, and in his travels, much of his time was devoted to interior design errands, purchasing prints in Paris and Rome, as well as shopping for the latest couture for Malé. Mario told him to let the real estate agent handle the legal transactions and management, but Manuel didn't have confidence in the relaxed Cariocas whose incompetence would elicit, to boot, unnecessary fees. To encourage Mario to move and to help entertain Malé, Manuel had handled everything. He never thought of the drain on himself, Mario says sadly. Amid these multifarious transactions Manuel searched the neighborhood for a bricklayer to do new tile work in the bathrooms and kitchen of his apartment, and found a sturdy-looking light mulatto, with the kind of boyish face Manuel liked, and whom everyone called El Chefao, or The Boss. He worked on the apartment, sometimes with a helper or two; Manuel enjoyed the company of these young men after work too, and offered them extra cash to help with their children's education. (Everybody was happy except for the occasional young female visitor, whom the bricklayers liked to pinch.) Manuel's attentiveness stimulated El Chefao to talk about himself:

> He had a story to tell: he had loved a woman, had to leave the town and she went crazy. I believed everything he told me, but a few days later, he began to introduce contradictions and variations on the story. Upon encountering a listener, he had taken advantage of the performance to project an ideal vision of himself. He told me how he was losing his house, his mother's house.

Here was an unreliable raconteur who played the role of several contradictory narrators. The one constant in El Chefao's ramblings was desire, intense sexual longing; also the perennial war between men and women and the man's obligation to be macho. El Chefao's rough, raw sexuality was adolescent, insecure, destructive: as this man's listener, Manuel felt like a voyeur but also empathized, and perhaps identified with his struggle against his role in life. Like Mark, El Chefao saw himself as an underdog, but, unlike Mark, he truly was an underdog. As the man spoke, Manuel heard a poignant lyricism, a potential literary voice, one that expressed emotions only in a repressed way, almost like a talking unconscious:

> This man didn't say anything directly; it was all metaphorical
> . . . And the result was very musical and colorful. But what
> was surprising was that he was also illiterate . . . It was like a
> wave of very beautiful peasant poetry, that I wanted to res-
> cue.[39]

The bricklayer's locutions were governed by the seductive rhythm of Brazilian speech patterns, sentences ending with a lilting "yes" or "no," which turned statements into questions.

The storyteller's extreme poverty meant he would accept Manuel's offer of money to stay overtime—money that would give El Chefao the possibility of building his own house. "I proposed a contract; in exchange for his permission to record the conversation on tape, he would receive a part of the royalties."[40] It was an intriguing experiment, something Manuel could play with, a provisional antidote to linguistic exile. While Carioca Portuguese was closer to his own language than English, Manuel's immersion in Portuguese was affecting his writing. But he felt more and more urgently that life came first, and he was not going to leave Brazil just to write. Also, even though the recently published *Eternal Curse* was poorly received by the critics, it was selling well, and Seix Barral clamored for more from their "Nobel candidate."

The bricklayer's semi-illiterate yet musical language synchronized somehow with Manuel's experience of linguistic displacement in yet another foreign language close to but not his own. Manuel's new literary experiment, to be called *Blood of Requited Love*, would involve writing in a mix of Portuguese and Spanish or *portuñol*. Manuel became the man's medium or echo, transposing his first person account into a disembodied third person, dramatizing both the individual's alienation from himself and an authorial presence. The Brazilian's speech was a language of (and subordinated to) passion, which was also the language of melodrama, and Manuel uncovered in it what Freud noted in the antithetical usage of primal words: "No" can mean "yes"; both words can mean nothing or the same thing. Out of El Chefao's ramblings, Manuel sculpted a repetitive echoing monologue within a real or imagined dialogue between the young man, whom Manuel named Josemar (a typically musical Brazilian name, meaning literally Joe-sea), and the girl, Maria da Gloria, whom he apparently deflowers brutally. Whether or not the text is a schizoid dialogue or narcissistic monologue remains unnervingly ambiguous from the novel's opening line:[41]

> —When was the last time you saw me?
> He saw her the last time ten, eight years ago . . . In the park, next to the church, right? She went to meet him, they had a date, or—how was it? . . . —And no one noticed that a girl of fifteen was going to a hotel?[42]

Who is speaking to whom? Did Josemar deflower Maria da Gloria in the hotel? The reader, the listener, is never quite certain, but what emerges is an epic of sexual obsession about a poor boy from the backlands of the State of Rio. "A Brazilian theme; the Argentine disappeared completely," Manuel said, but also suggested to his interviewer, "Perhaps [my struggle with Argentina is] so present that there's no need to embody it in a character."

It would appear that Manuel, about to turn fifty, and more accepting or resigned to the limitations of his affective life, returns in Josemar's story to his own old story about filial love that turns to hate. Josemar is a boy from rural Brazil whose real father dies, and who is rejected by a violent stepfather; the evil-stepfather melodrama runs parallel to the real or imagined escapades of a young Don Juan who cannot love. After his mother moves in with her new man, Astolfo, she sends Josemar away to protect him from Astolfo.[43] Why is Josemar rejected? "He didn't love you because you were different from the others. And I know why you were different." Josemar was whiter. "He didn't have the face of an Indian like the rest of them . . . even handsomer than the landowner's children, who were white like Josemar."[44] Racial resentment—bound up implicitly with class resentment—sends Josemar away from the place of his origin to seek a better life, in a town called Cocotá, and from there to Rio. As Coco was in love with the movies, Josemar is mesmerized by electricity when he first sees the lights of the city, like glittering stars. His ambition is to be an electrician, as Coco's was to make movies, but he doesn't have enough education to understand electricity, and settles for stonemasonry. Did Manuel imbue El Chefao's frustration with his own frustration at settling into a writing career, more plodding than the starry sphere of moviemaking? Was J(osé) M(ar) another Juan Manuel, a boy with a fair complexion, vulnerable sensibility, irreparable emotional scars? Josemar laments: "How can you ever love, if you can't love your father?"; another voice, in third person, speaks of Josemar's incapacity:

> "There are people who don't love anymore, your heart is dried up inside . . . up to a certain point in time the father's heart wasn't dried up, he'd been very good to the mother. Later he changed . . . But now his heart is dried up."[45]

A dried-up heart leads to the death of desire: "Once it's over, it's over."[46]

Perhaps the only place love could be requited was in writing. It is curious that both these later novels of his exile—*Blood* and *Curse*—were the results of interviews Manuel paid for, as he tried also, in different ways, to buy the love of the interviewees. For each novel, Manuel borrowed another's voice and words; each novel took the shape of a failed dialogue, fiction's body stripped down to its skeleton. Each novel addresses the need and impossibility not only of understanding but of hearing the other. Each attests to Manuel's exhaustive efforts and exceptional gifts as a listener.

Mario, who considers these "more mature" novels among Manuel's most interesting, was amazed at his uncanny ability to represent a purely Brazilian reality, at how quickly a fellow Argentine dominated Portuguese and Carioca slang. *Blood of Requited Love* was published simultaneously in 1982 in Portuguese (Rio de Janeiro, Editora Nova Fronteira) and in Spanish (by Seix Barral). In one of the few positive reviews, published in Mexico (where Carlos Monsiváis and Arturo Trejo Villafuertes organized a colloquium and book signing for Manuel, on a quick stopover between New York and Caracas), Emir cuts to the chase:

> What begins as the story of a Latin macho rapist, ends with a weeping boy; the novel begins with the voice of the raped girl, but ends with the voice of Mama. Oedipus in the slums of Rio.[47]

A mother's possessive love shapes and closes the novel: Maria da Gloria, a blonde, "the daughter of Italians," a woman possessed, is ultimately overshadowed by Josemar's mother.[48] Either could speak for both Manuel and Malé in the confusion of voices spewing at the end.

When Josemar leaves or fantasizes about leaving his mother's home "when the sky is most beautiful, at this hour, between two and three in the morning" (an insomniac hour Manuel knew well), death looms in his mind.[49] "He's not sure that suffering is worse than death. Death is the worst there is. Death is a terrible thing . . . because if a person dies people forget him."[50] Josemar's mother vacillates between feeling that heaven would be to "live forever with her son" and wondering if he was one of those "rebellious children . . . high strung . . . who don't love."[51] If living with Mama was, if not heaven, a reassuring comfort for Manuel, it was also a kind of anguish. Manuel himself lived in terror that Malé would die, and then what would he do? On the other hand, with her beside him, he himself was becoming an old woman, neglecting his own needs to attend to hers, and, like most old women, living (and even writing) vicariously through others.

the rocky road to oscar: the film

. . . glorious Silver Screen, tragic Technicolor, amorous Cinemascope, stretching Vistavisions and startling Stereophonic Sound, with all your heavenly dimensions and reverberations and iconoclasms.

—Frank O'Hara

In 1985, *Kiss of the Spider Woman* was released. Manuel was both excited and disappointed "like a mother whose child moves on."[52] Contrary to his expectations, it received kudos at the Cannes Film Festival and at the Tokyo Film Festival and was nominated in February 1986 for four Academy Awards: Best Film, Best Actor, Best Screenplay Adaptation, and Best Director. Somehow this unlikely production, with only two characters, "the queer and the commie," came up like a dark horse, alongside *Out of Africa*.

Babenco, relatively unknown except for *Pixote*, a feature-length docudrama about the plight of street children in Brazil, was nominated over Steven Spielberg, who that year had directed his dazzling war epic *Empire of the Sun*. William Hurt, in what is widely considered the crowning performance of his career, was awarded the Cannes Palme d'Or as well as the first Oscar for Best Actor ever won by an American for the portrayal of a homosexual. *Kiss of the Spider Woman* was the first independent film not only to receive four Oscar nominations but to win an Academy Award. Whether because of Babenco's charismatic energy, or because this film was a ticket to Hollywood, or out of mere idealism, everyone who worked on this difficult and challenging project stayed with it through thick and thin, even those who did not reap material profit.

The effect on Manuel's reputation as a writer was enormous—finally "la Metro" (Hollywood, that is) had rolled out the red carpet. If Manuel had been courting the movies for the first forty years of his life, the cameras were rolling for him now. Was he Gloria Swanson in *Sunset Boulevard* or (hopefully) Janet Gaynor in *A Star Is Born*? It was a dream come true, but also a nightmare, a roller-coaster ride—wonderful one moment, bad the next. At least one could always hope that it would be good once again.

ACT I: A TALE OF TWO COUNTRIES

SCENE I: ENTER BABENCO

Early in 1982, Hector Babenco, an Argentine documentary director living in São Paulo who had just finished his first successful feature film, *Pixote*, met American producer David Weisman through a mutual acquaintance, another young director, Arnaldo Jabor, a charming, handsome Brazilian whose sexy hit *Eu te amo* had also recently opened. Babenco was hoping to make his next film in Hollywood, and had just been with translator and agent Tom Colchie, who represented several Brazilian writers, to renegotiate the rights for Marcio Souza's novel, *Emperor of Brazil*. One of those exuberant South American sagas—more hysterical than historical—filled with wars, injustice, lusty heroes, lecherous patriarchs, and breast-heaving, hip-swinging *mulatas*, Souza's book would turn out to be too costly to produce. But during the meeting with Colchie, Babenco asked him if there was any novel of Puig's that could be made into a movie, and the literary agent replied, "I know of a great book that would be impossible to make into a movie, *Kiss of the Spider Woman*." Out of this meeting Babenco optioned his second choice, *Kiss of the Spider Woman*, which was the project he and Weisman discussed when they met in early 1982. Both knew that the time was ripe for Latin American magical realism to make it into the movies, and that co-productions south of the border could be cost-effective.

One of their primary challenges was the gay theme, which Babenco thought might be too much for mainstream audiences. They needed big-name actors to put this over, this unlikely love story about a political prisoner and a gay window dresser, who were, in essence, the only characters. Without stars they would be nowhere. Stars meant big bucks, but they also meant another worry for Babenco: as an Argentine expatriate working in the Carioca film industry and, as a Paulista—Babenco had married into an affluent Jewish family in Rio's rival cosmopolis—he was fearful of arousing xenophobic reactions to the project by hiring American actors.[53]

Meanwhile, *Pixote* had opened at the Public Theater, thanks to its film program director Fabiano Canosa (a Brazilian in New York who knew Manuel as well as Hector Babenco), and attracted a select, politically sensitive audience. After Vincent Canby gave it a rave review, *Pixote* received an award for best foreign film, but Manuel was skeptical about Babenco: "I was shocked by the NY critics award going to *Pixote*; it's such a coarse film. The director keeps asking for the *Spider Woman* rights but the money is not convincing."[54] He didn't think this unsophisticated director, who was not gay, would be particularly sensitive toward the gay theme. Manuel regarded him as a typical *porteño*, "opportunist."[55] They had become acquainted in Rio mainly because of Babenco's persistence— "I showed up with ice cream every time I came by for a visit; Manuel seemed more interested in the ice cream than in me," Hector recollects.

There had been a rash of theatrical productions of *Kiss* in Brazil and in Spain. The play didn't open in Stuttgart, because an actor walked out; but in April a highly regarded German director (Frank Ripploh, who did *Taxi Zum Klo*) asked to do the film version in Germany. Manuel was not thrilled: "She makes gloomy films." He was upset also that *Village Voice* writer Michael Feingold, who had taken on the English translation of the play three years earlier, was dragging his feet.[56] And since film offers continued to come but were "not too good as money goes," Manuel was hoping for a projected New York production to land a more attractive movie offer than Babenco's for exclusive rights.[57] Thus far, Manuel had granted him only a provisional option, gratis and without signing away rights, but Babenco returned from Hollywood and his meeting with Weisman with a new development: the prospect of a big actor in a starring role.

In an interview with Kevin Thomas of the *Los Angeles Times*, who asked Babenco which American actor he would most like to work with, Babenco cautiously mentioned Burt Lancaster, noting the actor's admirable work with Visconti in *Il Gattopardo* (*The Leopard*). Not fluent in English then, Babenco figured that Lancaster was a star to whom he could at least speak in Italian, or maybe French, and the Brazilians back home would not object to an American who had the good taste to work with European directors.[58] Last but not least, the legendary but elderly Lancaster represented a relatively inexpensive entrée into the international market.

SCENE II: EXIT BURT LANCASTER

Through Weisman, Babenco contacted ICM agent Michael Black, who worked closely with Ben Benjamin, Burt Lancaster's agent, who sent the script to Lancaster; four days later the actor, who had skimmed the book in one sitting, phoned Benjamin: he wanted the role of Molina. In his first meeting with Babenco and Weisman, the sixty-nine-year-old actor seemed eager for the part and inquired about Molina's age and looks—joking that if he played Molina, they'd have to borrow the actress who would play the mother from a nursing home. With Burt Lancaster in hand, Weisman had gotten a commitment from Richard Gere for the role of Valentín: Gere had recently taken an audacious career step from Hollywood onto the Broadway stage, playing an ill-starred gay lover in a concentration camp in *Bent* on Broadway. Playing a South American Marxist would be an intriguing change from his *American Gigolo* image; he would be working with screen legend Burt Lancaster; and, besides, he had a girlfriend in Brazil.[59]

Back in Brazil by mid-January 1982, Babenco again approached Manuel in Rio to buy the exclusive rights to direct *Kiss of the Spider Woman* with Burt Lancaster as Molina and Richard Gere as Valentín. An odd couple, Manuel thought, but it now looked as if he should take Babenco's proposal seriously. Gere's interest in spending time in Brazil was about to wane, in any case; Lancaster then wanted Martin Sheen, whose work he admired, but Sheen was not interested.

In New York Jane Holzer, an acquaintance of Weisman's and a socialite who ran with the Warhol crowd, put up funding for initial costs of the production in Brazil, and scriptwriter Leonard Schrader was hired: Schrader's previous credits included a collaboration with his brother Paul on Robert Towne's *Yakuza*, a detective film set in Japan starring Robert Mitchum. Babenco was still concerned about offending the Brazilian film industry by doing the movie in English, and was gladdened by a partial remedy: the distinguished Puerto Rican actor Raul Julia for the role of the young Argentine Marxist. Julia's agent, Jeffrey Hunter, and his partner Gene Parseghian loved the story, and felt that its witty and moving treatment of gay culture and Latin American politics was trailblazing, and upbeat. Parseghian asked in passing if Weisman and Babenco had considered his client William Hurt, and that if anything happened with Burt Lancaster, to keep Hurt in mind.[60]

For Lancaster, getting on in years, interesting roles were scarce. Rumor had it that, though a married man and the proud grandfather of thirteen children, the actor went on European holidays with a male friend and indulged, on these sorties, in cross-dressing. Widespread disbelief soon silenced these whispers, but a minor scandal erupted at the Cannes Film Festival when Babenco, to dispel the rumor, was misquoted by a French gay tabloid as saying that he had chosen Burt Lancaster unaware that the actor was gay, when he meant, simply, that he had no knowledge of such a rumor. Whatever the case, the role of Molina may have appealed to Lancaster at least in part because it was a safe way of acting out.

Following Manuel's own condensation of the novel into a stage play, the scriptwriter decided early on that, unlike in the novel, the sex between the men in the cell was going to happen only once, not over the course of several nights, as in the novel. Audiences would be grateful and, as it stood, would still be embarrassed when the camera cut to the candle as they could hear Molina's voice saying "Let me lift my legs." Lancaster reportedly didn't go for this discreet cutback of the sex scenes, and came up with a supposedly commercial, inadvertent *Cage au Kiss* kind of script with his dialogue coach, in which there would be an extended, almost soft-porn seduction scene between Molina and—as Lancaster put it, apparently oblivious to the other character—"the kid." Even before these alarming developments, the film's creators were already concerned about the actor's age. Rejecting his rewrite of the script would be a graceful way to disengage. Babenco, agitated under-standably by competing versions of the script in English, kept pushing to take the version most faithful to Manuel's play back to Brazil and translate it into Portuguese, repeating on numerous occasions that he was fed up with "this Hollywood shit," and that he was going to use Brazilian actors. Crew members on the São Paulo set heard Babenco utter indignantly on more than one occasion that he was no "Hollywood whore."

Fortunately for the film, Lancaster's ill health (heart disease, which Manuel mistook for cancer) caused him to abandon the project early on, at which point Manuel hoped that the actor's exit would also free his book from the "la Great Babenko":

> It seems the film is off, thanks God, Burt Lancaster is in bad shape it seems . . . He had a written agreement with la awful Babenco and his family met la awful to give her the bad news. He had been operated on 3 years ago, big C of course, and the thing came back . . . Such a romantic couple Lancaster (69) and . . . Raul Julia.[61]

Pleased that a distinguished actor like Raul Julia—a Broadway superstar, and a nice person to boot—was on board, Manuel still had grave reserva-tions. In August 1982, meanwhile, Mario Fenelli's mother had died, and Manuel was worried about his old friend. He called Rome to encourage him to come to Rio as soon as possible; Mario would also send the money needed to close the deal for his apartment.

SCENE III: ENTER WILLIAM HURT

When Burt Lancaster was finally out of the picture, the suggestion made by Gene Parseghian, William Hurt's agent at Triad, could now be explored. Soon after sending over the latest version of the script to Hurt, an actor no-tably drawn to challenging roles, Mr. Parseghian called Weisman with the good news that Hurt was interested. Mr. Weisman informed him that the director was equally enthusiastic, though, in truth, Babenco barely knew the blond, blue-eyed American actor. When Manuel heard that they had signed on Hurt, he replied, "In my bed maybe, but not as Molina!" By then Babenco had further appeased his Brazilian conscience, by recruiting the country's top female star, Sonia Braga, who was thrilled to make an American movie, though she wanted her role to be more substantial.

Eager not to lose time, Babenco returned to Manhattan for a meeting at William Hurt's apartment with Julia and Weisman to discuss the role. The director was flustered because he had nearly missed the plane in São Paulo and his suitcase hadn't arrived. In this first meeting they spoke briefly about the role but mainly about Hurt's concerns: he and Raul together had already screened *Pixote* and were worried about the garish colors, "third world stuff"; they didn't want to look like "yesterday's broccoli."[62] Hurt was reassured that they had lined up Rodolfo Sánchez (yet another Argentine exile), one of the best-paid cameramen in Brazil. Sánchez, like Sonia, was glad to have a crack at Hollywood. Considering that over half the scenes occurred within the four walls of a prison cell, the inventive camera work would be one of the film's greatest assets.[63]

Hurt accepted the part, and Weisman and Babenco left immediately for the airport. They had a meeting the next morning in Los Angeles with Ray Stark, éminence grise at Columbia Pictures: with Hurt and Julia in hand (and some initial funding), they could now hope for big studio backing. Stark, a very busy man, could see them in the morning before his first appointment; yes, he had read the script. An hour upon arrival from New York—Babenco, by now thoroughly exhausted, had taken the red-eye with Weisman—they were sitting across a wide desk from studio shark Stark, who remarked that the material was a great idea and would "make a good Broadway musical too," a suggestion that shocked his listeners at the time— a musical about torture in a Latin American prison? "How are you going to handle the diarrhea scene?" Stark queried Babenco, who turned on the charm: "I would never make a movie I couldn't take my children to see," and proceeded to praise the fabulous artists—Hurt, Julia, Braga—committed to this exciting project. After the interview, the mogul was convinced.[64]

Act II: (Maksoud) Plaza Suite

SCENE I: THE SCENARIO

At the time he signed *Kiss* to film—for a flat fee of around $100,000, the most he had ever been paid for any creative project—Manuel was handled by Maggie Curran, Lynn Nesbitt's assistant at ICM. For the mega-agency,

Manuel had been up until then a prestigious writer whom they wanted to retain, but not an income producer. Lynn, a high-powered agent with a businesslike affect, had negotiated the Knopf deal for the novel but, in Manuel's eyes, subtracted her fee and neglected his interests. While he understood perfectly the bureaucratic nature of the corporate world, he still believed individuals (publishers, agents) could make a difference if they really tried. He also felt compelled to control his terrain by delegating different projects, in different countries, to different agents. Lynn decided to place Manuel—"a Peter Pan, innocent in these matters"—in Maggie's "motherly" hands; she could best attend, as ICM agent Mitch Douglas put it, to his "sweet craziness."

Tensions would abound in the production of the film, and Manuel found himself, or placed himself, in the thick of it. He tried to exert his influence, while Babenco insisted, as most directors would, on control over the script. At the same time Babenco was often at odds with Weisman and Schrader, in part because of pressures from the home front: he didn't want it to appear that foreigners had co-opted his authority, putting him in danger of being locked out by the Carioca industry for allowing Americans to take over. Weisman and Manuel would try to bridge the language gap by translating Schrader's pages into *portuñol* for Babenco, who kept rejecting their drafts, which he considered too elaborate for the more condensed, universal message he was trying to impose. It often seemed contradictory that Babenco, complaining that they strayed from the original, at the same time vetoed Manuel's interference. The director's understanding of fidelity evidently diverged from the author's.

Manuel first met David Weisman on September 15, 1983, in Babenco's office, a suite at the newly built Maksoud Plaza Hotel, their production headquarters in São Paulo. On this occasion Manuel was explaining to those gathered in Babenco's room his vision of Leni, the glamorous chanteuse in the Nazi movie, by acting out the scene. Making one of his own oft-used gestures he showed Sonia that she should have both hands on one hip, in an arch forties kind of gesture, rather than a hand on either hip. They were scheduled to start shooting the film that month, on location at an abandoned prison. The Maksoud Plaza, named after its Lebanese owner, was São Paulo's ultimate luxury hotel, a striking exemplar of contemporary architecture in the heart of the bustling city. Towering over the adjacent Modern

Art Museum, it was the perfect *High Anxiety* à la Mel Brooks setting: on each floor all doors opened onto a circular corridor vertiginously suspended over a central atrium. Manuel's presence, his warm wit and intelligence, were a welcome diversion, considering the tensions already evolving between the director and his producer and scriptwriter. Sonia and Manuel got along well too: in Manuel's eyes she was the picture of glamour but also a simple Brazilian girl from humble origins, flattered to be treated as an equal by a great Latin American writer.

Manuel liked Weisman's tart wit too and enjoyed spending time with him; he certainly appreciated this quirky producer for being his first comrade in Hollywood and for finessing a deal with a major studio, Columbia Pictures.[65] Later, when the film triumphed, Manuel would lament, erroneously perhaps, that he accepted the sure advance instead of gambling on points, but at the time he did not believe that Babenco would actually make the film, and never expected him to engineer a hit.

Though Manuel expected to put up with the "horror show" for only a few days, between October and December 1983 he commuted back and forth between Rio and São Paulo; Weisman encouraged his input, and the two even composed the lyrics of an absurd cabaret song performed by Braga. Manuel's influence on the script was also felt in autobiographical nuances not explicit in the novel, as in the scene after Molina is released from prison, when Bill Hurt watches a movie on television with "Mother." Molina's constant worries about his mother's ill health in the novel had been reduced to one remark so that they added this touch, a typical scene from Manuel's everyday life—almost like a Hitchcock walk-on.

As the scriptwriter, Schrader (who had studied with Chilean novelist José Donoso at the University of Iowa, and who was acquainted with Manuel Puig's novels in English) was understandably nervous about meeting Manuel—and over the next months Manuel saw him only in the company of Weisman. The author, after all, might look upon him as the culprit betraying the original—or at the most would approve of only a fraction of the final result—even though Schrader had based the screenplay on Manuel's stage play (the only version Babenco knew when he took on the project) rather than adapting it directly from the novel. All involved (Manuel, Babenco, Hurt, Weisman) were type-A personalities, and Schrader was no exception. He appeared to be reclusive, or reluctant to venture out of the hotel into chaotic, polluted São Paulo. It didn't help that on location at the abandoned prison, the police who guarded the building—though there was nothing to guard—wore guns tucked under their shirts and, to pass the time, occasionally pulled them out and pointed them at members of the crew, laughing and saying, "Don't worry, we're here to protect you."

Manuel was reassuring to Schrader, as he was to everyone he came in contact with on the set; "la-ing" everyone—la Hurt, la Julia, la Great Babenko, as he called the director, and so on—was partly Manuel's way of dispelling the tension that he experienced as he watched the filming, of amusing others and putting them at ease. Even more to the point, it was his indirect way of trying, gently, to regain some control over the making of each scene, which, like a latter-day Scheherazade, he would dramatize for those willing to listen. Behind Manuel's humor was pain, most probably, as one observer recalls: "Manuel was sweet and patient, almost as if he were the wise parent dealing with spoiled children, but the stress he went through must have been terrible."[66]

Manuel's stress was heightened by the recent opening of the Buenos Aires production of *Kiss*. The reception was lukewarm, and Manuel blamed it on the Peronists, who once again held the reins, now that Galtieri had finally been dethroned. (The last gasp of the military regime had been the Falkland Islands War, which Borges described as "two bald men fighting over a comb.") The ban had finally been lifted on the book as well, but when the Spanish edition showed up on bookstore shelves, no reviews appeared. During that fall Manuel was also preoccupied with Malé's various ailments and his own gnawing fear of being HIV positive, as he confided in Howard, triggered by a skin rash, an "itch" or some kind of allergy, that wouldn't go away.[67]

The art of screenwriting consists of reducing everything rigorously to its concise essence. What happens in several pages in a novel needs to happen in thirty seconds in a movie. At least once a page—in the *Kiss* script—one of the relationships in the movie needed to change: Molina's relationship to Valentín, and Valentín's to Molina; also the spectator's relationship to each separately, as well as to the characters' relationship. Twice a minute, in well-wrought films, a relationship grows, or you see another dimension. Dialogue has to be spare, as Manuel understood when rewriting the dialogue in his stage version of *Kiss*; but, one of the challenges of writing the screenplay for *Kiss* was the fact that the novel itself was spare and used only two characters, one cell. How do you write a film where the characters are bored but the audience is not? One reason why the movie didn't bore its spectators is that each time the camera returned to the cell, the cinematographer shot the scene from a different corner. At the same time (despite Tom Colchie's caveat) the material did have moviemaking potential, partly because, according to Manuel's own ideas about the differences between novels and movies, the novel's structure is allegorical, reducing romance to a universal essence: two people meet, their love grows, is consummated, and ends with death.

Schrader had been as faithful as he felt he could be to the original dialogue, beginning the movie, as Manuel did the book, with Molina's voice; at the same time he had to translate a specific historical and regional frame into a more generic one, starting the film so that the English-speaking audiences, who would at first wonder where the action was taking place, would accept the convention of characters in a Latin American prison speaking English.

What holds the reader of the novel—storyteller Molina's elaborations and suspensions of his film plots to whet Valentín's appetite—had to be presented in compressed form, reduced to the essentials, through Zen-like concoctions, as when Molina gives Valentín the avocado, saying simply: "Enjoy what life offers you." Manuel took a whole page, if not the whole book, to say this in his original, by having Molina teach Valentín, little by little, the aesthetic pleasure of enjoying the fictional world of movies. The Zen seed in this way, of course, was already in the novel.

Faced with two guys talking about old movies in a prison cell, the writers decided to accent the Spider Woman motif, especially since Braga required her role to be more substantial. What the film did through visual storytelling was to project not only Woman's seductiveness, spinning Man in her web—but also the idea that all women are Greta Garbo, Rita Hayworth, or Sonia Braga to the men who desire them. This interpretation would please Braga and would be faithful to the novel's pervasive underlying thrust: Woman as Muse, Love, Death—fantasy, filmic, or flesh and blood. To the men who either dreamed about or identified with them, women were One. Braga would play the flashbacks (in the story told by Valentín about his past girlfriend) as well as Leni in Molina's Nazi film, and also the fantasy "Spider Woman." Spotlighting Woman would also suit most audiences by softening the gay male focus—which, without footnotes, would lose subtlety and complexity anyway.

The film was originally going to begin with Molina's narration of the last scenes of *Cat People,* under the assumption that the producers would obtain the rights because Len Schrader's brother Paul had directed the remake. After negotiating with Universal for almost a year, they received the news—a week before they were to start shooting—that Universal had refused to grant them rights to use *Cat People* footage or even to reshoot any scenes from the original classic. They would have to begin instead with the French Nazi propaganda movie, originally woven into the text twenty-five pages later. This meant a last-minute scramble to eliminate the first twenty-four pages, and introduce the Nazi movie on page 1.

In the first five minutes of the movie the audience had to be introduced to Molina; the gay audience would be with them, but to make general audiences laugh and get over their embarrassment, and then start to appreciate Molina as a human being, the scriptwriter, director, cameraman, and actor had to get the audience to accept or empathize with someone who was "different." Circling his hand over his head, Manuel suggested that Hurt could hide his all-American football-player look somewhat if he wore a turban and a kimono, as if he imagined he was some sort of geisha or odalisque. It worked, *grosso modo,* as Pauline Kael noted in her review of the movie: "William Hurt . . . is just about the only thing to look at . . . He first appears wrapping a red towel around his head as a turban—a Scheherazade flourish—and wearing the thick, coquettish makeup of an aging vamp." As Kael put it, Hurt's presence captured the spectator in part because he was so "physically miscast," hence making a "showy feat" of his performance, or as a friend of Kael's jested: "Hurt as Molina is like having a basset hound playing a Chihuahua."

From the very start of the shoot Hurt seemed justifiably nervous about this dicey role: it would be awkward to fail, and if he succeeded he might be typecast. Kael noticed this reserve in the performance: "Hurt holds back; he has a knotted, bunched-up presence."[68] As a spectator prejudiced by

Manuel's Molina, when I saw the movie in 1985, I agreed with her observation, though as the movie proceeded I found myself growing used to watching Hurt playing Hurt playing Molina. Because Manuel had definite ideas, naturally, about the kind of actor who should play Molina—his first choice was Jean-Louis Trintignant—his presence behind the scenes appeared to add further anxiety for Hurt.[69] The chemistry was not there, Manuel decided early on, after meeting Hurt over dinner with the director, producer, screenwriter, and Raul Julia at a restaurant near the hotel. They sat around the table reminiscing about their boyhoods, and Hurt quickly took center stage, recounting a traumatic incident when at age seven he was beaten up by some bigger boys in the schoolyard. They all listened attentively, but it became apparent that there was an uneasy tension between Manuel and Hurt. During the walk back to the Maksoud, Manuel was silent; he reportedly expressed his disappointment to intimates by claiming—only half in jest—that Hurt didn't understand how one could sometimes love those boys who beat one up in the school playground. Bill Hurt and Manuel Puig did not share the same sense of camp, evidently, which boded ill: Molina was a caricature, a certain kind of uneducated queen, and, as such, streetwise, but with a frilly touch of Carmen Miranda. Manuel saw that between Molina's earthy levity and Hurt's neurotic intensity yawned a huge abyss.

With Manuel and Weisman embroidering floridly on one hand, Babenco, with his limited English, felt beleaguered by the constant revisions of the script, and, on top of this, uneasy attempting to direct Hurt, an English-speaking Hollywood movie star.[70] Not only was the director in conflict with his producer and screenwriter but, to make things worse, after the first week of shooting, director and star got into a violent altercation and nearly came to blows; they did not speak to each other again. Hurt would no longer take instructions directly from Babenco. The director would have to address Hurt through a third person on the set: "Would you please tell Mr. Hurt . . ."

Back from a grueling session in São Paulo in mid-October, Manuel wrote to Malé, comforting her after the theater debut of *Kiss* in Buenos Aires:

> Every change suggested became a full-scale battle, but I've accomplished quite a lot; after New York [the first cut] there

will be more things to change, but a lot was accomplished. We'll see. The fights between the American producer and Babenco are a scream: they're always at each other's throats. The movie world is a HORROR. I've been very worried since our phone conversation on Saturday. You have to take better care, papa with the walking and mama not paying any attention to silly things like *Kiss* in B.A. The audience isn't ready for progressive things, that's why they reject it; the few that go applaud it enthusiastically; the others don't go to the theater because they do not support the work itself. With the critics, it's the same thing: it's the same shitty people. The point is, it's very clear that Peronism is back to stay; the nation is condemned to that fate.[71]

After returning to São Paulo for more script revisions in early November, Manuel expressed his displeasure more freely to a friend: "It was quite unpleasant. La Babenko is a freak woman. Now it seems la Hurt is really directing the film, they say she does a very bad pathetic believable queen but not funny, and that's bad news."[72]

Bill Hurt had taken over the direction of both himself and Raul Julia, and, without the humor, Manuel thought the whole thing would be a pointless cliché.[73] A few weeks later, referring to a "travesty in travesty," Manuel again wrote (exaggerating, as usual, for comic effect) that the film was going badly and that "la demented Hurt isn't in [sic] talking terms with la horrible Babenco. That will be something to watch." The summer before the shoot began in São Paulo, Bill Hurt and Raul Julia had begun rehearsals in New York, in a rented studio in the West Village.[74] Julia, a remarkable actor, needed a lot of preparatory coaching (as his agent forewarned Babenco and Weisman) to get the point of a role, but once he understood, he gave a great performance. Hurt was the exact opposite, brilliant, quick, he understood everything before you opened your mouth, but he didn't have Julia's vocal and gestural range. Glad to work with people who demanded perfection, and with a script he respected, Julia read the novel conscientiously every day in between takes, running into parts he didn't understand, like the enigmatic ending. Hurt, on the other hand, reportedly dispensed with reading the novel; he read his scenes and, ignoring Manuel completely, discussed

them with the scriptwriter.[75] In February, in a panel on Cinema and Literature at the Miami Film Festival, Manuel predicted, as Enrique Fernández
noted: " 'La Hurt was so bad that she'll probably get the Best Actor award at
Cannes.' (She did.)"[76]

Between the anti-climax of *Kiss* in Buenos Aires and the "Babenco fa-
tigues," Manuel was relieved to cross "the pond" (the Atlantic) again in mid-
November, with the first stop being Rome. Mario had finally sent him the
$22,000 that he had advanced for the purchase of the apartment; and want-
ing Mario in Rio sooner rather than later to help keep an eye on his parents,
Manuel picked up a huge suitcase from Mario to bring back to Ipanema,
lugging it with him to Germany for the opening of the theatrical production
of *Kiss* in Heidelberg.[77] "*Cómico*," he wrote to Emir some months later, "the
German composer Hans Werner Henze—who had produced Margot
Fonteyn's *Ondine*—wants to make an opera out of *Kiss*, a kind of gay *Tosca*
and wants me to do the libretto: it will be the first gay opera!"[78]

The opera never came to fruition, but it was only one among several
projects he was juggling at the time, including a treatment for the young
Brazilian director Bruno Barreto, "Good Luck Charm."[79] Back in Rio,
Manuel had his hands full with his parents, but it was also a festive Christmas on the beach, replete with visitors (among them, David Weisman and
Javier Labrada), and Mario was settling in. Manuel was about to make another escape, to a film festival in Huelva, Spain, but the ticket didn't arrive
in time, which meant he would be "nailed here [in Brazil] for 3 months at
least."[80] No matter what was going on in his life, however, Manuel tried to
keep everyone calm. (Lee Percy remarked that when he returned to Los
Angeles from Brazil, David Weisman was uncommonly courteous, and
even served tea to visitors at his house, a temporary transformation.) Meanwhile "la madwoman"—Manuel's invention of course—had become the
whole crew's code name for Babenco by the end of the shoot, as in "What is
the madwoman thinking?" or "What will la madwoman do now?"

The result of the first edits was a three-hour film that needed to be two; to
boot, early in 1984, Hector Babenco, who had not been feeling well, was diagnosed with lymph cancer. Thinking that he was soon going to die, he
wanted to be with his family, naturally, and disappeared for the next ten

months with these parting words to his cohorts: "You love this baby as much as I do. I leave it in your hands."[81] Weisman and Schrader would have to handle the final cut; back in Los Angeles, they recruited editor Lee Percy, who worked intensely with Schrader in an editing studio that summer, in some cases dubbing new dialogue that would go along with the actors' facial expressions. Len Schrader also flew to New York during this period to work with Julia and with Hurt, who was in a Broadway play with Sigourney Weaver and Harvey Keitel; because of Hurt's schedule, the dubbing sessions could only take place between one and six in the morning. With Braga, who was flown from Rio to Los Angeles, the dubbing was arduous because of her English. It took a whole day to work on the last, and in a way most important, line of the movie (and of the book): "This dream is short but this dream is happy." In her thick accent she kept mispronouncing "short" as "shirt." Percy and Schrader had to tape her repeatedly, and after multiple takes and infinitesimal sound splicings, they produced the final cut.

SCENE II: A DREAM (A NIGHTMARE?) COME TRUE

By the time *Kiss* was released in August 1985, Manuel had become royalty at international film galas. At the Miami Film Festival early in 1986, which was notably attentive to Hispanic and Latin American cinema, he met up again with the Cabrera Infantes, René Jordan, and other old acquaintances. Manuel had his own limousine and chauffeur and did endless shopping, filling the car with hatboxes and shopping bags, reserving all extravagance, as always, for his mother. The kitschy decor of the Miami hotel which hosted the visiting celebrities was perhaps best described by Alain Robbe-Grillet upon entering the lobby: "C'est un peu grandiose." On the way to a festival event, Manuel insisted that René accompany him in the limousine, making room among all the packages. Embracing the more formal René, Manuel remarked on the sorry state of his love life (in Spanish, in the feminine): "Oh, woman, how unhappy I am!" The limousine lurched to an abrupt stop as the Cuban chauffeur suddenly braked the car and stared at embarrassed René, the "woman" in the backseat.

Missing New York, where he hadn't been since October 1983, Manuel wrote to Howard when he returned to Rio: "It seems they have finally found a distributor . . .":

I'm traveling to Europe in May, it seems. I'm invited by a Dutch institution to lecture on censorship and from there I'd go to London where there is talk of a stage production of *Kiss of the S.W.* I haven't seen the film yet; the reports are quite contradictory, so of course I expect the worse. It has been cut down from 145′ to 115′ so you can imagine what that may mean. Anyhow the original structure of Leonard's script was all shaky so the cuts are not ruining anything immaculate to start with.[82]

Babenco had resurfaced in March 1985—fortunately, his cancer appeared to be curable—and when he screened the two-hour version, he remarked: "It's very good to leave a movie; you come back with fresh eyes, and it looks much better."[83]

Babenco sought a reconciliation with Manuel, hoping that he would approve of the film, but by now their relations were badly strained. Trying to get Manuel to attend the official screening in São Paulo, Hector called him on the pretext that Arnaldo Jabor wanted Manuel to be there. Hector then asked Manuel if he liked the final edit. "I don't like," Manuel reportedly replied. "I don't like the movie, and I don't like you. I don't know why you're bothering me." Hector pleaded with Manuel, insisting that he wanted him to be happy, that he would change it to please him, but apparently Manuel cut him off: "It's too late." Babenco believes this was their last conversation.

The film's heavy-handed naturalism irked Manuel. The last scene was a case in point: the stage play ended with the famous "kiss" good-bye and a hallucinatory voice-over much like the novel, which was less brutal than the movie, in which Molina's dead body is dumped in an alleyway and one of his assassins utters the words, "You fucking fag." In the penultimate letter he wrote to Emir, Manuel summarized his reaction to the film with damaging wit:

The movie: A hodge-podge, without the slightest subtlety. Babenco was a nightmare; no sooner did I give over the rights he vanished and to avoid my influence he fell into the claws of the U.S. scriptwriter (Paul Schrader's brother, boring and heavy-handed like him) and finally W. Hurt who completely colonized the idiot Babenco, and a typical "Schraderade" was the outcome, slow and lugubrious. Hurt playing the sad, tortured and neurotic . . . he is in real life. In the end, they excised the core of the story, which was the fag's joie de vivre and the humor. Julia is better, despite the fact that the character [the Marxist] no longer exists. Nor did they leave the motivations that make the story believable. The way it ended, Valentín could be bisexual or who knows what. In any case, what little was left appears to have touched people in a big way, so may it serve at least to sell more books.[84]

He was writing to an Emir already diagnosed with colon cancer, which may be why Manuel tried to keep the tone of the rest of the letter light and cheerful: "Just back from my lightning trip to London, Paris & Rome, with first stop in Amsterdam for a lecture that paid the ticket, and in Paris I found out through Severo that you were ill, and I never even remember you with a cold!" He hoped that Emir would recover, even though he had already heard the probable outcome from Emir's companion Selma, whom Emir would marry shortly before he died on November 11, 1985. Emir's fatal illness was one upset among others: Carlos's wife, Manuel's sister-in-law, had just committed suicide, and Malé was in a terrible state about not being in Buenos Aires with the rest of the family.

Not only had Babenco, in Manuel's opinion, not done right by *Kiss*, but a promised further payment never materialized because the production company Island Alive declared backruptcy, split up, and vanished. The other side of the equation, however, was the impact the movie's fame would have on Manuel's future. Manuel modulated his opinion for public consumption, responding to interviewers with an author's fatalism, alluding to the nasty old Hollywood story in which writers so often felt cheated fiscally as well as creatively:

> I did not like the movie; I found it too grim, too severe, but I liked the effect it had on audiences, so it is all right. What I like is that it presents the "queen" as a human being. Molina comes to think of himself as the quintessential queen. When I

sold it, I knew the vision in the final work would be that of the director, and not mine. The best thing is not to get too upset.[85]

Manuel's opinion would find further articulation, again, in Pauline Kael's review in *The New Yorker*. She compared the movie to the novel, describing the novel's vision: "More than a defense of escapism—it's an homage to escapism. The glory of the book is that the reader feels the power of fantasy." She adds:

> Puig isn't a sentimentalist . . . There is no authorial voice as such, and the motives behind what the men say are elusive. But there are undertones—subversive hints that the two men are using each other—which may or may not be picked up by a reader. They have definitely not been picked up by the movie . . . essentially about two men who give to each other and learn from each other . . . The movie is primarily the story of Molina's transfiguration through the power of love and happiness and a new self-respect—that is, his shedding of his effeminate mannerisms . . . This redemptive drama is as phony as the forties screen romances that Molina is infatuated with.

Kael conjectures that Babenco may have been trying to make the film politically correct:

> But its squareness is a betrayal of something in movie-loving gays: their carrying a personal theater of romantic fantasy inside themselves. Molina is the moviegoer as *auteur* . . . Babenco is reaching for something larger, something tragic and aggressively moral. The picture makes a show of its commitment to the highest human values. Puig's novel is saying that queens may be useless, silly window dressing, on the order of movie romances, but that can be lovely fun, can't it? It enhances life, makes it more rapturously giddy. Gay groups may consider this politically incorrect . . . [but] Puig's plea for

the indulgence of romance is much like that of Tennessee
Williams, and the novel speaks to that part of us which wants
more than is strictly essential—wants the delirium of excess.
Babenco . . . has steamrolled the romance and absurdity out of
the material.[86]

Babenco was, perhaps, more a producer than a director in that it was his
projection of confidence and charisma that mobilized the *Kiss* team to succeed, against all odds. After this success, Babenco moved on to option
William Kennedy's *Ironweed* (1987), but despite primo material, actors, and
technical backing, it was a flop. Manuel finally felt vindicated.[87]

Among Manuel's growing collection of admirers in the film world was
director Paul Mazursky, who was asked by Joan Cohen, one of Manuel's
video slaves, to deliver a shopping bag full of cassettes when he went down
to Rio that year to film *Moon over Parador* (1988).[88] Mazursky felt that besides his brilliance and unique wit, "Manuel had a purity, a wonderful fix . . .
He believed in his work so much that ambition took a second place." The
director tried to convince Manuel to make a cameo appearance as a Latin
American general in this satire, starring Raul Julia, Sonia Braga, and
Richard Dreyfuss. Manuel gently but firmly resisted: "In front of the screen,
always; in front of the camera, never."[89] After his experiences behind the
camera, with *Kiss*, Manuel completed his manifesto on why writing for the
screen was more difficult for him, and why his novels didn't "translate"
well.[90] His books were mainly spoken, with very little descriptive, visual
prose; it was all in the ear, not the eye. "I mostly *hear* the action." To a certain extent, his focus on the spoken word would fare better in the theater
than on film. Manuel's new projects included another spartan "two-
character solution," *Mystery of the Rose Bouquet*, a strange play about an invalid, a rich woman interned at an exclusive clinic who speaks obsessively
about death, and her nurse, a younger woman at the mercy of the older
woman's whims. A kind of mother-daughter psychodrama, the story plainly
revolves around his own filial bond and anxieties about mortality.

The success of *Kiss*, the film, snowballed into countless homages to
Manuel Puig: in Italy Manuel received, in 1986, his second literary award,
the Curzio Malaparte for best foreign novel for *Blood of Requited Love*. This
was particularly gratifying since the consensus among his critics was that

this was his worst book yet. Manuel was pegged glamorously by the Italians as a political dissident. "Puig is not a prophet in his own country," read one commentary on the winner of the Curzio Malaparte. In a letter to freelance film researcher Joan Cohen in Los Angeles, Manuel re-created the glamour with a touch of *All About Eve*:

> Well, enough dreams [chatter about movies]; I must preface my acceptance speech for the Curzio Malaparte award I just got in Italy . . . I'll thank everybody in Eve Harrington fashion. The truth is the only character I like in that film is Thelma Ritter's. One more truth: I really appreciate this award because it went to my last novel, *Blood of Requited Love,* which has been very roughly treated by critics.[91]

In Rome Malé and Mario stayed, as they always did, at the charming Hotel Due Torri, in a sidestreet adjacent to Piazza di Spagna; they lunched with the elderly Alberto Moravia and Argentine actress Elisa Galvé, had dinner with Mario and his friends Tony and Elvira at the Nerone; and the next day, a feast chez las Margas—Margherita's health was quite fragile by now—was de rigueur. Already in Milan, a production of *Mystery of the Rose Bouquet* was in the works, and *Under a Mantle of Stars* was about to open in Catania, Sicily.

Meanwhile, the adventures of *Kiss* the play continued. The opening of the French production was a gala affair, but it received mediocre reviews in *Le Monde*. Simon Stokes's production had better luck in London at the small West End Bush Theatre, except that: "London horror: *Kiss SW* was done with great success at an experimental theater off–West End and was going to transfer to [a more mainstream theater, but something went wrong] . . . The same occurred in NY: Richard Chamberlain was going to play Molina, but nothing happened."[92] Nino and Bensoussan accompanied Manuel and Malé to the opening night in Paris of *Le Baiser de la Femme Araignée,* directed by Armand Delcamp. Manuel had never let Malé see the movie or read the book—though she probably did anyway. He felt the homosexual subject matter would be too upsetting for her, but since she didn't understand French, and the Parisian debut was *très* chic . . . As they stood amid a dazzling circle of glamorous French actors and admirers like Jean-

Pierre Aumont in front of the elegant theater, the Studio des Champs-Élysées, Malé's main thrill that evening was gazing at Marlene Dietrich's apartment, directly across the grand avenue.[93] Manuel later remarked on the "delicacy" of the French production:

> Molina is played by a young actor, a good one but too young and handsome for the part. Since la Hurt did it, all the leading men want to do it, while it was destined for a Robert Duvall type. In Milan last week *Mystery of the Rose Bouquet*, again a delicate, not too dramatic production with two actresses who are OK but not starry enough. I've learnt my lesson with this play; it's only meant for monstres sacrés. It seems Edwige Feuillère wants definitely to do it in Paris, and I'd love Darrieux in the other part. It seems they are not enemies, so it could be . . . Just let me dream . . .[94]

Manuel's wish for Edwige Feuillère and Danielle Darrieux, both in their late eighties, to play a fifty-year-old and a seventy-year-old, did not come true in France, but in London he got his *monstres sacrés* with Gemma Jones and Brenda Bruce, and in 1989, he would have the thrill of working with Anne Bancroft and Jane Alexander, who starred in the premiere of Robert Anderson's production at the Mark Taper Forum in Los Angeles.

Meanwhile, in 1987, came the Efebo d'Oro Agrigento prize for the film *Kiss*. The ceremony took place in romantic Capri, and Sonia Braga joined Manuel there to receive a prize for her performance. All expenses were paid for both Malé and Manuel, so how could he not go, he exclaimed to Mitch Douglas, who handled theatrical rights at ICM; plus they were staying at a glamorous villa, the same "dazzling Villa Malaparte, stepped like a Mayan temple by Le Corbusier," where Jack Palance seduced Bardot in *Contempt*.[95] Too bad they didn't throw in a gigolo for good measure, he quipped to New York "daughter" Bruce Benderson.

By the mid-eighties, Brazil's economic situation was worsening and there were muggings everywhere, not only at night but on the streets and beaches in broad daylight. In May 1986, a friend of Mario's, Juancho, was stabbed in

front of Mario's building, and in March 1987, Mario's apartment was bur-
glarized while he was in Belém after which his tenant wanted to leave;
Mario had to stay at Manuel's apartment until they installed window gates.
When not traveling abroad, home and routine were one and the same for
Manuel. Mario, on the contrary, traveled all over Brazil, from Angra dos
Reis and Parati to Mato Grosso and the Amazon. Manuel admired and al-
most envied his friend's time and freedom to travel to remote natural won-
ders.

Even when he traveled all expenses paid, Manuel preferred staying with
friends rather than in an impersonal hotel. In this case, it wasn't parsimony
but preference for being cared for by friends like "Becky" in Mexico City,
Nino in Paris, and la Bruce in New York, who understood his movie needs
and provided the shelter of a shared sensibility. By now he had acquired all
the Mexican movies he wanted and was on to a new kick, Spanish Franco-
era propaganda flicks; this obsession would lead to a (still unproduced)
screenplay about Madrid during the Spanish Civil War.

As Tito, an Argentine friend in Rio, put it: "Fame frightened or inhib-
ited Manuel a bit. He preferred being among friends, rather than in front of
crowds, which is why he hid himself behind his characters, his imitations.
He had a strong personality with clear opinions and perspectives, but was
shy, introverted."[96] While this observation is valid, Manuel did enjoy being a
celebrity, but increasingly evaded public receptions which he suspected
would be tedious.

There were few outings to theaters in Rio: the city was getting too dangerous for Malé, now eighty. Except for afternoon excursions chauffeured
by Aristides, Rua Aperana was the hub of the Puigs' social life, where, for
Manuel, it was reassuring to have Mama, "sisters," and "daughters" around
the house watching a movie. But old friends could also prove to be a waste
of time, and Manuel often felt torn between avoiding loneliness and maintaining strict control over the time he spent with visitors. His rigidity in
managing his time was part of an upbringing in which everyday life had its
regimen, but it was also part of getting older—and his way of imposing the
discipline necessary both to write and to shepherd those he needed around
him.

In Rio, despite the fact that he had no deep friendships among the "superficial Cariocas," there was a cozy group of regular companions, among

them Hugo Gutiérrez Vega. A Mexican diplomat and poet who was then cultural attaché in Rio, Hugo had known Manuel since Manuel's Cinecittà days, when Hugo had his first diplomatic assignment in Rome. He and his wife, Lucinda, and Silvia Oroz and her boyishly handsome husband, Alfredo, were regulars at the Puig cine club.[97] These were unpretentious fellow cinephiles with whom Malé and Manuel could relax: Hugo, a witty conversationalist, amused Manuel with his gossip. Manuel confided to Hugo his fears about the rash that wouldn't go away, and Hugo convinced Manuel to come along with him to have the HIV test, done by a gay doctor in whom Hugo had total confidence. The doctor gave both men a complete checkup and a round of blood tests. When the results came back a few weeks later, Hugo called the doctor for both of them, and then called Manuel with the good news: he was negative, and, apparently, the rash was, as the doctor had suspected, a fungus from the polluted Ipanema beaches. For Manuel the relief was enormous; according to Hugo, from then (1986) until he left Brazil, Manuel abstained from any risky activity.

The cine club, which met on Monday, Wednesday, and Friday evenings, was especially meaningful for Silvia Oroz, an Argentine film scholar in Rio since 1979, who swallowed up every bit of history Manuel imparted during these video viewings. Manuel lent her name to the Silvia in what would be his last novel: *Cae la noche tropical*. Like Malé, Silvia Oroz, whom Manuel called La Pechocha (lower-class Argentine slang for "pretty" in the forties), was from La Plata; Manuel's nickname was Hada [fairy] and Silvia's husband, Alfredo, was Elf. Having moved to Rio around the same time as Manuel, Silvia, a comforting friend from home, recalls:

> He had classified our movies in three types: films, movies, flicks. The first were auteur productions—Fellini, Godard, etc.—we never watched those. The movies were good routine melodramas (Hollywood forties etc.); and the flicks were the unbridled melodramas like Ninón Sevilla's *Aventurera*, or Leticia Palma's *Hipócrita*. Our sessions, two or three per week, concentrated on Mexican and Spanish melodramas. We had another category for the masters, that is, Dreyer, Ozu, Mizoguchi, Ulmer—quirky, not mainstream, but eccentric geniuses of cinema. The words *vista* (flick) and *cinta* (literally,

tape, but meaning movie) were what the lower classes in Argentina in the forties and fifties called the movies.

Manuel generously made copies for her students—"he was so sweet to us." Hugo Gutiérrez Vega remembers Manuel would play films in organized series: Italian neorealism one week ("Silvana Pampanini" . . . "Mangano" . . .) and then German musicals of the thirties. While Hugo and Manuel, sometimes also Tito and Mario, watched esoterica, the ladies would be watching a classic Hollywood melodrama on the other television set.

Manuel's increasing rigidity came to seem despotic, though, to those family members and friends (Alfredo Gialdini, Hugo Sottotetti, Felisa, Felipe, and others) who came from Buenos Aires and other parts of the world to visit. Manuel was relieved, for instance, that Alfredo had bonded with Mario over the years, so that he could send the two of them out on *paseos*. It was hard for his devoted friends not to feel hurt, but they were also worried about Manuel.

Brazil was getting on his nerves. Mario, who spent six months each year in Brazil during the period Manuel lived there, believed Manuel was always driven to move on by loneliness:

> Manuel had few close friends in his life. He said that I was the "only one." That's not true, but I can be proud of having been the one closest to him throughout his life. For thirty-four years we were inseparable friends despite the fact that we never lived in the same city—except during the Brazil period (1981–89) we could spend more time together because I would spend six months out of the year in Rio, where I had an apartment near his . . . In Rio he never established an important relationship. He felt anguished by solitude and that was the real reason for his move to Mexico.[98]

finale

kiss, the musical

Lyricist Fred Ebb was in Los Angeles when the Oscar-nominated *Kiss of the Spider Woman* came to a Westwood theater in 1985; with composer John Kander, Ebb had created *Chicago* and *Cabaret* (this last with director Harold Prince), among other hit musicals. After attending the film on opening night, he made a beeline for the nearest bookstore, picked up the novel, and read it straight through the same night. The story had "loyalty, passion, compassion": he could visualize the dramatic clash between the bleak cell and a fantasy world of escape.[1] The timing was right (for both a homosexual love story and a Latin American political plot) and John Kander agreed; they called Harold Prince, whose distinguished credits also included *Evita*, *Sweeney Todd*, and *Phantom of the Opera*, and he agreed; Prince called librettist Terrence McNally of *The Ritz* and *Lisbon Traviata* fame, who also saw the "big emotions, the universal theme" of love and fantasy conquering all, transcending gender and politics.

Manuel meanwhile had been selling options for the musical version of *Kiss* to all comers—including Hans Werner Henze for a projected German opera—to the dismay of Mitch Douglas and ICM. Before Ebb and Kander had brought the project to Prince's attention, Fran and Barry Weissler, producers of *Grease* and other Broadway revivals, had rushed to option the work for a mere $5,000 after seeing the movie, but they were still sitting on it, because they couldn't come up with a Molina. "He didn't seem to realize competing productions would cancel out the effectiveness of one good one," Mitch Douglas later commented, referring to Manuel's "Zero Mostelian wackiness."[2] In September 1985 Hal Prince phoned Manuel in Rio to commission him to write the book (as musical scenarios are called). This meant Manuel would receive royalties for an original script as well as rights as the original author of the novel—a substantial sum.

A "musical buff," as Prince soon discovered, Manuel certainly knew who Kander and Ebb and McNally were—and politely concealed any skepticism. Prince then approached Mitch Douglas at ICM. With consummate diplomacy, Mitch disposed of the Weisslers' option by returning the $5,000 and, over the next few years, would gently restrain Manuel from responding to the many post-Oscar solicitations for stage productions throughout the United States and Europe, convincing him that, until the musical came out, it would be better, in most cases, to withhold permission.

Manuel first met with Prince in New York in October 1985, and charmed the Broadway entrepreneur from the moment he walked into his office. Right off the bat he told Prince that he didn't like the way the film had been done—the awkward narration of a movie within a movie which Prince also found "clumsy." "If Manuel had liked the film, I wouldn't have taken on the project." But the director soon decided that Manuel "didn't know the first thing about how to write a musical, and would come into my office and dance the numbers!" Manuel spoke about movies in general in this first meeting, Prince recalls: he was "hooked on the more innocent ones—Astaire and Rogers, Hayworth as both quintessential sex symbol and innocent dupe," the spirit of which Prince and his team would strive to incorporate into the musical version.

In early September 1986, after the award ceremony at Capri in August, Manuel passed through London to see Prince, who was between rehearsals of *Phantom*:

> La Prince of Sheer Delight is still interested in the project but the contract is taking forever. I don't understand why—she keeps writing to me and I made the huge mistake of writing the libretto before signing anything, so if it all collapses I will have the frustration plus the waste of time & energy. According to her this [the collapse of the project] will never happen, but . . . La casting problems killed or at least postponed for decades the straight (?) non-musical play so imagine, a simple operation of 2 actors couldn't be done, so what about a mamooth [sic] musical.[3]

By early 1987, after more talks with Prince, Manuel was apprehensive that
the musical could turn out to be even more of a mess than the film. His remarks to friends were like darts:

> La Prince back in harness: In London I saw *Phantom*, pure
> plastic, *Evita* a masterpiece in comparison. No story: since it's
> all singing there is no way to establish the precedents, he's just
> a creature living in the opera cellar, no explanation for any-
> thing. La Prince's job is great, all visuals fabulous but that's
> hardly enough.[4]

Ebb and Kander, "la horrible" couple, were already writing the opening
number—" 'Bedeviled Woman' it's called; it refers to the film la fag is
telling. The first song . . . it stinks!"[5] By August it was established that "a
horror" (McNally) and not Manuel would write the book:

> The Prince (I should say Prinz) thing continues. They have
> called another writer to do the final draft, a horror that did
> *The Ritz* and *The Rink*: what a mess. I had to accept that be-
> cause otherwise I would have had to move to N.Y. for a year,
> and I couldn't take that.[6]

Though Prince had assured Manuel that they weren't going to do that
"trashy thing" in the movie with one woman playing all the female roles, after the preview of the musical (with a bevy of scantily dressed nurses dancing around the dying Valentín) bombed, the Prince team went precisely for
the film's "all women are Woman" device. The Woman's name in the musical was Aurora (Dawn), an ironic label: she appeared to be Life, but she was
really Death. ("Aurora" was a private joke of Manuel's too, the alias of a
homosexual transvestite prostitute famous in the tango halls of La Boca at
the turn of the century.) Another problem of the musical in its first incarnation was the insertion of film story lines, long digressions that diffused the
dramatic tension.[7]

The musical previewed at the State University of New York in Purchase, as part of the liberal arts college's sponsorship of a New Musicals
workshop series. Manuel was staying with Bruce Benderson in the East Village, and Prince sent a limousine to take him up to Westchester County for

opening night, May 24, 1990. Manuel brought an entourage, including Bruce and Howard, for moral support. Previewing *Phantom of the Opera* on the same night in Chicago, Prince was unable to be there but had sent Manuel a warm telegram: "Hope you like what you see. The word is excellent and the future bright."[8]

The function of the Purchase series was to introduce and workshop experimental musicals.[9] Chita Rivera came to opening night in Purchase as well, accompanying her good friends Ebb and Kander. From the start they had been thinking of *Kiss* as a vehicle for Chita, the charismatic Latin crossover diva par excellence. Chita was at first hesitant, not only because she was approaching sixty but because she had not understood (or perhaps not liked) the film. She saw weaknesses in the Purchase production (though she tried to suppress her disappointment, in solidarity) but was drawn right away to the role of Aurora.

Frank Rich of *The New York Times* reviewed the preview, after it had been running for a few weeks, and panned it; the presence of the press during this trial run was a setback for *Kiss* and also had a disruptive effect on the New Musicals series: the other musicals which were to follow were canceled. Mitch Douglas had been holding back rights meanwhile, even when an agent from the William Morris agency called him in April 1989, offering Richard Gere for Valentín and Harvey Fierstein for Molina. But, after the Purchase setback, early in July 1990, Mitch started releasing production rights again, to selective provincial or summer stock theaters in the United States. After four years of suspense, the musical was a failure. What Manuel could not know at that moment was that it would make it to Broadway, and become a huge success.

the tropical night falls

He stowed away in an English ship.
They say his eyes were crying,
the eyes of Juan Manuel . . .

With the silence of ponies

they bade them farewell.

He never saw home again

but died faraway, in a foreign land

—Homero Manzi, "Juan Manuel"

Manuel's final home away from home was on Orquidea Street, Cuernavaca. Here "the failure of the musical really poisoned the last days of his life," an American friend in the Mexican city noted, but then again, stress of all sorts plagued Manuel from 1988 to the disappointing Purchase debut in May of 1990.[10] Not least were the arrangements attending the exhausting move of Malé and himself over four thousand miles. Longtime acquaintances like Mario, Nino, and Tom Colchie, who saw Manuel in the year prior to his death, were all struck by how haggard he looked. This was why he didn't want to be seen, Guillermo Cabrera Infante believes, the last time he was in London. Manuel excused himself for not visiting Guillermo and Miriam by explaining that the meeting with Prince took longer than he had expected because of the director's whims and there was no time before the flight out.

Aside from the fact that his goddesses were disappearing—Hayworth had died, after many years with Alzheimer's, in May 1987—Manuel worried constantly about losing Malé. After his cousin Susana's early death from cancer in 1986, her mother, Carmen—Malé's last surviving and dearest sister, the chatty maternal aunt whose voice is the first to be heard in Manuel's first novel, *Betrayed by Rita Hayworth*—had come to live with Malé in Rio, where Mario could also help comfort her. Carmen died several months later, still deeply mourning the death of her beloved daughter.

Tropical Night Falling, Manuel's last book, begins with two sisters speaking about the sadness of twilight and how the death of the day reminds them of the loss of loved ones, evoking also their own impending fates; they repeat almost word for word the soliloquy uttered by the mistress of the house in Manuel's play *Under a Mantle of Stars*, written immediately before he composed *Tropical Night*:

This time of the day always frightens me, the death of the day. Because it's not always certain the sun will rise again. One day or another, things die. That afternoon when I was waiting for you . . . it was growing dark . . . and for me the dawn never came again.[11]

When asked to translate the novel, at first I found it oppressively gloomy and difficult to stick with, but Manuel's mischievous humor still sparkled in the subtle kernels of semi-senile chatter between the two cranky, endearing old ladies. Published in 1988, *Tropical Night Falling* (as we titled it) was conceived, Manuel explained,

> more than anything, because for the first time, very close to me, are persons who have entered their old age. I've had to bring my parents to live with me because they've suddenly turned very old and dependent economically on me. I have realized that old age is the epic age par excellence, since you are no longer master of your near future. You have to consult death on everything. And these people are not only taken by surprise by age with these terrible problems, but are also living in times when fundamental changes are happening.[12]

The querulous conversations between Nidia and Luci, elderly Argentine expatriates in Rio de Janeiro in the eighties, echo the dialogues of at least two inseparable duos, Manuel and Malé, and Malé and Carmen.

The hope for transcendance permeates Luci and Nidia's conversations, but *Tropical Night Falling* has a decidedly melancholy air. *Wuthering Heights*, the ultimate romance about love beyond death, made into a film which Manuel tried to imitate in his very first script in the fifties, gets a curtain call in this final novel. His second excursion to the misty literary Yorksire moors in 1986 with Malé is thinly disguised in the reminiscences of the two Argentine ladies.[13] When Manuel presented the novel at the 92nd Street Y in May 1990 (introduced by his friend Alfred Mac Adam), he said it was about "how old people need someone young to love." One can assume that he was referring not only to his mother but also to himself, as a childless individual, living vicariously through younger friends, also concerned about love in his mature years, about being left alone by his aged mother. The title, like a stage direction, gives the feeling of the curtain falling on the last act. Manuel's ambivalence is evident as he records and chuckles at their clichés but also feels the grip of their sentiment. Like all of his fiction and plays, *Tropical Night* is embroidered with movies and melodrama: the sisters associate the tragic fate of Vivien Leigh in *Waterloo Bridge* with the desperate lives of servant girls and itinerant workers in Brazil.

As the novel begins, the two sisters peer voyeuristically into the rear window across the way, into the apartment and life of a forty-five-year-old Argentine psychiatrist named Silvia, who is an alter ego for Manuel, too, in her promiscuous midlife lust for love—or lust. They construct their own version of her story, using this third person as a screen, but finally invade that screen, getting into the plot that is part truth but partly elaborated by their tireless minds. If writing novels was Manuel's therapy, in which he played both analyst and analysand, his last fictional self-portrait was this female psychologist. Enamored of her own Freudian clichés, Silvia strives to seduce her elusive (and hopelessly unworthy) love object, whose behavior she rationalizes with psychobabble like "He himself had matured, gotten a little older, but inside he continued to harbor what he was before, a young boy who wasn't allowed to speak."[14] Silvia—there are a couple of Silvias in the old ladies' conversation and so they always clarify with "this Silvia"—is also Manuel's mischievous caricature of his Argentine women friends in Rio who, apart from Silvia Oroz, were all shrinks in exile, middle-class *porteñas*.[15] A figure of pathos and mockery, a specialist in other people's intimate lives, Silvia in her obtuseness personifies the very human quality of blindness to one's own inner workings—like most of Manuel's characters, and like Manuel himself.

After Manuel sent the manuscript off to press, he focused on the task ahead: if his decision to move to Rio de Janeiro had been swift, the decision to leave was even swifter. Brazil was *maravilhoso*, but, Manuel wrote in his last letter to Angelo Morino—dated July 6, 1990—as he and Malé were settling into Cuernavaca, "Rio turned into a nightmare: poverty, beauty and AIDS! What a combination." The muggings and street violence were a constant worry, particularly considering octogenarian Malé's daily walks to the beach, and Manuel panicked about the economic climate and falling property values. His sense of isolation was exacerbated by the frequent mail strikes. The beautiful boys were thieves or, more tragic, were dying of the plague, as was Nestor Perlongher, another respected Argentine writer in Brazil. During his last hectic months in Rio, Manuel tried to help a semiliterate acquaintance who had AIDS (with the multicultural and very Brazilian name of Overland Airton Gayoso) to publish an autobiographical book on the subject.

Malé, perhaps self-centered, considered the main reason for the move to be Manuel's concern for her well-being; Mario thought Manuel was mostly driven by his own solitude, and later thanked his "lucky stars" that he hadn't completely uprooted himself from Italy. (He had maintained his walk-up apartment in Albano Laziale, a southern suburb of Rome, on the margins of the formerly glamorous I Castelli.)

"Rio is fabulous for la sex but no friendships (lasting ones) flourish here, a very peculiar matter" was how Manuel explained his decision to Howard in New York.[16] Amilcar, the black construction worker, was a dependable romeo but also was married; they would never live together. Manuel worried not only about the ways in which economic instability and poverty infected urban life with violence, but also about disease; as his rash convinced him, not even the beach was safe.

In Mexico Manuel had a strong network of intimate and intelligent accomplices, with la Becky as the most dependable of his daughters, ready to be his permanent roommate when the dreaded day (of Malé's death) arrived. Javier and Agustín Gil, and other good friends in Mexico City— Miguel Sabido and Hugo Gutiérrez Vega among them—awaited him with open arms. (A talented director of serious theater, Sabido was now mainly a commercial producer for Televisa.) Mario, and even his brother Carlitos and family, could be tempted to join them there once they had settled.

With the cultural atmosphere of the Southern Cone (Argentina, Uruguay, Chile) poisoned by years of military dictatorship, and Castro's Cuba crumbling with the fall of the Soviet bloc, by the mid-eighties Mexico City had become the most vital cultural hub in Latin America. The connections and prestige Manuel had already established there with writers, and in film and theater circles, together with his international fame after the success of *Kiss of the Spider Woman*, as a play directed by Ripstein as well as the Oscar-winning movie, all made Mexico an attractive alternative. He could live in Spanish again, which was essential to him as a writer and a considerable convenience for Malé, whose impaired hearing made it more and more difficult for her to understand foreign tongues.

Mexico would also be a short plane ride from Los Angeles, where director Robert Allan Ackerman was working on a stage production of *Mystery of the Rose Bouquet*, scheduled for the next fall season. In February 1989, Manuel had made a detour to Santa Barbara on one of his Hollywood trips to work with me on the translation of *Tropical Night* for Simon & Schuster, our first collaboration in a decade. Manuel by now had hired his friend and translator Tom Colchie as his agent, partly to make up for what Tom (paid only that fee of $2,500) had not earned from *Kiss of the Spider Woman*, partly because he finally seemed to realize he wasn't doing the right thing by himself and his work by penny-pinching. He asked Tom to make sure that I received royalties; Tom felt at the time that Manuel's attitude toward money and friends had changed. He wasn't doing his usual faux-seductive act, Tom remembers: "Perhaps Manuel sensed that he was not long for this world."

Nidia, in the last scene of *Tropical Night Falling*, smuggles out an airlines blanket as she descends a plane from Buenos Aires to Rio, visiting her old friend Silvia. True to (his) character, Manuel had brought me a house present, a PANAM blanket; he may not have liked to spend, but he liked to give. He was staying near hip Melrose Avenue with David Weisman, who was about to release *Naked Tango*, a new film based on an idea that Manuel had developed in his unproduced play *Tango Musik*. (When this film appeared at the New York Film Festival a year later, in September 1990, it was "dedicated to the memory of Manuel Puig.") I went to pick him up at Weisman's house. Expecting a stranger to open the high wooden gate, I was pleased to hear a familiar voice exclaim, "Ay la woman!" followed by Manuel himself, playfully hiding his face like Count Dracula at the first rays of dawn. For some reason I was surprised by how changed he seemed in the six or seven years since I had last seen him. More round-shouldered, slighter or shorter, his thinning hair almost all gray, he looked tired, middle-aged, not the young Manuel I remembered.

In May 1989, Malé had a successful cataract operation. Because he wanted her to have the best medical care, Manuel had also considered moving to Los Angeles—after all, he would be working more and more exclusively on film and theater projects—or even to New York. But in the States the cost of living was much higher, he couldn't drive, and it would be problematic for Malé to live among English-speakers. Most of all, he urgently needed to live in his own language; because of his concern about writing in *portuñol*, before he sent *Tropical Night Falling* off to press, he asked

Venezuelan journalist May Lorenzo Alcalà, then cultural attaché in Rio, to revise the Spanish.

Relatively inexpensive, Mexico was more stable than most Latin American countries, in part because of its shared border, history, and trade agreements with the United States. But, because both mother and son had hypertension, the air of the capital city was too polluted and the altitude too dangerous. Cuernavaca seemed an ideal solution. Nestled in a valley, Cuernavaca, despite tourists and urban sprawl, still conserved its luxuriant aura as a resort where celebrities had homes or vacationed; it was a good place to retire. Malé and Manuel could live in complete comfort, near caring friends. After finding and buying a home on three acres of land, Manuel now had to undertake the arduous task of selling his property in Brazil and moving his household, that is, his two households and his octogenarian mother.

Meanwhile, for *Mystery of the Rose Bonquet*, Ackerman was seeking to cast *monstres sacrés* whom Manuel venerated; among the few hardies of this variety left in Hollywood was Luise Rainer, and Manuel wrote her a gently persuasive letter—touching base with yet another legend. Even though he did not hear from Rainer until after Anne Bancroft had accepted the role of the older woman, and after the play opened at the Mark Taper Forum, she did respond with great warmth and respect:

> December 12, 1989
>
> Dear Mr Puig:
>
> Thank you for your kind note. I am so sorry not to have felt induced to perform in your lovely play. My husband of 45 years of happiest togetherness had died recently and I could not face reliving in this part the sad and frustrating emotions that I needed to get rid of in my life! Write *another* play for me and if I feel it is right I shall do it. Anyway you have a great gift!
>
> With kindest good wishes,
> Luise Rainer

This letter, from an actress he idolized as a child half a century earlier, must have delighted him.

Opening night in November 1989 at the Mark Taper Forum in Los Angeles was a gala event at which the audience (including Gena Rowlands, Sally Field, and Ann Miller) almost outshone the stars on stage. Flanked by tall blond Daryl Hannah on his left and by Bancroft's comedic spouse Mel Brooks on his right—Daryl held his hand affectionately during the performance—Manuel watched the play enraptured. The performance went smoothly, even though, as Manuel accurately noted, the Mark Taper "was not the best place for that kind of intimate play."[17] Quite minimalist—one set, two actors—the play came off a bit flat, and Anne Bancroft's imitation of a refined, upper-class accent was uneven. Most of his readers who have seen the play agree that it was a minor piece compared to his novels; nonetheless, the American debut was an apotheosis, with standing ovations for Bancroft and Jane Alexander every night. "Now let's hope that it continues its career in New York," Manuel wrote Howard, concerned about Bancroft's devotion to her motherly (also grandmotherly) duties: "Bancroft is the problem because she won't let her son alone until June when he graduates." The play turned out to be one of the Mark Taper's biggest hits, though director Bob Ackerman remarked to Manuel that it had done better critically in London, where Gemma Jones had been "heartbreaking" as the muse, and that Jane Alexander, in this same role, should be replaced for Broadway, perhaps by Woody Allen's latest discovery, Dianne Wiest.

Manuel was also shuttling back and forth to Rome, working on an English-language film script about the eighteenth-century northern Italian priest/composer Antonio Vivaldi. In his first letter to Howard from Cuernavaca (upon returning from opening night at the Mark Taper in Los Angeles) he wrote:

> We spent two months at a lush villa by the sea in Santa Marinella (1 hour away from Rome) near the place where Ingrid [Bergman] and Roberto [Rossellini] had their nest. The villa was the summer house of the producer [Davide Rampello] who wants me to do a script on Vivaldi. It all went very well professionally and 2 weeks ago we landed finally in Mexico.[18]

On the same day (September 5, 1989) that Manuel and Malé passed through Rome on their way to Santa Marinella, intending to visit Mario and the

Muzis to celebrate the successful conclusion of Malé's surgical procedure, Margherita Muzi died.

Interviewed by an Italian reporter in Santa Marinella, Manuel had been asked why he had been chosen to write the story of the "Prete Rosso"; Manuel replied that he was known for the "thriller element" in his novels, and they needed to re-create the story of a man who disappeared for twenty years. Vivaldi's sexuality was something of a mystery as well, but Manuel did not mention his interest in this enigma in front of Malé. Describing Manuel's "fake Hollywood-style villa," the journalist attempted camp but ended up with kitsch:

> A ray of sun filters through the open window. Two chocolate-colored girls with Portuguese accents bring coffee on a silver tray. Puig's mother, a lovely lady dressed in turquoise satin, comes in and briefly interrupts us to talk animatedly about her father, and Verdi's melodramatic opera seen at the Teatro Colón in Buenos Aires. After her enters Anita Laurenzi, Puig's favorite actress and star of *Mystery of the Rose Bouquet* [in Italy] and of his farce *Under a Mantle of Stars*, shown in Catania and directed by Sandro Sequi. There's an aura of Fellini's *Dolce Vita*, on the white sofa the writer, small and vivacious, looks like an overgrown child lovingly spoilt by his women, while we sense the imposing presence of this outrageous villa. Puig calls it a *"femme fatale* of stone," replete with corridors and hidden dangers like Gloria Swanson's house in *Sunset Boulevard*.

cuernavaca, city of eternal spring . . .

Melodrama is the theme of a brief (two-page) dialogue which was found at Manuel's death in a trunk full of unpublished papers.[19] This dialogue between a teacher and "her" student served as a pretext for Manuel to explain his view of the difference between drama and its "debauched" form, melodrama. While dramas are serious works, often with somber endings determined by the characters' defects or virtues, in melodrama, *la forza del destino* intervenes: the hero or heroine's life is destroyed by a stroke of bad luck. The *maestra* notes that the women in melodramas are always good women whom fate has mistreated. (Her speech is lightened by a mischievous footnote, pointing out that such a destiny can be heightened by "Max Steiner's prophetic chords, or ominous lighting by J. Fipee.") Melodrama, whether a maudlin tango sung by Libertad Lamarque or a hysterical Hollywood flick starring Joan Crawford, was reality—or as Manuel would couch it in Lacanian jargon for the benefit of his compatriots: "Melodrama is the language in which the unconscious speaks." Manuel identified with ill-fated divas Rita Hayworth in *Gilda*, Garbo in the *Grand Hotel*, Lana Turner as doomed starlet in *Ziegfeld Follies*, in brief, with female martyrs. Thoroughly modern, he was also thoroughly old-fashioned: we are marked by destiny, whether we call it genes or fate, from early childhood.

Manuel's new residence at 210 Orquídea, toward the top of a gently sloping street lined with tall iron gates and stone walls overgrown with warm-hued bougainvillea, in the exclusive neighborhood of Las Delicias in the hills of Cuernavaca, was a large deluxe property, though run-down. Between the purchase and renovations, it ended up costing nearly $750,000: on three thousand square meters of land over four levels, there were several structures, among them a mostly glass-block main house built in the fifties and a two-story lodge called the bungalow: the top floor was the guest quarters, and the first floor a loft-sized studio with high windows, lined with lilac tiles. The final touches on this studio, the most opulent space Manuel ever worked in, were completed less than a week before he died. A gardener's cottage on a lower level housed the caretaker and his wife, the housekeeper, and their children; and on the bottom level, a tennis court was transformed into an Olympic-sized pool for Malé and Manuel's daily aerobics. Working with a landscape architect and the caretaker, Adán Mendiolo García, Manuel added fruit trees and tropical plants to create a veritable Garden of Eden; he did a lot of the actual planting himself. The pool was built by an architect he nicknamed Tom Cruise—perhaps his last crush. Manuel renovated the early fifties ranch-style main house, adding teakwood louvred doors on the closets, and revamping the bathrooms with the pastel tiles of the region, having his own done in refreshing pale shades of blue and green. When May Lorenzo Alcalà came to visit Manuel in the spring of 1990, he showed her around the grounds with pride and commented: "You know, May? I'm 56 years old; I think the time has come for me to enjoy what I worked so hard for."[20] On another occasion Manuel had remarked to a friend: "Your fifties are your best time, it's when you know your limitations and you're still young enough to enjoy what life has to offer." The City of Eternal Spring promised to be the perfect place to settle down.

In January 1990, at the age of eighty-three, Baldomero Puig died in a nursing home in Buenos Aires after a long period of crippling dementia. For Carlos, who had had a close relationship with his father, this was a sad loss (and the relief of a great burden), but Baldo's death seemed to pass unnoticed by Manuel, and by Malé too, who had been estranged from her husband several years already. For intimates it felt eerie, as if mother and son both were really Bette Davis in *The Little Foxes*, where Bette stands motionless, ignoring her dying husband—in close-up her face a frigid mask—as he (Herbert Marshall) gropes helplessly for his heart pills, out of reach and too late to save him.

A month after Baldo's death, Manuel took Malé on a trip to Japan while the house in Cuernavaca was filled with workmen. Since his first trip to the Far East in 1965—Bangkok, Hong Kong, Macao, and Tokyo—Manuel loved Japan, not only its majestic Fujiyama and its exquisite aesthetics in everything from daily life to the ritual No theater, but also its publishers' and readers' enthusiasm. It seemed at first uncanny for his books, so Argentine, so anchored in Western culture, to be understood in Asia, especially when *Betrayed by Rita Hayworth* was translated into Japanese from the English version. But Japanese audiences liked movies and the tango too, and found in Puig a voice that spoke to their own sexual and political concerns; indeed, a major theater in Tokyo would be among the first to request rights to stage Hal Prince's successful Broadway musical *Kiss of the Spider Woman*.

On this last visit, in which he and Malé toured the country for almost a month, Manuel was treated as an honored writer (he wrote in a postcard to Alfredo Gialdini, his old crony from university days in Buenos Aires), and he appreciated the Japanese people, "their courtesy and humility, so unlike the Argentines." After dinner one night, in their hotel suite in Kyoto, Manuel was suddenly convulsed with vomiting spells, and for the next several days had acute diarrhea. He attributed it to something he ate, Japanese food, and didn't bother to see a doctor. His cousin Bebé conjectures that the attack, following shortly upon Baldomero's death, had to do with Manuel's repressed guilt over his non-reaction to the final loss of his father. But whatever its psychological roots, Manuel's intestinal ills would later be diagnosed medically as stemming from an infected gallbladder.

When mother and son finally settled into their new home in Cuernavaca they began receiving regular weekend visits from "Rita's daughters," Miguel Sabido, and other friends whose company they enjoyed. Everyday life could now begin, with Don Adán and family to take care of things. Manuel adored Don Adán: a taxi driver, Adán would help his wife tend the garden, but Manuel doubled his wages so that he would work exclusively for him, as chauffeur and caretaker. There were playful flirtations with errand boys at the local *mercado*, but Manuel also enjoyed going to the main square in town before lunch to have a *cafecito* at "La Universal" or "La Parroquia," and to take in the local color, the outdoor market under the shade of the trees. Everywhere the eye could rest on graceful colonial vistas, everywhere there was an earful of mariachis. Up the thoroughfare from the square beside a church at the top of a hill stood a baroque altar to the Virgin called Calvario—Calvary. A few blocks away was the most fabulous hotel in town, Las Mañanitas, where one could sip margaritas and watch majestic white peacocks strut ceremoniously across the vast lawn dotted with swaying *palmeras*. Manuel dressed as always in *trapos* (rags) to go on errands—to the bank, stores, post office—although he was chauffeured around town, a contrast which apparently endeared him to Don Adán, who would gently reproach Manuel for wearing old sandals and carrying his money in a crumpled brown paper bag.[21] Manuel was evidently faithful, as ever, to his manias.

the kiss of death

Carlos Puig came to visit Manuel and Malé in the new house in June to escape the Argentine winter. While there, he struck up a romance with Manuel's editor, a young woman who headed the Seix Barral office in Mexico City, and played tennis at the local club. Though he didn't think much of it then, he remembers that his brother was extremely irritable, and attributed it, in part, to the stress from the move as well as the failed musical. Later, after the sudden succession of dreadful events in July, he interpreted that irritability as a bilious symptom, in keeping with Manuel's digestive problems in recent years.

Before his brother's arrival, Manuel had just completed an imagined conversation between two cinematic legends: the dying Max Ophüls and the immortal, alas mortal, Greta Garbo. (Manuel and Garbo would die within months of each other.) In "The Eyes of Greta Garbo," the title piece of his posthumously published *Gli Occhi di Greta Garbo*, Greta Garbo and legendary director Max Ophüls together contemplate the afterlife. Greta's reminiscence of her father here is curiously affecting, and her remark about looking forward to Paradise, so as to be rid, once and for all, of the critics, clearly reflects Manuel's own feelings on the matter: "The critics won't be there either. They are excluded, by definition, from Paradise."[22]

On Sunday, July 15, Manuel took his midday swim, *muy* Esther Williams, in his brand-new blue-tiled pool. Javier and Miguel Sabido were down for the weekend—that night they viewed one of Javier's newest videos on Manuel's giant screen—and Javier remembers that Manuel reclined on the chaise and said, "Now the glamour begins." If Manuel had AIDS and knew he was terminally ill, as many people conjectured after his death, why would he have spent eight months renovating a house, preparing it for guests and parties, Javier later asked. In early August Manuel was expecting a visit from the Yugoslav writer, set designer, and producer Milena Canonera, with whom he was drafting the script for a project he was very excited about, *Madrid 1937*, and had already invited several friends from abroad to visit his new home.

On Monday, July 16, Manuel was awakened by pains and chills, followed by intensifying spasms of vomiting and diarrhea. Instead of trusting the advice of his "daughter" Javier and Sabido and immediately checking in to the best hospital in Mexico City, or even being flown to Houston, Texas, Manuel telephoned several specialists and hospitals in Cuernavaca and deliberated for two days. Adán reportedly said that Manuel drank tea and refused to do anything "because his regular doctor in Cuernavaca was on vacation."[23] By Wednesday the pain was excruciating and he was so weak that he had to be carried to the car by Adán. At the clinic he finally chose, Central Quirúrgica Las Palmas, he was taken directly to the X-ray room and diagnosed, by Dr. Samuel Mejía Miranda, a reputable urologist in Cuernavaca, with an inflamed gallbladder that had to be removed before it ruptured: emergency surgery was performed the very afternoon he was admitted. The surgeon's usual anesthesiologist was not available, however, so that the anesthesiologist customarily on weekend duty had to be called in. The operation lasted over four hours, and at one point Manuel's heart stopped, but they brought him back. Because no stones were found, Malé requested a biopsy after they removed the gallbladder. The test for cancer was negative: the inflammation had enlarged the gallbladder and the pain had been caused by its pressing against his liver.

The next morning Javier showed up at the clinic. Malé looked at his face as he entered breathless and pale and said, "No te gusta, ¿verdad?" (You don't like this place, right?). Javier immediately tried to reassure her: "No, no, it's that I just arrived." But he was visibly appalled by the clinic's shabbiness, its low ceilings, small dark rooms, and bare furnishings; a disquieting sign over the reception desk read: "Pre-payment Required."

Contrary to the interpretation that Manuel had chosen an obscure hospital because he had something to hide, Luciana Cabarga, a film production manager and location scout—and Manuel and Malé's closest friend in town—explained to me that the clinic they chose was then the best in Cuernavaca for surgery.[24] Because of its location in Las Palmas, an old exclusive residential neighborhood where Lucy lived, Manuel chose it also as a convenience for her, so that she would be able to accompany Malé to the hospital every day. The problem was, as Javier, Miguel, and other Mexican friends insisted, that the only hospital in the whole country to be trusted was El Angel in Mexico City; Javier and Miguel argued with Manuel and offered to arrange everything with their doctors. But worried about leaving Malé alone in Cuernavaca, Manuel did not want to drag her to Mexico City either, and he was much more afraid, he told them, of being operated on in Mexico City because of the altitude and because of his previous frightening experiences there with high blood pressure and heart palpitations.

Parsimony (or at least bargain hunting) might also have played a role in Manuel's delay, and, as Guillermo Cabrera Infante commented with tart rigor, Manuel's fatal flaw was "not his limp wrist but his tight fist." Hugo

Gutiérrez Vega agrees reluctantly, adding, "Manuel still thought of himself as a young person" (relative to Malé, certainly) and "did not consider a gallbladder operation to be that serious." We do think of gallbladder surgery as fairly routine, but any long operation under anesthesia is potentially dangerous. One need only recall Andy Warhol's startling post-operative death in New York (due to mismanaged private care) after gallbladder surgery or, more recently, jazz drummer Tony Williams's death at fifty-one of a heart attack, two days after gallbladder surgery in San Francisco.[25]

After Manuel's death, rumors continued to multiply: conjectures that he was, at the very least, HIV positive but didn't know it, and that the doctors at the Central Quirúrgica hadn't known it either until it was too late. The international gay community rallied around the rumor disseminated by *Christopher Street* that the death had been hush-hush because the Mexican doctors—consistent with the Latino reluctance to admit to this stigma-tainted disease—had mistreated him upon discovering "AIDS complications" and, naturally, his Argentine family did not want it known: "Manuel Puig's death from AIDS complications . . . is symptomatic of the more general and universal repudiation of AIDS."[26] The fact that AIDS had afflicted several of Manuel's friends, who were also hermetically discreet about their illness, contributed to these rumors and allegations; around the time of Manuel's death Nestor Almendros was diagnosed with the plague and he kept it secret until his death, in 1992. Shortly after Manuel died, AIDS victim Reinaldo Arenas, in an advanced stage of illness, committed suicide. With all his friends gone, Severo Sarduy, terrified, knew his turn was next; his last writings bravely and meticulously confronted his own personal struggle with the virus.[27] Manuel had been invited and had agreed (according to Manrique) to participate in a PEN Club AIDS benefit—why else would Manuel, not famous for excessive altruism (according to Manrique), invest his time?

In Mexico, Ulalume González de León's version of Manuel's death was perhaps the most delirious: Manuel moved to Cuernavaca to flee from a group of Nazis in Buenos Aires who were persecuting him; these people infiltrated the shady clinic and had him killed. "If right-wing political fanatics were after Manuel," her fellow poet Manuel Ulacia remarked wryly, "Cuernavaca would hardly protect him." Silence in the Mexican press in the months after his death could be attributed to homophobia or machismo—

or possibly a more subliminal factor: Manuel was seen as almost an honorary gringo, an Argentine queer identified with Hollywood, an image that could easily provoke those with anti-Yankee proclivities. That his death was politicized by gay groups and other factions might have elicited a chuckle from Manuel in the afterlife: politics is in every corner of our lives; nothing's sacred, especially not death. Beyond Hugo Gutiérrez's testimony that Manuel had tested negative in 1986, acquaintances like Renata Schussheim and Felisa Pinto insist on AIDS as a remote possibility because of Manuel's hygienic fussiness. Besides, he did not deny the existence of AIDS, or his great fear of it, which he mentioned frequently in personal letters.

For whatever reason, says Carlos, Manuel suffered from pulmonary complications after the operation; Carlos heard this from both Aldo Navarro (the family solicitor in Cuernavaca) and Lucy Cabarga, whose account of his last days strikes me as the most coherent and detailed, thus far: "He initially recovered normally from the surgery, but he felt a sharp persistent pain in his throat; at first this seemed normal, a possible irritation from the anesthesia. But two days later it persisted, and he felt it [sic] too painful to eat." Lucy brought him honey and honey drops, hoping that they would soothe the soreness in his throat. She and Malé told the nurses to bring Manuel something he liked that was soft, like mashed potatoes, one of his favorite foods from childhood. This would be his last meal: at 9 p.m. on Saturday he could eat only four spoonfuls because the pain was so great. Lucy told him that she would bring papaya the next morning.

Two hours after Manuel swallowed the four spoonfuls of mashed potato, he suddenly began to choke and gasp; the staff rushed him into the operating room and attempted to respirate him, but his lungs were flooded and he had a heart attack. His heart stopped and this time there was no bringing him back; for Manuel, amid the palms, site of the final dream of desire and death in *Kiss of the Spider Woman*, the dawn never came again. At 4:55 a.m. on July 22, 1990, he was pronounced dead.

epilogue

"Maybe I shouldn't have taken him to the movies so much . . ."
—Malé Puig to a friend, 1998

When Lucy Cabarga drove to the funeral home in Cuernavaca later that morning, she found that she would only be allowed to enter in the company of the immediate family—and the coffin was like a jewel case, closed. After Javier had telephoned Carlos in Buenos Aires—eighty-three-year-old Malé was in a deep state of shock and would remain so for weeks—Carlos booked the next available flight and arrived in Mexico twenty-four hours after Manuel's death. Miguel Sabido made hasty use of his gifts as a stage director and orchestrated the modest ceremony, arranging Manuel's books around the foot of the coffin. Manuel's body had been injected with Formol so that, following Carlos's initial decision, it would be preserved for the voyage south, to the family plot in La Plata.

Javier had also notified the Argentine embassy in Mexico City, but the ambassador, Abelardo Ramos, a Peronist-Leninist, showed little interest. In her bereavement Malé remarked: "Just as well, better that the Peronists didn't come." However, as soon as SOGEM, the General Society of Mexican Writers, got wind of the sad event, the Argentine official changed his tune and sent an Argentine flag to honor the writer at the SOGEM library on Calle José María Velasco in Mexico City. Carlos and Javier accompanied the corpse in the funeral cortege from Cuernavaca, up the winding highway to the capital. The ceremony at the library was a distinguished affair, attended by many of Manuel's friends in high social and cultural circles, among them

Elena Urrutia; writers José Emilio Pacheco, Carlos Monsiváis, Vicente Leñero, Augusto Monterroso; theater people such as Rodolfo Echavarría Alvarez and Miguel Sabido, Gonzalo Vega and Hector Gómez (the actors who played Valentín and Molina in Ripstein's stage production); as well as several Argentines residing in Mexico at the time, including Tununa Mercado, Noé Jitrik, and set designer Eduardo Rossi. Unlike Abelardo Ramos, José María Fernández Unsaín, another Argentine in Mexico and president of the writers' guild, was an affectionate fan of Manuel's and created a friendly, almost homey atmosphere as Manuel's body lay in state, and writers and actors read pages of his works. Miguel Sabido insisted they open the part of the coffin that covered his smooth, serene face, "to show the world that he didn't have AIDS." Fernández Unsaín conversed with Manuel, gazing down at him: "Remember those times," he began gently, reminiscing over past dinner parties and good moments they had shared.

In order to take Manuel's remains back to Argentina, the family would have to return to Buenos Aires immediately, and Carlos was afraid Malé would not survive the stress of the trip. She had lost over ten pounds, still could not believe that her beloved son was dead, and kept repeating, "I won't take him back to Buenos Aires. I'll stay here with him." After the funeral Carlos explained to her that they could not return immediately to Buenos Aires: they had to settle Manuel's affairs and liquidate his assets, pack up and move his furniture and his worldly possessions back to their two apartments in Argentina. Manuel had died intestate, which made this process even more complicated. After Manuel had been dead for a week, Carlos realized that time was not on his side, and that they would not be able to travel with the body. After deciding on cremation, he and Javier accompanied Manuel's remains to the Panteón de Dolores, an enormous crematorium and cemetery overlooking the vast urban landscape of Mexico City. They brought the urn to Malé, who was in Sally Sloan's care; Sally hosted both Carlos and Malé at her house in San Angel Inn over the next six months while they stayed in Mexico. Cousin Jorge also made the trip to Mexico a few times, to keep Malé company when Carlos needed to return to Buenos Aires.

The urn that contains Manuel's ashes still stands on a mahogany shelf in the darkened study on Charcas Street in Malé's apartment, next to the desk where Manuel used to write. Beside it is a photo of Manuel in his early thirties, sitting at his desk, intensely hunched over a manuscript. Throughout his adult life, Manuel worried about his mother's health at least as much as he worried about his own—a preoccupation that surfaced throughout his writing, from the first novel to the last—and the cruel irony for both is that she outlived him. Now the City of Eternal Spring, the city of Manuel's death, had left him relatively young in her memory.

Manuel's work in progress at the time of his death included over twenty un-produced plays and screenplays; he stepped out of the limelight at the height of his global success. As his movie rights and theatrical agent Mitch Douglas told me, if he had lived, Manuel—up until then a bit player in the Holly-wood machine—would have earned more than he had ever earned in his entire career; moreover, the musical would have given him carte blanche for future projects both in Hollywood and on Broadway.

Two years after his death, *Kiss*, the musical, created by Terrence McNally, with music by John Kander and lyrics by Fred Ebb, opened with Chita Rivera. It was an instant Broadway hit and continued to be so for three years, later featuring Vanessa Williams and in March 1995 the Cuban-born Venezuelan soap star María Conchita Alonso. Thanks to Canadian producer Garth Drabinsky, the project did not die in Purchase; Drabinsky had given Hal Prince and his team a year to work on it, and by May 1991 he definitively committed his support. In toto, the producer was to spend, as the show evolved in production changes from Toronto to London and finally to New York City, seven and a half million dollars; only after the Tony Awards in the show's second year did he begin to earn back his in-vestment.

While Manuel had aesthetic reservations about the movie that made him famous, he would have probably gotten a huge kick out of the musical's glamour, ultra-kitsch extravagances, and Chita Rivera as the star. He might have even preferred, like Javier, the sexy younger female leads over veteran Chita—certainly he would have chuckled over the Venezuelan soap star's name Conchita—in venereal Argentine vernacular, "pussy." Javier Labrada (who saw the show on Broadway several times) said Vanessa was what was needed; she had everything Chita had and besides she was (young and) sexy. When María Conchita Alonso played Aurora, she was such a celebrity in

Venezuela that Venezuelan tourists bought weekend trips to New York that included tickets to *Kiss*.

Not only was the time ripe for a musical about a gay romance, but, by the nineties, the musical as a form had arrived at a self-reflective, postmodern stage as a cultural phenomenon which, like Hollywood, had been marked significantly from its very beginnings by gay talent and sensibility. *Kiss* spoke more directly than any other musical about "why gay men love musical theater, the uses of fantasy in gay culture, the invention of an alternate universe . . . Like Marxist Utopias, musicals imagine a better world" to live for rather than die for.[28] But Aurora (Dawn or Argentine transvestite) in her black widow's web also, ultimately, personified Death. The musical, more skeletal than the play or the film, in a way telescopes Manuel's odyssey from womb to urn, traces the labyrinth of this Theseus entrapped rather than liberated by Ariadne's thread. Death is the universal end but also the only path for one who, in some recondite zone of his psyche, cannot accept himself. Whether or not they did so intentionally, the creators of the musical spotlighted the book's subliminal, driving metaphor: the kiss of death.

The musical played everywhere, from Tokyo to Vienna to Los Angeles, but, in Hal Prince's opinion, no version has been more affecting than the one he directed in Buenos Aires. At forty dollars a ticket—an extravagance in a country where the peso is equivalent to the dollar in name only—the Argentine *Kiss* that played on Corrientes (counterpart of Broadway in Buenos Aires) was a runaway success. Writer Pedro Orgambide's Spanish translation of McNally's and Ebb's text also seemed more poignant to me, especially the scene in which Molina worries about his mother's sorrow at his death, imagining that she is thinking "How can you die on me of a silly stomachache?" During my visit to Buenos Aires on that occasion I had seen the real-life Malé struggle to go on living without her beloved son. Even more intense were the stylized dances suggesting prison torture, not Broadway clichés but traces of recent Argentine history shown to an audience whose memory was still painfully raw. When at the end of the play the dancing prisoners stepped forward with photographs of the "disappeared"—among them a photo of the actor who plays the guerrillero Valentín—one heard weeping in the audience amid a numb silence. In Buenos Aires, the famous kiss between the two men was notably, and predictably, chaste. Unlike the Broadway embrace, the actors barely touched—Valentín ever so lightly touched Molina's shoulder; Molina even more lightly touched Valentín's face—and the lights immediately went down. Cut.

Manuel Puig, as Juan Goytisolo wrote in his obituary, was not only a great writer but a "tenacious defender of the rights of women and homosexuals in a ferociously macho world, who, with honesty and dignity, captured reality despite the mists of fear and the bandaged eyes of ideologies."[29] With similar zeal Severo Sarduy eulogized Manuel as the "strongest" of his generation, the one whose gift for parody enabled him to face, more squarely than any other writer, the daily tragedy of Latin America. César Aira, one of Argentina's most talented novelists today, considers Manuel Puig a mentor who made the novel more vividly a continuum of reality, a "fuller literary machine." Beyond most novelists of his time, Manuel could still generate engaging stories and interesting characters; he cleverly sideswiped the ennui of postmodernity in his resurrections of popular genres, and he also evaded the clichés of the Latin American novel (that is, magical realism) by affirming the everyday and not resorting to magic tricks.[30]

Toto discovered "cinema paradiso" years before Tornatore's film, and stepped into the celestial sphere of movie stars decades before Mia Farrow's adventure with "explorer and poet" Tom Baxter in *The Purple Rose of Cairo*; Valentín found liberation in Molina's film tales before a glamour-girl poster became the threshold to a man's freedom in *Shawshank Redemption*.[31] Manuel was a writer ahead of his time, whose fictions foretold that the total fiction machine—the media—would not only consummate art as we have known it but would absorb all that we call reality.[32] Manuel's vision was deeply ambiguous, or rather *irreducible*, like those images or virtual existences he glimpsed in the fleeting, phantasmal experience of the movies: you return to the scene in a text by Puig you thought was there and it has vanished, as when you return to a moment you remember seeing in a movie, only to find that your memory was false. As a kind of double agent or spy (as Argentine writer Alan Pauls noted), both inside and outside literature, Manuel had almost rendered the critics, who haunted his steps, obsolete. With a naughty wink to his readers, he was always one step ahead. And though the spider woman's bite was deadly, Molina survives.

published works of manuel puig

NOVELS

La traición de Rita Hayworth. Buenos Aires: Jorge Alvarez, 1968.
Boquitas pintadas. Folletín. Buenos Aires: Sudamericana, 1969.
The Buenos Aires Affair: Novela policial. Buenos Aires: Sudamericana, 1973.
El beso de la mujer araña. Barcelona: Seix Barral, 1976.
Pubis angelical. Barcelona: Seix Barral, 1979.
Maldición eterna a quien lea estas páginas. Translated into Spanish by the author. Barcelona: Seix Barral, 1980.
Sangre de amor correspondido. Barcelona: Seix Barral, 1982.
Cae la noche tropical. Barcelona: Seix Barral, 1988.

PLAYS AND SCREENPLAYS

Bajo un manto de estrellas (two-act play) / *El beso de la mujer araña.* Stage adaptation by the author. Barcelona: Seix Barral, 1983.
La cara del villano / Recuerdo de Tijuana (screenplays). Barcelona: Seix Barral, 1985.
Vivaldi: A Screenplay (excerpt). In *Review of Contemporary Fiction* (Naperville, Ill.) 11, no. 3 (Fall 1991), 177–81.
Tango delle Ore Piccole. Translation of *Gardel, uma Lembrança* by Angelo Morino. Ed. Angelo Morino. Milan: Einaudi, 1993.
"Ball Cancelled," "Verano entre paredes," "La tajada," ms., in *Materiales iniciales para La traición de Rita Hayworth.* Ed. José Amícola and Graciela Goldchluk. La Plata: Centro de Estudios y Teoria Literaria, 1996. 27–230.
El misterio del ramo de rosas. Rosario: Beatriz Viterbo Editores, 1997.
La tajada; Gardel, uma Lembrança. Rosario: Beatriz Viterbo Editores, 1997.

MISCELLANY

"Growing Up at the Movies: A Chronology." *Review* 71/72 (New York, 1972), 49–51.
"Author and Translator: On Heartbreak Tango" (with Suzanne Jill Levine). *Translation* 2, no. 1–2 (1974), 32–41.
"Puig por Puig." *Zona Franca* 51–54 (May–June 1977), 49–54.
"Síntesis y análisis: Cine y literatura." *Revista de la Universidad de México* 37, no. 8 (December 1981), 2–4.

"Losing Readers in Argentina." *Index on Censorship* 14, no. 5 (October 1985), 55–57.
"El error gay." *El Porteño* (Buenos Aires) (September 1990), 32–33.
Gli occhi di Greta Garbo. Milan: Leonardo, 1991. Written by the author in Italian, translated posthumously as *Los ojos de Greta Garbo.* Barcelona: Seix Barral, 1993.
Estertores de una década: Nueva York '78: Bye-Bye Babilonia, 1969–70. Buenos Aires: Seix Barral, 1993. (Edited posthumously by the Estate of Manuel Puig.)
"La voz de una mujer," in J. Amícola, "El escritor argentino y la tradición borgeana" with the title "Recuerdo de Borges." *Espacios* (Buenos Aires 15) (December 1994–March 1995), 24.

Works in English

Betrayed by Rita Hayworth. Suzanne Jill Levine, tr. New York: Dutton, 1971.
Heartbreak Tango: A Serial. Suzanne Jill Levine, tr. New York: Dutton, 1973.
The Buenos Aires Affair: A Detective Novel. Suzanne Jill Levine, tr. New York: Dutton, 1976.
Kiss of the Spider Woman. Thomas Colchie, tr. New York: Knopf, 1979.
Eternal Curse on the Reader of These Pages. New York: Random House, 1982.
"The Black Detective," "The Sado-Masoch Blues," and "Classical Farrah." In *My Deep Dark Pain Is Love: A Collection of Gay Fiction.* Winston Leyland, ed., E. A. Lacey, tr. San Francisco: Gay Sunshine, 1983. 71–76. (Short stories from *Estertores de una década.*)
Blood of Requited Love. Jan L. Grayson, tr. New York: Vintage (Random House), 1984.
Under a Mantle of Stars: A Play in Two Acts. Ronald Christ, tr. New York: Lumen Books, 1985.
Pubis Angelical. Elena Brunet, tr. New York: Vintage (Random House), 1986.
The Kiss of the Spider Woman. In *Contemporary Drama: Latin America—Plays by Manuel Puig, Antonio Skármeta, Mario Vargas Llosa, Carlos Fuentes.* George W. Woodyard and Marion Peter Holt, eds. English adaptation by Michael Feingold. New York: PAJ Publications, 1986. 19–61.
Kiss of the Spider Woman: The Screenplay. Adapted by Leonard Schrader. Boston: Faber & Faber, 1987.
Kiss of the Spider Woman and Two Other Plays. New York: W. W. Norton, 1994.
Mystery of the Rose Bouquet. Allan J. Baker, tr. Boston/London: Faber & Faber, 1988.
"Cinema and the Novel." In *On Modern Latin American Fiction.* John King, ed. New York: Hill and Wang, 1989. 283–90.
"The Usual Suspects." Alfred J. MacAdam, tr. *Review* 44 (January-June 1991), 75–77. First published in *Chorus* (Italy), no. 8, September 1990, then in *Gli Occhi di Greta Garbo.*
"Relative Humidity 95%." In *A Hammock Beneath the Mangoes.* Thomas Colchie, ed., Andrew Hurley, tr. New York: Dutton, 1991. 66–77.
Tropical Night Falling. Suzanne Jill Levine, tr. New York: Simon & Schuster, 1991.

KEY TO ABBREVIATIONS

ERM   Emir Rodríguez Monegal
GCI   Guillermo Cabrera Infante
HM   Howard Mandelbaum
HT   Heartbreak Tango
MF   Mario Fenelli
MI   Materiales iniciales
MP   Manuel Puig
PA   Pubis Angelical
RC   Ronald Christ
RH   Betrayed by Rita Hayworth
SJL   Suzanne Jill Levine
SS   Severo Sarduy
SW   Kiss of the Spider Woman
TBAA   The Buenos Aires Affair

INTRODUCTION

1. The official words uttered upon Evita Perón's death in 1952.
2. Mike Deaver, *Behind the Scenes* (New York: Morrow, 1987), 101.
3. Olga Nolla, Manuel Ramos, and Manuel Puig, "Escritura y ensoñación," *Cupey: Revista de la Universidad Metropolitana* 5, no. 1-2 (September 1988), 64.
4. *International Herald Tribune*, August 14, 1985, 11.
5. See chapters 1–2, "Mita's Parents' Place, La Plata, 1933," and "At Berto's, Vallejos, 1933." And we "hear"—in chapter 4—only Choli's side of the conversation, from which we can infer Mita's omitted responses.
6. Some of his gay friends in Argentina insisted that I eschew his sexual life, as if it were nonessential to his identity.

PART I
THE PAMPA . . . PROMISES: 1932–49

GREEN PAMPAS, ARID PAMPAS
1. *RH*, 8.
2. Teresa Cristina Rodríguez, "Manuel Puig—O Rio è o verdadeiro paraiso terrestre, sonho de beleza e humanismo," *O Globo*, August 30, 1981, 8.

3. In 1937, Argentines owned more autos proportionately than the inhabitants of Great Britain and, with the exception of Switzerland and Hungary, had the highest number of doctors per capita.

4. Conversation with Alda (Bebé) Cortés, November 1995.

5. Letter from Bebé to SJL, July 1996.

6. *RH*, 82.

7. Interview, *Panorama*, August 26, 1969.

8. Excerpts (my translation) from his early draft of *RH* with the provisional title *Pájaros en la cabeza* (Birds in the Head), in *MI*.

MALÉ AND THE DELLEDONES

9. Alan Pauls, upon visiting Manuel in Rio de Janeiro in 1987.

10. "Russians" and "Turks" usually meant, respectively, Ashkenazi and Sephardic Jews, or, in general, Eastern Europeans and Middle Easterners. Between the years 1870 and 1940 immigrants represented 70 percent of the population in the capital and almost half in the provinces. Gino Germani, *Política y sociedad en una epoca de transición* (Buenas Aires: Paidos, 1968), 179.

11. Manuel alludes to the Delledonnes' sensitivity in the first chapter of *RH*, where (Clara's son) Ernestito expresses concern for the chicken Grandpa is about to slaughter.

12. *MI*, 243.

13. *MI*, 241.

14. *MI*, 238–39.

15. *MI*, 252.

16. *MI*, 236.

17. *MI*, 259.

18. *RH*, 7.

19. *MI*, 242–43.

20. *MI*, 254–55.

21. *MI*, 256.

22. A curious synchronicity is worth noting: the unknown columnist JLB in *El Hogar*, responsible for the section Foreign Authors and Books, would become Argentina's most famous author, Jorge Luis Borges.

23. *RH*, 87.

BALDO AND THE PUIGS

24. *RH*, 81.

25. *RH*, 220.

26. SJL's conversations with family members.

27. *MI*, 250–53.

28. *MI*, 252.

MADE AT THE MOVIES

Epigraph: Margaret Mead, "Tchambuli: Sex and Temperament," *Blackberry Winter: My Earlier Years* (New York: William Morrow, 1972), 230.

29. MP, "Growing Up at the Movies," *Review 71/72* (New York, 1972), 49.

30. George Hadley-Garcia, *Hispanic Hollywood* (New York: Citadel Press, 1990), 106. Latin America, then 10 percent of the world's population, constituted 20 percent of the foreign market royalties for American films.

31. Marysa Navarro, *Evita* (Buenos Aires: Planeta, 1994), 35–37.

32. Jorge Luis Borges, "On Dubbing," in *Borges in/and/on Film*, ed. Edgardo Cozarinsky, tr. Gloria Waldman and Ronald Christ (New York: Lumen, 1981), 62. Borges quips that dubbing creates "monsters who combine the well-known features of Greta Garbo with the voice of Aldonza Lorenzo . . . The voice of Hepburn or Garbo is not accidental; it is, for the whole world, one of their defining attributes. Similarly, it is worth remembering that miming is different in English than in Spanish."

33. The musical had begun to blossom in the Great Depression, as had the big band: musicians were cheap and many could be employed for little. *Some Like It Hot* (1959), one of the few "brilliant" post-golden-age films, in Manuel's view, recalls those hard times in clever slapstick: in this gender-bending farce, directed by Billy Wilder, two musicians trying to flee Chicago after they unwittingly witness the St. Valentine's Day Massacre, Joe (Jack Lemmon) and Jerry (Tony Curtis), are so desperate for work that they disguise themselves as "Daphne" and "Geraldine" to join a women's band.

34. See Jeanine Basinger, *A Woman's View: How Hollywood Spoke to Women, 1930–60* (New York: Knopf, 1993), *passim*.

35. RC, "Last Interview with Manuel Puig," *World Literature Today* (Autumn 1991), 577–78.

36. Basinger, *A Woman's View*, 112.

37. Another actress (aside from Dietrich, Garbo, Rosalind Russell, Tallulah Bankhead) who was bisexual (offstage) was Claudette Colbert, rumored to have beautiful young women companions. (According to Manuel, these actresses changed orientation as they grew older and became bored or disillusioned with men.) But although Colbert was quite pleasant in early comedies, she was the most limited of the stars, according to Manuel, and had only three facial expressions—which he, of course, could imitate.

38. Obituary of Greer Garson, *The New York Times*, April 7, 1996, 27. Her most famous role was Mrs. Miniver in 1942; other favorites of Manuel were *Blossoms in the Dust* (1941), *Madame Curie* (1943), *The Valley of Decision* (1945), where she plays a spunky Irish maid, and the lighthearted *Julia Misbehaves* (1948).

39. *Cartas de Manuel Puig,* published posthumously as "Bye-Bye Babilonia," in *Estertores de una década: Nueva York '78,* 113–14. After the publication of his first two novels he was invited by *Siete Días Ilustrados* (Buenos Aires cultural weekly) to contribute these chronicles of cinema and theater from Paris, London, and New York in 1969–70. While these campy letters did not aspire to serious criticism, they are

filled with judicious glimpses. In Paris he attended a revival of old American movies, rushing to see Rogers-Astaire in *Carefree*: "Finger-licking good: dialogue, music, choreography, sets, costumes, everything. Harvest of *36*," Manuel wrote, recapping the "glorious" Astaire-Rogers years from *Roberta* (1935) to *Irene and Vernon Castle* (1939). He advised: "It's not necessary to speak about Astaire, still well remembered, but his female lead needs to be properly credited, a charming pretty blonde who sang well and danced better; Astaire in his contract had 10 more close-ups per film than Ginger, and a dance number as soloist."

40. Basinger, *A Woman's View*, 195.

41. Xavier Labrada, interviewed by SJL, Mexico City, 1996.

42. *RH*, 34.

43. In *RH*, one can find a direct allusion to this incident: Lonely in boarding school and missing his mother, Toto writes a "school composition" (chapter 13) about *The Great Waltz*, "the movie I liked best," but he changes the plot. In the film Johann Strauss is torn between the love of two women, his faithful wife (Rainer) and a beautiful singer, Carla (Miliza Korjus). Toto's version subtly switches the principal triangle, and Carla's lover, the villainous Duke (Lionel Atwill), a secondary player, takes on a principal role as sinister father figure who steals her away from the younger, weaker man (Johann): an Oedipal triangle, it would appear, that suggests Coco's as well.

BLOOD AND SAND

44. MP's first TV interview, on *Identikit*, with Torre Nilsson (Buenos Aires, 1974): also Armando Almada Roche, *Cuando será el día que me quieras: Conversaciones con Manuel Puig* (Buenos Aires: Vinciguerra, 1992), 95.

45. *RH*, 42.

46. *RH*, 93.

47. *RH*, 59, 65.

48. *RH*, 121.

49. Germán García, a psychiatrist who left behind his career as novelist to direct the Freudian school in Buenos Aires, remembers Manuel explaining to him that when he realized he no longer *had* his mother, at age four or six—"sus gracias ya no le hacía gracia"—he realized that he had transitioned from wanting to have her to wanting to *be* her.

50. *MI*, 274. The horror film has been, by and large, a camp genre; *Frankenstein* and its sequel, for example, were directed by James Whale, one of many closeted gay artists in pre-Stonewall Hollywood.

51. MP, *Blood of Requited Love*, 27.

SIESTA TIME

52. Conversation with Ernesto Camoglio in La Plata, October 1995.

53. *RH*, 29, 58.

54. Based in part on statements by MP in Almada Roche, *Cuando será el día*, 95.

55. Ibid., 19.

56. Ibid., 92.
57. *RH*, 68.
58. *RH*, 32.
59. See *RH*, 94, for the fictionalized scene.
60. *MI*, 256.
61. *RH*, 10.
62. *RH*, 57.

I WAS NUMBER ONE AT SCHOOL
63. Almada Roche, *Cuando será el día*, 95.
64. *RH*, 140.
65. Almada Roche, *Cuando será el día*, 95. This interview contains some of Manuel's most explicit public statements about childhood experiences; his brother Carlos has suggested that this source is unreliable.

THE VALLEY OF DECISION
66. *MI*, 276.
67. Basinger, *A Woman's View*, 481–84.
68. MP to Malé, December 4, 1965.
69. *PA*, 60. I have slightly altered the translation.
70. Interview with her nephew, journalist Marcos Barnatán.
71. Toto tells Esther, in *RH*, 196, "You can't talk about anything with [girls his age], they're too young."
72. *TBAA*, 81.
73. Nolla, Ramos, and Puig, "Escritura y ensoñación," 76.
74. Ibid., 77.
75. Ibid.
76. MP, "Growing Up at the Movies," 50.

Part II
A Writer Is Born: 1950–61

BUENOS AIRES: AN AFFAIR TO REMEMBER
1. *La princesa que quería vivir* was the Spanish title.
2. *Éramos poco, y parió la abuela*, meaning, "as if we didn't have enough problems . . . ," was the remark uttered, according to Bebé.
3. He alludes to this episode in *TBAA*: Leo, the protagonist, is also a dropout from the School of Architecture.
4. MP, "Growing Up at the Movies: A Chronology," *Review* 71/72, 51.
5. Susan Sontag's apt alliteration alludes to the perverse erotic appeal of fascism, and also to its authoritarian attraction as an orderly antidote to social, economic, and political chaos.
6. Pamela Bacarisse, "Nationalism and Cultural Dependence," *Impossible Choices* (Calgary, Alberta: University of Calgary Press, 1993), 95–96.

7. Juan José Sebreli, *Buenos Aires: Vida cotidiana y alienación* (Buenos Aires: Ediciones Siglo Veinte, 1964), 71.

8. 1974; *Borges in/and/on Film*, ed. Edgardo Cozarinsky, tr. Gloria Waldman and Ronald Christ (New York: Lumen Books, 1988).

9. Author of late-nineteenth-century classics *The Moonstone* and *The Woman in White*.

10. MP, "Un recuerdo de Borges," ed. J. Amícola, *Revista Espacios* (Buenos Aires), no. 15 (March 1995), 25.

11. *TBAA*, 93.

12. One possible etymology of the term *camp* can be traced to Middle English *cam*, meaning "crooked" or "bent."

13. Wayne Koestenbaum, *The Queen's Throat: Opera, Homosexuality and the Mystery of Desire* (New York: Vintage, 1993); Christopher Isherwood, *The World in the Evening: A Novel* (London: Methuen, 1954), 126.

14. Koestenbaum, *The Queen's Throat*, 117.

15. *TBAA*, 81.

16. *TBAA*, 88.

17. Leo's grotesque character, beginning with his Russian name (common in melting pot Buenos Aires), seems partly a joke based on Manuel's adolescent "Russian" readings, such as Dostoevsky's *Crime and Punishment*, fraught with patricidal murderers and political hysterics.

18. *TBAA*, 91.

19. His glamour-tinged "Hitchcockian" (as he called it) English title also alluded to *A Foreign Affair* (1948), one of the few sophisticated postwar Hollywood comedies, about the American occupation of Germany. An older and even wiser Marlene Dietrich plays an ex-Nazi grande dame who is now a cabaret singer, a kind of composite of Hitler's pet filmmaker Leni Riefenstahl and France's Arletty, who was later disgraced for having been the mistress of a Nazi officer.

20. Armando Almada Roche, *Cuando será el día que me quieras: Conversaciones con Manuel Puig* (Buenos Aires: Vinciguerra, 1992), 33–34.

21. From my conversations with MP in the early seventies.

22. *TBAA*, 86.

23. *TBAA*, 92.

24. Tomás Eloy Martínez, "Manuel Puig: La muerte no es un adiós," *La Nación: Sección Cultura* (Buenos Aires), September 7, 1997, 2.

25. Jorge Salessi, "Medics, Crooks, and Tango Queens," *Every Night Life: Culture and Dance in Latin/o America* (Durham, N.C.: Duke University Press, 1997), 148–51. La Boca was "the mouth" of lust but also of "pederasty" and other polymorphous sexualities, fed by the white slave trade of foreign prostitutes (many of whom were lesbians) and "invaded" by Jewish and Italian men. All these "inverts" were also subversives threatening the hygiene and security of the state. Such a venereal hotbed had to be policed; like most societies, the Argentine *criollos* were xenophobic and associated foreigners with both moral and physical filth: the sexual was, implicitly, political.

26. Almada Roche, *Cuando será el día*, 99–100.

27. Germán Puig cites a comic version of this phrase, singing the lines from a famous bolero, "Only once in my life I loved," and replacing "loved" with "sucked": "Solamente una vez, *mamé* en la vida."

ESCAPE TO CINECITTÀ, OR HOLLYWOOD, ITALIAN STYLE

28. Anthony Quinn's memoir, *One Man's Tango*, quoted in *Roger Ebert's Book of Film* (New York: W. W. Norton, 1997), 504.

29. Moravia's famous novel *The Conformist*, in which a closet homosexual conforms to the fascist state to atone for his sexual guilt, would appear to be a precursor for Manuel's *The Buenos Aires Affair*, where fascist (Peronist) politics and homosexual guilt are interwoven in the actions of Leo, a psychopath.

30. Daniel Yakir, "Manuel Puig," in *Interview*, September 1985, 207.

31. MP to Malé, February 1957.

32. George Stevens, for example, was a great Hollywood director from the thirties (*Alice Adams*; *Swing Time*), but in Manuel's view his later work—aside from his somber masterpiece in 1951, *A Place in the Sun*, based on Dreiser's *American Tragedy* and enhanced by the beauty of Elizabeth Taylor and Montgomery Clift—was disappointing.

33. He saw Leander once in a personal appearance in Buenos Aires, in 1950. Aside from a small contingency of native *porteños*, the theater was packed with Nazi refugees to whom Perón had opened Argentina, journalist Felisa Pinto recalls: the event was both fascinating and horrifying, "pure kitsch." As the Swedish-born diva glided across the stage in a glistening green evening gown, the audience of Germanophiles gave her a standing ovation.

34. Nora Catelli, "Entrevista con Manuel Puig: Una narrativa de lo melifluo," *Quimera* (Madrid), no. 18 (April 1982), 22.

35. "Retrato del novelista desconocido," *Primera Plana*, no. 226 (April 25, 1967), 66.

36. Letters to Malé, in the sixties and the eighties.

37. Gustavo García and Andrés de Luna, "Rock, arañas, nenonas y manuelas: Manuel Puig en Nueva York," *Revista de la Universidad de México* 33, no. 7 (1978), 26.

38. Catelli, "Entrevista con Manuel Puig," 22.

39. Nestor Almendros, "El cine: Arquetipo literario," in *Manuel Puig: La semana de autor: April 24–27, 1990*, ed. Juan Manuel García Ramos (Madrid: Ediciones de Cultura Hispánica, 1991), 78.

40. Nestor Almendros, *A Man with a Camera*, tr. Rachel Phillips Belash (New York: Farrar, Straus and Giroux, 1984), 31.

41. Ibid.

42. Whether he was thrifty or poor, neither condition was acceptable to his Italian peers. Schoo, several years later, was one of the first Argentine journalists to acknowledge the artistic worth of *RH*, but, perhaps out of envy, he did spread this tale around Buenos Aires. Manuel returned the favor by christening "prissy" Schoo "la gran señora"—or "the great lady."

43. Yakir, "Manuel Puig," 207.
44. From London (April 1959) he wrote: "Mamá, how could you not like *Et Dieu!*"
45. MP, *Los ojos de Greta Garbo: Relatos*, tr. J. Amícola (Barcelona: Seix Barral, 1993); *Gli occhi di Greta Garbo*, 1991. "My dearest Sphinx," an imagined dialogue between Greta Garbo and a dying Max Ophüls (the legendary director of *Lola Montes*), gave the book its title.
46. MP, "Los desconocidos de siempre," *Chorus* (Italy), no. 8 (September 1990), 152–55; translated as "The Usual Suspects," *Review* 44 (January-June 1991), 75–77.

A FRIENDSHIP IS BORN

47. Birri later directed a movie based on a story by Gabriel García Márquez. The Nobel Prize–winning Colombian author had also been a starving student at the Centro Sperimentale in 1954.
48. Without realizing that Henri Barbusse, a writer praised by Borges, had already used the same conceit in *L'Enfer*.
49. MP to MF, May 1960.
50. The Argentine brand of pig latin is called *vesre* (*revés*, the word for "backward," spelled reversing the syllable order). In *vesre* Cubchapi suggests "gachupín," a derogatory Spanish American term for Spaniard, like "greenhorn," but also "Topkapi"—hence a comic image of Nestor, whose dry reserve contrasted with his taste for hotblooded Arab and Turkish lovers. Like Nestor and many gay men, Mario was drawn to Turkey and North Africa for their tolerance of homosexuality, their low cost of living, and their beauty.
51. Bazzoni was "Geisha"—always serving tea when Manuel came to visit.
52. MP to Malé, December 8, 1956. The Argentine contingency included Orlando "Luigi" Berlingieri, and satirist Juan Rodolfo Wilcock, an acquaintance of Mario's, from the elite *Sur* circle. Wilcock moved to Italy in the late forties, legally adopted an Italian boy he named Livio Baccho, and by the fifties was writing poetry exclusively in Italian, mostly popular balladry. Wilcock was a friend of Italian poet and filmmaker Pier Paolo Pasolini, who cast him as Caifas in his *Gospel According to St. Matthew* (1966).
53. MP to MF, September 1963.
54. MF to SJL, 1996.

FIRST SCREENPLAY

55. Luis Buñuel's delirious Mexican version, *Abismos de Pasión* (1950), brought out the necrophiliac excess of Heathcliff's "undying" love for dead Cathy.
56. MP to Malé, June 28, 1957.
57. Optioned first by RAI 2 for Italian television. MP to Stephen Harvey, MoMA, from Ostia, Italy, August 3, 1979.
58. MP to Malé, August 10, 1957.
59. MP, "Growing Up at the Movies," 51.

ARRIVEDERCI, ROMA

60. MP to Malé, June 14, 1957.

61. MP, "Growing Up at the Movies," 51.

62. MP to Malé, November 18, 1957.

63. MP to Malé, December 4, 1957.

64. Juan Goytisolo, "Living in Turkey," *Space in Motion* (New York: Lumen Books, 1987), 44–55.

65. MP to Malé, January 8, 1958.

66. In a letter from Málaga (January 18, 1958) Manuel gives his younger brother his impressions of Spain, beginning with Valencia, where he arrived by boat from Majorca. The "real Spain began in Valencia with its lovely corners, fried-food vendors on cobblestone streets." From Valencia he took the train to Madrid, and saw a "fabulous landscape with changing colors; the province of Cuenca had a reddish hue."

67. A famous Spanish music hall and film actress whose name Concha ("Shell") is slang in Argentina for "cunt."

68. Here and elsewhere I have occasionally changed the names of Manuel's lovers to protect their privacy.

69. In *El Hogar* Borges first published his now famous "condensed biographies" of great modern writers; *Para Ti* and *Maribel* were popular women's magazines which provided some of the raw material—lonely-hearts letters, fashion ads—for Manuel's second novel, *Heartbreak Tango*.

LONDON, LONDON

70. MP to Malé, February 1958.

71. MP, *Estertores de una década*, 100.

72. In conversation with SJL, New York, 1973. Both (Manuel alleged) were well hung, especially Brynner; with Baker there was a *coup de foudre* in the Soho restaurant where Manuel washed dishes, followed by "fellatio, I knew him" in the loo.

73. MP to Malé, June 25, 1958.

74. MP to Malé, May 15, 1958.

75. MP to Malé, July 1, 1958.

76. MP to Malé, June 15, 1958.

77. MP to Malé, June 7 and 15, 1958. *The Journey* (1959) was a trite cold-war melodrama directed by Anatole Litvak, with Yul Brynner and Deborah Kerr. Olivier, Havelock's first choice, had rejected the role, which confirmed to "those in the know" that the script was a "big bore."

78. MP to Malé, June 15, 1958.

79. MP to Malé, August 18, 1958.

80. MP to Malé, July 1, 1958.

81. MP to Malé, August 18, 1958.

82. MP to Malé. Told to SJL in conversation.

83. MP to Malé, December 1958.

84. Gathered from my conversations with HM, with whom Manuel discussed actresses at great length.

85. MP to Malé, September 9, 1958.

86. Frondizi's presidency in 1958 opened Argentina to foreign investments and triggered runaway inflation, frozen salaries, and workers' strikes.

87. MP to Malé, April 18, 1959.

88. Ibid.

ASSISTANT TO THE ASSISTANT

89. MP to Malé, July 15, 1959.

90. Ibid.

91. *RH*, 72–73.

92. *RH*, 72.

93. MP to MF, May 1960.

94. MF to MP, August 1960.

95. MF to SJL, May 1995.

96. Borges and Bioy Casares describe a Peronist rally, in which a Jew is stoned to death, in "La fiesta del monstruo" (1946), and Cortázar alludes allegorically to an authoritarian takeover in "Casa tomada" (1951).

97. See Graciela Goldchluk, "La construcción de una poética. Apuntes sobre *La Tajada* de Manuel Puig," ms., 1996.

98. MF to SJL, 1995.

99. She and Pato separated two more times, but always got back together.

100. MP to Malé, May 9, 1961.

PART III
THE SAGA OF *RITA HAYWORTH*: 1962–67

"MOVIE CITY" ONCE MORE WITH FEELING

1. MP to Malé, May 9, 1961.

2. Ibid.

3. Among them, producer Giuseppe Scotese and actor Antonio Cifariello; MP to Malé, July 3, 1961.

4. MF to SJL, 1995.

5. MP to Malé, October 1961.

6. Blassetti was a minor director of comedies and spectacles. Manuel found *Senso*, like most of Visconti's work after the fifties, stilted and ponderous; a young film critic in Cuba, his future friend Guillermo Cabrera Infante, shared this opinion, titling his review of the film "Denso" (Dense).

7. MP to Malé, March 4, 1962.

8. MP to Malé, June 21, 1961.

9. MP to Malé, January 18, 1962.

10. MP to Malé, February 1962.

11. Ibid.

12. Ibid.

MARIO, MENTOR

13. MF to SJL, 1995.

14. Nestor Almendros pointed out, in the spring 1990 Semana de Autor colloquium in Madrid, that *RH* preceded Gore Vidal's *Myra Breckenridge* (though not Walker Percy's *The Moviegoer*).

15. MF to SJL, 1995.

16. MP, "Cinema and the Novel," 286–87. Here he sums up the differences between the two media from his experience as a writer and as a spectator; this piece was first published as Manuel's preface to two screenplays he did in Mexico: one was never produced, and the other was a flop, changed drastically by the director. He agreed to publish them so they wouldn't be a "total waste"—a futile experience familiar to so many screenwriters—and, partly as a retort, he explained why he had begun writing fiction: it was less frustrating for a writer, who had more control over his own creation.

17. A twenty-six-page monologue, it was called "Pájaros en la cabeza" because he claimed it was composed of "automatic writing," of "whatever came into my head." The birds in his head were the voice of Aunt Carmen, Malé's sister, a voice that in the novel evolved into a cornucopia of voices, like the lavish threads of Malé's embroideries.

18. "Gallery of voices" was how GCI described his own novel, *Tres tristes tigres*. ERM applied the term also to *RH*.

19. Katherine Bouman, "Manuel Puig at the University of Missouri–Columbia," *American Hispanist* 2, no. 7 (April 4, 1977), 11–12.

20. MF to SJL, 1995.

21. In his first interview MP describes MF as his most demanding reader and editor and, with gentle irony, as "a great writer who doesn't want to be known," "Retrato del novelista desconocido," *Primera Plana*, no. 226 (April 25, 1967), 66–67.

22. Interview, *La Jornada*, Mexico, 1989.

FROM "QUEEN" TO QUEENS

23. MP to MF, November 26, 1962.

24. Anecdote recalled by Alfredo Gialdini, 1995.

25. MP to MF, February 27, 1963.

26. MP, *Kiss of the Spider Woman and Two Other Plays* (New York: W. W. Norton, 1994), 64.

27. MP to Malé, April 23, 1963.

28. MP to Malé, March 15, 1963.

29. MP to Malé, March 26, 1963.

30. MP to Malé, April 6, 1963.

31. Telephone conversation with María Barceló in Miami, 1995.
32. MP to Malé, April 17, 1963.
33. Nestor Almendros's recollections in *Manuel Puig: La semana de autor* (Madrid: Ediciones de Cultura Hispánica, 1991), 78.
34. MP, "Growing Up at the Movies," 71–72.
35. Ray Milland was well cast, particularly because his smile often seemed an ironic grimace, as if his female co-star had body odor (in this film as well as others: Hitchcock put Milland's unpleasant smirk to good use in *Dial M for Murder*).
36. MP to Malé, May 31, 1965.
37. GCI, "In a Pampas of Dreams," *The Guardian* (London), July 25, 1990.
38. Alejandro Varderi, "Letter from Manhattan," ms., 1992, 7.
39. MP to Malé, April 23, 1963.
40. MP to family, March 18, 1964.
41. MP to Malé, March 29, 1964.
42. Ibid.
43. MP to MF, March 1964. *The Deep Blue Sea* (1955), directed by Anatole Litvak, was based on a play by Terence Rattigan.
44. MP to MF, September 1963.
45. MP to Malé, March 24, 1963.
46. MP to Malé, September 28, 1963.
47. *Cuando los duendes cazan perdizes.*
48. The allusion is to an actress who played in *Joan of Arc*. MP to MF, April 18, 1964.
49. MP to MF, July 1965.
50. Rosa Montero, interview, "Caracol sin Concha," *El País* (1988), 31.

BIRDS IN THE HEAD
51. *MI*, 292: here Paqui sneaks off to hotel trysts with the man of her dreams (a traveling salesman); her father finds out and berates her.
52. MP to MF, January 26, 1964.
53. For Manuel, "realist" Arlt was more artificial, paradoxically, than "elitist" Borges and Bioy Casares, self-mocking satirists (who wrote under the pseudonym Bustos Domecq).
54. MP to MF, February 14, 1964.
55. Poetry reciter Berta Singerman.
56. MP to MF, February 14, 1964.
57. *RH*, 222. Revised translation.
58. MP to Malé, July 7, 1964.
59. MP to MF, September 1964.
60. Ibid.
61. MP to ERM, September 28, 1966.

MANUSCRIPT TO MARKET
62. MP to Malé, March 8, 1965.
63. Ibid.

64. *RH*, 197–98.

65. Chapters "Toto" (5), "Delia," "Mita," "Hector," "Paquita," "Cobito," "Esther" (7–12) were sent to Mario in February 1965.

66. MP to Malé, April 10, 1965.

67. See excerpt in *A Hammock Beneath the Mangoes*, tr. Andrew Hurley, ed. Thomas Colchie (New York: Dutton, 1991), 71–77.

68. Another discarded title was "De ese encuentro" (About That Encounter).

69. Told to GCI by MP.

70. MP to Malé, November 7, 1965.

71. MP to Malé, January 1966.

72. Alastair Reid, "Borges and Neruda," *The New Yorker*, March 5, 1997, 50.

73. Juan Goytisolo, "Manuel Puig," *El bosque de las letras* (Madrid: Alfaguara, 1995), 119.

74. Ibid.

75. MP to Mario, November 1965.

76. MP to Malé, November 13, 1965.

77. Ibid.

78. Goytisolo, "Manuel Puig," 119–20.

79. Almendros, *Manuel Puig*, 140.

80. MP, "Growing Up at the Movies," 51.

81. MP to family, February 1966.

82. First Cristina Ocampo, the French-speaking Anglo-Argentine wife of artist Miguel Ocampo (a nephew of Victoria Ocampo), whom MP knew from Rome days, and who would soon move to New York as cultural attaché.

83. Puig family archive, Buenos Aires.

84. David Thomson, *A Biographical Dictionary of Film* (New York: Knopf, 1995), 780.

85. MP to Malé, December 4, 1965. He would quote a key dialogue from *Dishonored* in *The Buenos Aires Affair*.

86. MP to Malé, January 8, 1966.

87. MP to family, January 19, 1966.

88. MP to MF, February 1966.

89. See Jorge Luis Borges, "The Argentine Writer and Tradition," in *Selected Non-fictions of Jorge Luis Borges*, ed. E. Weinberger (New York: Viking Penguin, 1999).

90. February 24, 1966: "Dear Miss Hayworth . . . You're mentioned in Chapter 5, your appearance is brief but extremely important since it becomes the crucial moment in the child's relationship with his father. This man seems uninterested in the little boy, absorbed as he is in his troubling business affairs, despite the child's attempts to capture his attention. Chapter 5 is the big turning point in the novel because it's there that the child ceases looking for his father and starts to replace him with another . . . image. This is the actual development: the child always goes to the movies with his mother, his father refuses to come along since he can't concentrate on the film, obsessed as he is with financial interests.

   "But in Chapter 5 he goes to see 'Blood and Sand' with his wife and child and enjoys the film and the new star (yourself) tremendously: he promises to come back to the movies more often. This is a moment of happiness and fulfillment for the child. But his father fails to keep that promise and the child resents it to the point of rejecting him. He rejects his father and all that he represents; symbolically the child resents his father liking Rita–Doña Sol, who betrays Juan Gallardo in the film. And the fact of Doña Sol being evil but beautiful at the same time confuses the child even more. Because of this symbolic moment, the phrase 'la traición de Rita Hayworth' came up as a possible title. I had suggested the title to Seix Barral most timidly but everybody loved it right away. For them it's excitingly new in a 'pop-art' way. Mr. Barral mentioned too that he had met you in Barcelona and thought that you were a lovely person and that you wouldn't object to such a thing. Before anything else I would like to assure you that your name is used in the title only as a symbol of screen seduction and that the novel in no way deals with your personal life and neither does it attempt to evaluate you as an actress." Quoted from rough draft on a Pan Am World Airways form, courtesy of the Puig estate.

91. MP, "Losing Readers in Argentina," 55–57.

92. Goytisolo, "Manuel Puig," 120.

93. Tomás Eloy Martínez, "Manuel Puig: La muerte no es un adiós," *La Nación: Sección Cultura* (Buenos Aires), September 7, 1997, 2.

94. Responding to Manuel's emphasis on actresses, Guillermo fanatically followed a British TV series ". . . called Sex Goddesses," he wrote to MP, "where they've shown Jean Harlow (*Red Dust*), Marlene Dietrich (*The Shanghai Express*, which I enjoyed more than I've enjoyed any movie in a long time, really impressed by Marlene Dietrich's beauty and the beauty of the frame. Miriam says von Sternberg *had* to be gay . . . Your authorized opinion is needed.) and next week there's Mae West, in *She Done Him Wrong*" (November 30, 1972). (All letters, written in a mixture of Spanish and English, retain *errata intact*.)

95. *Tango versus Bolero*—title of a radio program in Argentina in the forties—never materialized as a musical, though Manuel mentions it in *HT*. Eventually Manuel wrote a tango musical about Gardel, as well as "Amor del Bueno," about a Mexican *ranchera* singer.

96. Successor to *Cuadernos*, dominated by Spanish Civil War exiles.

97. MP to MF, November 1966.

98. September 22, 1966; ERM's and GCI's correspondence cited courtesy of the authors as well as of the Manuscript Division, Department of Rare Books and Special Collections, Princeton University Library. This first article was "A Literary Myth Exploded," *Review 71/72* (New York, 1972), published originally in *Imagen* (Caracas) 34 (1968).

99. MP to MF, October 1966.

100. José Donoso, *The Garden Next Door* (New York: Grove Press, 1992), 5.

101. MP to ERM, February 16, 1971.

ROMANCE PERCHANCE?

102. Kendrick to MP, August 19, 1966. The Jamaican's name has been changed to protect his privacy.

103. Kendrick to MP, October 28, 1966.
104. MP to Malé, January 4, 1967.
105. MP to ERM, September 28, 1966.
106. MP to ERM, April 11, 1967.
107. MP to MF, January 1967.
108. MP to ERM, May 17, 1967.
109. Ibid.
110. MP to ERM, January 10, 1967.

PART IV
TWILIGHT OF THE SIXTIES: HIS BRILLIANT CAREER: 1968–73

FRONT PAGE IN SWINGING BUENOS AIRES

1. "Retrato del novelista desconocido," *Primera Plana* (Buenos Aires), no. 226 (April 25, 1967), 66–67; "Diario de Esther . . . ," *Primera Plana*, 72–73.
2. MP to ERM, April 11, 1967.
3. Ibid.
4. MP to ERM, May 17, 1967.
5. A snobbish dig from the vitriolic Uruguayan Juan Carlos Onetti, despite (or in sync with) his populist vein.
6. ERM to MP, April 4, 1967.
7. Sánchez, the same age as Manuel, best known for his novel *Siberia Blues*, soon fell into obscurity.
8. In his book about *The New Novel* (1967), Carlos Fuentes would emphasize that a new literary language, created in part out of Latin America's vital, diverse vernaculars, was the greatest invention of the Boom writers.
9. ERM, "Una cosecha incesante" (An Incessant Harvest), *Mundo Nuevo* (Paris) 10 (April 1967), 4.
10. MP to SS, March 27, 1967.
11. ERM, "El folletín rescatado" (The Dime Novel Salvaged), *Revista de la Universidad de México* (1972), 29–30.
12. Oscar José Canale, "La chismografía en un libro inútil y perfecto," *Crónicas* (General Villegas), July 11, 1970, 3.
13. Peter Bogdanovich, "Introduction," *Who the Devil Made It* (New York: Knopf, 1997), 33. The legendary German filmmaker (1892–1947) moved to Hollywood in the thirties.
14. From my interview of Germán García, director of the Villa Freud Institute in Buenos Aires, November 1994.
15. The Ford Foundation was apparently funneling this money to the magazine through the Paris office of CIA front ILARI, or Latin American Institute of International Relations.
16. César Fernández Moreno, one of Emir's closest friends, was the son of Argentine

poet Baldomero Fernández Moreno. A staunch supporter of the Cuban revolution, César, a versatile writer and distinguished-looking man, was a cultural attaché affiliated, the same years as Julio Cortázar, with UNESCO in Paris, where he lived until his death in 1986.

17. MP to ERM, June 2, 1967.
18. As part of an increasingly restrictive cultural policy, Fidel censored, early in 1961, a twenty-minute documentary about nightlife in post-revolution Cuba called *P.M.*, filmed by GCI's brother Sabá Cabrera and photographer Orlando Jiménez Leal.
19. GCI to MP, August 8, 1971.
20. MP to ERM, January 24, 1968. For a cogent synopsis of the chaotic political events in Argentina, from the mid-sixties coup by Onganía to the return of Perón in 1974, see Edwin Williamson, *The Penguin History of Latin America* (London: Penguin Books, 1992), 471–75.
21. MP to ERM, December 12, 1967. Olympe Bradna was a transient American leading lady, formerly a circus bareback rider, whose most memorable flick was *The Knockout* (1941), which Manuel alludes to here, starring Anthony Quinn, about the rise and fall of a prizefighter.
22. See *Mundo Nuevo* 18 (Paris). MP to ERM, February 6, 1969.
23. My conversations with Felisa Pinto and Libertad LeBlanc, Buenos Aires, November 1995.
24. Conversation with Germán García, November 1995.
25. MP to ERM, November 3, 1967. While Manuel claimed he had been told that a Spanish linotypist stopped the works at Sudamericana, it was really an editor (López Llausás) whom Porrúa, editor in chief, had attempted to circumvent. See also MP, "Losing Readers in Argentina," 55–57.
26. Editorial Jorge Alvarez would be shortlived, but Alvarez's colleague Daniel Divinsky (imprisoned for several months during the "proceso") would perpetuate its spirit (and reissue *Mafalda*) under another rubric, Ediciones de Flor.
27. Edgardo Cozarinsky, "Un aprendizaje de la vida," *Primera Plana* (Buenos Aires), no. 226 (July 9, 1968), 68–69.
28. See René Girard, *Deceit, Desire and the Novel,* for discussion of triangular desire as the essential plot of the modern novel, beginning with *Don Quixote* and renewed in nineteenth-century realism by Flaubert's *Madame Bovary*.
29. Cozarinsky, "Un aprendizaje de la vida," 68–69; Emir's article, reprinted in *Review* 71/72 (New York, 1972) as "A Literary Myth Exploded," was first published in *Imagen* (Caracas) 34 (1968).
30. MP to ERM, December 24, 1968.
31. February 6, 1969; also, see MP, "Growing Up at the Movies."
32. MP to ERM, August 26, 1969.
33. MP, "Losing Readers in Argentina," 55.
34. MP (from Rio) to GCI, December 29, 1982.
35. MP to ERM, August 26, 1969.
36. MP to ERM, September 11, 1968. *Nanina* would also be censored in the repressive

seventies, but, as an immature work—the author himself admits—it would never reap international acclaim.

37. ERM to MP, August 19, 1968.

38. Bataillon also translated *Boquitas*, into *Le Plus Beau Tango du Monde*, but her resistance to slang and neologisms frustrated Manuel. From Paris, he relayed to GCI (April 21, 1971) his "Parisian misadventures": "I got here and the translator wasn't here, she had left me some chapters to revise, horrendously done, and had gone off on vacation to Switzerland, total craziness, lies, contradictions. I got desperate and asked the publisher to change translators, terrible complications . . . The delays didn't matter so much to me, what really alarmed me was to see those chapters in such bad shape. It seems that for fear that I would show up and wouldn't have anything to revise she did those 2 horrendous chapters in a rush." After Manuel recruited Albert Bensoussan to translate *Beso* (March 1977), Bensoussan, the most prolific translator of modern Hispanic fiction in France, became the designated French translator for Manuel's plays as well as his later novels.

39. MP to ERM, October 30, 1968.

40. The two friends worked swiftly, burning the midnight oil so to speak, on *Burn!*— a "boring" film about slavery in the Caribbean, by Gillo Pontecorvo, an Italian director he considered doctrinaire, and with an "unbearable" Marlon Brando.

THOSE LITTLE PAINTED LIPS

41. SJL, "Author and Translator: A Discussion of *Heartbreak Tango*," *Translation* 2, no. 1-2 (1974), 33–34.

42. By the same token Mabel—sentimental about love but driven by ambition—also caricatured a mode of being he obviously knew intimately.

43. MP, interviewed by Nora Catelli.

44. The idea came to him, in part, from a conversation with fashion reporter Carmen Díaz.

45. Jorge Luis Borges, "Historia del tango," *Evaristo Carriego*, in *Obras Completas* (Buenos Aires: Emecé Editores, 1974), 59–68.

46. The tango's distinctive move is "cutting" or suspending, a break in the motion manipulated by the male or dominant lead skipping a note, obliging his partner to lift and twine her leg around his; he leans her backward from waist up, his hips now against hers in "perfect fit."

47. Jorge Salessi, "Medics, Crooks, and Tango Queens: The National Appropriation of a Gay Tango," *Every Night Life: Culture and Dance in Latin/o America* (Durham, N.C.: Duke University Press, 1997), 168–69.

48. MP, *Tango delle Ore Piccole*, ed. and tr. Angelo Morino (Milan: Einaudi, 1993), viii.

49. It lasted through the end of the year, and was also staged in Italy as *Tango delle Ore Piccole*. Mario attended *Gardel* twice in Rio during the Christmas season; for him the high point of the second occasion was to accompany "superfamous Argentine star Amelia Bence" back to her lodgings; she was afraid to go alone because she was "in a dangerous neighborhood."

50. Manuel spent many afternoons in November 1967 with Bebé, probing her memory for poignant details of the daily life and harsh treatment of young servant girls in Villegas. They remembered a story from the late thirties about the upper-crust Caravera family, who sent their maid away to live in the country, all expenses paid, because she was pregnant and the father was a friend of one of their sons—or perhaps one of the Caravera boys themselves. This scandal, plus a news item about a pregnant girl who had killed her policeman lover, gave Manuel his subplot about Pancho and Fanny.

51. "Era para mi la vida entera"—from Alfred LePera's well-known tango "Cuesta abajo" (Downhill)—was also an early idea for the book's title, as Tomás Eloy Martínez recollects, in *La Nación* (Buenos Aires) September 7, 1997, 2.

52. "En nombre de este amor y por tu bien te digo adiós . . ." He explains to plodding German translator Wolfgang Luchting (Buenos Aires, November 20, 1969) why he has the lovesick Nené think "in bolero terms . . . but mostly LePera, popular tangos 'Cuesta abajo' (Era para mi la vida entera), 'Volver' (yo adivino el parpadeo / de las luces a lo lejos / van marcando mi retorno. Son las mismas que alumbraron / con sus pálidos reflejos / hondas horas de dolor); 'Melodía del arrabal' (barrio . . . barrio . . . / que tenes el alma inquieta / de un gorrion sentimental). One Luis Rubinstein tango; one Agustín Lara bolero [sic]." In French—thanks to the resources of the francophile Nino—Manuel came up with lively substitutions for Nené's monologue-dream of being reunited with Juan Carlos in heaven: she weaves in "bolero turns of phrase" (the *cursi* inverted syntax was the clincher) which Manuel asked Bataillon to replace with "phrases of postwar (WWI) French songs, à la Charles Trenet." (Courtesy Luchting Archive, Firestone Library.)

53. MP to ERM, December 12, 1967.

54. See B. Sarlo, *El imperio de los sentimientos* (Buenos Aires: Catálogos Editores, 1985).

55. See for instance, in *HT*, Episodes 4 and 5, which trace a whole day in April 1937, fleshing out the principal dramas in the lives of the five main characters, Nené, Juan Carlos, Mabel, Pancho, Fanny. In September, Mabel's father is disgraced in court, and, years later, Nené's indiscreet letters are sent to her husband. (See Josefina Ludmer, "*Boquitas pintadas*: Siete recorridos" in *Actual. Revista de la Universidad de los Andes* (Mérida, Venezuela) 2, no. 8-9 (January-December 1971), 11–22.

56. Phone conversation with Edmund White (July 1994), who had been amused as much by Barth's naïveté as by Manuel's guileless wiles; Manuel jolted Barth in a manner not unlike Jean Harlow's in *Dinner at Eight* when the bombshell shocks jaded dowager Marie Dressler by pronouncing brashly: "Ya know, I read a book the other day."

57. Henry James, Cozarinsky asserted in his doctoral thesis, reinvented gossip as a literary genre.

A BEST-SELLER

58. MP to ERM, January 1, 1968. The Miami-based Hispanic women's magazine *Vanidades* did serialize it in 1971, but in two issues as a literary work, not as pulp fiction.

59. Monegal, Castellet (the Spanish critic who had been a judge for the Breve prize), Maurice Coindreau, and a new literary confrere, the Chilean writer José Donoso (who had already been a Guggenheim Fellow), all wrote letters of recommendation for Manuel.

60. ERM to MP, August 17, 1972.

61. MP to SS, May 17, 1968.

62. Nino suggested to Manuel a possible English title for *Boquitas pintadas*—"Orchids in the Moonlight," from the early movie musical *Flying Down to Rio*. Buying the rights to quote this tango in English would prove prohibitive; publisher E. P. Dutton discarded the solution and Manuel resented Dutton's parsimony. A few years later Carlos Fuentes, who worked with agent Carl Brandt, secured the rights for his play *Orchids in the Moonlight*, an imagined dialogue between two Mexican film stars, Dolores Del Rio and María Félix.

63. Philip Core, *Camp: The Lie That Tells the Truth* (New York: Delilah Books, 1984), 81.

64. Claude Fell, "Argentine, réexamen d'un peuple," *Le Monde*, October 4, 1969.

65. MP to ERM, February 1970.

66. Enrico Groppali, interview, *uomini e libri* (Milan), April–June 1988, 79.

67. MP to ERM, February 6, 1969.

68. SJL conversation with Felisa, November 1994.

69. MP to GCI, August 6, 1969.

70. GCI to MP, August 20, 1969.

71. MP to GCI, August 6, 1969.

72. MP, "Bye-Bye Babilonia," in *Estertores de una década*, 134–37. What Manuel recorded in "Lunching with the Stars" during the filming of Truffaut's *Bed and Board*, starring Jean-Pierre Léaud, is a vivid sample. Through Nestor, Manuel met Truffaut and Léaud on the set and was invited to join them and two of France's most glamorous women, Catherine Deneuve and Jeanne Moreau, in a "lively conversation about the greats, which to them was trivia, of course." Manuel pinpoints their star qualities with finesse: Deneuve—blond, ethereal, pleasant with everyone—had "the masked simplicity of Garbo," while Moreau was "a challenging presence with an arched eyebrow behind thick clouds of smoke."

73. MP, "Argentinians in London," in *Estertores de una década*, 115.

74. Ibid., 102.

75. Ibid., 116–17.

76. Manuel lamented to GCI (April 10, 1971) about his love life, the French translator, Bertolucci's *The Conformist* . . . "and on top of all that, Secker & Warburg [the British publisher]!"

77. Feltrinelli had attempted to destroy a power transmission line.

78. MP to GCI, February 16, 1970.

79. The Center, located at 680 Park Avenue, is now the Americas Society.

80. GCI to "Mapuig" (October 1, 1971): "I had to reject the Italian translation. A disaster. The Portuguese translation too." The best (or, at least, respected) translators were still not good enough, but both writers would discover differences between

good and bad translators—the latter created more difficulties than necessary—when they compared notes: Manuel started working with GCI's first Italian translator, Enrico Cicogna, whom Manuel found "sweet," though, as the official translator of the Boom he worked too fast and carelessly, often delegating the text to a "negre"—a student then, Angelo Morino—who took over Manuel's opus in Italy after Cicogna died suddenly of cancer a few years later. Manuel didn't like translators to be too fast or too slow.

81. GCI to MP, October 1971.

82. From chapters 2, 5, 8, 15.

83. John Coleman, also a professor of Latin American literature at NYU, was introduced that December to Manuel, who was eager to meet the author of this glowing review, at a Christmas cocktail party at the center. The general hilarity, inebriation, and flirting almost sent John to his death: the stocky critic, provoked by Manuel's comedic but unmistakable overtures, attempted to slide down the elegant winding banister to the lobby, lost his balance, fell almost an entire floor, and landed on his back. Fortunately he survived this terrifying accident.

Manuel thanked Emir (nicknamed "Dino the Sheik") for putting him in touch with his new translator and supportive critic, casting "Greta" and John Coleman in a kind of *Sunset Boulevard* film noir romance with me as Silvana Mangano: "God save Dino the Sheik for having such good taste and catapulting into stardom the unique Silvana so Greta could admire her on the silver screen and accept the offer of a co-starring vehicle. It seems the production will be lavish."

84. On this visit to Mexico Manuel met fellow film buff–novelist Gustavo Sainz, who's "lovely and holds GCI high up on an altar, so his place in the MGM Cast needs to be changed; we now say 'Nestor Sánchez (Connie Francis)—Studios' overprotection killed her, no more starlets! and then Gustavo Sainz (Karen Black)—Miss Christie's contract doesn't allow MGM to employ starlets under 30, so the studio is obliged to disown talented Miss Black— Oh! and I changed Donoso: Deborah Kerr, [at first he had] every inch a lady, every inch a bore [to] 'at Oscar time she's always the bridesmaid and never the bride.' " MP to GCI, December 30, 1971.

85. The transcription here is a composite from Manuel's correspondence to GCI (December 1971) and to me (January 1, 1972).

86. Vicente Leñero, "Apostillas," *Medicina y Cultura*, September 1997, 55–56.

87. Oscar José Canale, "La chismografía en un libro inútil y perfecto," *Crónicas* (General Villegas), 1970, 3.

88. Felisa recorded the interview for a TV program called *Identikit* (1972).

89. Hearsay from Villegas—Susana Canibaño, Library, to SJL, March 7, 1996.

90. According to José Luis Chavarri, a former schoolmate who came to see him in Rio in 1986, Manuel did not return in the eighties. Juan Becerra, "La mirada sin cuerpo," *Página 12* (Buenos Aires, December 29, 1992), writes a tribute to MP "on the 60th birthday he never reached" in which Manuel—"the eyes without a body"—is like the ghostly narrator of Thornton Wilder's *Our Town*.

91. Armando Almada Roche, *Cuando será el día que me quieras: Conversaciones con Manuel Puig* (Buenos Aires: Vinciguerra, 1992), 93.

"THAT TANGO MADE MY HEART BREAK"

92. SJL conversation with GCI, December 1994.

93. Malé Puig in conversations with SJL, August 1997.

94. Greta Garbo speaks of black pearls in her sad soliloquy in *Grand Hotel*, filled with the foreboding that something terrible has befallen her beloved Flix (John Barrymore).

95. GCI to MP, May 12, 1973. *HT* was a heavy "heartbreak hotel" translation of light "Little Painted Lips." GCI had invented some airier titles for it back in 1969. In a letter of admiration, Guillermo wrote: ". . . charmed, amused, saddened was I by your From Babes to Bitches—which parodies not only the well-worn From Rags to Riches but also Babes in Arms" (September 23, 1969).

96. MP to SJL, January 2, 1972. *La Opinión*, the left-wing newspaper owned by Jacobo Timmerman, was targeted by the military dictatorship; Urondo, like Walsh, would be among those "disappeared" in the seventies.

97. Bruce Allen, in *Library Journal* (October 15, 1973), wrote that *HT* returned to the "Chekhovian" world of *RH* but this time as a seductive True Romance about "hopeless lifelong passion, illuminated by surrounding romantic subplots which broaden its lasting legacy of 'heartbreak' . . . Nené's unrequited, breast-beating obsession is banality incarnate: lovelorn cries and sombre tango lyrics fill the air. Even as Puig parodies chronicles of romantic desperation, he elevates this drab love-drama into an ironic grand passion by filtering its trite gaucheries through a comic glut of involved viewpoints and an ingenious montage of storytelling devices—a brilliantly articulated chaos of fragments which underlines the heady confusion of human loving and its pathetic evanescence. Even heartbreak fails to last forever . . . Puig knows *all* about his ambitiously daydreaming people; he renders their vitally grubby milieu with sympathetic clarity."

98. Reviews consulted include the above from *Library Journal*; Walter Clemons, *Newsweek* (November 26, 1973); Christopher Lehmann-Haupt, *The New York Times* (November 28, 1973); Michael Wood, *The New York Review of Books* (December 13, 1973).

99. John A. Coleman, in his 1971 *New York Times* review of *RH*, mentioned the "wheezy angst" of Ernesto Sábato and "nobly engagé" populism of writers from Roberto Arlt to the post-1968 Julio Cortázar.

100. MP, "Un recuerdo de Borges," ed. J. Amícola, *Revista Espacios* (Buenos Aires), no. 15 (December 1994–March 1995), 25; *Newsweek* (1973). For connections between Borges and Puig see also the review of *Le Plus Beau Tango du Monde* (Denoel) and *Le rapport de Brodie* (Gallimard) by Claude Fell, "Le Couteau et le Tango" (The Knife and the Tango), in *Le Monde,* August 4, 1972, 11.

101. From Buenos Aires to GCI, April 3, 1973: People laugh at Cortázar posing as militant, and "Cuba won't let him come anymore, he went to the embassy in Paris and they kicked him out." "The worst of all is the book that's just come out. 'Libro de Manuel' [A Manual for Manuel] is TERRIBLE; nobody's reviewed it yet because nobody wants to, nobody likes it. The biggest scandal: he announced that his royalties would go to the families of the political prisoners, and the book has been a box office flop!"

102. GCI's bon mot about writers and translators; see SJL, *Subversive Scribe* (St. Paul: Graywolf Press, 1991), for discussion of collaborative translation.

103. Katherine Bouman interview, in *American Hispanist* 2, no. 7 (April 4, 1977).

104. From Manuel, in Mexico, to Jack Macrae, August 22, 1973 (my file), trying to cajole Jack to take sides with him against associate Marian Skedgell, Manuel grumbled about Dutton's neglect: (1) his royalty was reduced to give a small percent to the translator; (2) they claimed there would not be a third printing of *Rita*, but then, later, when he left for Mexico (December 1972) to give copies to Hollywood people (among them, Rita Hayworth herself), the copies he brought were from a third printing, dated June 1972, and to boot ("el colmo"), he received a bill of $100 for changes in galleys—when "95%" were copyeditor mistakes.

105. The foe in this case was Goliath (height-wise) Saul Sosnowski, stationed at the University of Maryland. Emir wrote to Manuel (New Haven, September 21, 1973) about how upset he was at Manuel's letting himself be used (by Angel Rama's friend Sosnowski) to make statements aimed at discrediting Emir; see *Anales de Literatura Hispanoamérica* 1, no. 3 (1973); Sosnowski transcribed out of context Manuel's casual shorthand answers:

Q: How did you get to be translated into English?
A: Dutton had published Borges thinking it would be a prestige item and not make money. On the contrary they made a lot. So they needed something to give them a loss, a matter of taxes. They asked Prof. Rodríguez Monegal to recommend a new author to do someone a favor. [*RH* had already been rejected by 6 publishers] . . .
Q: Does Monegal still consider you to be a loss?
A: No, he always defended me. He took advantage [MP meant ERM took advantage of the opportunity to introduce MP]. There was extra money to make known a Latin American and he recommended me. [MP meant finder's fee, an erroneous assumption, as ERM clarified to MP in letter (September 21, 1973): "It was José and not I who got you the publisher"; Manuel also credits Coleman's review.]

106. MP to ERM and SJL, April 21, 1973.

107. Famous actresses played the roles, in several of Manuel's dialogue quotations, of important women in history—Garbo as Queen Christina, Dietrich as Catherine the Great, Shearer as Marie Antoinette.

108. June 22, 1973. The dream of the diva is an egotistic dream, Emir wrote in his review—both praising Manuel's novel and deconstructing its *auteur*—"Los sueños de Evita: A propósito de la última novela de Manuel Puig," *Plural* (Mexico), no. 22 (1972), 35–36: "It is also the dream of Evita, a dream she made a reality, paradoxically transforming this vain, *cursi* dream into collective fulfillment . . . a new version of Cinderella, in which all the frustrated women of the Pampa, and of that cement Pampa called Buenos Aires, can project their impossible dreams onto superstar Eva Perón." Emir promoted writers he believed in, but his need to prove himself as a displaced Uruguayan perhaps led him to overextend his energies, to

sacrifice his own creative talents. His mode of coping with the stress of exile was to become controlling, to take on a paternal role in his friendships. Manuel was allergic to fathers, and his visit to New Haven revealed that closeness was uncomfortable unless the boundaries could be made very clear.

LOSS OF A READERSHIP

109. Enrico Groppali interview, 1988.

110. *TBAA*, 97: It is tempting to infer correspondences between Manuel and both protagonists: in 1966–68 Leo establishes himself as a successful magazine director—those were the same years of Manuel's entrance into the local literary limelight.

111. Juan Manuel García Ramos, "Pubis Angelical el Palimpsesto," *Anales de Literatura Hispanoaméricana* 8, no. 9 (1980), 103–12.

112. "Lacan was hardly known in France and we had already given him all the recognition that he deserved . . . And the case of Bergman . . . his *Sommarlek* was a hit in Argentina before it was discovered in Paris, which was where it had its international launching . . . I remember that it was forbidden to minors and I couldn't see it, more or less around '54, and I was dying to go, because people could talk about nothing else" (interview with Reina Roffé, *Espejo de escritores* [1985], 140).

113. GCI to MP, June 15, 1973.

114. "Loss of a Readership," first draft of essay "Losing Readers in Argentina," ms., 4.

115. Daniel Yakir, "Kiss of the Spider Woman: Manuel Puig," *Interview*, September 1985, 207.

116. MP, "Loss of a Readership," 5.

117. Andrés Avellaneda, *Censura* . . . , vol. 1 (Buenos Aires: Cedal, 1986), 114.

118. Interviewed by Reina Roffé, *Espejo de escritores* (N.H.: Ediciones del Norte, 1985), 137.

119. César Aira, lecture, April 12, 1989, cited by S. Carcamo, "Manuel Puig in the Seventies," *Homenagem a Manuel Puig*, *Revista América Hispánica* 3, no. 4 (July–December 1990), 138.

120. MP, "Losing Readers in Argentina," 5.

PART V
EXILE: 1974–79

ADIÓS, BUENOS AIRES QUERIDO

1. MP to GCI, October 19, 1972.

2. Silvia Oroz, in *Melodrama: El cine de lagrímas en América Latina*, 127–28, citing Argentine directors Tulio Demicheli and Fernando Ayala, who worked in Mexico, where they claimed the studio technicians were more capable or specialized, and the technology more advanced.

3. Leopoldo Torre Nilsson, "Dios salve el rey," in *Del Exilio* (Buenos Aires: Ediciones de la Flor, 1973), 9.

4. *London Times*, September 25, 1974.

5. MP to SJL, October 7, 1974.

6. MP to GCI, October 6, 1974.

7. MP to SJL, January 1975.

8. MP to GCI, July 1974.

SPINNING THE SPIDER WOMAN

9. Silvana Castelli highlighted the kinky Leo and Gladys as "two young monsters lovingly tortured by their families and peers . . . Their affair fulfills their respective
dreams of brutalizing/being brutalized." In "Alchimista letterario cambia banalità
en oro," *Avanti*, January 13, 1974.

10. RC, "A Last Interview with Manuel Puig," *World Literature Today* 65 (Fall 1991),
571.

11. MP to GCI, August 3, 1975.

12. Luis Gusmán observed that while *SW* was a continuation in some ways of *TBAA*—
in its focus on sex and politics—Manuel made an "epistemological break" by cen-
tering the story around a homosexual affair.

13. "Loss of a Readership" (1984), draft of "Losing Readers in Argentina," ms., 6.

14. Laura Rice-Sayre, "Domination and Desire: A Feminist-Materialist Reading of
Manuel Puig's *Kiss of the Spider Woman*," in *Textual Analysis*, ed. Mary A. Caws
(New York: MLA, 1986), 246–47.

15. He told RC (see "A Last Interview with Manuel Puig," 573): "I realized the reader
wouldn't be able to judge the action without the appropriate information on the
origins or causes of homosexuality . . . It's only recently that we're starting to see
books that present an organized explanation of the origins of homosexuality. In
Freud, in Jung, in all the main psychoanalytic texts, the information is fragmented;
and, of course, it's destined for an elite audience for a very few specialists. General
information is very recent. In this respect I very much like Dennis Altman's *Homosexual: Oppression and Liberation*. It's easy to read and covers a lot. For instance, it
makes very clear, accessible comments on hard-to-read books like Marcuse's."

16. *SW*, 207–8.

17. Mary Ann Doane, *The Desire to Desire: The Woman's Film of the 1940s* (Blooming-
ton: Indiana University Press, 1987), 48–49. Another "reel" film that Molina recalls
is *I Walked with a Zombie* (1943); this Val Lewton–Jacques Tourneur masterpiece
of horror, based (very) loosely on *Jane Eyre*, is yet another brilliant metaphor:
Molina and Valentín can be seen as zombies, or walking dead men in prison, a life
in death, or death in life.

18. RC, "Interview of Manuel Puig," *Christopher Street*, April 1979, 28.

19. Elizabeth Pérez Luna, "Con Manuel Puig en Nueva York," *Hombre del Mundo* 3,
no. 8 (August 1978), 69.

20. RC, "Interview of Manuel Puig," 26.

21. Daniel Yakir, "Kiss of the Spider Woman: Manuel Puig," *Interview*, September
1985, 208.

22. Ibid.

23. See John Butt's review of *SW* at Bush Theatre in Movie Talk, *Times Literary Supplement*, October 4, 1985.

24. Allan Baker, letter to Manuel's agent.

25. MP to Malé, 1963.

26. See Marc Silberman on Theodor Adorno's analysis of this phenomenon in *German Cinema: Texts in Context* (Detroit: Wayne State University Press, 1995).

27. See Tina Rosenberg, *Children of Cain: Violence and the Violent in Latin America* (New York: Penguin, 1991), 94.

28. Mario also had exciting news, long-awaited: a film called *Le Orme* (1975), based on his story "Footsteps on the Moon," was finally being made by his friend Luigi Bazzoni and Victor Storaro—a rising star.

29. Manuel saw this film in the mid-seventies at MoMA (courtesy of Charles Silver, MoMA).

30. Silberman, *German Cinema: Texts in Context*, ix, 53. Sierck Americanized his name to Sirk in Hollywood, where the films he made in the fifties turned him into a cult figure for French and American intellectuals. These successful melodramas were, for the discerning spectator, scathing satires: "reliance on formulae, conventions, excess, exaggeration, and clichés" invites the spectator to read beneath the surface, as Sierck "plays off erotic excess against aggressive evil in a way that reveals the moral confines of cinematic illusions in an authoritarian society" (xiv). Sierck gave Leander her trademark roles: "the glamorous woman of the world with an independent nature, the femme fatale . . . who, despite everything—and here is the Nationalist Socialist twist—always reveals a warm heart or returns home in the end." Not only Nazi Germany: in postwar America too (64).

31. In 1973 Manuel brought me *Mein Leben für die Liebe* (My Life for Love), an arcane LP of Leander hits. Listening to her transgendered voice as Manuel mimicked her gestures, I felt it was clear that Zarah resembled a drag queen—the strong-actress type with whom queens identified before Stonewall. Bette Davis was subtle in comparison. Manuel overwhelmed film critic Joel Siegel, who, though he barely knew the famous Argentine novelist, felt honored to invite him to stay at his place in Washington, D.C., in October 1980. Manuel was to spend three weeks viewing the Library of Congress's newly acquired holdings in Nazi filmography. After each day's screenings, Manuel returned to his host's apartment brimming with fresh impressions and imitations of Zarah Leander.

32. See "Los desconocidos de siempre," in *Gli occhi di Greta Garbo*, where Manuel notes that Italian director Camerini's thirties comedies have been left to oblivion even though they are Lubitsch-like masterpieces.

33. "Destino" is preceded by another invented movie, about a South American playboy in France whose father, a wealthy landowner, had discouraged his son from hanging out with French radicals on the Left Bank. While leading a debauched life in the south of France, he falls in love with an older woman, and, when his father is held hostage by guerrillas back home, he recaptures his idealism and joins the revolution in his country. This narrative serves to help Molina understand Valentín's

struggles with his class (and mother and father) and to hope for Valentín's regeneration through love with "an older woman" (Molina).

34. S. Freedman, interview, "Manuel Puig and His Hollywood Lure," *International Herald Tribune*, August 14, 1985.

35. Tununa Mercado, "No me digas adiós," *La letra de lo mínimo* (Buenos Aires: Beatriz Viterbo Editores, 1994), 60. The final story Molina tells to his Marxist Valentine, a story that exalts the spiritual triumph of love against all odds, is a Mexican *cabaretera* which, like the Nazi movie, Manuel fabricated out of bits and pieces. He based it loosely on a "marvelous" Mexican flick, *Hipócrita* (1949), about the doomed affair of a beautiful cabaret singer, who gives up fame and fortune (a mafioso magnate lover) for an idealistic, hopeless, alcoholic journalist. *Holiday in Mexico* (1946), a Hollywood musical in which an ambassador's daughter (Jane Powell) falls in love with a famous musician (José Iturbi), was yet another inspiration, both for Molina's Mexican film and for Manuel's screenplay *Souvenir from Tijuana*.

36. Silvia Oroz, *Melodrama: El cine di lágrimas en América Latina*, 74.

37. Cf. Julia Romero, "The Melodramatic Imagination: National Life and Sentiment: On the writing of Manuel Puig," *Orbis Tertius*, 244–45: quoting MP interviewed by Elena Poniatowska, "Novedades," Mexico, October 23, 1974. He adds that "the equivalent of Ninón Sevilla in directors is Orol."

38. Oroz, interview of Ninón Sevilla, 1990, 95.

39. MP to GCI, December 12, 1974.

40. Interview, *Hombre del mundo* (1978), 104.

NEW YORK, NEW YORK

41. Jorgelina Corbatta, "Encuentro con Manuel Puig," *Revista Iberoaméricana* (April–September 1983), 123–24.

42. Bruce claims that his descriptions of bondage in "Slaves of Fashion" (unpublished) gave Manuel an idea for the ending of *PA*, where the futurist sex slave escapes sheathed in a latex body stocking and face mask.

43. MP to GCI, December 31, 1974.

44. MP, *Estertores de una década*, 26–28.

45. Gustavo García and Andrés de Luna, "Rock, arañas, nenonas y manuelas: Manuel Puig en Nueva York," *Revista de la Universidad de México* 33, no. 7 (1978), 25.

PUBIS ANGELICAL

46. MP to GCI, July 6, 1976.

47. Hedwig Kiesler, *Ecstasy and Me: My Life as a Woman* (London: W. H. Allen, 1967), 19, 23.

48. Cited in *TBAA*, 116.

49. *PA*, 61.

50. *PA*, 77.

51. "My summer has been very bad, full of complications, misencounters and sadness. Luckily I've been invited to the book fair in Frankfurt. I'm leaving the 23 [August]

and returning at the end of September. It appears there's money to continue the [Columbia University] workshop" (to José Kozer, August 20, 1976).

52. GCI, "In a Pampas of Dreams," *The Guardian* (London), July 25, 1990.

53. Manrique, who considers himself one of Manuel's "daughters," forgets to add "irony" to the eyebrow's list of duties, and proceeds to lay the mascara on thick: "The eyebrow was a curtain raised or lowered to expose eyes alive with fire; eyes that could warm you or make you feel faint with their coldness. He had what in some circles is known as Bette Davis eyes." Stavans and Manrique have subsequently exploited their acquaintance with Manuel Puig, claiming (Stavans, in *Transition*, 1997) to "out" him when he was already out, suggesting, in Manrique's case (see "The Writer as Diva," *Christopher Street*, July 1993), that—without concrete proof—Manuel died of AIDS but that neither he nor his family and close friends would admit it, and in Stavans's case, taking Manuel's gossip about others as the gospel truth.

54. MP to HM, June 16, 1977.

55. MF, letter to SJL, 1995. *PA* was Mario's least favorite of Manuel's novels.

56. See J. Amícola, *Manuel Puig y la tela que atrapa . . .* , 283.

57. RC, "Last Interview with Manuel Puig," *World Literature Today* 65 (Autumn 1991), 578.

58. Danubio Torres-Fierro, interview, *Memoria Plural*, 512.

HELL HAS NO LIMITS

Epigraph: John Keats reading Shakespeare, in 1818, quoted by Alfred Kazin in "All Critics Are Mortal," *Writing Was Everything* (Harvard University Press), reprinted in *Los Angeles Times Book Review*, June 14, 1998, 3.

59. See, for example, Ripstein's film *El castillo de la Pureza* (*The Castle of Purity*, 1972).

60. Yakir, "Kiss of the Spider Woman: Manuel Puig," 208.

61. Manuel said of this scene: "La Manuela incarnates the submissive, degraded part of women, so that women can identify with him; and the kiss provokes precisely the impact we want to produce on men."

62. "El Jinete," or "The Horseman"—one of Manuel's numerous (around thirty) unpublished story sketches, plays, scripts—which he also titled "Triste golondrina macho" (Sad Male Swallow), written in 1982, had elements similar to "La cara del villano," the screenplay Ripstein made into *El Otro*.

63. Directed by Terrence Malick.

64. MP, "Cinema and the Novel," 288–89. His scripts "La cara del villano" and "Recuerdo de Tijuana" were first published in Torino, Italy, by Editorial La Rosa as *L'impostore-Ricordo di Tijuana*, thanks to translator Angelo Morino. In the preface, especially written for the Seix Barral edition in 1985, Puig reconstructs in an essay his relationship with the movies, though the initial motive for the essay is to vent his rage at Ripstein for exploiting him as a writer and then taking over the projects they worked on, in dictatorial fashion.

65. MP to GCI, January 1, 1977.

66. In a letter to HM, commenting on Liza Minnelli's attempts to imitate the old-time

musicals in *Baryshnikov on Broadway* (1981): "All plastic, Liza does everything and it doesn't work, no real emotions. Behind it all, something died and all the pyrotechnics of choreography and vocal arrangements can't revive it."

67. MP to HM, January 2, 1982. "Mara's 'redeeming feature' was that she saw *Snow White* 8 times in 3 days in my video. And then went crazy for . . . Jack Oakie in *That Girl from Paris* and saw it 5 times in 2 days."

68. Interview, *Hombre del mundo* (1978), 106.

69. García and de Luna, "Rock . . . : Manuel Puig en Nueva York," 25; also, interview in *Hombre del mundo*, 68–72, 104–7. From 1976 to 1979, Manuel viewed the following (mostly silent, from the teens and twenties) romantic comedies, musicals, melodramas at MoMA, under the auspices of Charles Silver, director of the Film Studies Center, who gave me access to the list of screenings of these 16mm antiques, which include *Hotel Imperial*; *Student Prince*; *Flesh and the Devil* (Gilbert/Garbo); *Assunta Spina* (Italian, with Francesca Bertini); *Cenere* (Italian, Eleonora Duse's only film); *White Moth*; *Hoopla* (with Clara Bow); *Evergreen* (with Jesse Matthews); *The Sorrows of Satan* (with Lya de Putti, who had a glamorous German accent); and a classic romantic tragedy directed by Josef von Sternberg, *The Last Command*, with titles by Herman Mankiewicz, based on a Lubitsch idea, and starring Evelyn Brent and Emil Jannings. When accompanied by Malé, Manuel saw mainly operas and operatic comedies: *Rosita*; *Louise*; *Uberfall*; *Kiki*; *Variety*; *N.Y. Hat*. Tuned into the androgyny/bisexuality underlying the aesthetics of Hollywood, Manuel found the twenties, before censorship, more explicit, as in Asta Nielsen's *Hamlet* (1920): "It seems good, she plays a woman really; when she's born the King and Queen make her pass for a boy because the throne needs a descendant immediately. And Horatio is in love with her/him all the way, ashamed of his homo feelings, until in the end he embraces the dead Hamlet and feels a tit" (to HM, Rio, November 14, 1987).

70. Roberto Echavarren was "eye-witness" (October 1977).

71. GCI to SJL, September 6, 1979.

ETERNAL CURSE ON THE READER

72. Interviewed by Jorgelina Corbatta (1979), "Encuentro con Manuel Puig," while writing *Eternal Curse*, which came out first in Spanish—translated by himself—as *Maldición eterna a quien les estas páginas* (1980). In one of the last interviews of Manuel, he summed up the "two elements that need to coincide for me to write a book," reiterating in part statements made previously:

I have to feel a need to exorcise those personal obsessions. There are others I have no need to exorcise. Each of us has his own little masochistic game, and wants to continue with certain tortures until death, but there are some tortures that I do say, "Enough of this already." But I don't write a novel—since for me it's not only about writing but about communicating—if I have the sensation that that problem is not shared. That is, I'm interested in placing myself as one more victim of the collective unconscious . . . Yes, I'm very interested in clarifying certain things for myself and achieving certain stylistic things, but it has to be read too, if not there's not a certain libido flowing in this. Writing is a dialogue with another person.

73. Mark was, as Manuel told Bruce, "fearful of the baths." Trying to entice him with "petit bourgeois" food like packaged ham and Entenmann's coffee cake, "Manuel just didn't know the proper codes." Bruce advised him to try nonfat, whole grain "yuppie" food.

74. Merle in conversation with SJL, spring 1996.

75. Makes this remark, for example, in *Hombre del mundo* (1978), 72.

76. Hedy's "glamour and even the pleasure are at best ephemeral and superficial, at worst fraudulent" (Pamela Bacarisse, *Necessary Dream* [Cardiff: University of Wales Press, 1988], 135).

77. See Marcella Paul, "The Function of Illness in Manuel Puig's *Pubis Angelical*," *Chasqui* 17, no. 1 (May 1988), 31–41.

78. MP, *Eternal Curse*, 136.

79. To Angelo Morino in Italy, Manuel wrote, hoping he'd find out that Mark's family (of Italian origins) came from the same region as his grandmother, and hence that they shared a broken link to the past:

I fell madly in love with a gorgeous but crazy man—how I've suffered à la Lida Borelli, tearing my hair out and clawing the curtains, but finally I've lost him, DI-VINE, 36 years old, Italian background . . . He's not on speaking terms with his family, so I can't ask him. (April 27, 1978)

80. Random House jacket cover, New York, 1982.

81. Corbatta, "Encuentro con Manuel Puig," 20.

82. MP to Albert Bensoussan, February 5, 1983.

83. Bacarisse, *Necessary Dream*, 157, 198.

THE KISS OF SUCCESS

84. Andrés Avellaneda, *Censura, autorismo y cultura: Argentina 1960–83/2* (Buenos Aires: Cedal, 1986), 214.

85. Juan Goytisolo, *El bosque de las letras* (Madrid: Alfaguara, 1995), 121. Carvellis, Gallimard editor, supported the opinion of Bianciotti, the Spanish reader for the press, to veto *Kiss*.

86. MP to GCI, June 1977.

87. In MP's first letter to Bensoussan (March 7, 1977): "Didier Coste did the 3rd one and I prefer to forget that experience; he did it in 6 weeks thinking about every-thing but the book (I prefer to give him that excuse) and I had to rewrite the whole thing with Claude Durand, who was great." Durand, a translator, was editor at Seuil.

88. In *The New York Review of Books* (January 24, 1980), Michael Wood, an informed Anglo critic of Latin American literature, referred to the footnotes as an "elementary symposium on homosexuality" but recognized the effect Manuel was seeking:

this "activity at the foot of the page"—which included a "pastiche of a press-book for a Nazi movie showing the conversion of a slinky French singer to love for the Fuhrer and disgust for the degradations her cherished France is suffering at the hands of the villainous Jews"—"in conjunction with what goes on higher up, is not a simple equation between sexual and political repressions, but an intimation of the complicated lure of prejudice, whether political or sexual" (43). Robert Coover's *New York Times* review appeared April 22, 1979.

89. García and de Luna, "Rock . . . : Manuel Puig en Nueva York," 26.

90. Unlike Manuel, Severo never crossed over to a wider readership; his dense, baroque novels, long prose poems really, could only be appreciated by the happy few. Brimming with pop imagery like Rock Hudson's "measurements" and profane erotics—"ooh yummy, give it to me honey, in Sanscrit"—these textural collages, a kind of "action painting" writing, filled with satirical allusions to politics and philosophy, did not address the average reader.

PART VI
FLYING DOWN TO RIO: 1980–88

KISS, THE PLAY

1. Jaime Manrique cites a letter from MP (August 22, 1979), in "Writer as Diva," *Christopher Street*, July 1993, 16.

2. Ibid., 17.

3. MP to HM, June 1980.

4. Even when invited, Manuel griped. When Severo took him to lunch in Paris at a fancy St.-Germain restaurant on Seuil's budget, "fue un chasco": it was ridiculous, they served small portions that were so-so. On the other hand, he wrote Malé, "I took Nino out for couscous and it was fabulous" (written from Orly, June 9, 1981).

5. MP to Malé, October 10, 1983.

6. MP to Howard, April 1981. Out of this conference in Germany came a scholarly volume edited by José Amícola. In a letter to Malé and family (April 30) Manuel explained that the best university deals were in the United States and Puerto Rico, where they paid all expenses plus honorarium; but the conveniences of this trip were "1) pick up the Italian prize and stir up publicity; 2) pick up the royalties from the Italian theater production of Bacio; 3) see the videocassette market in Italy; 4) if I can finish, show Mario the latest version of my new novel [*Blood of Requited Love*]; 5) promote my books in Germany, where they're not doing that well; 6) see cassettes in Germany; 7) make stops in Paris to promote *Pubis*; 8) stops in Barcelona and Madrid to promote *Maldición* and the play *Beso*—I had to eliminate Yugoslavia and Vienna because the dates conflicted." All these stops, including an "annoying prize ceremony in Rome" and "tedious" talks at several German universities (Berlin, Hamburg, Göttingen, Frankfurt), occurred between May 16 and June 14. "All work," he wrote Malé.

7. See Peter Herzog and Gene Vazzano, *The Cold Flame. From Metropolis to Gold:*

Portrait of a Goddess (New York: Corvin, 1994). Author Herzog's prose sounds like the rhetorical hype Manuel weaves into *Pubis Angelical*: "This delirious dream is a woman who never smiles, is without pity in her eyes and, because of this, men love her and hate her at the same time. She is too beautiful to be loved, these men say; she is too unreachable, like an ivory tower, like a flower in its perfect beauty, like a star in the sky, shimmering. She cannot love and cannot be loved" (1).

8. Published as the already cited prologue "Cinema and the Novel."
9. MP to HM, April 20, 1981.
10. Alan Pauls, "La retrospectiva intermitente." *Encuentro internacional Manuel Puig*, ed. J. Amícola and G. Speranza (Rosario: Beatriz Viterbo Editores, 1998), 21–24.
11. "He had . . . lost his baby fat, and his hair had even stopped falling out. He would strut his svelte figure. 'Touch it,' he'd say, 'it's real woman's flesh' " (Manrique, "Writer as Diva," 18).
12. MP to HM, April 21, 1981.
13. Mattolini would continue to work with Morino, producing Manuel's last play, *El misterio del ramo de rosas*.
14. MP to Malé and family, May 20, 1981.
15. MP to Malé and family, June 9, 1981.
16. MP to HM, July 29, 1981.
17. MP to HM, June 1980.
18. *Christopher Street*, April 1979, 26. Christ, an ex-editor of *Review* magazine, had helped revise, along with Errol MacDonald, the translation of the novel, and was just starting Lumen Books. Christ translated *Under a Mantle of Stars* in the early eighties and tried to convince Manuel to let him do *Kiss* but could not offer enough money; nor did he have sufficient clout in literary/publishing/theater circles to produce it. After the *Christopher Street* spread, Manuel's celebrity brought a bid from Michael Feingold (*Village Voice* theater critic), who accepted Manuel's "advance" of $1,500 to translate the play, a deal made independently of ICM. By 1983 he still hadn't completed the translation, and Manuel fired "that bad penny." The English version was done by Allan Baker, in London, who also translated *Mystery of the Rose Bouquet*. Meanwhile Feingold published his unauthorized version in 1986, copyrighted under his name, claiming Manuel had given him the rights. In December 1986 Maggie Curran, Lynn Nesbitt's assistant at ICM, tried in vain to recover the advance, informing Feingold that, because his completed manuscript had never been delivered, the agreement between author and translator was void. But Manuel was finally at ease with this since the pirate publication brought attention to the play, which was then translated officially by Allan Baker, resulting in a good production in London. Myriad productions cropped up in the United States—in New York, Washington, D.C., and Los Angeles, in provincial theaters, university theaters, prestigious avant-garde theaters, and so on. Mitch Douglas at ICM considers the Williamstown, Massachusetts, summer stock production to have been the most effective, and, while Baker's translation was competent, Feingold's was actually written in more vivid, lively language. Again, Mitch felt Manuel's meddling in translations often worked to his disadvantage. Manuel's deals in Brazil and

the Hispanic world were handled by ICM as well by this point. Like Maggie, Luis Sanjurjo—ICM's dashing man in Havana from an upper-class Latin American family—put Manuel at ease, relatively. After Sanjurjo died of AIDS, Tom Colchie took over part of this detail. In Los Angeles, Manuel dealt mostly with Darris Hatch and Michael Black.

19. To Spanish actor Pepe Martín (October 1981), with whom Manuel worked on the production in Spain. In the Italian version the contrapuntal "multi-media" effect was a reasonable device, according to Morino, to substitute for the original's untransposable footnotes and multiple film plots.

20. Angelo Savelli's review, "Le Strategie del Ragno," cited in playbill of Italian production in Teatro Manzoni (February 1980).

21. MP to Malé, October 9, 1981.

22. *El Nacional* published a story that Manuel Puig was a hermaphrodite. The reporter was the young enfant terrible Pablo Antillano, scion of a distinguished Venezuelan family of letters and a protégé of Tomás Eloy Martínez. From Rio, June 29, 1980, Manuel admonished Guillermo and Miriam, after they had apparently remarked to Eloy Martínez in Caracas that Manuel had made love with women friends of theirs, who all claimed that Manuel was one of the best lovers they had ever had. They had told Eloy Martínez about this side of Manuel to defend him against Eloy's disparaging view of Manuel as a *marica* or what they perceived—in accord with Manuel's view—as the insidious envy common among Argentines in exile. In a tone somewhere between schoolmarmish and co-conspiratorial, however, Manuel scolded GCI for giving Eloy and his pals gossip which they then turned into a negative headline. Another friend's indiscretion produced further vicious gossip in August 1982, about Manuel's "romance with a bricklayer," El Chefao, published in a popular Argentine magazine called *Humor*. Manuel was upset with Felisa, who indiscreetly spread the news around when she returned to Buenos Aires from a vacation in Rio. Because homophobia and politics often colored the critical reception of his books, this publicized gossip revived the ever-present specter of censorship, always ready to pounce.

23. MP to Stephen Harvey, August 3, 1979.

24. MP to HM, June 16, 1981.

25. Francisco Umbral, *El País*, May 1, 1981. "Puig plays strong, like Genet and Marcuse, Freud and other defenders of sexual liberation. Here we witness a psychoanalysis, each is the patient and analyst of the other. The taboos and inhibitions break down, the hidden emotions are rescued, and finally the cry of human, sexual, political solidarity conquers individual morality to restore a common proposal of struggle."

26. Andrés Amorós, *Guía del Ocio*, May 3, 1981.

27. MP to HM, August 1979.

28. Manuel's version would be the basis for successive productions in Latin America, Europe, and the United States, as well as for the Hollywood screenplay. In a letter to Malé and family from Rio, Manuel was trying to decide which Parisian theater

group to accept and had asked the advice of his publisher, Gallimard, which, to his frustration, was indifferent. There was an offer in Chile but it was still politically problematic; the next Latin American production opened in Caracas, Venezuela (where experimental theaters flourished), on January 19, 1983. In Mexico, Ripstein was doing the production, but it was still held up over some concern about new president Miguel de la Madrid (taking over from López Portillo), who promised— or rather threatened—"moral renovation . . . But there's still no committee to censor previous commitments, so they'll take a chance, Mexico always so difficult, what garbage" (MP to Malé, December 17, 1982).

29. Cited by Vito Russo, in *The Celluloid Closet: Homosexuality in the Movies* (New York: Harper & Row, 1987), 285.

30. See (Feingold's "pirate") edition by George Woodyard and Marion Peter Holt, *Contemporary Drama: Latin America—Plays by Manuel Puig, Antonio Skarmeta, Mario Vargas Llosa, Carlos Fuentes* (New York: PAJ Publications, 1986), 69.

31. Including Emir Rodríguez Monegal and his future wife, Selma.

32. MP to HM, August 1981.

33. In Argentina, despite continued prohibition, Puig's novels circulated, and the film industry (Artediez Company) produced *Pubis Angelical*. De la Torre cast top Argentine stars Alfredo Alcón, who had played handsome Juan Carlos in the film *Boquitas*, now ten years later a slightly jaded Latin leading man in his late forties, perfect for the role of Pozzi, the ambiguous self-serving lover of Ana, and Graciela Borges, conventionally beautiful (with makeup on) but no Hedy Lamarr. The Uruguayan stage actress China Zorrilla played Ana's mother, and Buñuel's Silvia Pinal played Ana's friend in Mexico, Beatriz. The film places more emphasis on the political discussions between Pozzi and Ana, which were more relevant to the Argentine audience and, within the economic and technical production constraints of the national cinema, less intangible than Puig's subtle elaborations on sexuality and fantasy life. The forties melodrama and the science-fiction story required more elaborate and sophisticated artwork and direction; as suspected, it turned out to be a mediocre film.

34. MP to HM, December 1981.

35. See Joao S. Trevisan, *Perverts in Paradise* (London: Guernsey Press, 1986).

36. "La bataclana o la modista?" Patricio also did bit parts in Bruno Barreto's *Unhappily Ever After* and Argentine film *Naked Tango*.

37. RC, in a letter to SJL, March 14, 1996, explains his choice of this title because of "its resonance in the play—the appearance of the police, for example [calls into question legitimacy]—and how it covers so much of Manuel's work—the legitimacy of all desires, not including their fulfillment of course."

38. Ronald Christ Archives, University of Texas, Austin.

REQUITED LOVE

39. Jorgelina Corbatta, *Mito personal y mitos colectivos en las novelas de Manuel Puig* (Madrid: Orígenes, 1988), 102; see also *Crisis*, 35.

40. Ibid., 102.

41. See Flora Schiminovich, "El juego narcisista y ficcional en Sangre de amor correspondido," *Discurso literario* (Spring 1984), 295–301. The point of view of an obsessed narrator is narcissistic; the other is object of desire, projection, echo of himself; Maria da Gloria is left crazy, her subjectivity annulled, and only exists in Josemar's contradictory memories and fantasies.

42. MP, *Blood of Requited Love*, 3.

43. Ibid., 33.

44. Ibid., 26.

45. Ibid., 31.

46. Ibid., 148.

47. ERM, "Sangre de amor correspondido," *Vuelta* 6, no. 72 (November 1982), 34–35. This is the last novel by Manuel that Emir reviewed; Emir died, in New Haven, three years later.

48. MP, *Blood of Requited Love*, 20.

49. Ibid., 152.

50. Ibid., 196.

51. Ibid., 154.

THE ROCKY ROAD TO OSCAR: THE FILM

Epigraph: Frank O'Hara, "To the Film Industry in Crisis."

52. Hector Babenco, interviewed by Joseph Hurley on WBAI, 1985. My following reconstruction of the events leading to, during, and after the production of the film *Kiss of the Spider Woman* is based mostly on conversations with Manuel Puig and with several of those involved (including Hector Babenco, David Weisman, Leonard Schrader, Lee Percy, Patricio Bisso, Jolie Chain) as well as Peter Rawley, Mitchell Douglas, and the archives at ICM in New York. Another source is the introduction to the published screenplay by Schrader and Weisman (Faber & Faber, 1987).

53. Based on conversations with Hector Babenco.

54. MP to HM, January 2, 1982.

55. Ibid.

56. MP to ICM, January 1981.

57. MP to HM, December 2, 1981.

58. Also with Louis Malle in *Atlantic City* (1981).

59. Peter Rawley, interviewed by SJL, May 1996.

60. From my conversation with Gene Parseghian, July 1995. Parseghian's partner Jeff Hunter eventually left Triad and runs the William Morris Agency in New York.

61. MP to HM, May 27, 1983–July 21, 1983.

62. Quentin Crisp's description of the heroine's skin tones in Rainer Werner Fassbinder's sickly green-hued *Querelle*.

63. Bob Dawson, title designer, created, at Optical House in the United States, the sepia color effect in the "Nazi movie"—a kind of aquarelle to suggest the glamour of an old movie.

64. Columbia Pictures backed production company Island Alive, an overnight merger between Island Records—mostly reggae—and another small pop music company, Alive.

65. See Manuel's letters from Rio to Malé (who was still in Buenos Aires), October–November 1983.

66. Jolie Chain interviewed by SJL, June 1995.

67. MP to HM, October 19–26, 1983. The doctor finally diagnosed the rash as "scabies."

68. Pauline Kael, "Tangled Webs," *The New Yorker*, August 26, 1985, 62: "Hurt's . . . carefully constructed performance is all from the outside. There's nothing lyrical or iridescent about his Molina. Glamour doesn't hit a responsive chord in this guy's soul; his soul doesn't even vibrate sympathetically with the movie-goddess pictures on the wall of his cell. The role of Molina needs someone who can get lost in himself . . . there's no humor."

69. "Jean-Louis Trintignant would be the best Molina," Manuel remarked in May 1982 to Michèlle Ramond, a professor in Toulouse, and a quaintly eccentric lady whom Manuel nicknamed after one of his favorite French actresses, Danielle Darrieux.

70. Based on my phone conversation with Hector Babenco, May 30, 1999.

71. MP to Malé, October 19, 1983.

72. MP to HM, November 6, 1983.

73. As Manuel had advised Bensoussan, his French translator: "1) The main thing is Molina's tone: should be slightly ungrammatical or simply 'popular' with cheap, kitschy melodrama tendencies. But most impt. is his agile language, a special fluency within its awkwardness. 2) The Tobis-Berlin publicity [intended for international distributors of the Nazi film] should be extremely rhetorical, unintentionally comical. 3) The long monologue [in which Molina runs 'The Enchanted Cottage' through his mind] should have a certain musical, singsong tone."

74. From my conversation with Gene Parseghian, July 1995.

75. Raul Julia seemed nice but slow-witted, Manuel told me in conversation years later; for example, because he didn't notice it in the last ten pages, Julia wondered where the rowboat came from and kept exclaiming about the script, "But this is so different!"

76. Enrique Fernández, "The Spider Woman's Stratagem," *Village Voice*, April 4, 1986, 43.

77. Rio, November 7, 1983: Before embarking on this trip, Manuel wrote a portentous letter to the family in Buenos Aires, revealing his worries about providing for his parents if he died: "If anything happens to me (cruz diablo) [God forbid]: Mario wired me $25,000 to N.Y. [bank] because he wants to bring money to South America; $22,000 remains in my safebox in the Bradesco Bank, to which Mother has the key."

78. MP to ERM, May 30, 1985.

79. About a romantic triangle: a married woman, a gigolo, and a transvestite [to be played by Patricio Bisso]. Manuel took his name off Bruno Barreto's released film

Alem da Paixao (Unhappily Ever After) "just in time; it was badly received at film festival" (January 1, 1985, to HM).

80. MP to HM, December 13, 1983.
81. From Lee Percy's recollections, July 1995.
82. MP to HM, March 18, 1985. Manuel's talk ("Losing Readers in Argentina") was published in *Index on Censorship* 14, no. 5 (October 1985). Manuel wrote to HM, October 19, 1984: "La 'Kiss of the SW' thank God didn't get into the NY festival, they wanted it badly because of Hurt-Julia both on Bway at the moment. But when they saw it . . . It would be marvelous if it didn't get released at all." And then, from Amsterdam, Manuel to HM, May 14, 1985: "Did I tell you already about the film? It's bad, no motivations, dull as hell, la Hurt a disaster, but at the Cannes Festival they think it's better than the other ones, so it may even get a prize!"
83. While praising Manuel's "natural" talent with dialogue, Babenco predictably downplayed the author's participation as both "good and bad, you know, the way life is . . . the film and the book are two different worlds, and maybe the film reaches further than the book in some ways." And Babenco's opinion of the screenwriter's contribution was similar: "Then I didn't know English so well" (interview, WBAI).
84. MP to ERM, May 30, 1985. (Emir died a few months later.)
85. MP, interviewed in *Boston Globe*, August 12, 1986, 49.
86. See Kael, "Tangled Webs," 61–63.
87. Babenco's *At Play in the Fields of the Lord* (1991) would be yet another box office disappointment, affecting the director's Hollywood career—and possibly, according to comments made by Leonard Schrader, impacting other South American projects and directors in Hollywood.
88. From 1985 on, Bruce Feldman, head of marketing at Universal, obtained films for Manuel, and then Joan Cohen, a film researcher for the Los Angeles County Museum of Art, took over as Manuel's main supplier in Los Angeles. Joan religiously sent him the *TV Guide*, and Manuel always marked the women's movies of the thirties—aside from the obscure Anne Harding, Constance Bennett was another of Manuel's favorites, Joan recalls. Manuel would call Joan, order films, and she'd meet Brazilian pilots at Holiday Inns and make the exchange. Joan would contact Hollywood friends traveling to Brazil, namely Denise Dinovi (who produced the remake of *Little Women*) and Paul Mazursky, who was working on *Moon over Parador*.
89. SJL, phone interview with Paul Mazursky, 1996.
90. See aforementioned "Cinema vs. Novel" essay.
91. MP to Joan Cohen, September 12, 1986.
92. MP to ERM, May 30, 1985. See review by John Butts, Movie Talk, *Times Literary Supplement*, October 4, 1985: Simon Callow took on the role of Molina in the British production, and captured "his businesslike tenderness, charm and breathless excitement about his relationship with his unhappy friend." The production, "touching and funny in the right combination, an impressive achievement," was a great success. (Valentín was played by Mark Rylance.) "The production is perhaps rather less sym-

pathetic toward the 'freedom fighter' than is the novel, and the play reminds us that people like Valentín did their bit to bring us Videla and Galtieri. For all his febrile idealism, books and theories, Valentín is in every way an emotional dwarf alongside his cellmate Molina . . . baffled by Valentín's abstract feminism."

93. The terror of AIDS—Manuel calls it "pest," from the French *la peste*—permeated the ambiance on this occasion.
94. MP to HM, November 15, 1987.
95. Phillip Lopate, "Brilliance and Bardot, All in One," Film View, *The New York Times*, June 22, 1997, 17.
96. Francisco Artuso (president of the Argentine Club in Rio), *Homenagem a Manuel Puig, Revista América Hispánica* 3, no. 4 (July–December 1990), 158.
97. Aside from Mario (and his friends), Hugo Gutiérrez Vega, Silvia Oroz, Iván Albuquerque, and respective spouses, and other embassy and theater cronies, Malé and Manuel saw with some frequency a few university friends such as Emir's companion Selma Rodríguez, Bela Josef and her husband, George, and Jorge Schwartz, an Argentine in São Paulo. May Lorenzo Alcalà, Argentine journalist and cultural attaché who had been transferred to Rio in December 1986, also joined the cine club and was a good friend during Manuel's last years.
98. MF to SJL, October 1995.

PART VII
FINALE

KISS, THE MUSICAL
1. SJL phone interview of Harold Prince, September 12, 1995; also phone conversation, later that month, with Fred Ebb; another valuable source on the musical was the American Theater Wing CUNY seminar, aired on WNYC (1994), featuring the production team of the musical, including Chita Rivera and Hal Prince.
2. In the zany plot of *The Producers*, Zero Mostel as Mr. Bialystock sells 50 percent and 100 percent of the profits (from his dreadful musical—and guaranteed flop—about Hitler) to twenty different backers.
3. MP wrote HM from Rio, July 30, 1986, before departing for Europe.
4. MP to HM, July 3, 1987.
5. MP to HM, August 1 and November 12, 1987.
6. MP to Bruce Benderson, December 9, 1987.
7. As Prince explains in American Theater Wing seminar on WNYC.
8. From Benderson's personal archive.
9. Prince explains in American Theater Wing seminar.

THE TROPICAL NIGHT FALLS
10. Sally Sloan, director of the Brady Museum in Cuernavaca, whom Manuel befriended through American journalists Alan Riding and Marlise Simons, with whom he had become acquainted in Brazil.

11. MP, *Under a Mantle of Stars* (New York: Lumen Books, 1985), 92.

12. Rosa Montero, interview: "Caracol sin concha," *El País* (1988), 31.

13. MP, *Tropical Night Falling* (New York: Simon & Schuster, 1991), 33: "Emily Brontë sat for hours and hours and gazed out at the moors, wondering why a man had built the house so far away among thorns, and imagining what he would be like . . . They call it a mirage on purpose, so that people don't go there and get lost in those endless moors."

14. Ibid., 46.

15. The island off the Brazilian coast where "this Silvia" goes with her lover to a conference for a few days follows a description Silvia's husband, Alfredo, reported meticulously: "Manuel made him describe it a million times, without telling him why. He deceived him, making him think it was to go there for vacation" (Silvia Oroz to SJL, February 12, 1997). Nidia's daughter's death from cancer was another factual referent, based on cousin Susana, who died November 26, 1987.

16. MP to HM, November 1988.

17. MP to HM, November 20, 1989.

18. Ibid.

CUERNAVACA, CITY OF ETERNAL SPRING . . .

19. Which he had intended for *Chorus*, a magazine in Italy that had commissioned Manuel in 1984, inspired by a cavalcade TV series directed by Dino Risi, to write about Italian cinema before neorealism. Manuel wrote linked dialogues in which the characters in each vignette spoke (or corresponded) nostalgically about the gems of the thirties and forties, directly in Italian, encouraged by Alberto Albarzino. These articles, the last galleys Manuel proofed, were published a few months after his death as *Gli occhi di Greta Garbo* (1991).

20. May Lorenzo Alcalà, *Manuel*. . . .

21. Jaime Manrique, "The Writer as Diva," *Christopher Street*, July 1993, 25; reproduced in *Eminent Maricones: Arenas, Lorca, Puig and Me* (Madison: University of Wisconsin Press, 1999).

THE KISS OF DEATH

22. MP, *Gli occhi* . . . , 99–101.

Max: "Greta: the last thing I want to see in this life is your face. I want to die in this moment."
Greta: "Don't say such things. My face is sad. Better a child smiling in the arms of his mother."
Max: "No, Greta, your face doesn't make me sad, on the contrary. In your eyes there is so much compassion!"
Greta: "Max, that compassion is not for you. I can't lie to you. I haven't even had compassion for myself."
Max: "When you came in here with those flowers, your arms were filled with compassion for me."

Greta: "No, in my arms I always carry my father, trying to give him strength. He had gotten sick from tuberculosis working on the frozen streets of Stockholm. He did any work, even cleaned the streets . . . I watched him die when I was fourteen. Since then he always occupies my arms. But it's all useless. I can do nothing to give him back his life."

23. Manrique, "The Writer as Diva," 26.
24. Manrique and a few others have suggested that Manuel was hiding away in Cuernavaca. Luciana, or Lucy—a contemporary of Manuel's—first met Manuel and Malé through their mutual friend Graciela Borges in a screening of *Pubis Angelical* in Buenos Aires, on one of Manuel's rare visits in the mid-eighties. Of German-Swiss Jewish origins, Lucy is fluent in at least five languages, including English. Between a polyglot wartime European background (including a narrow escape from the Holocaust) and her movie work, she was an interesting as well as warmhearted friend, a fellow exile who formed part of Manuel's small but solid cadre in Cuernavaca.
25. Williams was a young prodigy with the Miles Davis quintet (*Los Angeles Times* obituary, February 26, 1997).
26. See Jorge Salessi, *Every Night Life: Culture and Dance in Latin/o America* (Durham, N.C.: Duke University Press, 1997), 148–51.
27. See *Life Sentences*, ed. Thomas Avena (San Francisco: Mercury House, 1994).

EPILOGUE
28. Laurie Winer, review of the Los Angeles production, *Los Angeles Times*, December 28, 1995.
29. Juan Goytisolo, *El bosque de las letras* (Madrid: Alfaguara, 1995), 122–25. Goytisolo goes on to give other examples of Manuel's political integrity and deep ethical commitment. Time has shown that not only *SW* but lesser-known *Pubis* dissects "with exemplary penetration and ethical rigor the system of terror imposed by the Argentine military junta and the well-intentioned but ineffective struggle of the Latin American extremist groups in the 70s" much more effectively than other more obviously political books, such as Cortázar's *A Manual for Manuel*. When Perón came back into power, Goytisolo considered Manuel's common sense superior to the political engagement of many of his left-wing countrymen: "How can a man who spent twenty years in Franco's Spain reading *ABC* suddenly become left-wing?"
30. César Aira, *Paradoxa* (Rosario: Beatriz Vicerbo Editores, 1991), 27–29.
31. Stephen King's title for this story, which came out several years after Manuel's first novel, was "Rita Hayworth and the Shawshank Redemption."
32. See Alan Pauls, "La retrospectiva intermitente," *Encuentro internacional Manuel Puig*, ed. J. Amícola and G. Speranza (Rosario: Beatriz Viterbo Editores, 1998), 21–24. Among the many pilgrims from Buenos Aires to Leblón, Pauls, a young Argentine literary scholar with the air of a French intellectual (or a New Wave actor), sketched one of the more insightful portraits of this compatriot whose writing he admired, beginning with Manuel's nomadism. Pauls's excuse for visiting Rua

Aperana was to bring Manuel the manuscript of the study he was about to publish on *Betrayed by Rita Hayworth*, which, like all analyses of Puig, Pauls later comprehended, was old the minute it came out. Expecting a stimulating literary discussion peppered with political gossip, Pauls discovered he could not engage the novelist in a satisfying dialogue. After seeing Manuel's "cloning library"—as Pauls coined it— which consisted, aside from the vast eclectic *videoteca*, of multiple editions of his own books (in almost every conceivable language) and a shelf of biographies of actresses, actors, and film producers, Pauls pegged Manuel as a Howard Hughes of the literary world. This balding, effeminate eccentric compulsively squirreled videocassettes in his cul-de-sac just as the reclusive millionaire had stockpiled cans of Campbell's soup. All Manuel wanted to talk about were videocassette acquisitions, his latest interest being obscure Spanish films of the early Franco period— about which Pauls knew nothing. Regarding his disillusionment after meeting Manuel, Pauls wrote: "We insist upon knowing a writer whose work we admire, but that admirable work mocks any relation that can be established with him. It's a phenomenon of reciprocal anamorphosis, strange but fatal: the author is a parody of his work, the work is a parody of him. And if the persona of the author sprouts again (because the writer as persona is always a zombie awakened by the enthusiasm of his admirers), it's only because the impersonality, the neuterness of a great literature is also what makes it intolerable. Puig was an intolerable disappearance."

acknowledgments

This book could not have been written without the generous assistance of Carlos Puig, who gave me access to numerous boxes of unpublished papers and permission to cite hundreds of Manuel Puig's letters to his mother and family from 1955 through the 1980s; this voluminous body of correspondence constitutes a veritable journal of the years Manuel Puig spent outside of Argentina. I am enormously grateful as well to Malé Puig, Carlos's wife Viviana and daughter Mara, cousins Jorge and Hugo Puig, Alda (Bebé) Cortés, and Ernesto and Nelva Camoglio (in La Plata) for their memories, insights, and encouragement during my two sojourns (1995, 1997) in Buenos Aires.

Other friends, as well as writers, artists, filmmakers and critics, publishers and academic colleagues in Argentina, Brazil, Chile, Colombia, Mexico, Uruguay, and Venezuela deserve grateful mention, among them Alfredo Gialdini and Hugo Sottotetti; José Amícola, Graciela Goldchluk, and Julia Romero of the Puig Archive research group at the University of La Plata; César Aira, Homero Alsina Thevenet, Monika do Amaral, Marcos Barnatán, the late Adolfo Bioy Casares, Patricio Bisso, Gustavo Cobo Borda, Lucy Cabarga, Julian Cooper, Horacio Costa, Aline Davidoff, Alberto Díaz, Daniel Divinsky, the late José Donoso, Roberto Echavarren, Cristina Fangmann, Luis Gusmán, Germán García, Ulalume González de León, Noé Jitrik, Bella Josef, Javier Labrada, Jorge Lebedev, Libertad LeBlanc, Hector Libertella, Felipe López, Josefina Ludmer, Jorge Mara, Tomás Eloy Martínez, Tununa Mercado, Silvia Molloy, Carlos Monsiváis, Silvia Oroz, Alan Pauls, Ricardo Piglia, Marcela Pimentel, Felisa Pinto, Nélida Piñón,

Sergio Pitol, Arturo Ripstein, Gloria Rodrigué, Sally Sloan, Renata Schussheim, Vicki Slavuski, Ernesto Schoo, Roberto Souza, Jorge Schwartz, the late Alberto Tabbia, Danubio Torres Fierro, Manuel Ulacia, Luisa Valenzuela, Alejandro Varderi, and still others. The interviews and documentation provided by the citizens of General Villegas (cited in the early chapters of this book) in the Province of Buenos Aires were invaluable, and I express my thanks, not least of all, to angelical Patricia Barguera, Hebe Uriarte, Claudio Pringles, and the late lamented Susana Cañibaño.

Another individual without whom this biography would not have been possible is Mario Fenelli, Manuel Puig's longtime friend in Rome who not only gave me access to crucial correspondence, unpublished writings, and photographs but read the early drafts of my chapters on Manuel's breakthrough years as a young writer in the late fifties and early sixties. Mario has been almost a medium; after Malé, perhaps Manuel's closest kin. Guillermo Cabrera Infante, who has had a profound influence on my own endeavors as a writer, has supported this project from the very beginning, as have Juan and Luis Goytisolo: without these writers, as well as our dear departed friends Nestor Almendros, Emir Rodríguez Monegal, and Severo Sarduy, many friends and readers of Manuel Puig might never have known him.

Thanks always to Ben and Alice Lustgarten (and my godson Dan, the doctor). Still others who have lent a helpful hand, on both sides of the Atlantic, are: Hector Babenco; Pepe and Sylvia Martin; Jack Macrae; Peter Brooks; Tom Conley; Lee Percy; Gene Parseghian; Harold Prince; Corina Hughes and Irene Singerman of the American Theater Wing; Fred Ebb; Joan Cohen; Howard Mandelbaum; Bruce Benderson; Jeanne Heuving; Paul Mazursky; Diane von Furstenberg; Alastair Reid; Allegra Lewis; Enrico Mario Santí; Helene Webb; Eliot Weinberger; Edmund White; Susan Sontag; Mark and Inge Mirsky; Merle Kaufman; Marisa del Rio; B. Lampert, M.D.; Janet Walker; Leonard Schrader; David Weisman; Bill Stern; François Wahl; Isabelle Wagner; Italo Manzi; Michèlle Ramond; Milagros Ezquerro; Liliane Hasson; Inge Feltrinelli; Miriam Gómez; María Barceló; Angelo Morino; Maria Bonatti; Michi Strausfeld; Germán Puig; Carmen Balcells; Carina Pons; Seix Barral; Faber & Faber; Allan Baker; Ronald Christ; José Kozer; Dolores Martin and Georgette Dorn at the Library of Congress; Joel Siegel; Albert Bensoussan; Charles Silver at MoMA; Mitch Douglas at ICM; Peter Rawley; Graziana Ramsden; Peter Johnson; Don

Skemer, and their staff at the Princeton University Firestone Library; the Rockefeller Foundation and the wonderful people at the Villa Serbelloni in Bellagio.

Fellowships from the National Endowment for the Humanities and the John Simon Guggenheim Foundation gave me the precious time needed, and the Visiting Scholar Program at NYU and the University of California at Santa Barbara also graciously supported this project.

Certain individuals have selflessly given their time and expertise, reading draft upon draft: John A. Coleman, my agent and friend John L. Hochmann, René Jordan, editor Lorin Stein; the final form of this manuscript owes its existence, in large part, to the lucid talents and infinite patience of editor Natasha Wimmer at Farrar, Straus and Giroux. And thank you, Jonathan Galassi, for having faith in me.

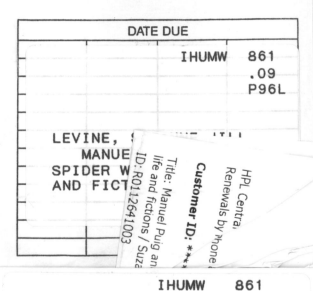